SEA BATTLES
in close-up:
World War 2

SEA BATTLES
in close-up:
World War 2

Martin Stephen
Edited by Eric Grove

Naval
Institute
Press

Reprinted 1991
Second Reprint 1993

Published and distributed in the United States of
America by the Naval Institute Press,
Annapolis, Maryland 21402

Library of Congress Catalog Card No. 87-63594

ISBN-0-87021-556-6

Manufactured in Great Britain

Acknowledgements

Both author and editor are indebted to the authors
of the original *Sea Battles in Close-up* series for all
their research; the views expressed in this present
work are, of course, not the responsibility of those
earlier authors, but are those of the present author
and editor.

The author owes a considerable debt of
gratitude to Robert Butler for providing access to
his unpublished and extensive research on the
escape of the *Scharnhorst* and *Gneisenau*, and for
sharing with him his intimate and detailed
knowledge of wartime naval operations. He is also
indebted to the staff of the Imperial War Museum,
and in particular to M. J. Willis, and to the United
States Department of the Navy and Robert
A. Carlisle. In addition thanks go to the staff of the
Public Record Office, the National Maritime
Museum, the Cambridge University Library,
Lancaster University Library, and the Ministry of
Defence (Navy). He has also received much
assistance from Adrian Vicary of the Maritime
Photo Library, Cromer; Robert Shopland, editor
of *Ships Monthly*, and the readership of that
magazine; Martin Edmonds, Lawrence James,
Frank Smith, the Real Photo Company, and
Charles Drury. Finally, his warmest thanks go to
Jenny, Neill, Simon and Henry for all their
patience and interest.

Editor's Note

The editor would like to thank David Lyon of
the National Maritime Museum for help in solving
specific carrier problems; Evan Davies and
Richard Kennell of BRNC Dartmouth, and
Michael Chapman of the Ministry of Defence
Library for assistance with the provision of
research materials. As usual Elizabeth was a great
help and support.

E. J. Grove

Contents

Introduction

Eight of the 10 sea battles covered in this book were the subject of individual volumes in the earlier Ian Allan 'Sea Battles in Close Up' series, produced in the early 1970s. These successful volumes have now become collectors' items. However, a significant amount of new information has come to light since the original series was published with the result that the earlier series can no longer be regarded as wholly accurate. The opportunity has been taken here to undertake extensive new research and as a result provide the most up-to-date and thorough coverage possible of 10 major sea battles in World War 2. The arrangement of each chapter roughly follows that used in the original Ian Allan series: a brief introduction is followed by detailed coverage of the events of each battle, a conclusion, and the provision of technical data on the major vessels involved in each engagement.

In a long and bloody war which, in naval terms, was ferociously active, it is no easy task to choose 10 sea battles from such a potentially long list. One relatively easy decision was to find space for two battles not covered in the original Ian Allan series — Barents Sea and Midway.

The Battle of the Barents Sea resulted in no major warship sinkings, and comparatively few casualties, yet it caused a crisis of major proportions in the German Navy, and broke the already fragile bond of faith between Hitler and his surface fleet. It is also the outstanding example from the war of how escorting forces can hold off heavier opponents, and also sums up many of the weaknesses shown by the German surface fleet throughout the war. Its final claim for inclusion comes from its being a curtain raiser for the sinking of the *Scharnhorst* a year later. There are even more compelling reasons for including the Battle of Midway, quite correctly seen as one of the most decisive naval engagements fought in any war.

The aim throughout has been to choose a representative set of battles from all theatres of the war, although a deliberate bias has been exerted in favour of 'big ship' engagements, partly because of the general interest in these but also because significant new information has become available on a number of them. Undoubtedly the most fascinating new information to have come to light

since the earlier Ian Allan books were published is that concerning ULTRA — or the British ability to decode certain German signals, in some cases more quickly than their intended recipients. Knowledge of the ULTRA secret was kept restricted to a handful of people in order to preserve security, and whilst the knowledge it gave did not always lead to the success that might have been expected, far better use was made of it than had been the case with code-breaking information supplied by the famous 'Room 40' in World War 1.

ULTRA had no part to play in the first battle covered here, that of the River Plate, but it has been possible to revise estimates of the strengths and weaknesses of the German *Panzerschiffe* design, providing some surprising new insights into these vessels. The performance of German armour, British gunnery technique, and the actions of Kapitän Langsdorff are all made subject to revised interpretations. This chapter also lays to rest the myth of Langsdorff having wrapped himself in the old Imperial Germany Navy ensign before shooting himself; and whilst not detracting from the brilliance of the British cruiser action, the chapter does attempt to put the importance of the action into perspective. Despite the fact that *Graf Spee* appears a rather less significant threat than has often been supposed if the damage inflicted by the vessel is compared with that inflicted by U-boats, the Battle of the River Plate is an obvious candidate for inclusion in a volume of this nature. The culmination of much prewar planning from both sides, it was one of the last classically simple ship-to-ship engagements ever to be fought, largely un-influenced by radar or the air and submarine threats that were to dominate so much of the later war at sea.

The attack on Taranto is included as one of two chapters on the war in the Mediterranean. Whilst the River Plate was in many respects a battle from an earlier age, Taranto marked the arrival of a new era in naval warfare. The opportunity is taken in this chapter to discuss at length the development of the Fleet Air Arm, its aircraft, and its carriers, culminating in a detailed discussion of the strengths and weaknesses of the armoured carrier in general and HMS *Illustrious* in particular. Torpedo protection on Italian battleships is also examined in detail and in the light of the most recent research, and the degree of blame usually apportioned to the Italian Navy lessened somewhat.

The Battle of Matapan proved a 'famous victory', and the coverage of it here takes full account of what is now known about Axis 'Enigma' codes. New light is thrown on the risks taken by Adm Cunningham in this action, and on the weakness of Italian rangefinders. It is possible that history has underestimated some of the weaknesses shown on the British side in this engagement, and been rather too harsh in its judgement of the Italian commander, Adm Iachino.

No work on sea battles of World War 2 would be complete without a section on the sinking of *Hood* and *Bismarck*. Recent years have seen a great deal of research into why *Hood* blew up so tragically, and full coverage is given in this chapter of such issues as *Hood's* above water torpedoes, ammunition storage, and flawed Dreyer fire control 'computer'. The design features which gave rise to the jamming of *Prince of Wales'* quadruple turrets are also discussed, and the weaknesses in *Bismarck's* design. Recent speculation on possible methods by which *Bismarck* might have made it into Brest are discussed.

The sinking of *Hood*, the escape of *Scharnhorst*, *Gneisenau* and *Prince Eugen* up the English Channel, and the loss of *Prince of Wales* and *Repulse* were arguably the three greatest disasters to be suffered by the Royal Navy throughout the war, if one accepts that convoy PQ17 was a tragedy belonging to a different category. The prologue to the chapter on *Prince of Wales* and *Repulse* provides a very full introduction to the war in the Pacific, seen in the light of recent historical research. It also gives a very full account of the nature of the damage that first crippled, and then sank, what was purportedly one of the best-armoured battleships in the world: salient detail about this damage has emerged over the course of several books on this engagement. Japanese torpedo design is also examined and some misconceptions about these and the 'Long Lance' torpedo are corrected. The absence of a fleet carrier with the force is shown here as being of less significance than has hitherto been supposed.

The famous 'Channel Dash' has been included here as an outstanding illustration of the importance of luck and human error in the outcome of any battle. The Germans had daring, good luck, and good planning on their side. The British had bad luck and bad planning on their side: a vast ration of heroic self-sacrifice from the latter could do nothing to avert the 'victory' of the former, a victory which was in effect a retreat by a defeated squadron. New information in this chapter includes that on ULTRA, the presence of a British agent in Brest, and the existence of a Signals exercise that added seriously to the confusion of the day.

The Battle of the Coral Sea is included here both as a major engagement in its own right, and as a curtain-raiser to the Battle of Midway. The performance of Adm Fletcher is studied anew in this treatment of the battle, and particular attention paid to Japanese and American aircraft and warship designs. The account of the Battle of Midway summarises recent research on this engagement, and analyses in the light of this the psychological and other factors which led to this massive defeat for the Japanese.

New information on the sinking of the *Scharnhorst* is largely centred on the information provided by ULTRA. Other information has emerged as a result of detailed research carried out on this engagement elsewhere. The new cocktail of facts and opinions leads to an enlarged awareness of how much luck played its part in this particular battle, and produces some worrying insights into the performance of *Duke of York's* main armament.

The major combatant nations were at varying stages of readiness when hostilities commenced in September 1939. The British were comparatively well off for aircraft carriers, having accepted the importance of these vessels, albeit in an essentially limited battlefleet support role. The latter meant that the provision of aircraft to fly off the carriers, both in numbers and quality, was far from satisfactory, a fact which in turn led the British to drop the successful *Ark Royal* design and opt instead for carriers with strong defensive armour. This extended the time necessary to bring new carriers into service, and gave an additional problem in terms of the supply of armour plate. As regards battleships, the new 'King George V' class vessels were mostly still on the stocks or some distance away from commissioning in 1939: *Prince of Wales* was never fully worked up during the whole of her short life. In the meantime the main battleship strength of the Royal Navy lay in World War 1 'Queen Elizabeth' or 'Royal Sovereign' class designs. A handful of the 'Queen Elizabeth' class were massively reconstructed, their only weakness after this being a top speed significantly under 25kt. But the dangers of using largely unreconstructed World War 1 vessels to fight in World War 2 were shown by the loss of *Royal Oak*, *Barham*, *Hood* and *Repulse*. The dangers were not the fault of the Admiralty. Had the money existed to reconstruct these vessels in the 1930s it would have been spent. The British had some excellent cruiser and destroyer designs available by the start of the war, although as in any war there were far from enough of them available. The escort situation was far less happy, and led to the hurried building of the famous 'Flower' class corvettes to plug the gap while larger and better-armed escorts came on stream.

In terms of what would now be called electronic warfare, the Royal Navy was either well ahead of the pack, or soon able to be so. It seems generally accepted that Asdic (Sonar) gave rise to over-confidence about fighting the submarine threat on the part of the Royal Navy, and impressive lists of vessels fitted with Asdic do not reveal how many of these were needed in home waters to act as escorts for units of the Home Fleet. Furthermore, Asdic in its primitive form was fixed in direction, lost contact at a crucial moment in the attack, and could not give a depth reading. Too much prewar faith in modern anti-aircraft systems such as the multiple pom-pom and the new generation of heavier dual-purpose weapons — notably, the 5.25in guns — gave rise to over-confidence about the threat to surface vessels from the air. Sadly, the Royal Navy had once again procured inadequate fire control equipment which was as flawed in the anti-aircraft role as its 'Dreyer' tables had been for anti-surface fire in 1914-18. Despite these wrong answers, however, the Royal Navy had not neglected to ask many of the right questions about anti-submarine or anti-air defences in the interwar years. It had also been in the forefront of radar use, and certainly by the time that *Bismarck* and *Hood* were sunk the accuracy and reliability of British radar provided a significant shock to the German Navy, which thereafter became almost obsessional about its own less-effective radar's emissions being tracked and used to hunt vessels. The Royal Navy had also learnt hard lessons from Jutland about night-fighting and gunnery control. Matapan is often seen as the triumph of British night-fighting tactics, but the sinking of *Scharnhorst* in many respects marks the apogee and reward of prewar naval developments, with the use of 'blind fire' gunnery radar, and the presence at North Cape of some of the finest battleship, cruiser, and destroyer designs of the whole war. Almost as important as any other factor was the realisation that the Royal Navy still considered itself the finest Navy in the world, a claim that its rivals might dispute, but which reflects the high morale present at the start of the war, and maintained throughout it.

Compared to the Royal Navy the German Navy was in a much worse condition at the outbreak of World War 2. The highly ambitious 'Plan Z' would have given Germany a navy of Wagnerian dimensions by the mid-1940s, but this was never to come near completion. The ill-fated German aircraft carrier, *Graf Zeppelin*, was never com-plted, and recent studies suggest that even had she done so her design was seriously flawed. As regards battleships, the three *Panzerschiffe* are discussed in detail in Chapter 1, but were not in any real sense battleships at all. The Germans themselves recognised this by redesignating the survivors as heavy cruisers later in the war. *Scharnhorst* and *Gneisenau* were effective vessels, but as developments of the World War 1 *Mackensen* design they showed rather too many features from an earlier age, as is discussed below. *Bismarck* and *Tirpitz* were not completed by 1939, and though very powerful vessels they have arguably been over-praised by those who have written of them in terms of myth rather than fact. German heavy cruiser design, exemplified in *Prince Eugen*, was excellent, though here again there were far too few vessels. The major weakness of German 8in cruisers was the unreliability of their high-pressure steam machinery and a limited range. Nor were German torpedoes sufficiently tested when war broke out, a fact which significantly reduced British losses in the early months of the war. German destroyers tended to suffer also from unreliable steam machinery and too great a weight of armament, a problem particularly noticeable in the twin-turret proposed for a number of later designs. The German E-boat (combined motor torpedo and gun boat) was a magnificent design, and schemes to evade treaty limitations had meant that German submarine design was well ahead. The German Navy was a highly professional, highly selective, and well-motivated force, although the surface fleet did suffer as the war progressed, and the U-boat arm attracted more and more men and resources. The absence of a separate air arm and the resultant need to rely on the Luftwaffe was to cost the German Navy dearly, though the reconnaissance service provided by the Luftwaffe was more effective than some commentators have supposed.

The Italian Navy had always been able to produce very fast and very beautiful warships, and some excellent fighting vessels were available to it at the start of the war. The 'Littorio' class battleships were very effective designs, their novel Pugliese system of underwater protection having received much atten-tion recently. It appears that its relative inef-fectiveness may have been the result of flawed installation rather than failure of the actual design. The Italians also went against their reputation for rather flimsy vessels in some of their heavy cruisers, and the design of the vessels sunk at Matapan was particularly noteworthy. However, there were serious weaknesses in Italian preparedness for a war against a technologically and tactically advanced opponent. The absence of radar, its own air arm, any night-fighting techniques, and weaknesses in gunnery-direction *materiel* severely hampered the Italian Navy in all its operations.

The US Navy was a well-balanced and well-provided force before Pearl Harbor, and remained so after it to a surprising extent. As with the British, actual carrier design was well advanced, and rather more so than the provision of aircraft to fly off the vessels. Whilst the American aircraft were by and large inferior to those used by their Japanese opponents at the start of the war (a situation that was to be dramatically reversed in later years), they were still ahead of the British. One reason was that larger aircraft-carrying capacity on board American carriers allowed for a degree of separation between the four types of aircraft needed — torpedo-bomber, dive-bomber, fighter, and spotter-reconnaissance — whilst the British attempted to kill three birds with one stone in the 'TSR' (torpedo-spotter-reconnaissance) Swordfish. The American fleet was committed, as was the British, to using a considerable number of older-design battleships or reconstructed vessels, and even the best of such conversions tended to suffer from low speed. However, new designs proved very effective, whilst a series of highly successful cruiser and destroyer classes were produced, numbers of which can still be seen in service today. American radar was soon to be put to effective use against an enemy who was largely to remain without effective radar to the end of the war. American weaknesses lay in their torpedoes, prone to be slow, run deep, not explode, or veer off course, and in their capacity to co-ordinate and launch large air strikes to maximum effect. Communications discipline was not all it should have been in the early stages of the war from American pilots, who lacked battle experience and training in comparison with the Japanese. ⸱

Ironically the Imperial Japanese Navy could be said to suffer from one of its main strengths. Its air crews and pilots — both carrier- and land-based — were an elite force, highly trained, highly professional, and highly committed. The opening phases of the war were intensely active for Japanese pilots, much more so than for the officers and men of the European navies. Unavoidable pilot wastage, coupled with scant regard paid to rescue services and a rather cavalier attitude to human loss, seriously reduced the number of trained pilots, and the Japanese élite force never managed the transfer (so successfully achieved by the American and British navies) into a mass force requiring mass recruitment and training. However, all this was only to become clear later on.

At the start of hostilities the Japanese had a large, well-supplied, and well-trained navy. The absence of radar was compensated for by excellent torpedoes. Those mounted in surface ships outranged the rest of the world's by a factor of three or more, and those provided for aircraft could be launched from a height and at a speed that an American or European pilot would have found unthinkable. Japanese aircraft were also excellent, in particular the Zero fighter. The Imperial Japanese Navy recognised with the US Navy that the vast distances of the Pacific would place a premium on air power, but with neither Navy did this interfere with the provision of the more traditional battleship-centred surface fleet. Japanese reconstructions and new designs of battleship were in many instances excellent, although no navy in World War 2 produced an effective method of reducing the tendency of World War 1 designs to capsize rather too readily. This being said, a disproportionate amount of resources were absorbed by Japanese battleships, in particular the 18in behemoths *Yamato* and *Mushashi*, resources which would have been better invested in carriers and escorts. Belated attempts to convert more vessels into carriers or seaplane tenders showed the truth of this when it was too late to affect the outcome of the war. Adm Yamamoto realised that his superb Navy was nevertheless one which could only afford a short war against a nation with overwhelming industrial superiority. The correctness of that reading never altered, but Midway effectively brought to an end any chance of the Japanese desire for a quick victory being achieved. The Royal Navy both patronised and seriously underestimated the power of the Japanese before and in the early stages of the war. The US Navy had Pearl Harbor to ensure that it never proceeded nearly as far down this path, but it was more than the good fortune of absent carriers at Pearl Harbor that was to lead to American victory. The Americans displayed a resilience, courage, and ability to learn fast that both surprised and dismayed the Japanese who found in the end that they had no counter to the USA's capacity to mobilise and deploy naval force on a massive scale.

World War 2 at sea had as one of its earliest battles a ship-to-ship engagement that was fought largely in terms that would have been well understood by any Admiral in World War 1. By 1945, primitive guided missiles were in use by both Germany and Japan, the first jet aircraft were in the air, and radar and electronic surveillance were vital and indispensable parts of naval warfare. Submarines were at sea that could outrun the majority of escorts then available, and most significantly of all the battleship had been relegated largely to a mobile shore-bombardment battery for the use of invading forces. The 10 sea battles covered in the following pages reflect accurately the changing nature of this most challenging of naval wars.

CHAPTER ONE

The Battle of the River Plate

The Panzerschiffe (Armoured Ship)

In the latter part of the 1920s Germany was still governed by the Treaty of Versailles as regards the size of her fleet, but at the same time she was beginning to flex her military muscles once more. Between 1923 and 1927 German ship designers struggled to produce new 'armoured ships' or *Panzerschiffe*, as allowed by the Treaty, that bore some resemblance to a post-dreadnought capital ship, but which at the same time did not too obviously exceed the Treaty limit of 10,000 tons. The designers faced the dilemmas of all modern warship designers: speed, firepower and armour protection are all interdependent, and on a limited tonnage one element of the triangle cannot be built up without a severe loss to one or both of the others. The result of their deliberations was the

Deutschland, laid down in 1929, launched in 1931 and commissioned in 1933. Two other vessels were built with incremental design improvements, the *Admiral Scheer* completed at the end of 1934 and the *Admiral Graf Spee* commissioned at the beginning of 1936.

The vessels were immediately dubbed 'pocket battleships' when they appeared, and caused considerable contemporary interest. In recent times writers have tended to emphasise their weaknesses such as relatively slow speed and comparatively light armour; of course, they also went considerably over their declared tonnage of 10,000 tons. Their design innovations were, however, noteworthy: welded construction saved weight — about 15% on the hull alone — and the diesel engines saved length and personnel, if not as much weight or total volume as had been hoped. The diesels also gave high endurance making the

Graf Spee: this photograph appears to have been heavily touched-up, for propaganda rather than security reasons. The distinctive German 'mattress' radar aerial on the foretop is still however clearly visible.
Real Photographs S1458

1458

ships excellent commerce raiders. The more rapid response of diesel engines also facilitated getting away from steam-powered warships in the immediate aftermath of a sighting.

Admiral Graf Spee

Builder: Reichsmarinewerft, Wilhelmshaven
(Laid down 1 October 1932; launched 30 June 1934; completed 6 January 1936)

Displacement: 12,100 tons (standard); 16,200 tons (full load)

Dimensions: 617ft × 71ft × 24ft

Machinery: 8 diesel engines, 2 shafts, 56,800shp, 26kt (28.5kt achieved on trials)

Armour: Main belt 3.15in, with 0.8in (upper) and 1.6in (lower) internal longitudinal armoured bulkheads; main armoured deck 1.8in; turrets 5.5in faces, 3.3in sides; barbettes 4.1in

Armament: 6 × 11in (2 × 3); 8 × 5.9in (8 × 1); 6 × 4.1in (3 × 2); 8 × 37mm (8 × 1); 10 × 20mm (10 × 1) (two transferred to *Altmark* on 1/9/39); 8 × 21in torpedo tubes (2 × 4); 1 × seaplane

Sensors: Seetakt FuMo22 radar on the foretop range finder

Complement: 1,124

Although the 'pocket battleships' were slower than cruisers, their armour was considered proof against 8in fire at ranges of 16-18,000m and their main battery of 11in guns was confidently expected to be able to pound any cruiser to pieces. At the time of their building only the British had battlecruisers that could outrun and outgun the German *Panzerschiffe*, and Britain was not officially regarded as the enemy for planning purposes. As answers to stringent design limitations these ships were highly creditable and innovative efforts. They required either a fully-fledged capital ship or a squadron of cruisers to defeat them and, with the whole of the ocean to play with, such a concentration was likely to prove hard to come by.

The three main weaknesses in their design were armour that proved less robust than expected in action, the lack of an armoured position for the captain in the foretop from where he might well have to fight the ship against multiple cruiser opponents, and the provision of only one aircraft. For a commerce raider the latter was an essential surveillance and target acquisition system. This shortcoming was compounded for *Graf Spee* in 1939 by her being fitted with a brand-new and unreliable Arado Ar196 seaplane. The Ar196 had a high landing speed, and alighted on the sea with such a shock that the hot radial engine was drenched. This led to persistent cracking of the cylinders and the final demise of the seaplane just at the point when her presence might have saved the ship.

Graf Spee Sails

By the time Grand-Adm Raeder knew that war with Britain was coming it was far too late to provide an effective fleet. The awesome Plan Z might have given him one by the mid-1940s but, as it was, in 1939 he had available to him only two 11in gun battleships (classified by the British as 'battlecruisers'), three *Panzerschiffe*, six cruisers and only enough U-boats to keep 10 on patrol at any one time.

The commerce raider posed a significant threat to the British Admiralty, not so much because the damage such a surface ship might do but more because such a vessel, with complete freedom of action, would tie down vast numbers of ships in hunting operations; *disruption* as much as *destruction* was the aim of the commerce raider. This being said, a great deal of destruction was possible given how thinly the resources of the British fleet were spread. In September 1939, as might be expected, the bulk of the British fleet was concentrated in home waters — seven battleships, three battlecruisers, four aircraft carriers and 21 cruisers. The Mediterranean was an unlikely area for commerce raiding, but with Italy's intentions far from certain it still needed strong cover; there were deployed three battleships, one aircraft carrier and six modern cruisers. In the North Atlantic were three old cruisers on trade protection duties. The South Atlantic Station deployed eight cruisers (half of them old), the America and the West Indies Stations had four, all modern, whilst the East Indies had the three impressive new ships of the 'Gloucester' class. The China Station, Australia and New Zealand between them mustered one old aircraft carrier and 11 varied cruisers. Given the huge areas of ocean that these ships had to cover, and the fact that three modern cruisers were a minimum for dealing with a *Panzerschiff*, it is hardly surprising that Grand-Adm Raeder's war plans envisaged the sending out of two such vessels into the trade routes before war started, with their necessary support vessels.

On 3 August 1939 the supply and support vessel *Altmark* sailed from Germany, followed by the *Graf Spee* on 21 August. A short while later the *Deutschland* was to sail, on 24 August, with her supply vessel, the *Westerwald*; the cruise of the latter was cut short on 1 November after she had inflicted minimal damage. Had *Graf Spee* sailed a day earlier she might have been spotted by RAF Coastal Command, whose aircraft had been flying reconnaissance sorties as part of a Home Fleet exercise until 20 August; but, given the standard of reconnaissance at that time, it seems unlikely. *Graf Spee's* commander was Capt Hans Langsdorff, 45 years old and carrying the reputation of being one of Germany's most able naval officers.

21 August-25 September

Graf Spee proceeded to break out unobserved through the Iceland-Faroes Gap, and on 1 September met *Altmark* southwest of the Canaries for refuelling. In company, and keeping off all main shipping routes, both vessels were in the South Atlantic a week later, war having been declared on 3 September. On 11 September as *Graf Spee* and *Altmark* prepared a transfer of supplies, the former's Arado seaplane reported HMS *Cumberland*, ordered from Freetown to Rio de Janeiro to deal with commerce raiders, steaming towards her. Langsdorff managed to slip away unobserved. The early stages of the operation were dominated by

GREENLAND
Denmark Strait
ICELAND
24/8
SCAPA FLOW
NORWAY
GOTENHAVEN
WILHELMSHAVEN
N. AMERICA
BREST
SAILED 21/8/39
28/8
AZORES
North Atlantic
GIBRALTAR
SUEZ CANAL
ALEXANDRIA
1/9
CANARY Is.
BDY
PAN AMERICAN NEUTRAL ZONE
DAKAR
C. VERDE IS.
FREETOWN
6/9
8/9
S. AMERICA
⒟ 10/10
Mozambique Channel
PERNAMBUCO (RECIFE)
11/9
Ⓒ 7.10
Ⓑ 5/10
Ⓐ
Ⓔ 22/10
Ⓖ 2/12
30/9
RIO
CAPE TOWN
Ⓗ 3/12
Ⓕ 15/11
MONTEVIDEO
Ⓙ 7/12
29/10
9/11
BUENOS AIRES
11/12
WAITING AREA
30/11
2/11
South Atlantic
4/11
BATTLE OF R PLATE
13/12/39
FALKLAND IS.

A	SS CLEMENT (SUNK)	B	SS NEWTON BEECH (CAPTURED)	C	SS ASHLEA (SUNK)
E	SS TREVANION "	D	SS HUNTSMAN "	H	SS TAIROA "
F	SS AFRICA SHELL "	G	SS DORIC STAR	J	SS STREON-SHALH "

Left:
The cruise of the Admiral Graf Spee — 21 August-13 December 1939.

Bottom left:
The 6in cruiser HMS Ajax.
Real Photographs S1632

politics and caution. *Graf Spee* had to loiter in an isolated waiting area, in the vain hope that France and Britain would make a quick peace after the speedy annihilation of Poland. Even after 26 September when German vessels were freed to attack individual British merchantmen they were not, for three more weeks, allowed to attack French vessels, warned not to alienate the Americans (whose naval patrols were discouraging operations close to the coast of North and South America), and tied to the regulations of International Prize Law. It was also emphasised to Langsdorff by the Naval Operations Staff that his ship was not to be fully committed to operations against enemy naval forces. This reflected anxiety about commanders unnecessarily throwing their ships away in premature and gratuitous combats, as was perceived to have taken place in the early months of the previous war. Langsdorff seems to have chafed at these orders, which he interpreted as forbidding him to take on escorted convoys.

26 September-12 December
Let off his leash, at least to some extent, Langsdorff headed immediately for Brazil, hoping to disrupt the significant food trade between South America and Britain. He found his first victim before noon on 30 September, the SS *Clement*, an ancient 5,050-ton tramp steamer. Langsdorff had disguised his vessel as the *Admiral Scheer, Graf Spee's* sister ship, and this later added confusion to an already confused situation. A burst of gunfire from the Ar196 stopped the *Clement* and her crew took to the boats. The Captain and Chief Engineer were taken back on board their ship and eventually to the *Graf Spee*; the rest of the crew were given the course to steer for South America. The German boarding party planted bombs on the vessel and tried to flood the ship, which seems to have been immobilised before abandonment in accordance with Admiralty instructions. The *Graf Spee* then attempted to begin the ship's sinking by firing a torpedo. Much to Langsdorff's embarrass-

ment two attempts to torpedo the old *Clement* failed and in the end it took no less than 25 5.9in and five rounds of 11in gunfire to send the merchantman to the bottom. As in all wars, 'nerves' and inexperience dominated such opening moves, despite the best peacetime training.

Shortly afterwards, *Graf Spee* sighted a neutral Greek steamer, the *Papelemos*. The two British officers were transferred and the ship allowed to continue on condition she made no radio report. Langsdorff sent a message to Pernambuco, using *Sheer's* call sign, to 'save the lifeboats of the *Clement*'. In this, as in his other successes against merchant ships, Langsdorff behaved with remarkable courtesy and generosity. The *Clement* had transmitted a radio signal before being sunk and Langsdorff determined to disguise his ship more heavily in future in order to take his quarry by surprise. The massive tower foremast was painted to appear like an allied tripod. *Graf Spee* also began to fly the French flag. In pursuit of his policy of causing maximum disruption Langsdorff headed off eastwards at 18kt, aiming to appear at widely differing locations as often as possible and sow confusion in the minds and planning of the British. His commerce raiding actions are summarised below:

Activities of *Graf Spee* up to 13 December with British Response

1/2 October: Crew of SS *Clement* land in South America; Admiralty learn for certain that at least one raider is at large, and think it is the *Admiral Scheer*.

5 October: *Graf Spee* captures SS *Newton Beech* (British 4,650-ton tramp carrying maize). Weak distress signal sent off. *Newton Beech* kept in company with *Graf Spee* as prison ship. *Newton Beech's* radio and confidential anti-raider instructions used to transmit bogus alarm calls.

Meanwhile *Deutschland* had sunk SS *Stonegate* off Bermuda, whose distress signal was picked up. Admiralty hope *Clement* and *Stonegate* have been sunk by only *one* raider. In response the British and French Admiralties form a series of hunting groups, as detailed below:

Initial Composition of British and French Hunting Groups

Name of Force	Composition	Type of ship	Area of operations	Detached from
F	Berwick	8in cruiser	North America	—
	York	8in cruiser	and West Indies	—
G	Exeter	8in cruiser	Southeast coast	—
	Cumberland	8in cruiser	of South	—
	Achilles	6in cruiser	America	New Zealand
	Ajax	6in cruiser		—
H	Shropshire	8in cruiser	Cape of Good	Mediterranean
	Sussex	8in cruiser	Hope	
I	Eagle	Aircraft carrier	Ceylon	China
	Cornwall	8in cruiser		China
	Dorsetshire	8in cruiser		China
K	Renown	Battlecruiser	Pernambuco	Home Fleet
	Ark Royal	Aircraft carrier		Home Fleet
L	Dunkerque	Battlecruiser	Brest	—
	Béarn	Aircraft carrier		—
	Gloire	6in cruiser		—
	Montcalm	6in cruiser		—
	Georges Leygues	6in cruiser		—
M	Dupleix	8in cruiser	Dakar	Mediterranean
	Foch	8in cruiser		
N	Strasbourg	Battlecruiser	West Indies	Brest
	Hermes	Aircraft carrier		Plymouth

HMS *Achilles* prewar with HMS *Orion* astern; *Orion* was another cruiser which had a very active war.
Maritime Photo Library (MPL)

Newton Beech's distress signal picked up by a merchant vessel and passed on to HMS *Cumberland* later that day. Capt W. H. G. Fallowfield failed to pass on the message ('SOS' rather than the prescribed 'RRR' for raider) to Freetown, presuming it had already been picked up. Under the circumstances, his decision to maintain radio silence was extremely unwise.

7 October: SS *Ashlea* (British, 4,222-ton steamer carrying sugar) surprised thanks to *Graf Spee's* deceptive appearance. No distress signal sent and more useful information captured by Langsdorff. *Ashlea's* crew transferred to *Newton Beech*; *Ashlea* sunk by scuttling charges.

8 October: *Newton Beech* proving slow and a liability: prisoners transferred to *Graf Spee* and prize sunk.

9 October: *Altmark* sighted by aircraft from HMS *Ark Royal* off Cape Verde Islands, but succeeds in passing itself off as the American SS *Delmar*.

10 October: SS *Huntsman* (8,196-ton liner with cargo of tea) captured; ship not sunk due to inability to accommodate prisoners. Prize crew put aboard and *Graf Spee* heads for rendezvous with *Altmark* in South Atlantic waiting area.

15 October: *Graf Spee* refuels from *Altmark*; latter made ready for prisoners.

17 October: *Huntsman* sunk after prisoners transferred to *Altmark*. In possession of secret Admiralty code for radio traffic, Langsdorff heads south to Cape-UK trade route.

22 October: SS *Trevanion* (5,299 tons carrying concentrates) captured and scuttled. Garbled distress message sent out. German Naval Operations Staff orders Langsdorff into Indian Ocean due to reported concentration of British naval forces and maintenance of 'no full commitment' proviso.

Meanwhile HMS *Caradoc* intercepts the German *Emmy Friedrich*, carrying supplies intended for *Graf Spee's* refrigeration plant for keeping magazines at safe temperatures. (Maintaining supplies of carbon dioxide and tropical oil put severe constraints on *Graf Spee's* ability to operate in tropical waters.) Survivors of *Deutschland's* victim SS *Lorenz W. Hansen* land in Orkneys and report being attacked by *Deutschland*; SS *City of Flint* arrives with prize crew in Murmansk (another of *Deutschland's* victims).

28 October: *Graf Spee* refuels from *Altmark* west of the Cape of Good Hope and transfers prisoners. At midnight Langsdorff begins his move into the Indian Ocean, passing south of the Cape on 3 November.

15 November: After 10 days of fruitless cruising on Cape-Australia and Cape-India routes, Langsdorff enters the Mozambique Channel; captures the SS *Africa Shell* (706-ton motor tanker in ballast), which he then scuttles. No distress call.

16 November: Langsdorff picks up warning of his presence in the Indian Ocean. Satisfied that he has created enough alarm in the area, Langsdorff heads back into the South Atlantic again. Once more he asks for the restrictions on his operations to be removed.

23 November: German battlecruisers *Scharnhorst* and *Gneisenau* sortie into Atlantic and sink armed merchant cruiser *Rawalpindi*, which mistakenly signals it is being attacked by the *Deutschland*. British Admiralty now convinced two raiders are at large, but think *Rawalpindi* episode may be one of them returning home. Hunting groups reorganised and reinforced.

23-30 November: *Graf Spee* back with *Altmark* in the Atlantic waiting area for engine overhaul. (The *Graf Spee's* diesels had been close to their maximum allowed running hours when war broke out and required frequent attention.) The vessel's appearance is also further disguised by a dummy forward gun turret and an extra 'funnel'. On 24 November Langsdorff explains to his officers that he is to return home for the required engine overhaul. He will also disobey his orders and 'commit himself fully' if he encounters enemy warships. As the ship will be on her way home the risk of limited damage would be acceptable. Notable successes are, however, required before returning as it is uncertain when another German ship would again be operating in the South Atlantic. At this point he decides to operate against the River Plate traffic before going home in the New Year.

2 December: Blue Star liner *Doric Star* (10,086 tons, cargo of meat, dairy produce and wool) sunk. Ship stopped by long range shots across bows. Repeated distress call sent out, picked up by SS *Port Chalmers* and relayed to Freetown. *Doric Star's* cargo would have been useful to Langsdorff but the ship's engineer had time to disable her engines. Giving the cargo liner so much time to take countermeasures may have been a surprising error of judgement: German sources suggest that Langdorff may have been looking for trouble. Ship's aircraft almost lost due to defects.

3 December: SS *Tairoa* (7,983 tons with cargo of meat, wool and lead) sunk as *Graf Spee* heads for River Plate. Distress call sent out and again picked up by *Port Chalmers*.

6 December: *Graf Spee* refuels from *Altmark*. She retains British Merchant Navy officers and radio operators on board but transfers 140 crewmen to *Altmark*.

7 December: SS *Streonshalh* (3,895 tons with cargo of wheat) sunk. Master refuses to send distress call so as not to endanger life. Confidential documents captured after being thrown over the side tell Lansdorff best position to intercept merchant ships out of the River Plate; he learns of convoy of four ships with naval auxiliary sailing from Montevideo on 10 December. Under Langsdorff's new interpretation of his orders he feels able to attack such targets.

9 December: With inspired guesswork Cdre Harwood orders *Exeter* (Falklands Islands) and *Achilles* (off Rio de Janeiro) to join with *Ajax* off the River Plate estuary.

11 December: *Graf Spee's* seaplane engine breaks down for the last time with no more spares available: the motor is jettisoned over the side although parts of the aircraft are retained on board. The false turret and funnel are removed as

they are a hindrance in combat. *Graf Spee* is stripping for action.

12 December: *Ajax*, *Achilles* and *Exeter* join forces 150 miles east of River Plate estuary.

13 December: Langsdorff sights *Exeter*, *Ajax* and *Achilles*.

The bare summary above does little to convey the utter confusion Langsdorff had sown. His handling of his cruise up to this point was faultless, and though he sank only nine vessels he had tied up a force of four battleships, four battlecruisers, six aircraft carriers and over 20 cruisers. To his immense credit not a single life was lost in the course of his attacks. On the other side, Harwood's reading of the situation was masterly. When *Doric Star* was sunk and the raider's position reported, *Graf Spee* was 3,000 miles away from the Plate. Guessing she would be tempted by the South Atlantic, Harwood had to choose between Rio de Janeiro, the Falkland Islands and the River Plate as to where she would hit next. To concentrate his force in the correct spot 24hr before the raider arrived was one of the most remarkable pieces of intelligent guesswork of the entire war.

Below:
Hunting Groups in the South Atlantic — 13 December 1939.

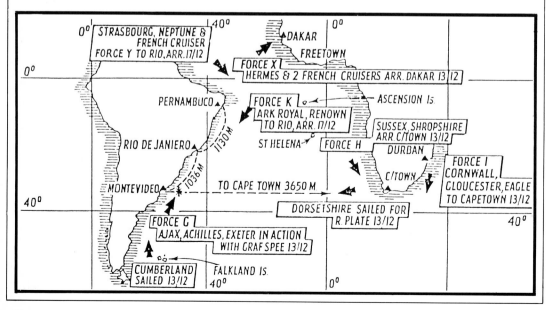

The Battle of the River Plate

Individually, Harwood's three cruisers were no match for *Graf Spee*.

HMS *Exeter*

Builder: HM Dockyard, Devonport
(Laid down 1 August 1928; launched 18 July 1929; completed 23 July 1931)

Displacement: 8,390 tons (standard)

Dimensions: 575ft × 58ft × 17ft

Machinery: Geared turbines, 4 shafts, 80,000shp, 32kt

Armour: Sides 3in (5½in on part of magazines); tower deck 1.5in over machinery; 3in over magazines; turrets 1in

Armament: 6×8in (3×2); 4×4in (4×1); 6×21in torpedo tubes (2×3); 2×aircraft (Vickers Supermarine Walrus in 1939)

Complement: 630

Notes: The 1922 Washington Naval Treaty limited cruisers to a maximum of 10,000 tons with guns not over 8in. The British Empire built 13 'County' class cruisers, but found the cost too high and so moved down the scale to the smaller 'B-type'. Only two were built, half sisters, *York* and *Exeter*; after considering reverting to 10,000-ton ships, the British were forced to concentrate on the smaller cruisers of the 'Leander' class, two of which were *Ajax* and *Achilles*.

HMS *Ajax* and HMS *Achilles*

Builders:
Ajax — Vickers-Armstrong, Barrow
(Laid down 7 February 1933; launched 1 March 1934; completed 12 April 1935)
Achilles — Cammell Laird
(Laid down 11 June 1931; launched 1 September 1932; completed 6 October 1933)

Displacement: *Ajax* 6,840 tons (standard); *Achilles* 7,030 tons (standard)

Dimensions: 554.5ft × 56ft × 16ft

Machinery: Geared turbines, 4 shafts, 72,000shp, 32.5kt

Armour: Sides 3-4in; deck 1.25-3in; turrets 1in

Armament: 8×6in (4×2); 4×4in (4×1); 8×21in torpedo tubes (2×4); 1/2 aircraft (*Ajax* was carrying two Fairey Seafox floatplanes; *Achilles* was not carrying the Walrus amphibian with which she had been fitted on transfer to the New Zealand Division)

Complement: 570

Notes: *Achilles* was attached to the New Zealand Division of the Royal Navy in March 1936; she was transferred to the Royal New Zealand Navy (and became 'HMNZS') when the latter was created on 10 October 1941.

0552-0614

Langsdorff's first sighting of the full extent of the British force threw him into a quandary. Although reminded by his navigation officer of his standing orders not to engage even inferior forces, he had already decided to fight what escort he found; this was, in the event, his fundamental error. He was, however, not expecting all the three ships sighted to be cruisers. Once he had thrown away the advantage confered by his more responsive engines, an advantage compounded by his earlier sighting of the British ships, he had no option but to fight; with a foul bottom *Graf Spee* could not make even her top speed of 26kt, and the enemy cruisers therefore had an advantage of over 8kt. Commentators have suggested he should have turned away from the British and used his superior main armament for as long as possible, while the British were still out of range. However, this would have allowed him presumably to bring only his three aft 11in guns to bear, an insufficient number for accurate fire control. Langsdorff could afford neither to miss nor to waste ammunition. His armour was proof against 8in shells, the most powerful available to the British. Moreover, at close range he could use both his main armament on the heavy cruiser and his secondary 5.9in armament on the smaller British ships; as such, his decision to close his enemy was the correct one.

At 0600 Langsdorff altered course towards his enemy, at his full speed of 24kt. *Graf Spee's* difficult engines appear to have had a smoke problem, and as she increased speed a cloud billowed forth from her funnel. It was soon sighted by the British, at 0614 and 2min later, *Exeter*

signalled 'I think it is a pocket battleship'. These were exactly the circumstances for which RN cruiser squadrons had prepared before the war and Harwood had rehearsed his tactics particularly well. They were simple and effective: *Exeter* would form the Second Division, *Achilles* and *Ajax* the First. The two Divisions would separate to exploit the pocket battleship's restricted armament layout and to split enemy fire. *Exeter* would flank mark for the other two cruisers whilst they fired as one group, passing range and elevation details over radio. Ever since the lessons of Jutland had been first absorbed, the Royal Navy had spent much time developing the technique of concentration firing. Sadly, damage to radio equipment only allowed it to work for just over 20min.

0615-0637

Graf Spee swung to port at 0615 so as to be able to bring both her 11in turrets to bear on HMS *Exeter*. At 20,000yd she was in a good position to engage. At 0616, as soon as Capt Bell of *Exeter* had decided the smoke was that of a pocket battleship, he rang down for full speed and bore away to the westward. That no signal was needed shows how clearly understood Harwood's orders had been. *Ajax* and *Achilles* headed on a course of 240° to close the range. Bell first intended to engage *Graf Spee* to port, but, seeing that this might cause difficulties for Harwood, he moved further round to a course of 280° before opening fire to starboard.

The British thought that Harwood's tactics had been successful in causing the *Graf Spee* to divide its main armament between the two Divisions, but

HMS *Exeter*, scuttled after receiving heavy damage from Japanese cruisers, 1 March 1942.
Bur Mar Hist vd Marinestaf

the Germans at first concentrated their 11in guns on *Exeter* and their 5.9in on the First Division. At 0618 *Graf Spee* opened fire and *Exeter* replied with 'A' and 'B' turrets at 0620 at a range of 18,700yd. At 0622 *Achilles* opened up, joined by *Ajax* a minute later. At Jutland, German fire, directed by long base-length rangefinders, proved very accurate in the opening stages and little had changed in 1939. *Graf Spee's* second 11in salvo found the range and her third salvo of six rounds straddled *Exeter* at 0623; splinters killed the starboard torpedo crew, and damaged both Walrus aircraft. Another of *Graf Spee's* shells reportedly went right through the deck and out the side, abaft of 'B' turret, without exploding. The Germans later regretted not using armour-piercing shells against *Exeter*, but it is an open question whether the increased penetration of these rounds against the cruiser's protected spaces would have been counterbalanced by incidents such as this; the German HE rounds were effective enough. *Exeter* had fired eight salvoes, the third a straddle, when an 11in shell scored a direct hit on 'B' turret.

As well as putting the turret out of action, it swept the bridge and conning positions with a hail of splinters, killing all on the bridge except Capt Bell and two others. Wounded in the face, Bell proceeded to the secondary conning position aft, with a party of messengers to carry steering

Below:
The Battle of the River Plate — 0614-0740.

orders to the after steering position. *Exeter* was hit twice more forward, and damaged by more splinters, though she remained capable of steaming at full speed. After drenching the after control position with petrol the two damaged aircraft were jettisoned.

At this point Langsdorff made his first serious mistake. By 0630 he had hit *Exeter* badly, but he himself had been hit several times and was increasingly worried by the rapid, accurate and concentrated fire of the two light cruisers; moreover, as an old torpedo specialist himself, he was acutely worried by the torpedo threat. Accordingly, he shifted his main armament to *Ajax* and *Achilles* at 0630. His 11in broadsides had been accurate, and a few more minutes of concentrated fire on *Exeter* might well have finished her off, as events a short while later were to prove. As it was, *Ajax* and *Achilles* were hit only by splinters, largely as a result of masterful ship handling.

In a typically aggressive manner *Exeter* fired her starboard tubes under local control at 0632, and her port tubes at 0643. To avoid the first attack, and still worried by the threat of the other two cruisers, now ranging at 13,000yd, Langsdorff at 0637 made a sharp turn to port of 150°, making smoke. This marked the beginning of the end.

0638-0740

After turning, *Graf Spee* concentrated its main armament again on *Exeter* and inflicted two more crippling hits: one knocked out 'A' turret, the other started a bad fire amidships, putting out of action the fire control circuits and gyro-compass repeaters. Later another hit forward caused a 7° list, again (and quite remarkably) with none of this

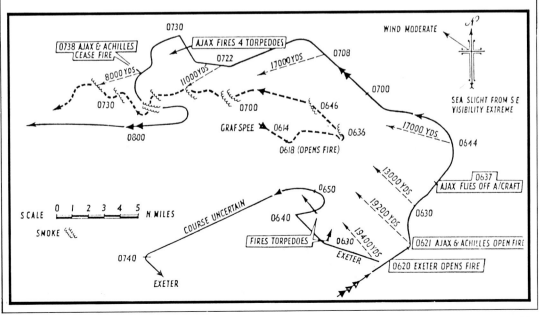

affecting her engine room or speed. Had Langsdorff continued his sweep to port he might have polished off *Exeter*, which now had only 'Y' turret firing in local control. Instead the torpedo threat drew him back to *Ajax* and *Achilles*, which he engaged at 17,000yd.

At 0637 *Ajax* had launched her Seafox aircraft to spot fall of shot. Her pilot realised his radio was tuned in to 230kcs, the reconnaissance rather than the spotting frequency, and signalled the flagdeck to this effect. Alas, the message never reached the wireless office. As a result it was not until 0649 when the aircraft returned to the correct spotting frequency (3.8mcs) that radio contact was established. Before this, at 0646 *Achilles* had lost her wireless link and so had reverted to individual control for her guns, rather than concentrated firing with *Ajax*. The Seafox was not aware of this, reported *Achilles'* salvo to *Ajax*, and as a result *Ajax* was correcting not for her own fire but for *Achilles'*. Until the mistake was realised *Ajax* fired consistently over.

Graf Spee's secondary armament appears to have made little impact on the course of the battle up to this point. The reason may have been the absence of effective protection for secondary gun crews, causing a high casualty rate amongst them and hence inaccurate fire. After Langsdorff's alteration of course to 120° away from his enemy the battle turned into a chase. At 0710 Harwood tired of the long range of the engagement and turned westward to shorten it, increasing to full speed; this effectively halved his fire. As his after turrets could no longer bear, Langsdorff made a turn to port at 0716 under cover of smoke and Harwood interpreted this as an attempt to finish off *Exeter*. Accordingly he turned to starboard to uncover all his guns and rescue the stricken ship. *Graf Spee* was hit amidships and the remains of the Arado caught fire. This regained Langsdorff's attention and he swung back to starboard to resume his main armament bombardment of the First Division at 11,000yd. He straddled *Ajax* with three salvoes and at 0725 *Graf Spee* landed a hit which put both *Ajax's* after turrets out of action.

Suddenly the battle had gone into overdrive.

Left:
HMS *Cumberland* as rebuilt in 1935-36 with additional armour and large aircraft hangar.
Real Photographs S1135

Ajax turned to starboard and fired four torpedoes at 9,000yd, Langsdorff swung away and then back again to fire his own vessel's four starboard tubes. *Ajax's* Seafox reported the tracks, and Harwood swung away to avoid them.

Graf Spee was now headed firmly west, making occasional smoke and blazing away with her entire armament, including her 4.1in AA guns firing time-fused shells. At 0738 Harwood heard that *Ajax* had expended all but 20% of her 6in ammunition. The report was in error; it was only 'A' turret that was so down on ammunition. The actual position was much healthier, but what he heard and the fact he had only three guns in action (a hoist having failed in 'B' turret) persuaded Harwood to break off the action at 0740, swinging away east under smoke. He planned to shadow and close in again at nightfall. The range at this time was down to 8,000yd, and *Graf Spee's* fire was still accurate, as a hit that collapsed *Ajax's* topmast and lost all her radio aerials proved. *Exeter* had broken off the action at 0730 when flooding put 'Y' turret's machinery out of action. Her casualties

were 61 men killed and 23 wounded, she was unable to shoot, had more holes in her than a sieve, and her mainmast was held up by little more than faith and defiance of the laws of gravity.

The view from Langsdorff's bridge was clearly very different. The bare facts were that *Graf Spee* had 40% ammunition remaining, 36 dead, six seriously wounded and 53 other wounded. Langsdorff himself had been wounded due to his having directed operations from the unprotected foretop gallery. *Graf Spee* had been hit by three 8in and 17 6in shells. One 8in round, most unnervingly for the Germans, had penetrated the main armoured belt within the internal armoured bulkheads: a few inches lower and it would have entered the machinery spaces. Another of *Exeter's* rounds penetrated two decks and destroyed the water purification plant. It might have been better if the 6in cruisers had used HE shells as their AP rounds could not penetrate *Graf Spee's* armour. Nevertheless, *Ajax* and *Achilles* had peppered her superstructure and given her a large hole in her bows. *Graf Spee's* bakery, gallery and most

Above:
The damaged main armament director control tower of HMS *Achilles*.
Imperial War Museum (IWM) HU203

Below:
British Shell Hits on the *Graf Spee*

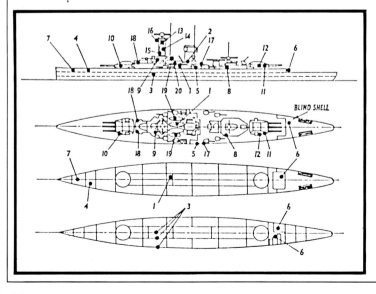

BLIND SHELL

Note:
Nos 2, 3 and 15 are 8in shell hits by HMS *Exeter*, the remainder are 6in hits by HMS *Ajax* and HMS *Achilles*.

Positions of British shell hits on the *Admiral Graf Spee* (from p215 of *The Drama of the* Graf Spee *and the Battle of the Plate*, compiled by Sir Eugen Millington Drake (Peter Davies, London, 1964).

Notes:
Perhaps the most important hit was number 3 which penetrated the main belt and demonstrated *Graf Spee's* unexpected vulnerability to heavy cruisers. The major damage actually inflicted was a large hole in the bows, the galley, refrigeration and water purification plants and, most importantly, the loss of the engine-oil purification machinery. She was, however, still able to fight even with all her hits. Thanks to the early disabling of HMS *Exeter* her main armament and machinery were untouched. Nonetheless, Langsdorff could not calculate that he would be safe from HMS *Cumberland's* fire, which had the potential for inflicting lethal, or at least disabling damage.

importantly, her plant for purifying fuel oil had been wrecked. The loss of the oil purification plant was serious as it was far from clear that *Graf Spee's* poor engines could make the Atlantic crossing without it. The hole in the bows also complicated the ship's inherent problem of wetness in a head sea. Although *Graf Spee* remained seaworthy she was no longer in a fit condition for a long ocean voyage. There was thus good reason to visit a neutral port for urgent repairs.

Graf Spee might have continued the action against the British cruisers and dealt with both, but all her high explosive main armament rounds (the most effective against light cruisers) had been expended. She only had 40min worth of armour-piercing rounds remaining and all these and more might have been necessary to deal with Harwood's well-handled ships. Certainly there would have been precious few rounds left to give *Graf Spee* protection from the overwhelming might of Anglo-French sea power commanding the oceans on the homeward voyage. *Graf Spee* had not got the speed to avoid being dogged by Harwood's cruisers until inevitably heavier forces arrived. If Langsdorff fought he was doomed, if he did not fight he was doomed. His humanitarian instincts were appalled by the thought of his crew suffering more casualties to such little purpose. Wounded, his nerve no doubt shaken by the persistence of his opponents, Langsdorff took the obvious way out. He had to have time to think — he headed for Montevideo.

0740-2350

At 0814 the hard-working *Ajax's* Seafox was

Below:
The *Admiral Graf Spee's* approach to Montevideo.

ordered to find *Exeter*, who was not answering on radio and tell her to close on the flagship. *Exeter* was duly found and at 0910 the aircraft signalled to Harwood that she was 'badly damaged, but is joining you as best she can'. At 0916, surprisingly late in the day, *Cumberland* was ordered to leave the Falklands. It was rapidly becoming a tradition for British warships to be called into action from the Falklands when they were least ready for it; the battlecruisers at the first Battle of the Falklands were coaling when Von Spee's squadron was sighted, and *Cumberland* had her boilers opened up to repair brickwork when she was called up. Despite this she left Port Stanley at 1000, Capt Fallowfield having raised steam on his own initiative when he heard of the action commencing, thus making up to some extent for his mistake on 6 October.

Neither *Ajax* nor *Achilles* had radar, and *Graf Spee's* had insufficient bearing accuracy and range to be of any use beyond search and preliminary target acquisition in conditions when visibility was less than 15,000m. The River Plate action was thus fought without any modern electronic aids. At 1005 *Achilles* was unfortunate enough to draw three salvoes from *Graf Spee* when she drew in to 23,000yd: *Achilles* quickly retired to a more cautious distance. Brief flurries of action and news enlivened the long day. At 1107 *Exeter* signalled her plight to Harwood. She could still make 18kt but only one 8in gun was available in local control; a single 4in gun was also available. Twenty minutes later came the laconic 'All guns out of action'. HMS *Exeter* was clearly of little further use to Harwood and he ordered her to the Falklands at 1340; she turned south at 1510.

Just over half-an-hour later a merchantman was sighted with a silhouette akin to that of a German

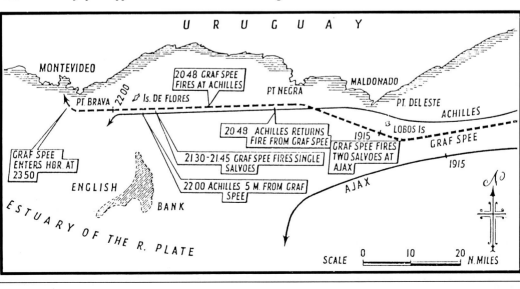

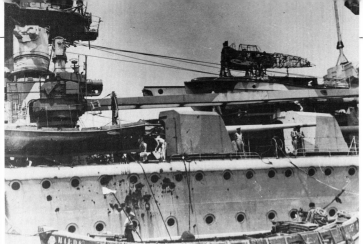

heavy cruiser, causing more than a few flutters on
the British light cruisers before the SS *Delane* was
correctly identified. At 1915, near the Uruguayan
coast, *Graf Spee* suddenly turned and fired two
salvoes at *Ajax* from 26,000yd. Grand-Adm
Raeder had responded to Langsdorff's signal
detailing his intention to enter Montevideo with
the curt reply 'Agreed'; Harwood knew for certain
at 1900 that this was her intention, and split his
forces accordingly — *Achilles* to follow her in, and
Ajax to patrol to the south of the estuary in case
Graf Spee doubled back.

At 2048, still 50 miles out, *Graf Spee* fired three
salvoes at *Achilles*, to which the British ship
replied with five. Between 2130 and 2145 *Graf
Spee* fired three final salvoes, but her shadower
was able to keep at 10,000yd as the German ship
was silhouetted against the lights of Montevideo.
She dropped anchor shortly before midnight.

The Plate estuary offered three possible exit
routes for *Graf Spee* across a hundred-mile width.
Harwood had one cruiser with only splinter
damage, and one minus half its main armament
(between them the two ships had lost 11 killed and
five injured); *Cumberland* would not arrive for
24hr. Harwood was man enough, no doubt, to
wonder if his immediate promotion to Rear-Adm,
the award of the KCB, and the award of the CB to
the captains of the three cruisers might not be a
little premature. He had won the *first* Battle of the
River Plate, but his enemy could still slip past him
all too easily — or overwhelm him. Harwood
estimated that *Graf Spee's* chance of a successful
escape were 70-30 in her favour.

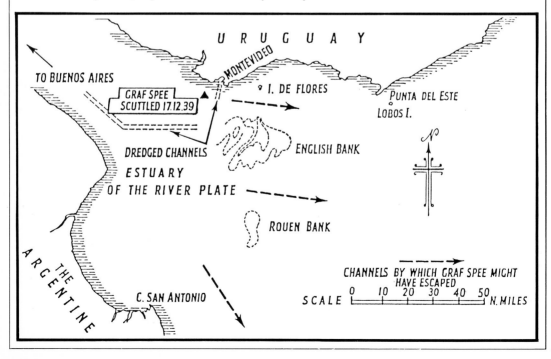

Montevideo: 14-16 December

When *Graf Spee* dropped anchor in Montevideo a whole new set of characters and issues came into play. On the one hand was Langsdorff, the German Minister Otto Langmann and his naval attaché Capt Dietrich Niebur; on the other hand was the British Minister Eugen Millington-Drake and his naval attaché McCall. In the middle was General Alfredo Baldomir — President of Uruguay, his Minister for Foreign Affairs Dr Alberton Guani, and the Minister for Defence General Alfredo Campos. The Uruguayan Government had to guard their country's neutrality, attempt to keep friendly relations with Britain, but also take account of the vociferous pro-Nazi element in their population.

The law, as defined by the Hague Convention of 1907, was straightforward enough. A belligerent warship could remain in a neutral port for only 24hr, unless it had suffered damage, in which case it could be allowed to make repairs *only* to render it seaworthy. It was not allowed to 'add in any manner whatever' to its fighting capacity. The Germans wanted a stay of 15 to 17 days, to repair damage and make her capable of a long voyage. The British started by arguing that as *Graf Spee* had sailed over 300 miles at full speed to reach Montevideo she was clearly seaworthy, and should leave after 24hr. In the meantime a Uruguayan technical team inspected *Graf Spee* on the 14th, after Langsdorff had freed his miraculously uninjured British prisoners, landed his dead for burial, and sent his seriously wounded for hospital treatment.

Early on the 15th the British realised that by pushing for *Graf Spee* to leave early they were forcing themselves over a cliff edge. Harwood wisely signalled on the 15th that the last thing he wanted was an early departure, when his forces would have been augmented by only one 8in-gun cruiser, the *Cumberland*, which joined Harwood at 2200 on the 14th. The British Admiralty had acted fast enough in sending reinforcements. The following ships were ordered to the Plate in support:

Vessels Ordered to River Plate

Ship	Type	Point of origin	Arrival time at River Plate
Dorsetshire	8in cruiser	Cape Town	21 December
Shropshire	8in cruiser	Cape Town	23 December
Renown	Battlecruiser	Off Pernambuco	19 December
Ark Royal	Aircraft carrier	Off Pernambuco	19 December
Neptune	6in cruiser	Off Pernambuco	19 December

From the above it is clear that the British would not have a concentration of force available until 19 December. The result of all this was a mind-boggling display of shadow-boxing from both sides. The Germans wanted a stay of 15 days but did not want to make this too clear in case they revealed the extent of *Graf Spee's* damage to the British. The British wanted the ship interned, but if that was not possible they wanted its sailing to be delayed until the 19th. However, to press for that day too earnestly might well reveal the weakness of the forces waiting outside for *Graf Spee*. The British therefore planted stories that both *Ark Royal* and *Renown* were already off the Plate estuary, tried to appear eager to get *Graf Spee* out of Montevideo and at the same time held up their sleeve the ace that they were later to play magnificently: the Hague Convention forbade a belligerent warship to leave port less than 24hr after the departure of a merchant vessel flying the flag of an adversary, and there were British ships in Montevideo.

15 December

On Friday 15 December Langsdorff buried his dead. Alone of those at the gravesides he gave the old naval salute, all the others giving the Nazi salute. Pictures show a furious Otto Langmann directing a baleful glare at Langsdorff. The British prisoners attended the funeral, and placed a wreath on the coffins of the German dead, inscribed 'To the memory of brave men of the sea from their comrades of the British Merchant Service'. Thereafter the blows fell thick and fast on to Langsdorff. His own Embassy reported that *Ark Royal* and *Renown* had left Cape Town on 12 December, when in fact they were at that time far to the north. Then one of *Graf Spee's* gunnery officers reported a definite sighting from *Graf Spee's* Director Control Tower of *Renown*, *Ark Royal* and several destroyers. These reports, planted British rumours, and genuine over-eagerness on the part of observers, convinced Langsdorff that superior British forces were waiting for him. It is sometimes assumed that these reports were the deciding factor in his decision to scuttle. This is not so. At 1300 on 17 December Langsdorff heard definitely and beyond any shadow of doubt that *Ark Royal* and *Renown* had entered Rio de Janeiro, 1,000 miles away from the Plate. It did not make him change his mind. Both vessels were faster than his own, British shadowing forces were waiting for him, and there was still nothing he could do except postpone the evil day.

Then Langsdorff heard the decision of the Uruguayan Government: *Graf Spee* was to be allowed a 72hr stay, meaning that he would have to leave on the evening of 17 December.

16 December
Langsdorff had three options open to him, all of which were widely discussed by his superiors and Hitler. *Graf Spee* could be interned, break out and possibly fight her way to Argentina, a country which might be expected to be more sympathetic to the German cause, or scuttle herself. On 16 December opinion seemed to be moving towards the Argentinian breakout. All parties considered internment ignominious and unthinkable; a breakout was the preferred option, with scuttling (provided it could be done effectively) the second choice. This was the gist of the many signals sent to Langsdorff from Germany.

Then came the news that, probably more than anything else, tipped the balance in favour of scuttling: Langsdorff was informed that the British SS *Ashworth* had sailed from Montevideo at 1850 that evening; *Graf Spee* therefore could not sail until 1815 on the evening of 17 December, and his time limit expired at 2000 on the 17th. His best chance of escape was a sudden dash; now the British would know within an hour-and-a-half when he would have to sail. The British had sailed the steamer in order to keep *Graf Spee* in port; Langsdorff saw it merely as the British pinning him down to a departure time.

Perhaps the breakout to Argentina was never really a viable possibility. There was little reason to think Argentina would be more sympathetic than Uruguay, and in any event a battle in the shallow waters of the Plate might clog *Graf Spee's* cooling-water intakes and stop her, or shell damage cause her to ground and become a sitting duck. If hastily abandoned in shallow water, secret equipment such as her radar might fall intact into enemy hands.

17 December
At 0300 on 17 December Langsdorff returned on board *Graf Spee* from the German Embassy. The British, still only with *Cumberland*, *Ajax* and *Achilles*, were convinced *Graf Spee* would fight. Harwood's orders were identical to those issued to his force when *Exeter* was the heavyweight member of the group. They commenced with the phrase 'My object destruction'. No one was quite sure whose destruction was being referred to. This did not stop Harwood's men from requesting that they remain closed up at full action stations all night on the 16th despite Harwood's order that they could stand down to the third degree of readiness in order to get some sleep, after four days of frantic activity.

Various valuables were removed from *Graf Spee* in the morning, including her ship's bell.

Documents and equipment were destroyed and scuttling charges placed. 700 crew were transferred to the German tanker *Tacoma*, lying in the Roads.

At 1800 *Graf Spee* weighed anchor, and moved out with two Nazi ensigns flying, followed by the *Tacoma* a mile astern. Four miles out (a mile outside territorial waters) she altered course sharply to the west, dropped anchor and evacuated her crew. At 2200 she was torn apart by explosions. The British cruisers had not engaged immediately *Graf Spee* left territorial waters because of the lack of sea room and the risk of shells landing in Uruguay. But *Ajax's* Seafox saw the event, radioing '*Graf Spee* has just blown herself up'. Large parts of her torn and twisted hull remained above surface for several years. The Battle of the River Plate was over.

Aftermath
On the evening of 17 December Capt Hans Langsdorff said goodbye to his officers and men, wrote letters to his wife, his parents and the German Ambassador, laid out his ship's battle ensign and shot himself with his own revolver. In his letter to the German Ambassador he took full responsibility for the scuttling of the *Graf Spee*. He wrote that:

'. . . under the circumstances no other course was open to me, once I had taken the ship into the trap of Montevideo. For, with the ammunition remaining, any attempt to fight my way back to open deep water was bound to fail . . . Rather than expose my ship to the danger of falling partly or completely into enemy hands after her brave fight, I have decided not to fight but to destroy the equipment and scuttle the ship. It was clear to me that the decision might be consciously or unwittingly misconstrued by persons ignorant of my motives as being attributable partly or entirely to personal considerations. Therefore I decided from the beginning to bear the consequences involved in this decision.

'For a captain with a sense of honour, it goes without saying that his personal fate cannot be separated from that of his ship.'

Perhaps he could have broken free of his shadowers, met up with *Altmark*, and waited out the winter in isolation before returning to Germany. The fact that *Altmark* herself evaded capture until she was a hair's breadth from home is no proof that *Graf Spee* could have done the same. *Altmark's* existence was only realised when British prisoners told of her; a merchant ship is a great deal more innocuous than a pocket battleship and *Altmark* did not first of all have to break free from British cruisers. In any event, *Altmark* was finally

spotted on 15 February in the Norwegian fjords, and Capt Philip Vian defied Norwegian territorial water to board *Altmark* and release her 299 British prisoners, with the famous cry 'The Navy's here!'.

Uruguayan warships stopped the *Tacoma* from sailing out of the Plate estuary, but the *Graf Spee's* crew were transferred to Argentinian tugs. Argentina insisted on interning the vast majority of the crew. Several escaped, and one became Captain of *U162*, sinking 86,000 tons of Allied shipping (almost twice the amount sunk by the *Graf Spee*). In the long term some 500 of the *Graf Spee's* crew settled in Argentina.

Conclusion

Langsdorff's scuttling of *Graf Spee* was not in the British naval code of conduct. A British officer in his predicament would have been expected to chance his arm, attempt escape and, if necessary, go down fighting against superior odds. Yet this was a tradition forged in an atmosphere of quantitative advantages and on the assumption of superior fighting qualities. Fighting, even against the odds, usually meant winning. The German Navy, for all its technical qualities built into individual ships, could never make these assumptions. To them taking on overwhelming odds meant inevitable destruction and death. To a man of Langsdorff's instincts such useless loss of life was absolute anathema. *Graf Spee's* captain was a remarkable man who had handled his raiding cruise with consummate skill as well as humanity, sinking over 80% of all Allied tonnage accounted for by surface raiders in 1939. He was trapped, above all else, by the sheer ubiquity of the Allies' command of the sea in 1939, at least when the challenge was posed in traditional terms. Langsdorff's crucial mistake, as the German Naval Staff later recognised, was to have disregarded his orders to avoid all engagements with defended targets. Langsdorff could have got away when he first sighted the British and they had not yet seen him. To press on and engage was a personal decision, taken against higher authority. Having chanced his arm and failed he took the path of true honour to his grave.

From the British viewpoint the River Plate was a copybook and brilliantly-handled cruiser action. The British ships had done the job for which they were built in the way they had been trained. Surface raiders had been a high priority threat in the interwar period and forces and techniques

were developed to deal with them. Sadly for the British they were rather less well prepared to deal with the U-boat menace which, in the first four months of the war, accounted for over 12 times the ships and eight times the tonnage disposed of by the *Graf Spee*.

British Honours and Awards

Knight Commander of the Order of the Bath

Cdre Henry Harwood (who also received immediate promotion to Rear-Adm).

Companion of the Order of the Bath

Capt F. S. Bell	*(Exeter)*
Capt W. E. Parry	*(Achilles)*
Capt C. H. L. Woodhouse	*(Ajax)*

Distinguished Service Order

Cdr D. H. Everett	*(Ajax)*
Cdr R. R. Graham	*(Exeter)*
Cdr D. M. L. Neame	*(Achilles)*
Cdr (E) C. E. Simms	*(Exeter)*
Lt R. E. Washbourn	*(Achilles)*
Lt I. D. De'ath, RM	*(Ajax)*

Distinguished Service Cross

Lt-Cdr D. P. Dreyer	*(Ajax)*
Lt-Cdr R. B. Jennings*	*(Exeter)*
Lt-Cdr C. J. Smith*	*(Exeter)*
Lt G. G. Cowburn	*(Achilles)*
Lt E. D. G. Lewin	*(Ajax)*
Lt N. K. Tod	*(Ajax)*
Lt A. E. Toase, RM	*(Exeter)*
Surgeon-Lt C. G. Hunter	*(Achilles)*
Surgeon-Lt R. W. G. Lancashire	*(Exeter)*
Mid A. Cameron	*(Exeter)*
Mid R. W. D. Don	*(Exeter)*
Gnr R. C. Biggs	*(Ajax)*

Who also received immediate promotion to Cdr

Gnr H. T. Burchall	*(Achilles)*
Gnr E. J. Watts	*(Achilles)*
Warrant Engineer A. P. Monk	*(Ajax)*
Warrant Shipwright F. H. T. Panter	*(Ajax)*
Warrant Shipwright C. E. Rendle	*(Exeter)*

Conspicuous Gallantry Medal

AB G. Gulliam	*(Exeter)*
Stoker P. O'Brien	*(Exeter)*
Marine W. A. Russell	*(Exeter)*
Sgt S. J. Trimble, RM	*(Achilles)*

Left:
Graf Spee burning. Note the patch placed over the hole in the bows, and the clear view of the radar. *IWM A4*

Right:
Sir Henry Harwood, photographed as an admiral after the Battle of the River Plate. *IWM A13964*

Distinguished Service Medal

AB A. J. Ball	*(Exeter)*
Engineroom Artificer F. L. Bond	*(Exeter)*
CPO W. G. Boniface	*(Achilles)*
CPO Telegraphist W. L. Brewer	*(Achilles)*
Marine T. S. Buckley	*(Ajax)*
Master-at-Arms S. A. Carter	*(Exeter)*
PO H. V. Chalkeley	*(Exeter)*
Sgt R. G. Cook, RM	*(Ajax)*
LS L. C. Curd	*(Ajax)*
Sick Berth Attendant E. T. Dakin	*(Exeter)*
Chief Mechanician W. G. Dorling	*(Ajax)*
Boy A. M. Dorset	*(Achilles)*
PO A. E. Fuller	*(Ajax)*
PO C. H. C. Gorton	*(Ajax)*
AB H. H. Gould	*(Achilles)*
Shipwright D. Graham	*(Ajax)*
PO W. E. Green	*(Exeter)*
PO C. F. Hallas	*(Exeter)*
PO W. R. Headon	*(Achilles)*
PO J. W. Hill	*(Ajax)*
Chief Mechanician L. Hood	*(Achilles)*
Electrical Artificer J. W. Jenkins	*(Ajax)*
Joiner F. Knight	*(Exeter)*
AB R. D. Macey	*(Ajax)*
Engineroom Artificer J. McGarry	*(Exeter)*
AB R. McClarnan	*(Ajax)*
Chief Yeoman of Signals L. C. Martinson	*(Achilles)*
PO A. Maycock	*(Achilles)*
Stoker J. L. Minhinett	*(Exeter)*
Stoker F. E. Monk	*(Ajax)*
Stoker R. C. Perry	*(Ajax)*
Engineroom Artificer T. G. Phillips	*(Exeter)*
Sick Berth Chief Petty Officer C. D. Pope	*(Exeter)*
OD I. T. L. Rodgers	*(Achilles)*
Chief Mechanician J. A. Rooskey	*(Exeter)*
Chief Ordnance Artificer G. H. Sampson	*(Achilles)*
Sgt F. T. Saunders, RM	*(Achilles)*
AB E. V. Sherley	*(Achilles)*
PO S. J. Smith	*(Exeter)*
Plumber G. E. Smith	*(Exeter)*
LA E. A. Shoesmith	*(Exeter)*
Chief Stoker W. J. Wain	*(Achilles)*
Sgt A. B. Wilde, RM	*(Exeter)*
Stoker B. Wood	*(Ajax)*
Cook A. G. Young	*(Achilles)*

Many other officers and men of all three ships were 'mentioned in despatches'

CHAPTER TWO

The Attack on Taranto

The attack by aircraft from HMS *Illustrious* on the Italian fleet in their home port of Taranto on 11/12 November 1940 was a magnificent achievement in itself, paving the way for Pearl Harbor and marking the beginning of the end for the battleship as a dominant vessel. It was also a strike that came very near to not happening at all.

The Royal Navy and Air Power

The Royal Navy had been a pioneer as regards air power after World War 1. It had lost almost all of its officers who thought as airmen as well as seamen when the Royal Naval Air Service became an important part of the new Royal Air Force in 1918. Despite much 'air mindedness' of a limited

kind among naval officers, the Navy was not to recover from this until well into World War 2. Nevertheless, by the mid-1920s the Royal Navy could claim five operational aircraft carriers: *Furious, Eagle, Hermes, Courageous* and *Glorious.* Only one of these — *Hermes* — was purpose-built, the remainder being conversions of battlecruiser or battleship hulls, and aircraft-carrying capacity tended to be small, but this was still a significant force.

However, between 1928 and 1936 naval aviation hit the doldrums. Between 1928 and 1932 a mere 18 aircraft joined the Fleet Air Arm, and Britain did not bother even to use the 24,000 tons of spare aircraft carrier capacity allowed her by the Washington Naval Treaty. Defence economies

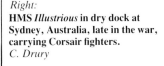

Right:
HMS *Illustrious* in dry dock at Sydney, Australia, late in the war, carrying Corsair fighters.
C. Drury

Far right:
A prewar picture of a Fairey Swordfish or 'Stringbag' — Mk I K5933 is illustrated.
Military Aircraft Photographs (MAP) 47/R29

were the major culprit, with both the Royal Navy and Royal Air Force finding better ways of utilising scarce resources (among them the cruisers that dealt with the *Graf Spee*). Nevertheless, another vital factor was the complex system of 'dual control' and dual manning set up as a compromise between the two services in 1924. The Royal Navy had an interest in keeping the 'Fleet Air Arm' of the Royal Air Force small so that it could be manned by the maximum proportion of naval officers.

The beginnings of naval rearmament began to solve the resources problems and in 1936 the new carrier *Ark Royal* was laid down. In 1937, after a major inter-service tussle, it was decided that the Fleet Air Arm should come back under Admiralty control; the administrative hand-over duly took place in May 1939. Nevertheless recent history had taken its toll. The major weakness was the absence of effective high-performance aircraft. The famous Fairey Swordfish, or 'stringbag', came into service in 1936. This biplane has won undying fame for its exploits, but it was undoubtedly obsolescent by contemporary aircraft standards almost before it

came into service. The great virtues of the Swordfish were its immensely rugged construction and its handling qualities. These allowed it to take the intense battering of carrier operations, take-off and land when other aircraft would be grounded (shown most clearly when *Ark Royal's* Swordfish took off to land a crucial hit on *Bismarck* when the flightdeck had a rise and fall of over 50ft) and manoeuvre extremely well. Its major weakness was that it was very slow.

The disappointing Devastator monoplane was substantially faster, but not by such a margin as to make up for its inferior robustness. The Japanese 'Kate', in service from 1937 and designed by dedicated naval airmen to a most ambitious requirement, was a remarkably advanced aircraft, head and shoulders above the rest, but in 1940 it was still serving side-by-side with the Yokosuka B4Y1 'Jean' biplane of very similar performance to the Swordfish. The key problem was that, given Britain's inability to produce new naval aircraft as well as new types needed by the RAF, the Swordfish was in service much longer than the others, although eventually in duties to which its qualities made it well suited. The Fleet Air Arm was, however, forced to retain it as a firstline torpedo bomber for about 2-3 years too long, in times of revolutionary developments in aircraft design.

Part of the Swordfish's problem was that it was a TSR (torpedo-spotter-reconnaissance) aircraft. To the naval officers who set the RAF the thankless (and often impossible) task of designing naval aircraft in the 1930s, spotting for the guns and finding the enemy fleet in the first place were at least as important as torpedo-dropping in the functions of naval aircraft, if not more so. The multi-purpose concept had been a suggestion of the naval airmen to obtain the most from a limited number of aircraft, but its effects were negative as the Naval Staff tried to combine only dubiously similar functions. The 'three-seat spotter fighter' never took to the air but the moderately adequate Skua intended to dive-bomb the enemy's screen of smaller ships was asked to double as a fighter. Given the structure of the 1924-39 Fleet Air Arm, observers tended to be senior to pilots; this, combined with the real problems of flying aircraft over the sea, seemed to make two seats mandatory for fleet fighters. A dubious RAF converted a Fairey light bomber into the Skua's successor. This was progress, at least it was not meant to bomb anyone, but at the time of its design fighters were only intended to knock down spotters. In the words of the C-in-C Home Fleet in 1938: 'Modern gunfire makes the air attack of fleets uneconomical'.

The British Naval Staff was, on the whole, satisfied with its aircraft. It wanted them in large part for the tasks for which it uses helicopters today: high performance in terms of speed was not a high priority. It was assumed that low performance was a natural consequence of modifications to operate from ships; combined with small numbers this fed low expectations. British carriers were not expected to fight for command of the air, certainly not to take on a land-based air force. Carriers were vulnerable: they might be relatively easily destroyed even by low performance aircraft. The battleships at sea could only be slowed down, or thrown into confusion in the vital opening moments of battle. In 1936 the Admiralty took the crucial decision to accept only 36 TSRs as the standard complement of British fleet carriers. This was half the complement of the superb *Ark Royal* laid down that year, but enough for expected fleet purposes given the availability of spotter-fighters in battle-ships and cruisers. Spreading aircraft around the maximum number of platforms would diminish the problem of carrier vulnerability, but the carriers themselves were also to be made as tough as possible. Thus, plans were approved for a new

fleet carrier design, the 'Illustrious' class. This ignored savings to be made in time and money by ordering more of the 'Ark Royal' class, as originally projected. It also put more strain on Britain's inadequate armour production facilities.

Illustrious was based on the idea that carrier-based fighters would be inadequate to defend the vessel against an enemy, and that British carriers would be operating both within range of enemy land-based bombers and on the edge of fleets vulnerable to enemy light forces. The resulting design therefore carried a huge anti-aircraft armament, and had an armoured hangar (see technical specifications below and at the end of this chapter). The effect of putting this armoured box on the carrier was a much-reduced aircraft carrying capacity, in the case of *Illustrious* 36 aircraft (36 TSRs or 24 TSRs and 12 fighter/dive-bombers). In the event of air attack the aircraft were to be struck down to the security of the hangar, and air defence left to the guns and the armour protection.

This decision has received a surprisingly good press largely due to the good performance of the ships against kamikaze manned missiles in 1945. When fully considered, however, it must be seriously questioned. The Japanese battleships *Yamato* and *Mushashi* proved that all the armour protection in the world (especially if its layout has design weaknesses) is not a real defence against sustained aerial torpedo attack, and AA guns on carriers always provided a problem for ship designers. Ammunition supply was a problem, and blast damage from gun muzzles potentially harmful to parked aircraft. *Illustrious* was seriously damaged after Taranto, when she was attacked on 5 January 1942 by elements of the German Fliegerkorps X flying Junkers Ju87B (Stuka) dive-bombers. *Illustrious* had allowed her combat air patrol to chase off after torpedo-bombers which had attacked earlier; but even with all her fighters she would have been hard-pressed to counter the attack. It would have needed at least a couple of squadrons of fighters (a US or Japanese carrier's complement) to break up such an attack.

As well as throwing into doubt the wisdom of having so few fighters this engagement has also raised the question of whether or not it was possible to strike down aircraft below with sufficient speed when faced with a surprise attack, as was the original design concept. Unlike shells, aircraft are large and bulky. They must go through large openings in order to move from 'magazine' (ie hangar) to 'launcher' (ie deck); here was the *Illustrious'* achilles heel. At each end of the box hangar with its 4½in armoured sides and ends were a set of large, thin doors leading into the lift wells. The 3in flightdeck armour was continued fore and aft on each side of the lift well for half the length of each relatively narrow lift. The rest of the deck on each side of the lift was armoured with 1.5in plate. The lifts themselves were, however, unprotected in order to make them easier to move (as was the flightdeck fore and aft of each lift). This meant that an unlucky bomb could penetrate the lift, explode in the lift well and the blast would pass into the hangar. Worse, if the ship was operating aircraft the doors might well be open with nothing but space between a lift, perhaps carrying a highly flammable aircraft and the equally combustible contents of the hangar.

This latter situation was the case on 5 June. Understandably *Illustrious* was trying to get more fighters into the air, not close down as an operational 'airfield'. The first serious hits, numbers 4 and 5 (see diagram on page 47) hit the after lift area just as a Fulmar fighter was being hoisted to the flightdeck. One hit the lip of the well, bounced down piercing the lift and exploded in the well. The other exploded on the lift demolishing the Fulmar. Whether the hangar doors were closed or not is unclear but the combined force of the bombs (two 550lb or one 550lb and one 1,100lb) would have overpowered the hangar doors anyway. The aft section of the hangar became a raging inferno of burning Swordfish and Fulmars.

To add to the carrier's woes the German 110lb (500kg) bombs were much heavier than *Illustrious*' upper hangar armour had been designed to withstand. Hit number seven went straight through the much-vaunted armoured deck and exploded inside the hangar, blowing a hole in the armoured floor and blasting forward through the forward hangar doors to buckle the forward hangar into the shape of an arch. Air rushed in to fan the flames but, although the internal metal fire screens were shredded causing fearful casualties, the fire did not spread into the forward part of the hangar. Nevertheless the ship's armoured protection had been well and truly defeated and *Illustrious* was only saved by heroic efforts on the part of her crew. It is true that a less strongly-constructed and protected vessel, and one with an 'open' as opposed to 'closed' hangar layout, might have been more seriously damaged still, and even foundered; it is also true that one with more fighters might well have taken less hits in the first place. Magnificent fire precautions that controlled the spread of the fire *inside* the hangar, and a high standard of training did much more to save *Illustrious* than her armour.

Despite all the shortcomings of its equipment the Fleet Air Arm in 1939-40 had a tremendous

Sir Dudley Pound, the controversial First Sea Lord who played an important role in the genesis of the Taranto raid. *IWM A16722*

spirit and belief in itself, a surprising number of enthusiastic officers who were prepared to squeeze the most out of what they had, and plentiful experience of operating carriers in a fleet context and at night. The Fleet Air Arm's ability to operate at night was a unique attribute for its time: it is even possible that its low performance aircraft were an aid in developing it. It was these virtues and their application in the right circumstances that were to create the great victory at Taranto.

The Mediterranean 1932-1940

In 1935 Mussolini's invasion of Abyssinia caused the idea first to be mooted in the British Mediterranean Fleet for a carrier-based attack on the Italian base at Taranto. No plan was prepared and there was no official discussion of any kind. The idea was resurrected in 1938 when the crisis over Czechoslovakia looked as if it might plunge Europe into war. The fleet commander, Adm Sir Dudley Pound, remembered the 1935 discussion and had the carrier *Glorious* under his command. Pound had little faith in the survival prospects of a carrier in the Mediterranean and wanted to get the

most out of her first. Capt A. L. St G. Lyster, *Glorious'* able and pugnacious captain, assured Pound that his Swordfish squadrons could carry out a night attack on Taranto. With the C-in-C's verbal authority Lyster had a conference with his senior airmen and told them to begin training with such an operation in mind. Secrecy was considered vital and no written records were kept, but when Pound became First Sea Lord in 1939 he took the idea with him. Indeed, the month before war broke out he wrote to Adm A. B. Cunningham, his successor in the Mediterranean, that 'I think there is a great deal to be said for making an attack by air on the Italian fleet at Taranto'.

When Hitler declared war on 3 September 1939 the British Mediterranean fleet consisted of three battleships, one aircraft carrier, three 8in cruisers, three 6in cruisers, one anti-aircraft cruiser, 26 destroyers, four escorts, 10 submarines and four minesweepers. When Mussolini failed to declare war on Britain immediately, ships were taken away from the Mediterranean theatre, but the situation altered dramatically in June 1940 when Mussolini declared war and France was defeated 11 days later. This latter fact meant that French ships could no longer cover the western Mediterranean, for

which eventuality the famous 'Force H' had to be assembled in Gibraltar.

The Admiralty found the man for the job in appointing Adm Sir Andrew Cunningham to command in the Mediterranean. Essentially a destroyer man, he brought total aggression and determination to the Mediterranean, remaining undaunted at a time when the disposition of forces put the British at a huge disadvantage. Cunningham was allocated one carrier, *Eagle*, which, according to prewar doctrine, had an all-TSR air group, 18 Swordfish. Local initiative supplemented these with three Sea Gladiator fighters, the agile single-seat biplanes which delighted FAA pilots had received, despite the doubts of their senior officers, in 1939. Although the Italians still relied on biplane fighters of their own, this was not much to set against the Regia Aeronautica, the Italian Air Force.

The Italians, too, were not without their problems: Mussolini had declared that Italy was one huge aircraft carrier, and denied the Italian Navy its own fleet air arm. The Italian Supreme Command was dominated by Mussolini and the Army, neither of whom understood naval matters. The Chief of the Italian Naval Staff,

Adm Domenico Cavagnari, had expressed grave misgivings to Mussolini when he heard of the impending declaration of war. In Cavagnari's view an offensive naval war against France and Britain would allow the latter's greater naval resources to make good losses. However, a defensive strategy would also allow France and Britain to exhaust Italian resources to little benefit for Italy. Cavagnari noted the shortage of Italian reconnaissance aircraft, the difficulties of working with the Regia Aeronautica and the inadequate state of air defence at Italian naval bases. He did not mention that no form of effective military co-operation had been worked out with Germany. With all his misgivings, Cavagnari opted for a defensive strategy in the Mediterranean. With both France and Britain opposed to him he was no doubt justified in this but, when France was knocked out of the war, his refusal to change his policy and opt for a more aggressive and offensive mode was of dubious validity.

Thus when war was declared both sides had their problems, but after the capitulation of France the balance of power swung very much the way of the Italians. The early days of the conflict saw both sides being reinforced, and a number of relatively inconclusive brushes which gave the moral advantage to the British. The main task of Cunningham's forces was to guard the convoy routes to Malta, keep the eastern Mediterranean open to shipping and harry the Italian forces. The Italians for their part were committed to supplying their army in Libya. Cunningham put to sea on 7 July 1940 to escort a convoy evacuating women and children from Malta and another carrying stores to Alexandria. Italian bombers hurled over 50 bombs at *Warspite*, but succeeded only in hitting the cruiser *Gloucestershire* with one bomb, on 8 July. On 9 July the British force brushed with an Italian escort force of two battleships and numerous cruisers, but after a 15in hit at extreme range from *Warspite* had demonstrated the superiority of modern British fire control, the Italian Adm Inigo Campioni broke off the action. On two further occasions the Italian fleet avoided action with the British. Several interesting features emerged from these scuffles: Italian reconnaissance was clearly inadequate, as was their high level bombing, and Italian aircraft showed a disturbing tendency to attack their own ships.

In August, Cunningham was reinforced by the modernised battleship *Valiant*, the new carrier *Illustrious* and two AA cruisers. At the same time the Italian fleet was augmented by the arrival of the two new battleships, *Vittorio Veneto* and *Littorio* (both with nine 15in guns and an excellent turn of speed), and the modernised *Caio Duilio*. These three ships were added to the two modernised battleships *Giulio Cesare* and *Conte di Cavour*, seven 8in cruisers, 12 6in cruisers, 61 large destroyers, 69 other destroyers and torpedo boats and 105 submarines.

The arrival of *Illustrious* brought more than air support. With it was Rear-Adm Lyster, ex-captain of *Glorious* and someone already familiar with the idea of attacking Taranto by air. On 13 September

the Italians launched a campaign aimed at Egypt. Italian strategy was no more offensive on land than at sea and they decided to dig in at Sidi Barrani, thus releasing the British fleet once again to turn its thoughts to attacking Taranto. General ideas could now become firm plans.

October-November 1940

The Italian navy complained fiercely about the lack of effective reconnaissance provided for them by the Regia Aeronautica but, until September 1940, the British were little better served. Their Sunderland flying boats were slow and lumbering. Then fast, twin-engined Martin Maryland bombers, diverted from France, were made available to the RAF in Malta as 431 General Reconnaissance Flight; the attack on Taranto, which hinged on effective reconnaissance, was now thoroughly viable.

Operation 'MB8'

Intensive training was necessary for the aircrews of *Illustrious* and *Eagle*, particularly in night flying, before their attack. They were reported as being ready by mid-October, and Trafalgar Day, 21 October, was chosen for the attack. Lt David Pollock, *Illustrious*' Intelligence Officer who had, on his own initiative undergone a course at the RAF's photographic interpretation unit in Cairo, was sent back to the Egyptian capital in a Swordfish for the latest photographs of Taranto. When he arrived to examine the photographs he found strange white blobs on the prints, which

Left:
The Italian battleship *Conte di Cavour* sunk in the attack.
IWM HU2058

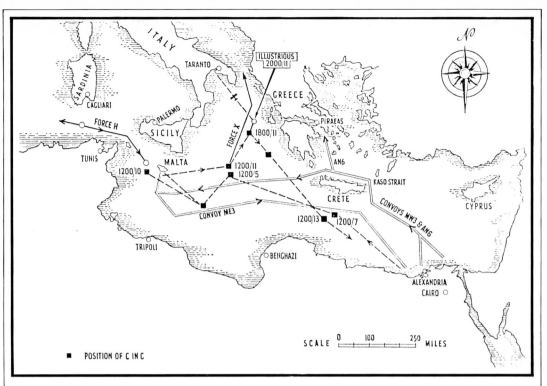

Above:
Movements of forces during Operation 'MB8'.

could only be hitherto unsuspected barrage balloons. Pollock, without permission and more concerned with the safety of the aircrews than with a reprimand, took the prints back to *Illustrious*. The photographs were later returned, with no one appearing to notice. A revised plan of attack was rapidly prepared; Pollock's discovery was a stroke of fortune, but the balance of British luck was bad — a serious accident took place in *Illustrious*. The Swordfish carried a crew of three, but to increase its range of 450 miles, a 60gal tank could be fitted into the observer's seat of the aircraft. This was being done when a mechanic slipped on the greasy cockpit floor. As he fell his screwdriver brushed across two live terminals, there was a spark and petrol dripping from a badly-drained tank ignited. The mechanic was blasted across the hangar, his own Swordfish and one other destroyed, and five others soaked by the salt water sprays that came on immediately to control the fire. *Illustrious* and all British carriers had some of the best hangar fire precautions in the world, and the fire was out in a few minutes. The five drenched aircraft had to be stripped down to almost every last wire to free them from the effects of the salt water. The operation had to be postponed.

The second blow to strike the operation was the rejection of an Italian ultimatum to Greece, and an appeal from Greece for British help on 28 October. This required a fuelling base to be set up in Crete, and troops to be transported to Piraeus. The third blow came when the elderly *Eagle* had to report a breakdown in her fuelling system that was beyond self-help. Out of the operation, five of her Swordfish and eight of her crews were transferred to *Illustrious*, thus giving the latter a theoretical strike force of only 24 aircraft. The RAF had already expressed worry that a few Fleet Air Arm planes attacking Taranto would only succeed in putting the wind up the Italians and reduce the chances of success for a major land-based strike. Success heals all wounds but, when *Eagle* dropped out, the RAF might well have been proved correct; two dozen aircraft was a desperately small force with which to plan a major air attack.

Nothing could illustrate better the demands placed on Cunningham's forces than Operation 'MB8'. Operation 'Judgement', the attack on Taranto, was only one part of an operation which involved six separate forces adding up to five battleships, two carriers, 10 cruisers and 30 destroyers. The second carrier was *Ark Royal* which, as part of 'Force H', covered the western end of the Mediterranean. These forces were being deployed to cover no less than four convoys between 4-11 November, as well as the arrival from England of the battleship *Barham*, cruisers

Berwick and *Glasgow*, and several destroyers. The plan had the following elements:

Operation 'MB8'

Operations 'Coat' and 'Crack'

Barham, *Berwick* and *Glasgow* and three destroyers on passage from England and carrying troops for reinforcement of Malta, as well as AA guns. 'Force H' to cover from Gibraltar to central Mediterranean (*Ark Royal*, *Sheffield*, eight destroyers); three of 'Force H's' destroyers as close escort to Malta, remainder of 'Force H' as distant support force, turning back 165 miles west of Sicily (Operation 'Coat'). In addition *Ark Royal* to launch bombing raid on Cagliari en route (Operation 'Crack').

Convoy MW3

Five merchant vessels from Alexandria to Malta; two more merchant vessels with supplies for base at Suda Bay to be routed with this convoy: escorted by AA cruiser *Coventry* and three destroyers.

Convoy ME3

Four empty merchant vessels awaiting passage from Malta to Alexandria, and to be escorted by *Ramillies*, *Coventry* and two destroyers.

Convoy AN6

Three merchant vessels with fuel from Egypt to Greece. This slow convoy was delayed by its even slower trawler escort.

Cruiser force

Ajax and *Sydney* ('Force B') to carry troops and equipment to Crete; *Orion* ('Force C' — Vice-Adm Pridham-Wippell) to carry RAF stores and supplies to Greece and then to inspect base at Suda Bay. All ships variously to rejoin flag before forming 'Force X' with two destroyers to raid the Otranto Strait on the night of 11 November.

Operation 'Judgement'

Adm Cunningham to sail with *Warspite*, *Valliant*, *Malaya* and *Ramillies* (battleships); *Illustrious*; *Gloucester* and *York* (cruisers) with destroyer escort to meet and cover Convoy MW3. *Ramillies* to be detached as escort for convoy. *Barham* force to be met, thereafter *Illustrious* to detach with *Gloucester*, *Berwick*, *York* and *Glasgow* and four destroyers to attack Taranto.

The plan for the actual attack was for two strikes of Swordfish to be launched approximately one hour apart, with 12 aircraft in each strike, six of which would be armed with torpedoes, the remainder with bombs and flares. The aircraft with bombs were there in the main to provide a diversion, it being felt that the barrage balloons and disposition of the Italian fleet gave a restricted number of torpedo launching positions. A change from the plan of 21 October was the earlier launching of the raid, the first strike being expected to hit at 2200. The torpedoes were to be armed with the Duplex pistol, which could explode either on impact or under a vessel's hull, being activated by magnetic

influence. The Duplex pistol performed badly in anything approaching a heavy sea, and in the relatively shallow waters of Taranto there was a danger that the torpedoes would hit mud and not metal, but the advantages of the dual strike capacity and the damage that could be inflicted by an explosion under the hull, plus the calm waters of Taranto, seemed to justify the risk. The earlier time had been ordered because it meant less chance of meeting enemy surface vessels leaving Taranto; the British feared surface sightings more than air reconnaissance, given the ability of *Illustrious'* fighters to drive off shadowing aircraft.

The plan was a sound one, and achieved the ultimate accolade of success. Its main risk was that surprise would not be achieved: if *Illustrious* was spotted so near to the Italian base and disabled by air attack she was without heavy support, and could be delivered into the lap of the Italian fleet. If she was spotted whilst waiting for her aircraft to return she and they might be placed in an appalling predicament. The other risk was the obvious one: earlier plans had envisaged a possible loss rate of 50% among the Swordfish. The main weakness of the plan was the presence of only 12 torpedo-carrying aircraft. The limited number of attacking positions was a valid point, but six aircraft in each strike in a harbour that would be well-lit by flares had neither the ingredients of a traffic jam nor blind man's-buff. The RAF had not come up with an effective design for an armour-piercing bomb in the interwar period, and the 250lb semi-armour-piercing bombs carried by the Swordfish displayed the features of many of their type — a tendency either to pass straight through a hull without exploding when meeting no armour, or failing to penetrate when they did.

The fact that the attack on Taranto was only one element in a massive movement of ships gave the plan one further invaluable asset. Up until the last few hours, when *Illustrious* separated from the rest of the fleet, the Taranto strike force was buried amidst a welter of ships engaged in what, to all intents and purposes, were normal convoy activities. Indeed, the sheer size of Operation 'MB8' added to Italian confusion. The Italians knew that naval forces from both Alexandria and Gibraltar were at sea by 7 November. They spotted a Malta-bound convoy on 8 November, together with Cunningham's covering force of battleships, and ordered nine additional submarines out to the area. Bombers failed to locate the fleet, and by 9 November they knew that the Gibraltar force was heading back westwards, and assumed that the force from Alexandria was duly heading back eastwards. Confusion was caused by a sighting on the morning of 10 November of a group of ships (actually *Barham*, *Berwick*, *Glasgow* and their destroyer escort) off Limos.

The Italians assumed correctly that this had broken off from the Gibraltar force, but did not know it was to rendezvous with Cunningham at 1015 on that day. They also spotted that afternoon *Ramillies* with the AA cruiser *Coventry* and two destroyers escorting a convoy of four vessels bound for Alexandria from Malta (Convoy ME3). Bombers failed to find this convoy.

As Brigadin, author of *The Italian Navy in World War II* and, in 1941, an officer serving in the Supermarina (or Italian Naval High Command in Rome) has written: 'If the British had not explained after the war what had gone on in those days, the Italians would not know what these movements had been.' However, it has perhaps been too easy for historians to dismiss Italian reconnaissance efforts in this period. With a huge area of ocean to cover, the Italians spotted several of the ship movements taking place, attempted to attack some of them and failed only in the one area that was crucial — keeping track of *Illustrious*. The mistake made was in some respects the same one as was made in very different circumstances by the aircraft from *Ark Royal* which fired torpedoes at *Sheffield* in the hunt for the *Bismarck*: having been told that *Bismarck* was the only ship in the vicinity the aircrews saw what they wanted and expected to see. The Italians were expecting that the force

from Alexandria would reverse course, as was standard British operational procedure, and in the absence of firm information this reasonable conjecture was assumed to be the truth.

Taranto

On the evening of 11 November the Italian base of Taranto housed all six of Italy's battleships, and a huge concentration of other forces. Doubts had been expressed about the wisdom of having all the fleet's capital vessels in one harbour, for what was rumoured to be an impending operation against Crete.

As might be expected, Taranto was well defended. It consisted of an inner harbour (Mar Piccolo) and an outer harbour (Mar Grande), with the battleships moored in Mar Grande. The Italians were well aware of the threat of air attack, and Taranto had a multi-layered defence. It was expected that air reconnaissance would pick up well in advance any threatening move to launch an attack on Taranto. As has been seen, this failed. The next line of defence was 13 sound listening posts placed strategically around the harbour. These did their job and alerted the harbour defences a full two hours before the attack when a cruising Sunderland, placed there to guard against the Italian fleet leaving harbour, was picked up. For close-in defence the base had 21 batteries of 4in guns, 13 ashore and eight on floating platforms, 84 heavy machine guns and 109 light machine

Below:
The attack on Taranto — 11 November 1940.

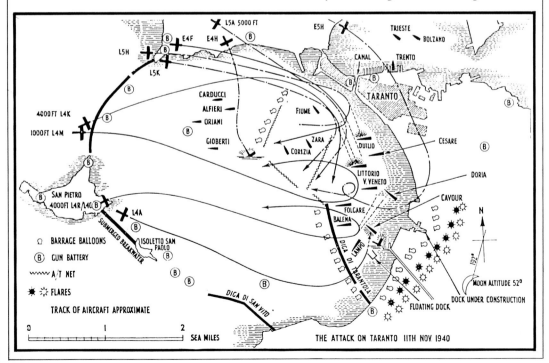

THE ATTACK ON TARANTO 11TH NOV 1940

guns. In addition the AA armament of vessels moored in the harbour could be called upon. The 4in guns were heading towards obsolescence, and the AA barrage thrown up by all these weapons was almost wholly ineffective. One reason was that the 22 searchlights on land and the many searchlights available on ships moored in the harbour did not appear to be used on the night of the attack. Another reason was that the AA guns threw up a box barrage, each gun blanket-firing at an allocated area — an inefficient and wasteful, albeit necessary, procedure. Firing discipline was bad: guns continued firing 15min after the last aircraft had departed, and warships ignored zones of fire to spray their own vessels.

Passive defence was provided by anti-torpedo nets and barrage balloons. Nearly 14,000yd of netting was needed to protect vessels in the outer harbour; on the night of 11 November 4,593yd were in position, 3,171yd waiting to be laid, and the remainder not available from an industrial complex which was not ready for Mussolini's war. The netting in any event only extended down to the level of a vessel's draught, allowing the Duplex pistols to run under the ships; the quantity in store lay there partly because senior officers resented the interference caused by the raising and lowering of netting to ships entering and leaving harbour. Of 90 barrage balloons only 27 were in position on the night of the attack. There had been problems with the supply of hydrogen, and storms had destroyed two-thirds of the total number in the first week of November.

Whatever else it may have been, Taranto was not taken unawares. British reconnaissance had warned the Italians of an impending attack, and ships were at readiness throughout the night with half their AA batteries manned, in addition to the 2hr alert warning provided by the listening posts.

The Attack on Taranto

Cunningham sailed from Alexandria at 1300 on 6 November and met Convoy MW3 at noon on 8 November. Reconnaissance aircraft and bombers found the fleet, but were either chased off or shot down by *Illustrious'* Fulmar fighters. By noon on 10 November Cunningham was 40 miles west of Malta, having met with *Barham* and detached her cruisers and destroyers to land their troops at Malta. Again the fleet was bombed, but without damage; it turned eastward, and by noon on 11 November was roughly midway between Malta and Crete. However, the jinx that affected the early stages of the attack was still in force. Between 10 and 11 November no less than three Swordfish aircraft had crashed as a result of engine failure, all from one squadron, and as a result of contaminated fuel taken from the tanker *Toneline*.

The attack force was now down to 21 aircraft from the original 24. All the crews were rescued; one of them (Sub-Lt Alistair Keith and Lt George Going) hitched a ride back on a cruiser's Walrus amphibian so as not to miss the attack. Cunningham's turn to the east suggested a normal return to Alexandria; what the Italians did not spot was Pridham-Wippell's Force X, detached at 1310 on 10 November and destined later to maul a convoy in the Gulf of Otranto, or *Illustrious* and her eight escorts detached at 1800 to make their attack on Taranto.

The revised plan called for two strikes, of 12 and nine aircraft respectively, six with torpedoes in each flight. *Illustrious* and her escorts would steam to position 'X', 38°12'N 19°30'E, 40 miles from Kabbo Point, Cephalonia, from where they would launch the first strike at 2200, giving them a total distance to Taranto of 400 miles on the round trip. The second strike would be launched at 2100, and the first recovered at about 0100 on 12 November, 20 miles from Kabbo Point. Each wave would be formed around one of *Illustrious'* squadrons: a toss of the coin decided which.

The two strike commanders studied the latest photographs of Taranto flown in via Malta and made their plans accordingly. Lt-Cdr M. W. Williamson, commanding officer of 815 Squadron and in charge of the first strike, proposed to approach Taranto at between 8,000 and 10,000ft. with his squadron split into three sub-flights. The first sub-flight would attack from the southeast, the second from the northwest, thus sandwiching the enemy battleships between them. The third sub-flight consisted of the bombers and flare-droppers, which would light up the harbour and then attack vessels in the inner harbour and shore installations. Lt-Cdr J. W. Hale of 819 Squadron, and commander of the second wave, decided on an approach in line astern from the northwest. This plan appeared more hazardous, as the flight path brought the aircraft over the heavy AA defences on the canal that separated the inner and outer harbours, and meant they had to drop down over a line of barrage balloons to the west of the anchored ships. Its advantage was from that angle the battleships overlapped each other, giving a higher likelihood of a hit if a torpedo veered off course. Given the 300yd spacing of the balloon cables, a 48ft-wingspan Swordfish had a 10 to 1 chance of avoiding them. Some pilots hoped to fly low enough to dodge the lighters to which the balloons were moored.

At 1945 *Illustrious* increased speed to 28kt, and shortly thereafter began to launch the first strike. Amongst their torpedoes, bombs and flares was an unusual weapon of war; *Illustrious'* Marine contingent had arranged for a pair of Royal Marine marching boots to augument the bomb load of the one Swordfish piloted by a Marine, Capt O. ('Ollie') Patch.

Williamson's flight clawed up to 7,500ft at a speed of 75kt. When they broke through the cloud cover four aircraft had lost touch — three bombers and one torpedo-armed aircraft. Williamson pressed on. At 2250 he saw the sky ahead lit up by the intense AA bombardment already being fired by the Italian defenders. At 1955 and at 2040 the alarm had been sounded at Taranto, as listening posts picked up the noise of the scouting Sunderland. At 2225 the noise of the incoming first strike was picked up, and a short while later the third alarm sounded and the barrage opened up. The Swordfish were flying in four V-shaped formations of three aircraft each. It was a clear night with a light wind and a three-quarter moon. As Williamson led his flight up the Gulf of Taranto he spotted the missing torpedo aircraft: L4M, piloted by Lt Swayne with Sub-Lt Buxall, which had lost contact in the clouds, had made its own way to Taranto, flying lower than the main flight and thus making better time. It had 'stooged around' for a quarter-of-an-hour waiting for the remainder of the flight.

Below:
The Fairey Fulmar (Mk II N4062 illustrated) was a useful addition to the Fleet Air Arm as an eight-gun carrier-borne fighter when introduced in June 1940. *MAP 71/R19*

Bottom:
HMS *Illustrious* at Malta in September 1943. Her AA guns are at near-maximum elevation in preparation for a raid. *MPL*

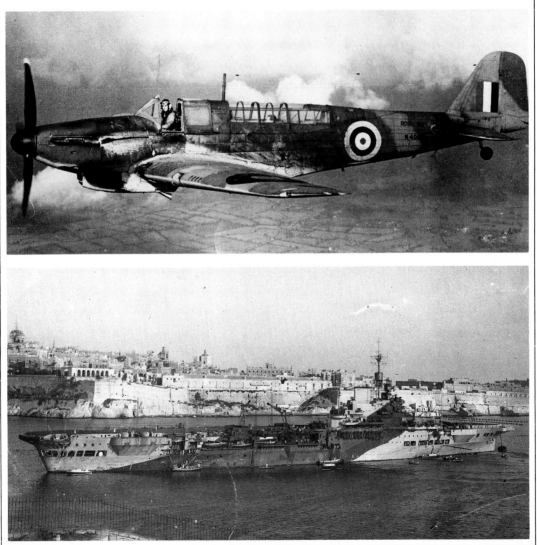

As Williamson approached he detached his flare droppers, L4P (Lt L. J. Kigell and Lt H. R. B. Janvrin) and L5B (Lt C. J. Lamb and Lt K. G. Grieve). Flying at 7,500ft L4P dropped its flares to the northeast at half-mile intervals, cruised around for 15-20min, and then dive-bombed the oil storage depot with the reserve flare carrier, L5B. Williamson in L4A, with L4C and L4R, headed for the centre of the outer harbour, and with three-and-a-half miles to go to reach the battleships moored at the eastern end of the harbour dropped through the box barrage and inferno of tracer in a shallow dive. He narrowly missed a barrage balloon; his observer, Scarlett, was amazed at Williamson's skill in avoiding the cable — actually, Williamson had simply not seen it. He swept over two destroyers, the *Lampo* and *Fulmine*, which opened up intense and accurate fire. Seeing *Conte di Cavour* looming in front of him he released his torpedo, banked steeply to starboard and dropped like a stone as machine gun fire from *Fulmine* inflicted fatal damage. Miraculously he and his observer escaped, were machine gunned as they spluttered on to a nearby dry dock, beaten up and stripped by dockyard workers, but eventually rescued by the Italian Navy who treated them with great courtesy, eventually packing them off to become prisoners of war. Williamson's torpedo ran true and exploded under the *Conte di Cavour* between the bridge and 'B' turret.

L4C and L4R crossed the breakwater at 30ft under an onslaught of fire. Too far south to attack *Vittorio Veneto* they both fired instead at *Conte di Cavour* from a range of 700yd. Both torpedoes missed and exploded near *Andrea Doria*, without damaging her.

Lt N. McI. Kemp in L4K was the leader of the second sub-flight. Swinging to port to come in from the north he also emerged unscathed through intense fire, and hugging the water he turned to starboard to launch his torpedo at 1,000yd against the starboard side of the battleship *Littorio*. Shortly afterwards Swayne in L4M — which had taken the opposite approach — launched his torpedo at 400yd against *Littorio's* port side. Kemp's torpedo struck the battleship just abaft of the forward turret, tearing a hole 49ft by 32ft. This did not defeat the ship's novel anti-torpedo protection, but flooding spread into the double bottom and was more extensive than it ought to have been. Swayne's torpedo from L4M hit almost immediately afterwards on the port quarter, abreast the tiller flat. The hole blasted by this torpedo was 23ft by 5ft, the rudder was partially destroyed, and the steering gear seriously damaged.

The final torpedo-carrying aircraft, one of

Below:
Andrea Doria was a new Italian battleship present at Taranto; she was not damaged. *IWM A19322*

Eagle's, E4F, piloted by Lt M. R. Maund, came in low from the northwest and fired at *Littorio*. The torpedo missed and exploded when it hit the ground on *Littorio's* starboard quarter, at about 2315.

The bombing group of four Swordfish had rather less success. Capt Patch flung his bombs (and pair of Marine boots) on a group of cruisers and destroyers moored against the jetty in the Mar Piccolo. He straddled the ships but made no hits. Meanwhile, L4L (Sub-Lt W. C. Sarra and Mid J. Bowker) was unable to pick up its primary target, so instead bombed the seaplane base causing a fire in the hangar which was not brought under control for 15min. L4H (Sub-Lt A. J. Forde and Sub-Lt A. Mardel-Ferreira) had lost contact with the main group, but arrived just as the first flares were being dropped. Aiming at the ships moored by the jetty his bombs again appeared to miss, and seeing no explosions he calmly turned round and repeated the attack in case his bombs had failed to release. Despite heavy fire from warships his aircraft was undamaged. The last bomber (E5Q) hit the destroyer *Libbeccio* but the bomb failed to explode. Its pilot, Lt J. B. Murray, headed back the way he had come in.

The last aircraft had departed from the first strike by 2335, but this did not deter the defenders from continuing to fire for many more minutes. Three out of six torpedoes had hit, one on *Conte di Cavour* and two on *Littorio*, both vessels suffering severe flooding; in addition a destroyer had been damaged and the seaplane base set on fire.

The Second Strike

When *Illustrious* turned head to wind to launch her second strike the last two aircraft, L5F and L5Q, taxied into each other. L5Q, undamaged, was allowed to take off; L5F was grounded. After fierce pleading from its crew (Lt E. W. Clifford and Lt G. R. M. Going) and some intense work on the aircraft, it was allowed to take off 24min after the others. In the meantime L5Q's long-range fuel tank parted its straps and fell off. The aircraft was forced to return to *Illustrious*, braving her fire before being recognised, and landing safely. By 2310 Lt-Cdr Hale sighted the cone of flak over Taranto; at 2355 he detached his flare droppers, L5B and L4F, which dropped their flares without incident and then bombed the oil storage depot, causing only small damage.

The five aircraft with torpedoes skirted the northern edge of the harbour. Hale dived through the flak and fired at *Littorio* at a range of 700yd. His north-south line of approach subjected him to land-based and destroyer fire from both sides, and then the fire from the battleships at the end of his route. E4H (Lt G. W. Bayley and Lt H. J.

Slaughter) followed Hale, but was never seen by the British again. The Italians reported an aircraft shot down making an attack on the cruiser *Gorizia*. Hale was luckier: his torpedo tore a hole 40ft by 30ft in *Littorio's* unprotected starboard bow. This made the flooding in the fore part of the ship much more extensive, causing her to be grounded. On his exit route Hale swung to avoid a lighter, not realising it carried the cable for a barrage balloon. L5H (Lt C. C. S. Lea and Sub-Lt P. D. Jones) followed Hale but was forced into a starboard turn by the flak. Flying low across the northern shore he fired at *Caio Duilio*, his torpedo struck on the starboard side, low down, abreast 'B' turret, ripping a hole over 800sq ft in area out of her side, flooding Nos 1 and 2 magazines, and requiring her to be beached to stop her foundering. He too made his escape, the height at which he was flying being symbolised by a near-collision with the mast of a trawler.

Lt F. M. A. Torrens-Spence and Lt A. W. F. Sutton in L5K made it down through the flak, but narrowly missed colliding with Bayley and Slaughter in E4H, witnessing what was probably that aircraft's explosive demise. They fired at *Littorio*, and on their exit hit the water with their undercarriage and flew right over two flak lighters; undercarriage, aircraft and crew survived with one bullet hole in the fuselage. Their torpedo probably hit the battleship on the starboard quarter but only caused a dent: it buried itself in the mud without exploding, causing some difficulty to the salvage operations. E5H (Lt J. W. G. Welham and Lt P. Humphreys) tried an angled shot at *Vittorio Veneto* but missed; control surfaces and the port wing were hit by flak both before and after launching its torpedo. The sturdy Swordfish still made it back to *Illustrious* safely.

Clifford and Going (the late arrivals in L5F), delayed in their departure, arrived after the main assault was over, flew round for a while and then dropped a stick of bombs over moored cruisers. One bomb hit the cruiser *Trento*, but went straight through it without exploding.

The second strike had scored a third hit on *Littorio*, hit *Caio Duilio* and dented a cruiser, all for the loss of one aircraft.

On board *Illustrious* there was a mixed feeling of triumph and disbelief that losses had been so small, tempered by the realisation that they might have to go through it all again on the night of 12 November. As one pilot remarked, 'They only asked the Light Brigade to do it once'. As it was, the suggestion of a second attack before the Italians had a chance to improve defences came to nothing when worsening weather made such a strike impractical. The pilots themselves recorded their impressions of the attack: multi-coloured tracer idling towards them and suddenly picking up

speed to race past; the stench of cordite, feeling the actual blast from the muzzles of guns as they flew over them. Perhaps most vivid of all was the impression of the cone of fire thrown up round Taranto by the area bombardment, a roof of shell-fire through which it seemed as if they might never pass unscathed.

Aftermath

Illustrious met up again with Cunningham and the remainder of the fleet at 0700 on 12 November, to be met by the traditional signalled understatement from a C-in-C: 'Manoeuvre Well Executed'. It took time for the full details of the damage to the Italian fleet to work through, not in fact until a faithful Maryland had flown over the base and taken pictures. In the meantime *Illustrious* shot down three lumbering CANT Z-501 flying boats with her Fulmars, for the British were still in range of Italian aircraft. Using radar to full advantage, the Italian aircraft were shot down before they could make sighting reports. The fleet reached Alexandria on 14 November with Adm Lyster still deeply regretting that the absence of *Eagle* had reduced the impact of the attack. Winston Churchill, *The Times* and King George VI poured congratulations on Cunningham and his fleet. The Fleet Air Arm had arrived — and a new era in seapower.

The Italians, however, were more concerned with the losses of the old era. *Conte di Cavour* was worst affected: her crew had difficulty containing the flooding and, after being towed towards the shore, she was abandoned at 0545. She finally settled with her stern on the bottom two-and-a-quarter hours later. This was the end of *Cavour's* active career. She was not refloated until July 1941, and repairs on her at Trieste were still incomplete when Italy signed the armistice in June 1943. She was scuttled and then raised by the Germans, only to be sunk yet again in an air raid on Trieste. The poor old hulk was raised again in 1947 and mercifully scrapped in 1950-52. *Duilio* was luckier; her repairs were complete by the middle of May 1941 and she survived in the postwar Italian Navy until 1957. The better protected *Littorio* was back in service by March 1941. However, at a crucial period in the war, Italy's battleship strength had been halved, from six to three vessels.

Less calculable, but almost as important, was the strategic loss, with the remaining vessels having to be moved further north and so further away from the areas in which the British fleet would have to be met; there was also the savage blow to morale and prestige. As a result of Taranto — and the failure of the Italian fleet to bring the British to action off Cape Spartivento a fortnight afterwards — wholesale and sweeping changes were made in the Italian naval command.

Conclusion

There was no shortage of scapegoats for Taranto on the Italian side. The Regia Aeronautica totally failed to spot a major British force steaming to within range of Taranto. Inefficient industry and truculent commanders ensured an inadequate anti-torpedo net line, although even with all nets laid the Duplex pistol might have succeeded in running under them; bad weather took out the barrage balloons at a crucial time. Of these the Regia Aeronautica took the most blame, their reconnaissance failure effectively unpinning the whole defence plan for Taranto, which hinged on sighting a threatening force. The Regia Aeronautica was not blameless; it had inadequate aircraft, crews badly-trained for maritime reconnaissance, and weak liaison with the Italian Navy.

Half a century on, however, it is time perhaps to broaden the analysis. It was not that the Regia Aeronautica failed to send out aircraft, rather that those sent out were shot down or driven away by the British, whose carrier-based fighters allowed them to achieve 'local' air superiority. The lumbering CANT flying boats were exactly the

Left:
Another view of the sunken *Conte di Cavour*.
IWM HU2059

Below:
HMS *Illustrious* after being hit by German Stukas in the Mediterranean, 1941. Beyond the very obvious hole in the flightdeck, shrouded in smoke, can be seen the tangled wreckage of her lift. *IWM A9793*

45

aircraft with which Royal Navy's low performance fighters had been designed to deal. Combined with radar the Fulmar could even neutralise the faster, more modern Italian bombers. In the three days before the raid, persistent attempts to locate *Illustrious* by air were foiled. As the British record showed, supplying the Italian Navy with its own fleet air arm need not have given Italy's maritime aircraft sufficient performance to deal with the British combat air patrols. Italy's industrial and production base was even more inadequate than Britain's. A unified air force with all the operational and organisational problems it brought in its wake was therefore perhaps more a result of the general weaknesses of a nation's air power than a cause of defects in specific areas.

The British plan had the hallmark of genius. It capitalised fully on known enemy weaknesses, made the best possible use of available forces and had the ultimate virtue of survivability, mincing to nothing several potential spanners thrown into its works. It married technical innovation (the Duplex pistol and radar) with the older virtues of training and sheer courage, and came out on the right side of the age-old equation that balances likely risk with likely gains. Equally, the risk would have been significantly less and the damage possibly much higher if the British had for their use more aircraft with a longer range and greater payload. Just over a year later, the Japanese, stimulated by Taranto, were to show what a fully-fledged air fleet could really do to an enemy naval base.

HMS *Illustrious*

Builder: Vickers-Armstrong, Barrow
(Laid down 27 April 1937; launched 5 April 1939; completed 25 May 1940)

Displacement: 23,000 tons (standard)

Dimensions: 743.25ft × 95.75ft × 24ft

Machinery: Geared turbines, 3 shafts, 111,000shp, 30.5kt

Armour: Main belt, hangar sides and bulkheads (except end doors) 4.5in; flightdeck above hangar and both sides of lifts to half their length 3in; rest of flightdeck to just fore and aft of lifts 1.5in; hangar floor 3in, hangar deck ends 1in

Armament: 16×4.5in dual-purpose (8×2); 48×2pdr (6×8); 8×40mm (8×1); 8×20mm (8×1)

Sensors: Type 79 (Air Warning) radar

Aircraft: 36 (24×Swordfish, 12×fighters)

Complement: 1,392

Notes: Diagram below shows bomb (and crashed Stuka) hits on *Illustrious* after Taranto. *Illustrious* was delayed completion for two months to allow fitting of radar. Her armour came from the Vitkovice works in Czechoslovakia; her design philosophy is discussed above.

Below:
HMS *Illustrious*, near-missed by a *kamikaze* attack. The armoured hangar afforded more protection for this threat than it did from bombs. *C. Drury*

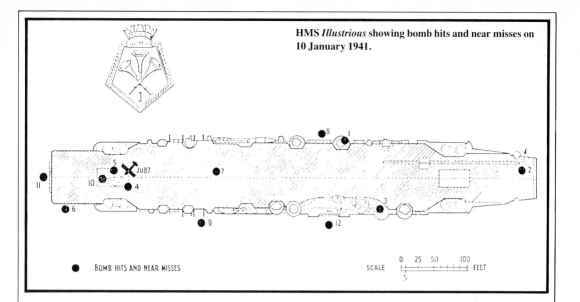

HMS _Illustrious_ showing bomb hits and near misses on 10 January 1941.

● BOMB HITS AND NEAR MISSES

SCALE ├──┼──┼──────┤ FEET
0   25 50   100

Littorio

Builder: Ansaldo, Genoa
(Laid down 28 October 1934; launched 22 August 1937; completed 6 May 1940)

Displacement: 40,723 tons (standard), 45,237 (full load)

Dimensions: 780ft × 108.1ft × 31.4ft

Machinery: Geared turbines, 4 shafts, 128,200shp, 30kt (over 31kt on trials)

Armour: Main belt 14.17in total, decks 6.14-6.65in total, turrets 14.96in front, 5.12-7.87in sides

Armament: 9×15in (3×3); 12×6in (6×2); 4×4.7in; 12×3.5in (6×2); 20×37mm; 24×20mm

Aircraft: 3

Complement: 1,920

Notes: The 'Littorio' class of fast modern battleships consisted of _Vittorio Veneto, Littorio_ and the slightly different Group 2 ships _Roma_ and _Impero_ (which was never completed). They were well designed with a novel system of underwater side protection developed by Pugliese. This consisted of a hollow cylinder on each side of the armoured citadel backed by a 40mm curved bulkhead made of high strength steel. The system was supposed to absorb the energy of an exploding warhead of up to 772lb, twice the weight of the 388lb warhead of the British Mk XII 18in aerial torpedo, but its effectiveness was lessened by poor construction, notably the use of rivets rather than welding. The connection between the system and the bottom of the ship was a particular weakness which probably explains _Littorio's_ excessive flooding in the double bottom spaces from her first hit. The damage control equipment was also inadequate, which helps account for the very extensive flooding the ship suffered in her forward spaces when hit beyond the anti-torpedo protection.

Conte di Cavour and Caio Duilio

Builders:
Conte di Cavour — R. Arsenale, Spezia
(Laid down 10 August 1910; launched 10 August 1911; completed 1 April 1915)
Reconstructed October 1933-June 1937 by Cantieri Riuniti dell'Adriatico, Trieste
Caio Duilio— R. Arsenale, Castellamare
(Laid down 24 February 1912; launched 24 April 1913; completed 10 May 1915)
Reconstructed April 1937-July 1940 by Cantieri del Tirreno, Genoa

Displacement: _Cavour_ 23,619 tons (standard), 29,100 tons (full load); _Duilio_ 23,887 tons (standard), 29,391 tons (full load); _Cavour_ 611.5ft×91.8ft×28ft; _Duilio_ 613.2ft×91.8ft×27.7ft

Machinery: (after reconstruction). Geared turbines, 2 shafts, 75,000shp, 27kt (_Cavour_), 26kt (_Duilio_) — forced draughting increased the speed by a knot in each case

Armour: Main belt 10in; deck (after reconstruction) 3.1-3.9in

Armament: 10×12.6in (3×2 and 2×2); _Cavour_ 12×4.7in (6×2); 8×3.9in (4×2); 12×37mm (6×2) and 12×13.2mm machine guns (6×2); _Duilio_ 12×5.3in (4×3); 10×3.5in (10×1); 15×37mm (6×2+3×1); 16×20mm (8×2)

Complement: _Cavour_ 1,236; _Duilio_ 1,495

Notes: These ships were of two related different classes. _Cavour_ was name ship of the first class of Italian dreadnoughts. She had two sisters _Giulio Cesare_ (at Taranto but undamaged) and _Leonardo da Vinci_ (sunk by internal explosion in 1916). _Duilio_ was one of the two 'Andrea Doria' class: her sister also came through unscathed. The very extensive reconstructions were successful enough but reflected Italian priorities in putting speed before protection. Pugliese underwater protection was fitted, but insufficient beam limited its effectiveness. By the standards of 1940 these were vulnerable ships.

CHAPTER THREE

The Battle of Matapan

**HMS *Warspite* of the 'Queen Elizabeth' class of 15in-
battleships.** *Ministry of Defence (MoD) (Navy)*

The Battle of Matapan, fought on 28/29 March 1941, was both a great victory and a story of lost opportunity. Perhaps even more than Taranto, which was first conceived as far back as 1935, it showed the hallmark of the man who was to become Admiral of the Fleet, Viscount Cunningham of Hyndhope KT, GCB, OM, DSO. Known universally as 'ABC', Cunningham was a man totally without cant or humbug, adored by those who served under him and with a total commitment to daring and aggressive tactics. He knew when to take risks but also how to plan with meticulous detail. His overriding principle was that the enemy were there to be defeated, and that this could only happen if the respective vessels met, preferably at pointblank range. He was also lucky, as have been all great commanders, and the 'Nelsonian' tag has been applied to him frequently; it fits Cunningham better than many. Both men did a great deal to create their own luck.

The Mediterranean Situation

The situation facing Cunningham was still bleak at the start of 1941. Malta (which had been declared indefensible before the war) and the territory taken by General Wavell's December 1940 offensive in North Africa both demanded supplies. Most importantly the decision was taken to send troops from Libya and Egypt to Greece, an operation that would demand the full attention of the Mediterranean Fleet when it began in March 1941. Cunningham was concerned about the vulnerability of these movements to Greece. Taranto had reduced battleship strength by a half, to three vessels, but German involvement in the Mediterranean was increasing with Hitler's decision (clearly indicated by British signals intelligence) to stiffen his Italian allies and begin planning for an offensive through the Balkans which would conquer Greece, and threaten the whole of the Eastern Mediterranean. One early result was *Illustrious*, as already described, being put out of action by German Stuka dive-bombers in January 1941. This lost Cunningham his only armoured carrier, but exactly two months later the new carrier *Formidable*, third member of the 'Illustrious' class, joined Cunningham at Alexandria. It did not take the C-in-C long to use her.

The First Phase

By March 1941 the now famous Government Code and Cypher School at Bletchley Park had cracked both the Luftwaffe 'Enigma' codes and the little-used Italian Navy 'Enigma'. These gave Cunningham and the Admiralty in London warning that an operation into the Eastern Mediterranean was due to take place on 26 March. The C-in-C therefore took action. A southbound convoy from Piraeus was cancelled, a northbound convoy turned round (after nightfall to reduce suspicion) and Vice-Adm, Light Forces, H. D. Pridham-Wippell, with Force 'B' of cruisers and destroyers ordered to be southwest of Gaudo Island, Crete, by 28 March. Cunningham with the main fleet would sail after dark on the 27th. At 1220 on the 27th confirmation came from a flying boat of three Italian cruisers and a destroyer at sea 80 miles east of Sicily, heading southeast towards Crete. Operation 'Lustre', the convoying of British troops from Egypt to Greece, had been going on since 4 March. *Formidable* had returned three days earlier from a sweep to protect these troop movements, and Pridham-Wippell was on the same duty in the Aegean with the four light

Right:
HMS *Warspite*, with torpedo bulges and 0.5in machine guns atop 'X' turret clearly visible.
Real Photographs S1123

Below right:
HMS *Valiant* seen during late 1939.
Paul Silverstone Collection

Below:
HMS *Formidable* being launched on 17 August 1939.
MPL

cruisers *Orion*, *Ajax*, *Perth* and *Gloucester* and the destroyers, *Ilex*, *Hasty*, *Hereward* and *Vendetta*. Where there were Italian cruisers and destroyers there might well be battleships, hence his decision to sail with his full force. Pridham-Wippell was ordered to move his dawn rendezvous further east so as to provide him with battleship cover at the earliest possible moment. Cunningham's aim was decisive action: he did not want to scare off the Italians and so had to wait until dark, as planned. Moreover, Cunningham went to great pains to disguise that he and the fleet were sailing at all. It was known that the Japanese consul acted as an Axis informant on British movements.

So Cunningham went ashore to play golf on the afternoon of the 27th carrying a suitcase; other senior officers left their vessels; a supper party was aired abroad and invitations sent; awnings were spread on board the flagship, *Warspite*. Suspicions thus having been allayed, all was hurriedly cancelled and collected in, and *Warspite* sailed at 1900 on 27 March. With her were the fully-modernised battleship *Valiant* and the old and lightly-modernised *Barham*, and the destroyers *Jervis*, *Janus*, *Nubian*, *Mohawk*, *Stuart*, *Greyhound*, *Griffin*, *Hotspur* and *Havock*. This force then met with *Formidable* which had sailed during the afternoon to land on her aircraft. The Germans believed that only *Warspite* was operational at this time and had effectively instructed the Italians to disrupt British convoys whilst the British were in a weakened state. Their one actual weakness was that *Warspite* had passed too close to a mudbank on leaving Alexandria, clogging her condensers, and was therefore restricted to a speed of 20kt.

The main battlefleet was 150 miles south of Crete by dawn on 28 March, at which time (0555)

Above:
HMS *Formidable* was one of six vessels of the 'Illustrious' class. *Real Photographs S1484*

Formidable launched reconnaissance patrols in the likely direction of enemy forces. *Formidable's* two TSR squadrons largely were equipped with the Albacore, built to a 1936 'TBR' specification that combined the torpedo and dive-bombing roles. From the same stable as the Swordfish, the new aircraft was another biplane but the engine was of almost twice the power and an enclosed cockpit nearly doubled the ceiling (20,700ft as against 10,700ft) as required for dive-bombing operations. The new engine and aerodynamic refinements gave a 20kt advantage in speed (161mph as distinct from 139mph), and a greater range (930 miles as distinct from 546 miles).

At 0720 one of these aircraft reported a force of four cruisers and four destroyers, steering southwest off Gavdo Island, over 100 miles northwest of the main British battlefleet. At 0739 a second aircraft reported four cruisers and six destroyers in a position roughly 20 miles from the first sighting. Both Italian and British commanders at Matapan recognised the uncertainties of aerial navigation over the sea and were unwilling to give complete credence to aircraft reconnaissance reports. Pridham-Wippell's force of four cruisers and four destroyers had been ordered to rendezvous by 0630 off Gavdo Island, and both he and Cunningham assumed that the sightings were actually of the British cruiser force, or at best of one Italian force; the discrepancy in positions could be accounted for by understandable navigational error given the distance from the carrier. Both were wrong — there were two Italian cruiser forces at sea in the area. The first, and nearest to Pridham-Wippell, consisted of the three 10,000-ton cruisers *Trieste, Trento* and *Bolzano,* with

three destroyers *Corazziere, Carabiniere* and *Ascari.* To the northeast was a second force of the 10,000-ton cruisers *Zara, Fiume* and *Pola,* the 8,000-ton cruisers *Garibaldi* and *Abruzzi,* and the destroyers *Gioberti, Alfieri, Oriani, Carducci, Da Recco* and *Pessagno.* Astern of these, as yet unsighted, was the 15in-gun battleship *Vittorio Veneto,* flying the flag of Adm A. Iachino, and escorted by the destroyers *Granatiere, Fuciliere, Bersagliere* and *Alpino.* Iachino had sailed from Naples at 0900 on 26 March, largely in response to German nagging, and in the hope not of a fleet engagement but rather of disrupting convoys and making a show of force. It was the *Trieste* group of cruisers that had been sighted by the flying boat, but Iachino was reassured by the fact that the British signal (which he intercepted and could decipher) made no mention of any other forces; and also by the fact that his own reconnaissance aircraft had reported, quite accurately, that the British fleet was in harbour at 1400 on 27 March. At 0643 *Vittorio Veneto's* aircraft had spotted Pridham-Wippell's cruiser force only 50 miles from *Vittorio Veneto* and, sniffing both an easy prey and a possible convoy, Iachino cracked on speed to 30kt. Pridham-Wippell knew he had been spotted and, to avoid further sightings, steered away at 20kt.

At 0804 a sighting report from one of *Formidable's* aircraft amended the earlier report of four cruisers and four destroyers to four cruisers and six destroyers. Cunningham had little time to

Top:
**The Fairey Albacore torpedo-bomber (L7111 illustrated)
was intended as a replacement for the Swordfish. In the
event, the worth of the Swordfish was such that it
remained in service alongside, and eventually outlasted,
the later design.** *MAP 47/R46*

Above:
**Both the Italians and the Germans produced battleship
and cruiser designs with strikingly similar profiles; hence
at Matapan a heavy cruiser was erroneously reported as a
'Littorio' class battleship. Illustrated is the Italian cruiser
Garibaldi.** *IWM AX10A*

weigh this up before all doubt was removed. At
0824 he received a report from the cruiser *Orion* of
three unknown vessels steaming east at a distance
of 18 miles. In fact the vessels had been sighted by
Orion at 0745 and identified by 0755, and were the
Trieste group of three 8in-gun cruisers and three
destroyers.

Pridham-Wippell's response to the sighting was
to alter course to 140° from his previous 200°, this
heading southeast towards the main British
battlefleet. There were logical reasons for his
turning away from the enemy force. Although he
had numerical superiority the three Italian cruisers
outranged him with their 8in guns, and their
advantage in speed meant that theoretically they
could choose their range and shell the British
cruisers without themselves being fired upon.
Pridham-Wippell's move also took the Italian
force into the arms of Cunningham to the
southeast. This being said, his turn away from the
enemy could be questioned. Pridham-Wippell had
36×6in guns against the Italian 24×8in. His course
away from a faster enemy allowed the Italians to
fire on him for a lengthy period without his being
able to return fire. *Gloucester* had been suffering
engine trouble the night before, and though it did
not appear to be affecting her there was always the

risk that she might drop back and fall into the Italian force's grasp. A lunge at the enemy to close the range as rapidly as possible would have been far more typical of Cunningham's aggressive policy. Nevertheless, this could well have induced the *Trieste* (and any other Italian forces in the area) group to turn away which would have lost the main battlefleet its chance of an annihilating victory. The main problem with applying this long-hallowed principle of leading the enemy on to the guns of the main fleet was that a powerful force of British cruisers running away was so unusual as for it to be only a matter of time before someone on the Italian side smelled a rat. Iachino certainly could not understand the behaviour of the British. Knowing as we do now that there were two other forces near to Pridham-Wippell when he turned away it can be argued that, had he paused to engage in a *melée*, he would have been trapped by the oncoming Italian forces. However, Pridham-Wippell did not know of these forces at the time and his turn away was, in any event, heading him into a sandwich trap plotted by Iachino. His course away from the enemy strained morale in his squadron, and exposed his ships to continuous fire with little chance of retaliation.

Perhaps Pridham-Wippell well understood Italian gunnery weaknesses. The old rangefinders of the Italian cruisers proved almost useless in the prevailing atmospheric conditions; and when they opened fire at 0812, their initial salvoes fell well short. However, it was not long before the speed of the Italian force brought them closer to the British. *Gloucester*, at the end of the line, was forced into 30° alterations of course to dodge the salvoes. In addition the destroyer *Vendetta* developed engine trouble; she was detached amidst the smoke being made by the British force in the hope that she would escape unnoticed, a manoeuvre which succeeded. At 0829 *Gloucester* fired three salvoes at the pursuing Italians, now at 23,500yd. The salvoes fell short, but caused the Italians at 0837 to alter course to stay out of 6in-gun range. They then turned back on a parallel course to the British ships to continue their inaccurate 8in bombardment.

Cunningham did not appear unduly bothered when he heard of Pridham-Wippell's contact and apparent flight. At 0832 he ordered his fleet to increase speed to 22kt, the most *Warspite* could manage with her condenseritis, and the most the largely unmodernised *Barham* could manage at the best of times. As it was, someone clearly had sharp words with *Warspite's* engines — shortly afterwards she was able to steam at 24kt again. At 0851 Cunningham ordered *Valiant*, with the destroyers *Mohawk* and *Nubian*, ahead at best speed to give assistance to Pridham-Wippell. A torpedo strike had been ranged on *Formidable*, but it was held back for fear that it might alert the main Italian fleet, if it was out, to the existence of a strong British force in the area. Though rarely remarked on, this was perhaps the second largest gamble Cunningham took in the whole engagement. Pridham-Wippell's cruisers could have been in trouble. Cunningham did not know for certain that the Italian battleships were at sea. Had one of the cruisers been crippled, with a torpedo strike waiting on *Formidable's* flightdeck, and the Italian battlefleet not been at sea, Cunningham would have had to answer some very serious questions. As it was the Italian cruisers ceased fire and drew away northwest at 0855, Iachino hoping thereby to draw the British cruisers under the guns of *Vittorio Veneto*.

At around 0900 both commanders received relatively accurate sighting reports. Iachino was told of a British carrier, two battleships, nine cruisers and 15 destroyers at sea. Because the position was the one he had been in at 0745 when

Below:
Both German and Italian destroyer designs favoured heavy armament at the expense of sea-keeping qualities. The snaking line running after is furled awnings, seen here on the Italian destroyer *Vittorio Alfieri*, sunk at Matapan. *Real Photographs 1260*

Above:
HMS *Mohawk* of the 'Tribal' class.
Real Photographs 1103

the sighting was made, and because of undue confidence in his intelligence assessments that the British main force was still in harbour, he assumed it was his own ships that had been seen. Pridham-Wippell received a signal at about the same time of three Italian battleships at sea; he, too, discounted this because his own force had been a mere seven miles away from the reported position at the time of sighting, and assumed that the aircraft's position was incorrect. Navigation on or over the sea was far from an exact science in the pre-electronic aids era. When Pridham-Wippell later met the C-in-C, their navigating officers were 10 miles apart in their calculations. In the finest traditions of the service the senior officer's navigator was deemed correct! Whatever his true position, Pridham-Wippell's instincts were correct: the aircraft had mistaken the 'Garibaldi' class cruisers for 'Cavour' class battleships of similar silhouette and armament arrangement. Four minutes after the Italian cruiser had turned away Pridham-Wippell signalled their change of course. He duly turned himself to shadow and steamed northwest, signalling the position of the *Trieste* group of cruisers at 0921 and again at 0936.

At the Battle of the River Plate a spotting aircraft's radio, tuned in to the wrong frequency, had caused trouble. Similar problems struck again when, at 0917, *Gloucester's* Walrus aircraft sighted

the second, *Zara* group of cruisers, also turning northwest like the *Trieste* group. Off the Plate the spotter had been on the reconnaissance frequency. Now the opposite effect occurred: the use of a spotting frequency meant that the signal never got further than *Gloucester* which failed to pass it on. This was a pity, as it would have significantly clarified Cunningham's appreciation of the situation.

With the cruiser action broken off, Cunningham recalled *Valiant* and her destroyers at 0918, and the fleet returned to *Barham's* best speed of 22kt. At 0849 Cunningham had sent a signal to Maleme, on Crete, ordering a land-based aircraft torpedo-strike. This throws some doubt on one explanation of his holding back for a time of *Formidable's* own strike, to avoid alerting the Italians. As Maleme flew Swordfish it seems unlikely that the Italians would have spotted the difference between these and carrier-based aircraft. In fact, Cunningham was holding back *Formidable's* aircraft for the situation to clarify itself and the chance of meeting heavier forces. He was most concerned not to commit his aircraft prematurely and scare the Italians off. In effect, he was quite deliberately letting Pridham-Wippell's cruisers be used as live bait. Against Italian opposition this was not as unduly risky as it might seem. Cunningham shared with Nelson the genius of knowing when an enemy's limitations put normal prudence and caution at a discount.

At this stage in the action neither commander was aware of any enemy battlefleet at sea. Iachino

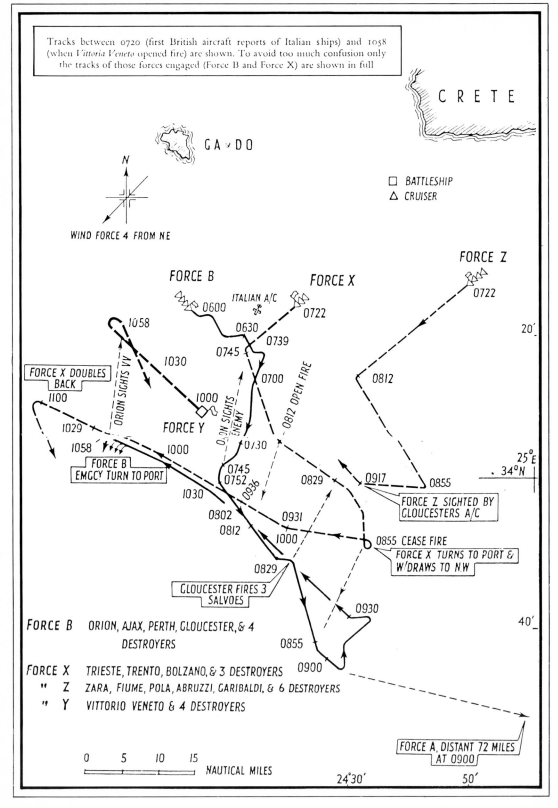

Tracks between 0720 (first British aircraft reports of Italian ships) and 1058 (when *Vittorio Veneto* opened fire) are shown. To avoid too much confusion only the tracks of those forces engaged (Force B and Force X) are shown in full

CRETE

GAVDO

N

WIND FORCE 4 FROM NE

□ BATTLESHIP
△ CRUISER

FORCE Z
0722

FORCE B
0600

FORCE X
0722

ITALIAN A/C
0630
0739
0745
0700

1058
1030
1000

0812

0812 OPEN FIRE

FORCE X DOUBLES
BACK
1100

1029

1058

FORCE B
EMCGY TURN TO PORT

ORION SIGHTS VV

FORCE Y

ORION SIGHTS ENEMY

0730

1000
1030

0745
0752
0936

0829

0917   0855

FORCE Z SIGHTED BY
GLOUCESTERS A/C

0802
0812

0931
1000

0855 CEASE FIRE
FORCE X TURNS TO PORT &
W/DRAWS TO N.W

20'

25°E
34°N

0829

GLOUCESTER FIRES 3
SALVOES

0930

0855
0900

40'

FORCE B   ORION, AJAX, PERTH, GLOUCESTER, & 4
           DESTROYERS

FORCE X   TRIESTE, TRENTO, BOLZANO, & 3 DESTROYERS
 "   Z   ZARA, FIUME, POLA, ABRUZZI, GARIBALDI, & 6 DESTROYERS
 "   Y   VITTORIO VENETO & 4 DESTROYERS

FORCE A, DISTANT 72 MILES
AT 0900

0   5   10   15
                    NAUTICAL MILES

24°30'   50'

had discounted sightings of British battleships, had steered his own flagship to the north and was hoping thus to lure Pridham-Wippell's cruisers into a position between *Vittorio Veneto* and the heavy cruisers, a lethal sandwich. Cunningham was chasing after an Italian heavy-cruiser force in the hope that it might lead to something larger.

At 0939 Cunningham finally decided to use his aircraft to take the pressure off Pridham-Wippell and he signalled *Formidable* to launch an air strike on the enemy cruisers, both those being shadowed by the British ships and any others sighted. The carrier launched a torpedo-striking force of six Albacores escorted by two Fulmars, a force that was later to exert a decisive influence on the battle. A Swordfish was also launched to observe results. Meanwhile the Maleme strike force, ordered at 0849, had not set off until 1050, because orders had to be passed via the cruiser *York*, beached in Scuda Bay after being damaged by an Italian explosive motor boat.

Vittorio Veneto in Action

A measure of doubt was rapidly resolved when at 1058 *Orion* sighted unknown vessels 16 miles to the north. The major unknown vessel was *Vittorio Veneto*, which opened fire with her 15in guns on Pridham-Wippell's cruisers at 1059. Action was speedy: the cruisers turned to race south to the main British fleet, still 80 miles distant, and Iachino similarly turned his cruisers round, ordering the *Trieste* force to engage the British from starboard. For the second time that day

Left:
Action off Gavdhos — Phase 1: 0722-1058.

Below:
The Italian battleship *Vittorio Veneto*, Iachino's flagship at Matapan. She was a well-armed and well-protected design; her eventual fate was to be scrapped between 1948 and 1950. *IWM CM5337*

Pridham-Wippell's cruisers were 'legging it' back to the south, but this time pursued by a new, fast and extremely powerful battleship with heavy cruisers in attendance. The range was soon down to 12 miles, accurate fire being received from the Italians and splinter damage from near-misses being caused to *Orion*. The situation was made even more desperate when the long-suffering *Gloucester* was left out of the smoke screen and repeatedly straddled, a situation not remedied until the destroyer *Hasty* was detached to fill the smoke gap. *Gloucester's* failing engines responded to the stimulus of being bombarded by 15in shells, and held up; the surprise was that more British ships did not fall prey to mechanical breakdown. One destroyer had sailed minus most of its rudder plates, another with empty oil tanks forward because of ruptured tanks. All the British vessels were showing signs of a hard war.

It was only a matter of time before one of the British cruisers was hit. Instead, in an appearance that was at least equal to anything achieved by the Seventh Cavalry, *Formidable's* strike force arrived. It had already passed Pridham-Wippell's cruisers on its way to find the Italians, and been fired on, despite frantic attempts at self-identification. Other opposition had come from the Luftwaffe but the pair of escorting Fulmars shot down one Ju88 and forced another to flee. With a speed of 90kt against a 30kt headwind and *Vittorio Veneto* steaming at 30kt it took time for the Albacores to get in position to avoid the destroyer escort. They launched their attack at 1127, sending two torpedoes ahead of *Vittorio Veneto* and four astern. Pridham-Wippell, immersed in his smoke, did not see the attack and carried on his headlong rush for a while. Then he emerged to see an empty sea. Despite not being hit, Iachino had broken off the action and turned away. Taranto had left its mark, and his fear of being crippled by an air attack had been enough to cause him to break off the action. *Vittorio Veneto* had fired 94×15in shells in 29 salvoes, and was

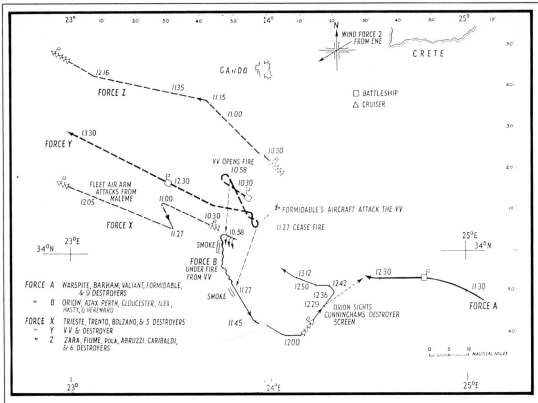

Wind Force 2 FROM ENE

CRETE

☐ BATTLESHIP
△ CRUISER

FORCE Z
1216
1135
1115
1100

GAVDO

FORCE Y
1330

1030

VV OPENS FIRE
10 58
1030

FORCE X
FLEET AIR ARM
ATTACKS FROM
MALEME
1205
1100
1230
1030
1127
10.58
1127

FORMIDABLE'S AIRCRAFT ATTACK THE VV
1127 CEASE FIRE

SMOKE

FORCE B
UNDER FIRE
FROM VV

34°N   23°E

25°E
34°N

FORCE A   WARSPITE, BARHAM, VALIANT, FORMIDABLE,
& 9 DESTROYERS
"   B   ORION, AJAX, PERTH, GLOUCESTER, ILEX,
HASTY, & HEREWARD
FORCE X   TRIESTE, TRENTO, BOLZANO, & 3 DESTROYERS
"   Y   VV & DESTROYER
"   Z   ZARA, FIUME, POLA, ABRUZZI, GARIBALDI,
& 6 DESTROYERS

SMOKE
1127
1312
1250   1242
1236
1229
1230
1130

ORION SIGHTS
CUNNINGHAMS DESTROYER
SCREEN

FORCE A

1145
1200

0   5   10
NAUTICAL MILES

23°   24°E   25°E

Above:
The British cruisers in retreat and the first air strike on
Vittorio Veneto **from** *Formidable*.

unlucky not to score at least one hit. Iachino proceeded on a course of 300° with his fleet, at 28kt. During the chase of the cruisers his speed and that of Cunningham's force had brought them together at 50kt. By this time Cunningham was roughly 45 miles away from the Italian force, but since Iachino's turn away the Italians had at least a 6kt advantage over him. The Maleme force of three Swordfish attacked the *Trieste* group at 1200, but also missed with their torpedoes. This time Pridham-Wippell did not turn to follow the Italians, but, with Cunningham's concurrence, headed on to meet up with Cunningham and the main battlefleet at 12.24. Aircraft would now be used as less risky means of finding the enemy.

The Waiting Time

The British battlefleet was steaming with turrets trained northwards, expectantly awaiting the enemy to come into sight. Off Calabria, in July 1940 Cunningham had waited too long to launch his spotting aircraft, considered absolutely vital to exploit fully the British advantage in long-range shooting. The fleet gunnery officer prevailed upon Cunningham to get the spotters into the air and

they were duly launched at 1215. *Warspite* launched two Swordfish floatplanes, one to act as action observer to give the C-in-C an accurate tactical assessment. All this reflected current Admiralty doctrine on the operational use of aircraft in battle. Another important function was throwing the enemy into confusion and, if possible, disabling him at the outset of a gunnery action. Cunningham was holding back *Formidable's* second wave for such an eventuality, but the first strike had to be landed back on, and by 1230 the carrier could wait no longer. She was duly detached for flying operations. To allow the first strike to land back on, the three Albacores and two Swordfish of the second wave, with two escorting Fulmars, were launched to patrol until the fleet action began at the expected hour of 1330. As *Formidable* tried to catch up the rest of the fleet, no less a personage than her Captain spotted an Italian SM79 torpedo-bomber making a run on his ship. The lookouts and gun crews were preoccupied by lunch and lulled into a false sense of security by the sunny weather. Sworn at by their Captain the crews of the multiple pom-poms forward of the bridge opened fire. The rest of the AA armament soon joined in and the Italian dropped his torpedo and wheeled away. As *Formidable* turned to 'comb' the first track a second SM79 attacked. Again the carrier heeled over to face end-on to the threat. Both torpedoes missed, a fortunate escape for *Formidable*.

At 1305 Cunningham ordered Pridham-Wippell ahead with his cruisers to 16 miles, maximum visibility range. *Formidable* rejoined the Fleet at 1400, thus creating one of the more remarkable sights of World War 2 — *Warspite*, *Valiant*, *Formidable* and *Barham* in line ahead with attendant escorts at 22kt, with a scouting force of light cruisers thrown out ahead. Here was exactly what the Royal Navy had prepared for since Jutland: a British fleet in hot pursuit of a weaker, fleeing foe. Some things were the same, notably the battleships, two of which were Jutland veterans. Others were new, such as the carrier and her aircraft and, most notably, the Fleet's considerable expertise in continuing the action after dark.

1330 came and went but the Italians were not yet overhauled. Indeed touch was temporarily lost due to the scarcity of aircraft for shadowing duties on board *Formidable*. Three Albacores from the first wave were eventually launched at 1400 and did not regain contact until just before 1500. The design features in the 'Illustrious' class of carriers which gave rise to small aircraft-carrying capacity have already been noted, but the presence on board *Formidable* of a mere 27 aircraft (13 Fulmars, 10 Albacores and four Swordfish) gives a clue to why such an apparently flawed design was adopted in the first place: the aircraft were simply not available to put on the carriers. The RAF had overriding priority for the products of the aircraft industry. The third service now made a contribution to the battle and sent bombers from Menidi in Greece to attack the Italians. Two Blenheims made the first attack on Iachino's force at 1425, and thereafter attacked regularly until 1645. The attacks failed to score any hits — a regular feature of high level bombing from both sides in the war — but indirectly one of the bombing strikes was to make a major contribution to the success of *Formidable's* own strike.

On the Italian side there was a spurious certainty about the situation. At 1200 Iachino had received a report that *Formidable* had sailed from Alexandria and just launched a strike against him. Influenced by misleading German intelligence of damage to two out of three of Cunningham's battleships, and accurate reports from the same source of the presence of the complete British fleet in Alexandria on the 27th, Iachino chose to believe *Formidable* had only just sailed, and that the British battleships had not sailed at all. He made the classic ostrich-like error that because enemy ships had not been seen they could not be there. Not until 1425 did he receive from Rhodes a reconnaissance aircraft report of the presence of both a carrier and a battleship sailing course 200°

at 1215, 80 miles to the east of him; this was followed at 1504 by a Radio Direction Finding fix on an enemy ship 170 miles to his southeast. Iachino chose to believe the DF report as intrinsically more accurate, and convinced himself that the force of one carrier, one battleship and four cruisers was far astern.

Vittorio Veneto Hit

By 1519 the second strike from *Formidable* had worked itself into a position from which it could attack the Italian battlefleet. Its commander, Lt-Cdr J. Dalyell-Stead, had only five aircraft, three Albacores and two Swordfish, but RAF Blenheims were beginning a high level bombing raid as he made his approach, and this was to prove crucial, as happened later at Midway when the positions were reversed. There a torpedo strike distracted fighters and gunners and let in the dive-bombers; at Matapan the torpedo aircraft were able to make a low level approach for a considerable while without being spotted. By pure fluke Britain's divided air power was making the type of co-ordinated attack impossible from British carriers alone. Fluke or not, it worked. The three Albacores launched on the port side at *Vittorio Veneto*, the two Swordfish from the starboard side, out of the sun. In accordance with long-standing doctrine the Fulmar fighters made supporting strafing runs at the battleship, which distracted gunners and look-outs and gained valuable seconds. However, by the time Dalyell-Stead came to launch, the gunners were back on target. Shortly after releasing his torpedo and attempting to cut across the bows to the starboard side of *Vittorio Veneto* his plane was cut down, and he and his crew killed. His sacrifice was not in vain: a torpedo hit the Italian battleship above the inboard of the two propellers on the port side, just over 20ft below the waterline.

Only a few months later two great warships — *Bismarck* and *Prince of Wales* — were to be lost partly through torpedo hits on the unprotected stern. *Vittorio Veneto* might have added a third to this list. Both port shafts were put out of action as were the auxiliary rudders on either side of the ship. Flooding was extensive: by 1530 some 3,500 tons of water had entered *Vittorio Veneto* and she was dead in the water. A significant flaw in the *Vittorio Veneto's* otherwise relatively sound design was placing the pump rooms at each end of the ship beyond the ship's armour or anti-torpedo protection. The destruction of the after pump room and the lack of portable powered pumping equipment was a major cause of the progressive flooding that endangered the ship. The static battleship was also more vulnerable to high level bombing and at 1530 a bomb from a Blenheim

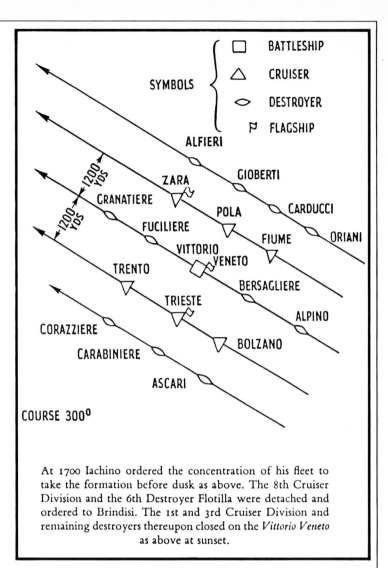

SYMBOLS {
☐ BATTLESHIP
△ CRUISER
◇ DESTROYER
⚑ FLAGSHIP
}

1200 YDS
1200 YDS

ALFIERI
GIOBERTI
ZARA
CARDUCCI
GRANATIERE
POLA
FUCILIERE
FIUME
ORIANI
VITTORIO VENETO
TRENTO
BERSAGLIERE
TRIESTE
ALPINO
CORAZZIERE
CARABINIERE
BOLZANO
ASCARI

COURSE 300°

At 1700 Iachino ordered the concentration of his fleet to take the formation before dusk as above. The 8th Cruiser Division and the 6th Destroyer Flotilla were detached and ordered to Brindisi. The 1st and 3rd Cruiser Division and remaining destroyers thereupon closed on the *Vittorio Veneto* as above at sunset.

Right:
Concentration of Iachino's forces at dusk.

Far right:
The Italian destroyer *Vincenzo Gioberti*. *Real Photographs 1265*

exploded close to the stern. This disabled the steering gear and added further to the flooding. If all this was not enough, Cunningham was a mere 3hr steaming away, 65 miles astern.

At 1558, with some understatement, a shadowing Albacore reported that the enemy had made large decrease in speed. The situation still seemed confused to Cunningham due to conflicting reports from aircraft. At 1600, just before he received the Albacore's welcome news, he ordered *Formidable* to prepare a maximum effort strike for dusk. Cruisers, the C-in-C felt, would provide more reliable shadowing; at 1644; Cunningham ordered Pridham-Wippell's ships to press on and gain touch with the enemy, stationing the destroyers *Nubian* and *Mohawk* at maximum visibility range to act as a visual signalling link between the two forces.

Meanwhile, Iachino's problems were the greater: at 1600 he received a signal from his High Command putting the enemy battlefleet 170 miles to his southeast. Fearing — quite rightly — a destroyer attack, he bunched his fleet, with both the *Trieste* and the *Zara* group of cruisers now present, round his injured flagship. Meanwhile, as heroic damage control parties struggled with inadequate equipment to contain the flooding, the starboard steering gear and shafts were coaxed back into life. Counter-flooding restored trim. By 1820 *Vittorio Veneto* was making 16kt. Iachino's conduct up to this point, and that of *Vittorio Veneto's* crew, cannot seriously be faulted. He had been more unlucky than incompetent in his interpretation of confused sighting reports. His facility in this regard was, in fact, little worse than Cunningham's and the latter had many more intelligence-gathering assets at his disposal. Iachino's initial deployment off Gavdo might have proved a well-planned and executed trap for the British cruisers. His breaking off the action for fear of air attack was shown to be fully justified when he was hit later: it also confirmed to the Italian 'fleet in being' doctrine.

Having been hit, Iachino's decision to group his force round the flagship, thus presenting a steel wall between it and its attackers, were exactly right, and his tactics for opposing the next strike were innovatory and effective. He was also right in fearing a destroyer attack; given the situation it is hard to see that anyone could have done better. As for his vessel and crew, although the flooding showed up weaknesses in the battleship's internal subdivision as well as damage control facilities, it was no mean feat to get *Vittorio Veneto* moving so soon and at such speed after a major hit on her stern.

At 1735 *Formidable* launched a third strike of six Albacores and two Swordfish, the aim being to attack at dusk and use the bad light to the aircraft's advantage: the size of this strike is a sad comment on the state of the Fleet Air Arm in 1941. The inexperience of the available observers in *Formidable's* aircraft had already significantly contributed to Cunningham's problems. Happily for the C-in-C, *Warspite's* Swordfish floatplane, launched earlier as action observation aircraft, had not flown to Crete as ordered but had returned to the flagship which had recovered the aircraft at the remarkable speed of 18kt. This aircraft was launched again at 1745 together with its able and experienced observer, Lt-Cdr A. S. Bolt. Bolt's competent reporting, which began at 1831, finally provided Cunningham with the accurate information on the disposition and course of the Italian fleet. Bolt only erred, understandably, in his estimates of the Italians' speed, which at between

12 and 15kt was probably slightly less than *Vittorio Veneto* was actually making. Cunningham's plan was for the cruisers to make contact, and then for his destroyers to launch an attack on the Italians, the main battlefleet coming up to support as necessary. This was precisely the eventuality Iachino had planned for when he closed up his fleet round the flagship.

Orion spotted the Italian fleet at a range of 10 miles at 1918. *Formidable's* aircraft and two Swordfish from Maleme had joined up and cruised around waiting for the right conditions of light: at 1925 they attacked. Iachino had decided to make smoke when the aircraft attacked, and at the same time shine searchlights at the aircraft in the hope of blinding them. These measures, plus a withering AA fire from the massed fleet and the close company they were keeping, split the attack up. It did have one result, and a dramatic one: the cruiser *Pola* was hit amidships on the starboard side between the engine and the boiler room — three compartments flooded and the main engines stopped. Amid the smoke and the confusion she dropped out of line at 1946, just as the attack was ending, unseen both by Iachino and the British. Iachino had certainly heard of *Pola's* injury by 2018, when he ordered Vice-Adm Cattaneo to turn back with the cruisers *Zara* and *Fiume*, together with four destroyers, to render such assistance as was necessary to *Pola*. This was Iachino's major, and perhaps his only, mistake during the action. He wanted a flag officer on hand to assess the situation, and in sending two heavy cruisers and four destroyers he must have assuaged his own feeling of helplessness at not being able to do more. He knew all three cruisers well, had a deep personal attachment and admiration for Cattaneo and would have had many questions to answer if he had left *Pola* unsupported. Cattaneo disagreed; he wanted to send only two destroyers back,

fearing quite rightly what the cruisers might head into. The Italian ships were not supplied with flashless cordite, nor had they trained in night-firing or acquired the necessary equipment and techniques to undertake it. Iachino stuck to his earlier decision, despite a signal from Cattaneo. *Zara* and *Fiume* turned out of line with four destroyers — *Alfieri, Carducci, Oriani* and *Gioberti* — and headed southeast at 16kt straight into the British fleet, 50 miles away.

Once he had given this order, carried out at 2100 and which lost him the Battle of Matapan, Iachino then gave the order that saved the rest of his fleet. At 2048 *Vittorio Veneto* and her consorts altered course 23° northwards, to 323°. This course change, and his speed of 19kt, were to lose him from British sight for the rest of the engagements. The Fleet Air Arm had not succeeded in 'fixing' the main enemy unit, but it had created the conditions for a major success.

Two hours earlier, Cunningham had also faced a decision as to whether or not to send his own forces into unscouted darkness without being entirely sure what they would meet. Cunningham's plan was to denude his three battleships and *Formidable* of all except four destroyers, and send these on to attack what he thought was the crippled *Vittorio Veneto*, wrongly plotted as proceeding at 13kt rather than the 19kt she was actually making. Fearful of Iachino's formation, the prospect of destroyer and submarine attacks on the battleships and the danger of German air attacks the following day, Cunningham's staff officers expressed their misgivings. According to his autobiography, *A Sailor's Odyssey*, the C-in-C 'paid respectful attention to this opinion' and decided to think it over after supper. Capt S. W. C. Pack quotes a more colourful account given by the fleet gunnery officer, according to whom Cunningham listened, and then accused his staff officers of being 'a pack of yellow livered skunks. I'll go and have my supper now and see after supper if my morale isn't higher than yours'. Over his meal Cunningham must have pondered the well-known British expertise in night action, practised and developed in the Mediterranean over a decade or more since the era of Adm Chatfield's command in the early 1930s. On the other hand, the fleet was rusty in its night action techniques and a confused melée was possible. Cunningham's aggressive instincts, and his know-ledge that even inadequately trained British crews had a more than significant advantage over the totally unprepared Italians, made pressing on the only possible decision for 'ABC'. At 2037 the second and fourteenth destroyer flotillas, already in position ahead of the battleships, were ordered forward to find and 'attack enemy battlefleet with torpedoes'.

Pridham-Wippell's cruisers saw *Formidable's* strike at a range of about 15 miles. At 1949, with darkness upon them and visibility down to four miles, the Vice-Adm, Light Forces, slowed to 20kt, 'in order to reduce bow waves'. At roughly the same time Iachino ordered increased speed to 19kt. Presumably this action was taken because of the prevailing belief that *Vittorio Veneto's* speed was a mere 13kt, and hence the cruisers might blunder into his force, ruining the surprise element for the destroyers. Throughout this part of the action the planned destroyer attack, led by Capt P. J. Mack in *Jervis*, cramped Pridham-Wippell. The destroyers, of course, were still steaming ahead to a position for *Vittorio Veneto* that gave her somewhere in the region of 30-mile head start, without realising that the real distance was almost twice that. Mack had decided on an extremely bold plan of action. He would go to northward of the battleship, then turn back and pass down *between* the cruisers and the battleship, hoping thus to make the enemy fire at each other in the confusion. Cunningham later criticised Mack's plan as it was bound to lead to problems with Pridham-Wippell's cruisers.

The Battle Begins

At 2015, *Orion* spotted an unknown vessel on radar roughly six miles ahead of her; at 2040 Pridham-Wippell had established that the vessel was stopped. He signalled its position to Cunningham, and then sped on. His reasoning was that if this was the Italian battleship she was duly 'fixed' and the destroyers would be about to attack; the result might be, as one who was there put it, 'an all-British battle'. In any case it was up to him to follow the main body. Mack in *Jervis* did not receive this signal, with the result that the destroyer group raced on at 28kt on a course that converged with Pridham-Wippell. Pridham-Wippell, about to spread out his cruisers again in a search pattern, refrained when he realised the destroyers' heading and the possibility of mistaken identity. There was a case of mistaken identity, but not of the variety expected by Pridham-Wippell. At 2145 *Ajax* reported three unknown vessels on her radar five miles to her south. These must have been the *Zara* and *Fiume* group heading back to *Pola*, but Pridham-Wippell assumed it was Mack's destroyer group and Mack, too, thought it was his own vessels. Pridham-Wippell turned to the north at 2202, in order to clear Mack's destroyers, thus putting himself even further away from *Vittorio Veneto*. To cap it all, *Vittorio Veneto* sent off a red flare at 2243, sighted by *Orion* and *Gloucester*. Mack also sighted it, but was happy to leave it to Pridham-Wippell, who changed course 9min later,

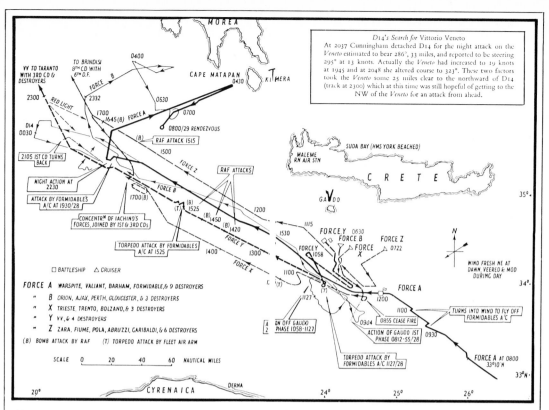

MOREA

CAPE MATAPAN
KITHERA

0400

TO BRINDISI
8TH CD WITH
6TH D.F.

FORCE B

0430

0630

0700

VV TO TARANTO
WITH 3RD CD &
DESTROYERS

2300

RED LIGHT

2332

0800/29 RENDEZVOUS

1700

1645(B) FORCE A

DI4
0030

(B) RAF ATTACK 1515

1500

2105 IST CD TURNS
BACK

FORCE Z

NIGHT ACTION AT
2230

FORCE Z

RAF ATTACKS

ATTACK BY FORMIDABLE'S
A/C AT 1930/28

1700(B)

(B) 1525

(T)

CONCENTRⁿ OF IACHINO'S
FORCES, JOINED BY IST & 3RD CDS

(B) 1450

(B) 1420

FORCE Y

1200

TORPEDO ATTACK BY FORMIDABLES
A/C AT 1525

1400

1300

FORCE Y

FORCE X

1100

1530

1115

FORCE Y 0630
FORCE B
FORCE Z

FORCE Y
1058

FORCE
X

0722

□ BATTLESHIP   △ CRUISER

FORCE A   WARSPITE, VALIANT, BARHAM, FORMIDABLE, & 9 DESTROYERS

"   B   ORION, AJAX, PERTH, GLOUCESTER, & 3 DESTROYERS

"   X   TRIESTE, TRENTO, BOLZANO, & 3 DESTROYERS

"   Y   VV, & 4 DESTROYERS

"   Z   ZARA, FIUME, POLA, ABRUZZI, GARIBALDI, & 6 DESTROYERS

(B) BOMB ATTACK BY RAF   (T) TORPEDO ATTACK BY FLEET AIR ARM

(T)

(T)

1127

FORCE A

1200

1100

TURNS INTO WIND TO FLY OFF
FORMIDABLES A/C

A
2

ON OFF GAUDO
PHASE 1058-1127

0904

0855 CEASE FIRE

ACTION OF GAUDO IST
PHASE 0812-55/28

0930

TORPEDO ATTACK BY
FORMIDABLES A/C 1127/28

FORCE A AT 0800
33°10´N

33°N·

SCALE   0   20   40   60   NAUTICAL MILES

20°

CYRENAICA   DERNA

24°

25°

26°

35°

34°

33°N·

WIND FRESH NE AT
DAWN, VEERED & MOD
DURING DAY

N

SUDA BAY (HMS YORK BEACHED)

MALEME
RN AIR STN

C R E T E

GAVDO

D14's *Search for* Vittorio Veneto
At 2037 Cunningham detached D14 for the night attack on the *Veneto* estimated to bear 286°, 33 miles, and reported to be steering 295° at 13 knots. Actually the *Veneto* had increased to 19 knots at 1945 and at 2048 she altered course to 323°. These two factors took the *Veneto* some 25 miles clear to the northward of D14 (track at 2300) which at this time was still hopeful of getting to the NW of the *Veneto* for an attack from ahead.

Above:

Overview of the battle up to the night action.

Below:

HMS *Jervis*, Mack's flotilla leader, which sank *Zara*.
IWM A10479

only to withdraw when he received a signal at 2332 from Cunningham ordering all forces not engaged with the enemy to withdraw to the northeast. This signal was made when the battlefleet had smashed two Italian cruisers and two destroyers, and Cunningham wished to leave the field clear for the destroyers to attack. Mack in *Jervis* asked if it referred to him, and was told to carry on as before until he had engaged the enemy. Pridham-Wippell did not ask, and turned away, thereby losing the battlefleet its last slim chance of regaining touch with the Italians, at 2332 just over 30 miles ahead of both the cruisers and Mack's destroyers.

However, before all this, the battleships had already inflicted a crushing defeat on the Italians.

Battleships in Action

At 2100 Cunningham had received *Ajax's* radar report. Unlike Pridham-Wippell and Mack, Cunningham did not assume this sighting referred to the British destroyers. He thought it was the crippled Italian battleship, and steered to 280°, 20 miles away from the reported position. At 2203 *Valiant's* radar sighted a stopped vessel eight or nine miles off the port bow. By 2210 *Valiant* was able to report a ship of at least 600ft six miles off the port bow. Cunningham ordered a 40° alteration in course, thus moving his whole battlefleet towards an unidentified enemy much in the manner of a commander of light forces in the

Above:
A prewar view of HMS *Greyhound*, a 'G' class destroyer. *MPL*

Bottom:
The Italian cruiser *Zara* was sunk at Matapan. Note the unusual catapult arrangements *forward* of the main armament. Unusually for Italian vessels the cruisers sacrificed speed for relatively heavy armour protection, and stayed afloat for a creditably long time after their pounding at Matapan. *IWM HU2689*

Channel. At 2220 *Valiant* reported a ship bearing 191° off the port bow, at 4½ miles. Then at 2223, the destroyer *Stuart* gave the night alarm. There, steaming across the bows of the British fleet and completely unaware of their presence, was a line of Italian warships: the destroyer *Alfieri*, the 8in

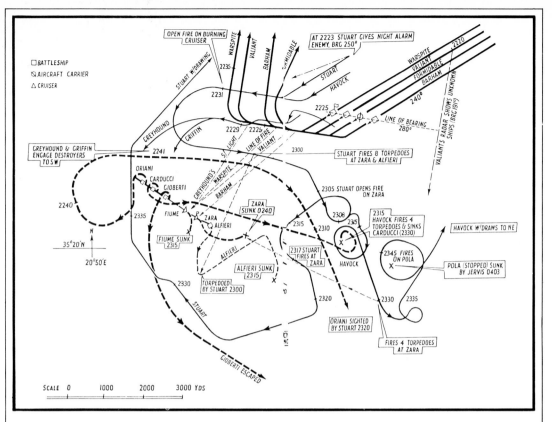

Above:

The night action.

cruisers *Zara* and *Fiume*, the destroyers *Gioberti*, *Carducci* and *Oriani*. Using short-range radio, and with remarkable precision, the battlefleet turned to 280°, almost parallel and opposite to the Italian force, to open its 'A' arcs. In Cunningham's own words:

'I shall never forget the next two minutes. In the dead silence, a silence that could almost be felt, one heard only the voice of the gun control personnel putting the guns on to the new target . . . one saw the turrets swing and steady when the 15in guns pointed at the enemy cruisers. Never in the whole of my life have I experienced a more thrilling moment than when I heard a calm voice from the director tower — "Director layer sees target"; sure sign that the guns were ready and that his finger was itching on the trigger. The enemy was at a range of no more than 3,800yd — pointblank.'

The port wing destroyers were told brusquely to get out of the way. At 2227 *Greyhound's* searchlight shot out to capture one of the cruisers

in its beam, its splash showing also the outline of the leading destroyer, *Alfieri*, and the other cruiser. It was a massacre. *Warspite* at 2,900yd and *Valiant* at 4,000yd fired at *Fiume*, turning her into a sea of flames and blowing 'Y' turret overboard, trained fore and aft as were all the other turrets. In a remark remembered by several witnesses later, the Flag Captain, a distinguished gunnery officer and more used to the uncertainties of long-range firing, exclaimed 'Good Lord! We've hit her!' Indeed they had. *Valiant* shifted fire after her first salvo, when 'X' and 'Y' turrets ceased to bear on *Fiume*, and slammed an amazing total of five 15in broadsides into *Zara* in the space of 3min. *Warspite* shifted target similarly after her second broadside.

Formidable was ordered out of line as a liability shortly before fire opened. Behind her *Barham*, whose Captain saw the stranded *Pola* fire a flare to guide her rescuers in, was about to open fire on her when she saw *Greyhound's* searchlight illuminate *Alfieri* and fired into her instead. Then she fired six 15in and seven 6in salvoes into *Zara*. *Griffin*, which had stumbled into the line of fire, was told to 'Get out of the way, you bf!' by the C-in-C. There can never have been a few minutes like it in history, nor will there ever be such again. *Fiume* and *Zara*, little more than flaming wrecks, reeled out of line, the only wonder being that they did not blow up and sink there and then.

At 2231 the three undamaged Italian destroyers swept in, at least one launching torpedoes. Fire was shifted to them, and to *Havock* who had failed to switch on her fighting lights and was straddled by *Warspite's* 6in guns. A slight case of over-enthusiasm was visible in this quarter when the same 6in guns nearly opened up on *Formidable*, caught to the north in *Warspite's* searchlight, with the order countermanded only just in time.

At 2238 the four destroyers left with Cunningham were ordered to finish off the cruisers. As a result of receiving the night alarm signal from Pridham-Wippell and Mack, who had unknowingly sighted *Vittorio Veneto's* flares, Cunningham believed they were in action with the main Italian fleet; consequently he sent the signal discussed previously, ordering all those not actually engaged in sinking the enemy (that is, his four destroyers) to retire northeast, leaving the field clear for Mack's destroyers. The signal was badly worded as it was not intended that Pridham-Wippell should turn away. Cunningham and his staff never thought that Pridham-Wippell would disregard all peacetime training and lose touch with the enemy.

Cunningham's four destroyers were to have a wild night of it. *Griffin* and *Greyhound* chased off after the three Italian destroyers, found them, fired on them, but lost them when the Italians put on speed, made smoke and disappeared to the south at 2320. *Stuart* and *Havock* had made for the crippled cruisers, and at 2259 sighted one stopped and one circling (*Fiume* and *Zara*). *Stuart* fired all eight torpedoes at both ships, saw an explosion on *Fiume*, but also saw *Zara* start to limp away, ablaze as she was. She therefore fired on *Zara*, was rewarded by a dramatic explosion, but then saw an Italian destroyer passing down her starboard side only 150yd away. *Stuart* fired two salvoes at her, then caught sight of *Zara* at 2317 and shifted fire to her. In the meantime she was witness to the sudden capsize and sinking of the destroyer *Alfieri* at 2315. *Stuart* twice sighted destroyers again, but lost them on both occasions. The first destroyer which had passed so close to *Stuart* was *Carducci*, which ran into *Havock* at 2315. *Havock* fired four torpedoes with one hit, then opened fire, sinking *Carducci* at 2330. At the same time she sighted the two cruisers *Zara* and *Fiume*, fired her remaining torpedoes at them (four in number), but missed. Not abashed by this she opened fire, but at 2345, in the light of a star shell fired to illuminate *Zara*, saw the stopped *Pola*. She identified her as a 'Littorio' class battleship, and withdrew to the northwest. Mack in *Jervis*, 60 miles west-northwest, thought he was at that moment crossing the Italian fleet's line of advance. He received the mistaken identification at 0030 on 29 March and

Below:
Pola disabled.

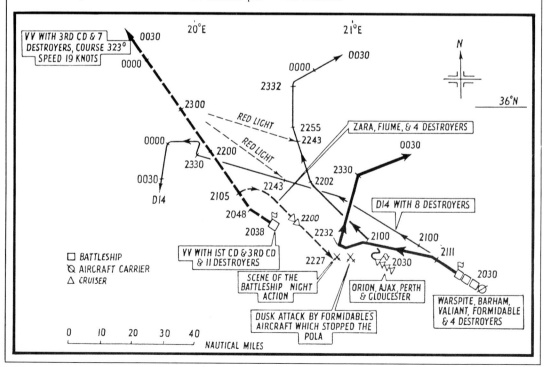

immediately turned southeast, thereby steaming directly away from Iachino. A signal correcting 'Littorio' to '8-inch cruiser' was sent 8min after the first signal, but not received by Mack until 0134, by which time all chance of catching up with the Italian main fleet was gone. Mack arrived at the burial ground of the Italian cruisers at 0200, and was drawn by her fires to the abandoned *Zara*. He picked up survivors, and fired four torpedoes from *Jervis* into *Zara* at around 0240; three were reported as hitting, and *Zara* slowly turned over and sank. *Fiume* had sunk at around 2315.

At 0140 *Greyhound* and *Griffin*, rushing to *Havock's* signal, found the cause of it all, *Pola*, drifting; three-quarters of her crew had gone and the remainder were half drunk on the upper deck. She took no offensive action, and had her guns trained fore and aft, possibly to avoid retaliation but more likely because she had lost all electrical power. At 0325 Mack arrived, went alongside *Pola*, and took off 257 Italian survivors. One torpedo from *Jervis* at 0340 and two from *Nubian* caused an explosion from which *Pola* sank, at 0403. *Fiume* had sunk some time before *Zara*. The destroyers hastened back to the main battlefleet; by 0700 all units were back within sight of the flagship.

The Italians had lost three modern 8in cruisers — *Zara*, *Fiume* and *Pola*, and two destroyers — *Alfieri* and *Carducci*, and approximately 2,400 officers and men. That more men were not lost is in part due to Cunningham, who allowed a message to be forwarded via Suda Bay to the Italians.

Conclusion

After Matapan the Italian fleet stayed in harbour until August 1941. It did not add its weight to the air attacks that were such an ordeal for Cunningham as Greece and Crete were evacuated. As the C-in-C himself put it 'these later operations may be said to have been conducted under the cover of the Battle of Matapan'. From the Italian viewpoint the battle was merely added proof of the qualitative inferiority of their fleet, with its total inability to use its main armament after dark due to its lack of radar and a closely-integrated air component; numbers meant little given these crippling disadvantages. The Italian Navy had progressed little beyond the stage of the Battle of Jutland in its operational techniques. Yet Iachino made one seriously wrong decision: to send back the 1st Cruiser Squadron. It was both an honourable and understandable response, if an unwise one; in coldly rational terms air reconnaissance, even had he interpreted available information correctly, put the British fleet at least 25 miles further away than it was. Both

commanders had to take risks on inadequate and contradictory information: Iachino gambled and lost, Cunningham gambled and won. The overwhelming superiority of the British fleet in night-fighting did, however, weight the dice in the latter's favour.

Cunningham's handling of the situation was masterly, but the British had weaknesses as well. The first mistake was the insufficient priority given to naval aviation which left *Formidable* with such a diminutive strike force aboard. The second was the slow speed at which the British fleet advanced out of Alexandria. The desire to concentrate forces is quite understandable, but here Cunningham's aggressive instinct let him down. Had *Formidable* and *Valiant* cracked on speed immediately, and not waited on *Warspite* and *Barham*, an annihilation of the Italian fleet, rather than a severe blow, might have been possible. Possible also would have been the destruction of important Italian units; that too would have been a gamble. Perhaps most open to question is the handling of Pridham-Wippell's cruiser force. Although both its turns from the enemy were understandable, the British cruisers lost sight of their enemy twice, lost them a third time, and then broke off the chase in response to a signal from the Commander-in-Chief when they were in pursuit of the one lead that might have led them to the main Italian force. They lacked just a little of the sparkle that one might have expected from Cunningham's 'eyes of the fleet'.

When it is remembered how *Bismarck* was trailed through a long night and shadowed it is hard to explain how an Italian force that was within easy range of carrier and land-based aircraft, and in sight of them for much of the day, was lost so easily. The answer lies in difficult wind conditions, inexperienced air observers and the inherent difficulty of accurate speed estimation compounded by a fortuitous increase in speed and change of course from *Vittorio Veneto*. If Pridham-Wippell had closed up on his enemy when he saw the tracer of *Formidable's* dusk attack, and if he had run the risk of either long-range fire from the Italian force or a surprise lunge at him from cruisers it might have been a very different battle. Signals procedure was also not as good as it might have been. In the understandable excitement of action Cunningham's badly-worded signal to retire to the northeast caused Pridham-Wippell to break off. Identification was a persistent problem, notably when *Havock's* signal caused Mack's flotilla to steam away from the enemy, but anyone who has tried to identify a ship at sea in the most peaceful of conditions must sympathise with those trying to sort out the identities of ships of very similar appearance in war.

Cunningham's aggressive 'up and at 'em!' attitude won him a great victory, and a deserved one. The success of such methods depended, however, on a sufficient margin of technical superiority: where that did not exist disaster might ensue and, only a short while after Matapan, in the Denmark Strait, it did exactly that.

British Destroyers at the Battle of Matapan

A representative sample of the various destroyer types is given below.

'Queen Elizabeth' Class Battleships

Builders:

Warspite — Devonport Dockyard
(Laid down 31 October 1912; launched 26 November 1913; completed March 1915)

Valiant — Fairfield
(Laid down 31 January 1913; launched 4 November 1914; completed February 1916)

Barham — John Brown
(Laid down 24 February 1913; launched 31 October 1914; completed October 1915)

Displacement: *Warspite* 31,315 tons (standard); *Valiant* 31,585 tons (standard); *Barham* 31,350 tons (standard)

Dimensions: *Warspite* 639.4ft×90.5ft×28.8ft; *Valiant* 639.75ft×90.5ft×28.75ft; *Barham* 639.75ft×90.5ft×30.75ft

Machinery: Geared turbines, 4 shafts, 80,000shp, *Warspite* 23.5kt, *Valiant* 24kt. *Barham* 75,000shp, 22.5kt

Armour: Main belt 13in (4in ends); deck over magazines 5in

Armament: 8×15in (4×2); *Warspite* 8×6in (8×1); 8×4in (4×2); 32×2pdr (4×8); 16×5in machine guns (4×4). *Valiant* 20×4.5in (10×2). *Barham* 12×6in (12×1); 8×4in (4×2); 16×2pdr (2×8); 2×21in torpedo tubes (2×1)

Sensors: Type 279 radar (*Valiant* only)

Aircraft: 2 (*Barham* 1)

Notes: Amongst the most successful design of battleship ever built, all five vessels in the class were extensively modernised after World War 1, but *Warspite*, *Valiant* and *Queen Elizabeth* were given complete reconstructions, after which their only real weakness was a relatively low top speed. *Warspite* had received no less than 13 heavy shell hits at Jutland, and survived.

'Tribal' Class

Builder: Thornycroft
Nubian — (Laid down 1936; launched 1937; completed 1938)

Displacement: 1,959 tons

Dimensions: 377ft×36.5ft×9ft

Machinery: Geared turbines, 2 shafts, 44,000shp, 36kt

Armament: 8×4.7in (4×2); 4×2pdr (1×4); 8×.5in machine guns (2×4); 4×21in torpedo tubes (2×4)

Complement: 190

Notes: This type was built in response to larger destroyers being constructed abroad during the 1930s. *Mohawk* of this type was also present at Matapan.

'G' and 'H' Class

Builder: Denny
Havock — (Laid down 1935; launched 1936; completed 1937)

Displacement: 1,340 tons

Dimensions: 323ft×33ft×8.75ft

Machinery: Geared turbines, 2 shafts, 34,000shp, 36kt

Armament: 4×4.7in (4×1); 1×3in AA; 8×.5in (2×4); 4×21in torpedo tubes (2×4)

Complement: 145

Notes: *Greyhound* and *Griffin* of the 'G' class had a displacement of 1,335 tons. *Hasty*, *Hereward* and *Hotspur* were also present at Matapan.

'J' Class

Builder: Hawthorn Leslie
Jervis — (Laid down 1937; launched 1938; completed 1939)

Displacement: 1,760 tons

Dimensions: 356.5ft × 35.7ft × 9ft

Machinery: Geared turbines, 2 shafts, 40,000shp, 36kt

Armament: 6 × 4.7in (3 × 2); 1 × 4in AA; 4 × 2pdr (1 × 4); 2 × 20mm (2 × 1); 8 × .5in machine guns (2 × 4); 5 × 21in torpedo tubes

Complement: 218

Notes: These were the first class of British destroyers constructed with longitudinal framing — a cost-saving measure which gave excellent strength to the hull. *Jervis* was a leader; *Janus*, also at Matapan, had a complement of 183. Anti-aircraft fit varied.

HMAS *Stuart*

Builder: Hawthorn Leslie
(Laid down 1916; launched 1917; completed 1918)

Displacement: 1,530 tons

Dimensions: 332.5ft × 31.75ft × 9.25ft

Machinery: Geared turbines, 2 shafts, 40,000shp, 36.5kt

Armament: 5 × 4.7in (5 × 1); 1 × 3in AA; 2 × 2pdr (2 × 1); machine guns; 6 × 21in torpedo tubes (2 × 3)

Complement: 183

Notes: An old 'Scott' class flotilla leader transferred to the Royal Australian Navy in 1933.

HMS *Formidable* was built by Harland & Wolff, laid down on 17 June 1937, launched on 17 August 1939 and completed on 24 November 1940. Other details are as for *Illustrious* (see Chapter 3).

Vittorio Veneto was built by CRDA (Trieste), laid down on 28 October 1934, launched on 22 July 1937 and completed on 28 April 1940. Other details are as for *Littorio* (see Chapter 3).

Left:
HMS *Barham*, one of the less modernised 'Queen Elizabeths'. She came to a well publicised and explosive end later in 1941. *IWM HU2869*

'Zara' Class Heavy Cruisers

Builders:
Zara — OTO, Muggiano
(Laid down 4 July 1929; launched 27 April 1930; completed 21 October 1931)
Fiume — Stabilimento Technico
(Laid down 29 April 1929; launched 27 April 1930; completed 23 November 1931)
Pola — OTO, Leghorn
(Laid down 17 March 1931; launched 5 December 1931; completed 21 December 1931)

Displacement: *Zara* 11,680 tons (standard); *Fiume* 11,326 tons (standard); *Pola* 11,545 tons (standard); 14,300 tons; 13,944 tons; 14,133 tons respectively, full load

Dimensions: 557.2ft × 62.8ft × 19.4ft

Machinery: Geared turbines, 2 shafts, 95,000shp, design speed of 32kt; trials speed 33-35kt; normal sea speed 29kt

Armour: 3.9-5.9in belt; 2.75in deck; 4.7-5.9in turrets

Armament: 8 × 8in (4 × 2); 14 × 3.9in (6 × 2 + 2 × 1 for starshell); 8 × 37mm (4 × 2); 8 × 13.2mm (8 × 1)

Aircraft: 2

Complement: 841

Notes: The 'Zara' class were yet another treaty-limitation heavy cruiser that exceeded the 10,000-ton limit, but the result was a batch of four fine vessels. Unusually for Italian design they sacrificed speed and range for weight of armour, and they also carried a heavy AA battery. They had the unusual feature of a catapult forward of 'A' turret, a measure adopted to economise on hull length. The battering that *Zara* and *Fiume* took before sinking suggests excellent watertight integrity and design, although a very large number of ships in World War 2 refused to be sunk by gunfire, and had to be dispatched by torpedoes.

'Oriani' Class Destroyers

Vincenzo Gioberti — Laid down 1936; completed 1937
Vittorio Alfieri — Laid down 1936; completed 1937
Alfredo Oriani — Laid down 1935; completed 1937
Giosue Carducci — Laid down 1936; completed 1937

Displacement: 1,675 tons (standard)

Dimensions: 350ft × 33.6ft × 11.2ft

Machinery: Geared turbines, 2 shafts, 48,000shp, 39kt (designed); sea speed 33kt

Armament: 4 × 4.7in; 8 × 20mm; 6 × 21in torpedo tubes

Complement: 206

Notes: Designed for high speed, these powerful vessels were not very good sea-keepers.

CHAPTER FOUR

The Sinking of *Hood* and *Bismarck*

Operation 'Rheinubung' (Operation 'Rhine Exercise')

By April 1941 Grand-Adm Raeder thought that he would soon have four major surface ships able to launch raids on British convoys in the Atlantic. The magnificent new battleship *Bismarck* would have finished working up, and with her in the Baltic was the 8in-gun cruiser *Prinz Eugen*. These ships would be able to team up in mid-Atlantic with *Scharnhorst* and *Gneisenau* currently in Brest. Several ships had already made successful break-outs, British reconnaissance was still inadequate and the concentration of force would be awesome. Plans went awry when *Scharnhorst's* refit took longer than expected; *Gneisenau* was hit in harbour, first by an air-launched torpedo and then by four bombs, and *Prinz Eugen* ran over a mine. *Prinz Eugen* would soon be ready again, however, so Raeder settled on a raiding force of two ships,

Bismarck and *Prinz Eugen*, with a start date in May.

He faced at least two opponents to his plan: Hitler was so worried about the risks to capital ships and relations with the United States that he was not told of the operation until 22 May, when both ships were at sea, despite having inspected them at Gdynia shortly before they sailed; Adm Lutjens, the commander of the force, wished to wait for a greater concentration of strength before such an operation. Raeder refused to listen, perhaps realising that the coming Russian offensive would draw resources away from the Navy and make such operations less possible.

Below:
Bismarck, as new; some of her AA armament appears to be not yet fitted. *Real Photographs S1737*

Bismarck photographed in Norwegian waters from *Prinz Eugen*, just prior to the breakout. The distinctive camouflage was painted out shortly after this photograph was taken. *IWM HU374*

Bismarck

Builder: Blohm und Voss
(Laid down 1 July 1936; launched 14 February 1939; completed 24 August 1940)

Displacement: 41,673 tons (standard); 49,136 tons (full load)

Dimensions: 820.3ft × 118.1ft × 28.5ft

Machinery: 12 × 825psi boilers, geared steam turbines, 3 shafts, 136,112shp, 30.1kt (maximum 29kt normal)

Armour: Main belt 12.6in; upper belt 5.72in; upper deck 1.97in; main deck 3.15-3.74in; slopes between main deck and bottom of belt 4.3in; turrets 14.17in front, 8.66in sides, 12.76in back, 5.12-7.09in roof

Armament: 8 × 15in (4 × 2); 12 × 5.9in (6 × 2); 16 × 4.1in (8 × 2); 16 × 37mm (8 × 2); 16 × 20mm (16 × 1)

Sensors: Three 'Seetakt' FuMo23 radar sets for search and limited fire control mounted on the directors; radar detection receiver; passive warning sonar array

Aircraft: 4

Complement: 2,065

Notes: *Bismarck* was essentially a reworking of World War 1 designs. The combination of high speed and wide beam, making her a very stable gun platform, was perhaps her greatest strength, and the excellence of her watertight sub-division. However, the provision of a 'splinter deck' of 2in armour to explode armour-piercing shells before they hit the main deck was generally considered obsolete by 1939, as a main belt low down in the ship allowed communications and superstructure to be heavily damaged, even if engine rooms and magazines were protected. British and American designs raised the main horizontal armour to deck level. *Bismarck* also had a clumsy combination of anti-surface vessel secondary armament and a tertiary layer of anti-aircraft weapons, as distinct from the British *King George V* designs which had dual-purpose 5.25in secondary armament.

Prinz Eugen

Builder: Germaniawerft, Kiel
(Laid down 23 April 1936; launched 22 August 1938; completed 1 August 1940)

Displacement: 16,974 tons (standard), 19,042 tons (full load)

Dimensions: 679.1ft × 70.6ft × 21.7ft

Machinery: Geared turbines, 4 shafts, 132,000shp, 32.5kt

Armour: 3.25in-1.5in main belt; 1.25in-0.5in deck; 0.75in torpedo bulkhead; 6.25in-2.25in turrets

Armament: 8 × 8in (4 × 2); 12 × 4.1in (6 × 2); 12 × 37mm (6 × 2); 8 × 20mm; 12 × 21in torpedo tubes (4 × 3)

Sensors: GHG passive surveillance sonar; 60 hydrophones on each side of the bow. Also 3 'Seetakt' FuMo23 radars mounted on the fire control directors

Aircraft: 3

Complement: 1,600

Notes: *Prinz Eugen* was first of the second group of 'Hipper' class heavy cruisers to be laid down, although the only one to be completed. She and the two ships of the first group are considered some of the most effective of the interwar 8in-gun cruisers officially built to the Washington Treaty of 10,000-ton standard — perhaps not surprisingly as they exceeded treaty limitations by about 50%! Their Achilles heel throughout the war was their high-pressure boilers, and as raiders they lacked endurance. *Prinz Eugen* was a 'lucky ship' and survived the war to be expended in atomic bomb tests. Her large passive sonar system — the most advanced in the world at the time — was a major contribution to her good fortune.

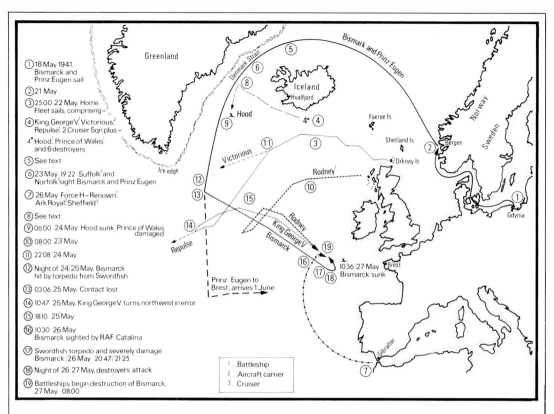

1. 18 May 1941, Bismarck and Prinz Eugen sail
2. 21 May
3. 2500 22 May, Home Fleet sails, comprising –
4. King George V.² Victorious,² Repulse¹ 2 Cruiser Sqn plus –
   4* Hood¹, Prince of Wales¹ and 6 destroyers
5. See text
6. 23 May, 1922 Suffolk³ and Norfolk³ sight Bismarck and Prinz Eugen
7. 26 May Force H – Renown,¹ Ark Royal,² Sheffield³
8. See text
9. 0600 24 May Hood sunk, Prince of Wales damaged
10. 0800 23 May
11. 2208 24 May
12. Night of 24/25 May, Bismarck hit by torpedo from Swordfish
13. 0306 25 May. Contact lost
14. 1047 25 May, King George V turns northwest in error
15. 1810 25 May
16. 1030 26 May Bismarck sighted by RAF Catalina
17. Swordfish torpedo and severely damage Bismarck, 26 May 2047/2125
18. Night of 26 27 May, destroyers attack
19. Battleships begin destruction of Bismarck, 27 May 0800

1...Battleship
2...Aircraft carrier
3...Cruiser

18 May–21 May

Bismarck and *Prinz Eugen* sailed in darkness from Gdynia on the night of 18/19 May 1941. ☐1 Their instructions were to break out into the Atlantic and harry British convoys. The British were worried about *Bismarck* and the code breakers of Bletchley Park had detected increased Luftwaffe activity that seemed to indicate a major naval

Above:
Overview of the sinking of the *Bismarck* (map numbers keyed in to text).

Below:
The Swedish cruiser *Gotland* that first sighted the two German vessels. *Real Photographs S610*

Above:
HMS *Antelope*, one of the destroyers sailing with the *Hood* group. *Real Photographs S300*

movement. As it was, both German ships were sighted by the Swedish cruiser *Gotland*: her report was soon passed on to London the following morning, 21 May. Two RAF Spitfires were sent to take a look at the Norwegian coast and at 1300, less than 2hr after their arrival, *Bismarck* and *Prinz Eugen* were photographed at Bergen. Bletchley Park, which was still taking days to translate naval 'Enigma', confirmed the ship's destination at about the same time. At 1828 a signal reporting both the ships and their mission was sent to all naval commands including Adm Sir John Tovey, C-in-C Home Fleet at Scapa Flow. The distribution of the command at the time was as follows:

British Ship Dispositions 21 May 1941

At Scapa Flow

Battleships/Battlecruisers (3)
King George V (Adm Tovey C-in-C), *Prince of Wales*, *Hood* (Vice-Adm L. E. Holland, Second in Command and Commander 'Battle Cruiser Force')

Aircraft Carrier (1)
Victorious

Cruisers (4)
Galatea (Rear-Adm A. T. B. Curteis), *Aurora*, *Kenya*, *Neptune*

Fleet Destroyers (9)
Active, *Antelope*, *Achates*, *Anthony*, *Electra*, *Echo*, *Punjabi*, *Icarus*, *Nestor*

At Sea

Cruisers (6)
Norfolk (on patrol, Denmark Strait), *Suffolk* (refuelling, Iceland), *Birmingham* and *Manchester* (patrolling Iceland-Faroes Gap), *Arethusa* (on passage to Iceland), *Hermione* (on passage to Scapa)

Destroyers (2)
Inglefield and *Intrepid* (on passage to Scapa)

The battlecruiser *Repulse* was in the Clyde at the time preparatory to joining with *Victorious* for convoy escort duties.

Some of this apparent strength was misleading: *Prince of Wales* still had civilian workmen on board trying to cure problems in her quadruple 14in turrets; *Victorious* was not fully worked-up either and had only nine Swordfish and six Fulmar aircraft embarked, remaining space being taken up by crated Hurricanes; *Hood* was known to be inadequately armoured against plunging fire.

At 0052 on the morning of 22 May, acting on Tovey's orders, the 'Battle Cruiser Force'. of *Hood*, *Prince of Wales* and six destroyers (*Electra*, *Echo*, *Anthony*, *Icarus*, *Achates* and *Antelope*) steamed out of Scapa for Iceland, where they would be in a position to cover both likely escape routes into the Atlantic, either via the Iceland-Faroes Gap, or the Denmark Strait.

HMS *Hood*

Builder: John Brown
(Laid down 31 May 1916; launched 22 August 1918; completed 15 May 1920)

Displacement: 42,462 tons (standard), 48,360 tons (full load)

Dimensions: 860.6ft × 104.2ft × 28.9ft

Machinery: Geared turbines, 4 shafts, 144,000shp; designed speed of 31kt, reduced to 29½kt at time of loss

Armour: Main belt 12in maximum, reducing to 6in maximum forward and aft; forecastle deck 1.25-2in, upper deck 0.75-2in, main deck 1-3in, lower deck 1-3in; turrets 15in front, 11-12in sides and back, 5in roof

Armament: 8×15in (4×2); 8×4in (4×2); 24×2pdr (3×8); 16×0.5in machine guns (4×4); 4×21in torpedoes in twin above-water mountings; 100 UP projectiles (5×20)

Sensors: Type 284 gunnery radar

Notes: *Hood* was laid down the day Jutland was fought but her design was changed to such an extent by the battle that she was laid down again on 1 September 1916. Unfortunately, due to the conviction that no battlecruiser had been sunk by direct penetration of the magazines, the requests of Beatty and Jellicoe that her horizontal protection be increased were ignored by the material departments of the Admiralty. *Hood*, while a fine ship, well protected for her time and more a fast battleship than a true battlecruiser, was still assessed as basically a pre-Jutland ship by the Director of Naval Construction in 1918. The interwar Naval Staff, however, understandably persisted in viewing her as post-Jutland and she was not a candidate for early modernisation, plans only being drawn up at the end of 1938. This would have significantly increased *Hood's* protection to bomb or plunging long-range shell fire. Her three sisters, *Rodney*, *Howe* and *Anson* were all cancelled in 1918.

The first three mistakes of the battle appear to have been made at this point, the first two by the Germans. Lutjens appears to have made it clear before his departure that he did not intend to stop off in the Norwegian fjords. It is a bit of a mystery why he did so 2, as by so doing he placed himself in range of British aircraft and thereby risked damage as well as the loss of surprise. It seems most probable that he was waiting for bad weather to cover his final sortie. Secondly, though *Prinz Eugen* refuelled off Bergen, *Bismarck* did not. She had sailed 200 tons short as a result of a broken fuel line, and she had used over 1,000 tons of fuel already and, as events turned out, that fuel — or lack of it — was to exert such an important influence. The third mistake with benefit of hindsight, seems to have been Tovey's. He knew that *Prince of Wales* was not fully worked-up and that *Hood* was weakly protected against plunging fire; nevertheless, he had little choice. Only four capital ships were at his immediate disposal: *King George V*, *Hood*, *Prince of Wales* and *Repulse* and only one, the flagship, was in the first-class condition. It made sense to combine the strongest, *KGV*, with the weakest, *Repulse*, and let numbers two and three form the other striking group, especially as *Hood* was the natural flagship of the advance portion of the fleet. Tovey clearly had to remain behind in Scapa until *Bismarck's* movements became clearer.

Bismarck and *Prinz Eugen* had sailed at about 2300 after having painted out camouflage. After they had left the port behind them they saw the first explosions of a British air raid, a reassurance that their departure had not been spotted in the foul weather, as indeed it had not.

HMS *Hood* still with her original secondary armament of 5.5in guns; these had been removed by the time she was sunk. *MoD (Navy) Q397*

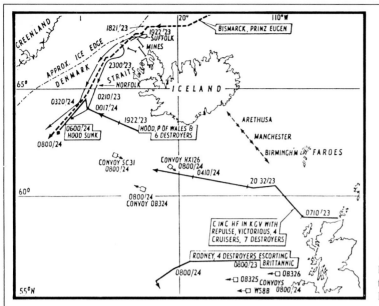

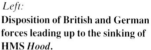

Left:
Disposition of British and German forces leading up to the sinking of HMS *Hood*.

22 May

Reconnaissance let down both sides on 22 May. British pilots were unable to see through the murk, and a German pilot who made it to Scapa Flow wrongly reported the Home Fleet at anchor, being fooled by dummy vessels. It was not until late that evening, at about 1930, that Tovey had confirmation of the German ships' departure, as a result of a sortie by a Maryland training aircraft sent out on the basis of private initiative by the commander of the Royal Naval Air Station at Hatston in the Orkneys. The aircraft had flown at wavetop height across the Bergen approaches and not hit anything! As a result *Suffolk* was ordered out to support *Norfolk* in the Denmark Strait, *Arethusa* to support *Manchester* and *Birmingham* in the

Iceland-Faroes Gap ③. At 2300 Tovey set sail as follows:

Ships Sailing with Adm Tovey, 2300 22 May

Battleship
King George V

Cruisers
Galatea, Aurora, Kenya, Hermione

Destroyers
Inglefield, Intrepid, Active, Punjabi, Nestor, Windsor, Lance (detached later due to boiler trouble)

Ships Joining 0710 23 May

Battlecruiser
Repulse (from Clyde)

Destroyers
Legion, Sagvenay, Assiniboine

23 May

Tovey had to cover three possibilities with his ships: a breakout through the Denmark Strait, through the Iceland-Faroes Gap, or *Bismarck* turning north into the Arctic Circle, refuelling and waiting for fuel shortage to send the British ships scurrying back to harbour. A tanker was in fact waiting to the north of Lutjens. Tovey suspected that the Denmark Strait would be used but he could not be sure. Indeed the German command at Group North recommended the Iceland-Faroes

passage. Lutjens finally decided otherwise. The Denmark Strait is a narrow passage only some 30 or 40 miles wide, bounded by the ice-edge to the north and in 1941 by a British minefield to the south, but Lutjens had used it before with success. It was the furthest breakout point from Scapa and he had been falsely informed that the Home Fleet had not sailed. In addition fog seemed assured for the area, and Lutjens did not know that some British cruisers at least carried effective search radar. Tovey, with the responsibility for Britain's Atlantic lifeline at his disposal, could not gamble. He positioned his own squadron to cover the Iceland-Faroes Gap, with *Hood* and *Prince of Wales* off Iceland to cover the northern passage ④.

Bismarck Sighted

At noon on the 23rd *Bismarck* and *Prinz Eugen* entered the narrowest part of the Denmark Strait ⑤; they had steamed at less than full speed, despite the advice of meteorologists, and found unusually clear weather in the channel they were forced to sail. *Norfolk* and *Suffolk* were patrolling some 15 miles apart. It was *Suffolk* that sighted the two German ships visually at 1922, at a range of seven miles ⑥. At full speed *Suffolk* turned and steered into the mist on the edge of the minefield to the south. The Germans made contact at about the same time on radar and sonar but were unable

Below:

The ill-fated HMS *Prince of Wales* which, throughout her brief life, had a reputation as a jinxed vessel. *MPL*

Above:
HMS *Norfolk* which, with HMS *Suffolk*, was the first British warship to sight *Bismarck* and *Prinz Eugen*.
Real Photographs S416

to engage on such imprecise information. *Norfolk* was less lucky when she joined *Suffolk* an hour later, and the first shots of the battle were fired at a range of six miles. *Norfolk* scuttled away, none of *Bismarck's* five salvoes hitting her. The two cruisers shadowed from astern.

HMS *Norfolk* and HMS *Dorsetshire*

Builders:
Norfolk — Fairfield
(Laid down 8 July 1927; launched 12 December 1928; completed 30 April 1930)

Dorsetshire— Portsmouth Dockyard
(Laid down 21 September 1927; launched 29 January 1929; completed 30 September 1930)

Displacement: 10,400 tons standard (approx)

Dimensions: 632.7ft oa × 66ft × 17ft

Machinery: Geared turbines, 4 shafts, 80,000shp, 32.25kt

Armour: 1-4.4in around ammunition spaces, 1in side and turrets

Armament: 8×8in (4×2); 8×4in (4×2); 16×2pdr (2×8); 8×0.5in (2×4); 8×21in torpedo tubes (2×4)

Sensors: *Norfolk:* Type 286P radar

Complement: 710

HMS *Suffolk*

Builder: Portsmouth Dockyard
(Laid down 30 September 1924; launched 16 February 1926; completed 31 May 1928)

Displacement: 10,310 tons standard (approx)

Dimensions: 630ft oa × 68.4ft × 16.25ft

Machinery: Geared turbines, 4 shafts, 80,000shp 31.5kt

Armour: 4.5in belt added at reconstruction

Armament: 8×8in (4×2); 8×4in (4×2); 8×2pdr AA guns (2×4); 4×20mm AA guns. Torpedo tubes removed

Sensors: Types 279 and 284 radar

Complement: 679

Notes: One of the seven 'Kent' class cruisers, reconstructed 1935-38.

Radar

Norfolk was fitted with a Type 286P radar, with fixed aerials. *Suffolk* was better off, with a fixed aerial Type 279 radar for air warning, but also a Type 284 rangefinding radar on her rotating main armament director. Nevertheless she had a blank spot over the stern which radar did not cover. *Bismarck* had three 'Seetakt' radar sets but they suffered from two drawbacks common to all German radar of the time: First, they were not accurate enough for 'blind fire' gunnery control, and secondly they were very prone to damage from gun blast or bad weather. *Bismarck's* salvoes directed at *Norfolk* duly disabled through their vibration *Bismarck's* forward radar, and Lutjens

instructed *Prinz Eugen* to take station ahead to cover the area ahead on both sonar and radar. The change in positions was also ordered so as to allow *Bismarck's* heavier main armament to have a clear arc of fire at the cruisers which were shadowing from astern. As German code-breakers embarked in the ship deciphered the British messages (somewhat more easily than the British were able, at this stage of war, to unscramble German naval codes) the effectiveness of the British radar became apparent. This, in addition to the pressure in *Bismarck* of a simple radar detection receiver, gave the Germans their unpleasant surprises about British radar efficiency. These had a considerable effect on Lutjens' morale.

When the two German ships were sighted, Holland and the Admiralty picked up *Suffolk's* sighting report; Tovey had to wait an hour for *Norfolk's* signal. Holland was 300 miles distant from the German ships, Tovey 600; on hearing the news, Holland ordered an increase of speed to 27kt, and a course of 295° that should bring him to interception in the early hours of 24 May. If this plan had worked he would have found the two German ships silhouetted against the setting sun. He faced a problem in that *Hood* needed to close with the enemy as rapidly as possible in order to ensure a flatter shell trajectory from the German ships which would hit *Hood's* side rather than deck armour, whereas *Prince of Wales* was better suited to a long range engagement. The course of 295° Holland was steering might have allowed him to cross Lutjens' 'T' and bring his full weight of broadside to bear, and would certainly have allowed him to meet *Bismarck* head-on. Tragically, the situations were to be reversed.

The situation at this point for Tovey was still worrying: the German ships might turn on their shadowing cruisers, or simply lose them in the bad weather that produced all sorts of problems for radar operators. More worrying was the fact that no less than 11 British convoys were at sea on 23/24 May, including the troop convoy WS8B, which had already lost *Victorious* and *Repulse*; the latter joined Tovey at sea on the 23rd. Thus at 0500 Force H, under the command of Vice-Adm Sir James Somerville, was ordered to sail north

from Gibraltar [7] to cover the convoy. Force H, consisting of the aircraft carrier *Ark Royal*, the modernised battlecruiser *Renown*, the cruiser *Sheffield*, and the destroyers *Faulknor*, *Foresight*, *Forester*, *Foxhound*, *Fury* and *Hesperus*, was destined never to meet its convoy, but to meet and ensure the destruction of *Bismarck* instead.

24 May
Just before midnight on 23/24 May, *Suffolk*, already having clutter problems on her radar because of a snowstorm, saw *Bismarck* advancing towards her, turned away, and lost contact. Lutjens was determined to throw off his shadowers; he did not succeed permanently, but the loss of contact for almost 3hr occurred at a crucial moment as the 'Battle Cruiser Force' closed in. At 0203 Holland hauled *Hood* and *Prince of Wales* round to the southwest [8], fearing that if *Bismarck* had reversed course or turned south he might pass astern of him and have the Atlantic before her. When contact was regained by *Suffolk* at 0247, Holland was on an almost parallel course to *Bismarck*. He had lost his lead over the German ships, a situation accentuated when *Bismarck* and *Prinz Eugen* made a slight alteration to the west, in order to continue hugging the ice edge. Holland's destroyers, now detached from the capital ships, in fact narrowly missed sighting *Bismarck* because of the bad weather. By 0340 the two British ships were running almost parallel with the Germans on a slightly converging course, whilst by 0400 *Bismarck* was only 20 miles northwest of *Hood*.

Prinz Eugen picked up the noise of the British ships at a range of 20 miles, on her ultra-sophisticated passive sonar array. *Prince of Wales* made a visual sighting of the German vessels at 0537. Before this, at 0440, Holland had ordered a 40° turn to starboard to close the range, and he followed this at 0549 with a further 20° turn. When *Hood* opened fire at 0552 [9] enough mistakes had already been made to seal her fate. First of all, one mistake was an ironic misjudgement on the part of the Germans: standing orders forbad a cruiser to engage a capital ship, and had Lutjens realised what his opponents were (reports suggest he thought he was against two cruisers right until *Hood* opened fire) he may have had to order *Prinz Eugen* to disengage. Secondly, *Norfolk* and *Suffolk* were never ordered to engage *Prinz Eugen*, although Capt Leach on board *Prince of Wales* knew this to be Holland's intention. *Prinz Eugen's* fire was to prove crucial in the coming engagement. Thirdly, Holland's course of 280° was the worst of both worlds. It was not a head-on approach that would have narrowed the range in the quickest possible time, yet it allowed the German ships to fire full broadsides whilst the British could only use their forward main armament. This should have been 4×15in from *Hood* and 6×14in from *Prince of Wales*, but it was known that one of *Prince of Wales'* guns would jam after one round. A final problem with the diagonal approach was that it produced just the conditions of changing rate of change of range with which *Hood's* old and flawed Dreyer fire control computer could not cope.

Two further errors were to contribute to the tragedy. Tovey had considered signalling Holland to order him to place the better-armoured *Prince of Wales* in the van to absorb punishment. He refrained, and *Hood* received the full attention of both German ships. Nor was *Prince of Wales* allowed freedom of manoeuvre, but was instead tied to following *Hood's* course at close range. As if this was not enough, Holland mistakenly identified the leading German ship, *Prinz Eugen*, as *Bismarck*. *Prince of Wales'* gunnery officer spotted the error and shifted his fire in time. *Hood* signalled 'shift object one right' before opening

fire, but the message did not get to her own gunnery officer in time. Her opening salvo at least was directed at *Prinz Eugen*: it was fired at 0552½ and fell wide. *Prince of Wales* joined in half a minute later and her first salvo went over *Bismarck*.

Hood Sunk

Lutjens, for some unaccountable reason, delayed replying and Capt Lindemann eventually took his own initiative. *Bismarck* fired her first salvo at 0555; her first two were wide, but her third straddled *Hood*. *Prince of Wales* had fired nine salvoes, straddling *Bismarck* with her sixth, although persistent machinery problems frequently reduced her to three-gun salvoes. In an ironic echo of Jutland in reverse, a number of *Bismarck's* shells failed to explode, but not so *Prinz Eugen's*. The German cruiser had begun the action with her fire control well set up thanks to the ship's sonar warning. Thinking she was to engage cruisers she had high explosive shells loaded; these were probably the best to use against battleships also, as they could deal with vulnerable but vital external mountings such as fire control equipment. *Hood* was very vulnerable to HE rounds. She had recently been refitted with the Unrotated Rocket Projectile, a parachute anti-aircraft weapon that was a passing fad with the Royal Navy at the start of the war. Ready-use ammunition was stored in thin steel lockers on the deck. Someone who served on *Hood* shortly before her last cruise reported that standing orders were for large quantities of 4in ready-use ammunition also to be stored on deck, similarly unprotected, because in her Mediterranean and African service rate of fire was a higher priority

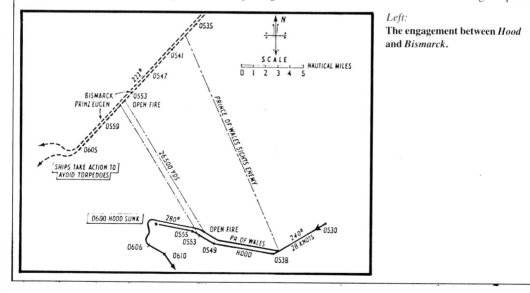

Left:
The engagement between *Hood* and *Bismarck*.

Above:
HMS *Hood* exploding, taken from *Prinz Eugen. Prince of Wales* can just be made out to the left of *Hood.*
IWM HU385

than magazine security. There is no evidence that this practice was rescinded when *Hood* sailed against the *Bismarck*. In any event, a hit from *Prinz Eugen* started a massive fire aft which gave *Bismarck's* optical rangefinders a better assessment of bearing and range. At 0600, with smoke pouring from her, a full salvo just fired and the ship in the process of turning to open her 'A' arcs and bring her full broadside to bear, a huge explosion from the after end of the ship split *Hood* in two ⑨. As her bow and stern pointed mutely up into the air, observers saw her spit out a last 15in salvo before she sank at 0600. There were three survivors, picked up later by destroyers, from a complement of 1,418.

The sinking of the *Hood* has been the subject of two formal enquiries and a vast amount of conjecture. Conventional wisdom is that the ammunition fire was not a cause of the explosion, but that a 15in shell from *Bismarck* plunged through her thin deck armour and penetrated the 4in magazine, which then blew up igniting the main magazine. It seems probable that this was one of the eight rounds of *Bismarck's* fourth salvo. A fashionable and plausible modern view is to suggest the possibility of an underwater penetration. There is, however, a more fascinating — and slightly disturbing — explanation: Goodall, the Director of Naval Construction in 1941, felt that the explosion, the centre of which was at the base of the mainmast, 65ft away from the nearest magazine, might well have had a completely different cause. The first hit (from *Prinz Eugen*) in this area and consequent fire seemed to have caused serious damage below, as well as on deck; the officers' quarters were furnished within the original non-fire-proofed wood. In this part of the ship was 4,000lb of ill-protected explosive in the

shape of eight torpedo heads for the above-water tubes. Further hits by one or more 15in shells in this area might have proved fatal. Goodall concluded that if one or more of the torpedoes had gone up in sympathy, 'the result would be an explosion where it was actually observed. Such an explosion could break the ship's back, already weakened in this neighbourhood by the earlier damage'.

If *Hood's* above water torpedoes were indeed her Achilles heel the irony is especially acute. D'Eyncourt, the DNC, had waged a constant battle during *Hood's* construction to have these vulnerable fittings removed. He came close when it was decided to increase the ship's magazine protection. In order to provide spare weight the armour around the torpedoes was removed. They were retained for trials purposes only to be taken out before the ship went to war. However, the extra armour was never fitted. It was thus possible to add the 3in box torpedo protection again during *Hood's* large repair in 1929-31; the torpedoes became 'war fittings' again, despite the misgivings of the DNC's department. Goodall, one of *Hood's* designers, was expressing a long-standing departmental view on her vulnerability when he made his 1941 diagnosis.

Capt Leach in *Prince of Wales* had to swing sharply to starboard to avoid the wreck of the *Hood*, an illustration of how closely his orders tied him to the flagship. His vessel quickly received the concentrated fire of both German vessels, and was hit seven times. A 15in shell passed through the bridge without exploding, but fragments of the plates at the shell's point of entry, pieces of the shell's ballistic cap and shattered bridge equipment killed or wounded most of the personnel except for the Captain and Chief Signals Yeoman. Hit number two glanced off the base of the forward 5.25in director, again without exploding, but cutting the electric leads and putting both the directors out of action, one permanently. The third hit was a 15in shell which struck the starboard aircraft crane and exploded abaft the after funnel, sending splinters to lethal effect around and below. The fourth was an 8in shell which traced a destructive path through the upper part of the ship but which did not explode. It was thrown overboard. Hit number five was the most serious; a 15in shell dived underwater, pierced the hull below the water line and let in 400 tons of water. It was defused back in harbour. Hits six and seven were 8in shells which hit the ship and exploded below the waterline, adding to the flooding.

At 0613 Leach broke off the action, retiring under cover of smoke. Three reasons were given — the fact that the ship was not fully worked up, the continuing troubles affecting the main armament and the probability that a concentration of force against *Bismarck* would be brought about later. As it was, *Prince of Wales'* after 14in turret jammed as she turned away, leaving only the two guns of the troublefree 'B' twin turret in action. It was another 4hr before Leach considered his main armament ready for action once more, and even then all 10 guns were still not operational.

Below:
HMS *Prince of Wales* retires as shell splashes still fall around *Hood*'s funeral pyre. *IWM HU384*

HMS *King George V* and HMS *Prince of Wales*

Builders:
King George V — Vickers-Armstrong, Walker-on-Tyne
(Laid down 1 January 1937; launched 21 February 1939; completed 30 September 1940)

Prince of Wales — Cammell Laird, Birkenhead
(Laid down 1 January 1937; launched 3 May 1939; completed 19 January 1941)

Displacement: *King George V* 38,031 tons (standard); 42,237 tons (full load); *Prince of Wales* 43,786 tons (full load)

Dimensions: 745ft × 103ft × 29ft

Machinery: Geared turbines, 4 shafts, 100,000shp, 28kt

Armour: Main belt 13.73in-14.71in machinery and magazines; turrets 12.75in face, 6.86in sides, 5.88in roof; deck 4.9in-5.88in over machinery and magazines

Armament: 10 × 14in (2 × 4, 1 × 2); 16 × 5.25in DP (8 × 2); 32 × 2pdr (4 × 8), 4 (*Prince of Wales* 3) UP rocket projectors; 1 × 40mm AA in *Prince of Wales*

Sensors: Type 279B (air warning); Type 284 (main armament direction). *King George V* Type 271; (surface warning) *Prince of Wales* Type 282 (2pdr direction); Type 285 (5.25in direction)

Aircraft: 2

Complement: 1,543 (as flagship)

Notes: Designed to comply with the 1936 London Naval Treaty, they were the most heavily protected battleships for their size in the world, sacrificing armament to armour. The desire to make the magazine system as flash-tight as possible resulted in complex safety interlocks, insufficient clearances and, hence, a propensity for the quadruple turrets in particular to jam. Clearances were later increased but it took considerable efforts to make the system fully reliable. The ships were also very wet forward because of the desire to fire the main armament at minimum elevation straight ahead.

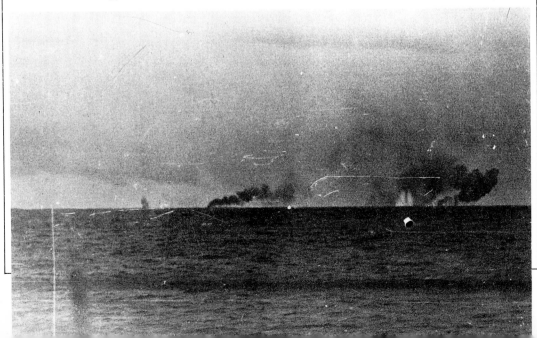

Admiral of the Fleet Sir Dudley Pound and Vice-Adm Tom Phillips both appear to have considered Leach's action in turning away to have been ill-advised, yet Tovey, Wake-Walker (who took over command at sea when Holland went down with *Hood*) and Leach himself felt that breaking off the action was the only sensible course. When, after the engagement, Pound announced he was going to court-martial both Leach and Wake-Walker, Tovey announced that if this took place he would haul down his flag and appear as the prisoner's friend. No more was heard about the affair. Damage to *Prince of Wales* was not major; the real problem was that Leach simply did not have a complete battleship to fight with, because of the wholly inadequate performance of the 14in turrets, and he stood in danger of losing the Navy its second capital ship in a day. It is more interesting to speculate why Lutjens did not pursue *Prince of Wales* and destroy her as well. The answer is that he did not know it was *Prince of Wales* (the Germans were convinced she was *King George V*, and so for all they knew were facing a fully worked-up and efficient vessel), nor did he know what other vessels were in the vicinity or whether, in an extended battle, he might fall prey to the cruisers' torpedoes. Perhaps the final and decisive element in his decision not to pursue the British (a decision much lamented after the event by Hitler and by German historians) were his strict orders not to engage in avoidable conflict with capital ships.

Bismarck's Damage

Prince of Wales retired to join company with the still-shadowing cruisers; *Hood's* destroyers, still deployed on their search pattern to the north, were ordered to pick up survivors from the battlecruiser and a flurry of signals went out from the Admiralty in London. *Bismarck* had been hit three times by *Prince of Wales*. One hit amidships carried away a boat and damaged the aircraft launching gear, but did not explode. Of the two more serious hits, one penetrated the armour belt below the waterline, destroyed a dynamo and put a boiler room with two boilers out of action. The third, and eventually fatal, hit did not explode, but in passing right through the ship from the port bow it penetrated two oil tanks and by flooding pumping gear cut off a further thousand tons of fuel. The holes were below the bow wave, not the waterline itself, and the damage control parties pleaded with Lutjens to reduce speed. The Admiral refused to do so immediately due to the tactical situation. Eventually, however, he felt able to slow down and ordered *Prinz Eugen* to drop back and examine what sort of wake of fuel oil *Bismarck* was leaving: it was quite severe. The result of the flooding from both hits was to leave *Bismarck* down 3° by the bow and listing 9° to port. Speed was now limited to 28kt.

The Admiralty Responds

Reaction from the British to the loss of *Hood* was swift. Tovey with *King George V*, *Repulse*,

Below:
Bismarck down by the bow after taking a shell hit from Prince of Wales. The faint marks of her earlier camouflage scheme can still be seen just under 'Caesar' turret.
IWM HU400

Above:
**HMS *Victorious* with the cruiser HMS *Newcastle*.
Victorious launched the first air strike against *Bismarck*,
but the one torpedo hit failed to slow her.** *MPL*

Victorious and five cruisers was 360 miles away to the southeast. Various vessels, including the old battleships *Ramillies* and *Revenge*, were ordered to break off from their duties and steer to converge with *Bismarck's* course. More significantly, the *Rodney* [10], just out of the Clyde and escorting the liner *Britannic*, was ordered to leave one destroyer behind and steer for *Bismarck*. She took the destroyers *Somali*, *Tartar* and *Mashona* with her. *Rodney* was relatively old, desperately in need of repairs and so below her designed speed of 22kt. Because she was on her way to a refit in Boston, USA, she had her decks packed with crates and cases of spare machinery and equipment, as well as having a party of wounded servicemen on board on their way to Canada for convalescence.

HMS *Rodney*

Builder: Cammell Laird
(Laid down 28 December 1922; launched 3 September 1925; completed August 1927)

Displacement: 33,730 tons (standard)

Dimensions: 710ft oa × 106ft × 29.6ft

Machinery: Geared turbines, 2 shafts, 45,000shp, 23kt

Armour: 13in-14in belt; deck 6.25in over magazines, 3.75in over machinery; turrets 16in face, 9-11in sides, 7.25in roof

Armament: 9×16in (3×3); 12×6in (6×2); 6×4.7in (6×1); 24×2pdr (3×8); 2×20mm (2×1); 8×0.5in (2×4); 2×24.5in torpedo tubes, below water

Sensors: Radar Type 279

Complement: 1,314

Notes: Built to treaty limitations, and sacrificing speed for armour and firepower; turrets grouped forward as weight (armour)-saving device. Contrary to a popular belief the larger 'battlecruisers' they replaced would also have had this layout.

Lutjens had two choices: damaged and with lost fuel he could not now proceed out into the Atlantic; he could either double back through the Denmark Strait or the Iceland-Faroes passage and head home for Germany; or he could head for France. The latter was 600 miles further, but it meant he did not have to pass again through the back yard of a very angry and alerted British fleet. He should also have sea room to dodge his shadowers and it would allow him to team up with *Scharnhorst* and *Gneisenau* in France.

Meanwhile, a barbed game of cat and mouse was being played between Lutjens and his shadowers. Tovey was dogged by the fear that *Bismarck* (the extent of whose damage he did not know) might still break out, and so steered southwest, a course which was the best compromise for all three of Lutjens' options. At 1440 Tovey detached *Victorious* and four cruisers (*Galatea*, with Rear-Adm A. T. B. Curteis, *Aurora*, *Kenya* and *Hermione*) to get in position as quickly as possible so as to be able to make an air attack, maximum range for which was 100 miles. *Bismarck* had been under aircraft surveillance at intervals since the meeting with the *Hood* and at 1535 a Catalina reported her 15 miles ahead of her shadowers. At 1711 *Prince of Wales* was ordered by Wake-Walker (who himself had been prodded by London) to try and slow down *Bismarck*; *Suffolk* was also ordered at 1809 to close to within five miles of the enemy. Lutjens had, by this time, decided to detach *Prinz Eugen* into the Atlantic and head himself for France. To cover his consort he turned sharply in a rain squall at 1839. A sharp radar watch on *Suffolk* saw what was coming, and turned the ship away as *Bismarck* loomed out of the mist and fired at her, at a range of about 10 miles. *Bismarck's* near-misses started rivets aft, but did no other damage; in reply *Suffolk* fired nine salvoes, most of which were short, and *Prince of Wales* and *Norfolk* joined in the fire at 15 miles range. Two guns on *Prince of Wales* went out of action almost immediately. In the fracas *Prinz Eugen* (whose Captain appeared to be opposed to Lutjens' splitting of the force) made her escape, and *Bismarck* settled back on a south-southwesterly course leading the British ships over a patrol line of U-boats halfway between Greenland and Newfoundland. Adm Wake-Walker appears to have been aware of this danger, as he ordered his ships to zig-zag. Sadly, and perhaps for fear of *Bismarck* turning once more and savaging a cruiser, he also ordered an inefficient line-ahead formation for his vessels, which was later to have disastrous consequences.

Victorious Attacks

Victorious all this while had been steaming at 28kt towards the German vessels. At 2210 she launched a strike of nine Swordfish aircraft. The squadron was led by Lt-Cdr Eugene Esmonde, who was later to be awarded a posthumous VC for his attack on the *Scharnhorst* and *Gneisenau* in the Channel Dash. They picked up *Bismarck* on radar at 2327, sighted her at 2330, and then lost her in thick cloud [11]. The United States coastguard cutter *Modoc* was nearly attacked, but with *Norfolk's* help the final attack was launched at 2350 [12]. Eight aircraft launched torpedoes (one had become lost in the cloud), and one hit was reported on the main armour belt of *Bismarck*, on the starboard side abreast the bridge. The torpedo seemed to have run shallow, and it did minimal direct damage, most of its blast being directed upwards. What did do harm was the shock effect both of the torpedo and the AA guns and the radical manoeuvring by *Bismarck* which opened up the old wounds made by *Prince of Wales*. The damaged boiler room had to be abandoned and with the bows even further down in the water speed was reduced temporarily to 16kt. All the Swordfish, remarkably, returned safely despite a breakdown in *Victorious'* homing beacon. Two Fulmar shadowers flown off at 2300 were forced to ditch, but even more remarkably their crews were later picked up.

25 May

During the air attack contact was briefly lost by Wake-Walker, but it was re-established by 0116. Fourteen minutes later *Prince of Wales* and

Bismarck spat a couple of salvoes at each other. At 0306, however, *Suffolk*, leading the shadowers, made her last contact with *Bismarck*. *Suffolk* had been zig-zagging 30° on either side of her course, losing touch with *Bismarck* on the edge of the outer leg [13] but regaining it later. At 0306 *Bismarck* turned almost a complete circle, steadied on a course of 130° to the southeast, and cut across the wake of her pursuers. Lutjens had made extravagant claims about the number of Swordfish shot down (27 according to one account), but his ship was short of fuel, and his young crew were becoming exhausted. The obvious presence of a British carrier within range, and the shock of even an ineffectual torpedo hit, made him decide to take the shortest route back to Brest, even if this meant failing to draw his pursuers over the waiting line of U-boats. At 0605 Tovey heard the news that contact with *Bismarck* had been lost. He did not have enough aircraft or ships to search everywhere, felt he had to guard against a break-out into the Atlantic and so mistakenly concentrated searches to the south and west.

Now the focus shifted to British intelligence sources: Bletchley Park could not help due to the delays in decoding Naval 'Enigma', but other forms of radio intelligence could — notably direction finding and signal analysis. The British had already taken note of *Bismarck's* tell-tale radio signature and at 0854 were given a potentially excellent fix when Lutjens sent out a long signal detailing his victory over the *Hood*. He had failed to realise the British had lost touch. Perhaps he was given erroneous or misleading information by his onboard code-breakers. More likely, or in addition, he interpreted receipt of radar signals as meaning the enemy were getting reflections (an understandable error with electronic warfare in its infancy). Perhaps, as von Mullenheim-Rechberg has speculated, he was just depressed. Group West signalled Lutjens that he really was out of contact and must keep radio silence.

The damage had been done, yet the Germans almost 'got away with it'. Tovey had insisted that the Admiralty's Operational Intelligence Centre (O/C) pass on to him the bearings rather than the actual position of the enemy ship, because he had with him two direction finding-equipped destroyers who, if they picked up a signal, would provide a better cross-bearing than that from shore bases alone. Mistake number one was that the destroyers had had to detach to Iceland for refuelling. Mistake number two was that the bearings were wrongly plotted in *King George V*. The inexperienced plotters in the flagship wrongly put *Bismarck* 200 miles north of her actual position, which suggested she was heading back through the Iceland-Faroes Gap. Thus at 1047

Tovey set off northeast, whilst all the while Lutjens was headed southeast [14].

What followed was a classic demonstration of the fog of war. The sequence of signals was this:

1023 The correct O/C view of *Bismarck's* movements is signalled to Tovey, Somerville and Wake-Walker: they are told to assume *Bismarck* is heading for France. It takes until 1108 to send all the signals.

1047 Tovey broadcasts wrongly-plotted position of *Bismarck* to Fleet. *King George V*, *Prince of Wales*, *Victorious* and cruisers turn northeast. *Norfolk*, *Edinburgh* and *Rodney*, stationed to south, decide to cover possible course of *Bismarck* to France.

1054 Admiralty obtain third D/F fix on *Bismarck* suggesting she is heading for France.

1100 Somerville with Force H signalled by Admiralty to assume *Bismarck* headed for France.

1108 *Rodney* signalled by Admiralty to assume *Bismarck* heading for France. Admiralty, confused by Tovey's course, decide to give him the benefit of the doubt.

Left:
A fine bow view of HMS *Rodney*, showing the massive bridge structure that became a standard feature in all modernised or new British capital ships.
Real Photographs S1107

Right:
**An unusual aerial view of *Rodney*
showing main and secondary
armament layout.**
Real Photographs S1561

1244 Flag Officer Submarines disposes six boats
on assumption *Bismarck* headed for Brest.

1320 U-boats transmission picked up, wrongly
assumed to be relayed from *Bismarck*, but
held to confirm her course towards France.

1401 Tovey receives signal from Admiralty on
basis of 1054 D/F fix confirming *Bismarck's*
movement towards France.

1428 *Rodney* receives unexplained Admiralty
signal ordering her to conform to Tovey's
signal of 1047, implying *Bismarck* was
heading for Iceland-Faroes Gap and going

against all previous signals. *Rodney* con-
tinues to steer northeast.

1548 Tovey changes course to east-southeast,
implying *Bismarck* headed for France. Then
intercepts Admiralty signal to *Rodney* timed
1428, turns to steer compromise course of
080°.

1630 Tovey signals Admiralty asking if it is their
opinion that *Bismarck* is headed for the
Faroes.

1805 Admiralty signal their error to *Rodney*.

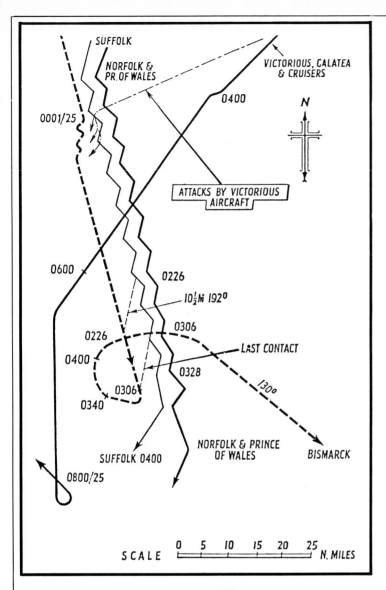

SUFFOLK

NORFOLK &
PR. OF WALES

VICTORIOUS, CALATEA
& CRUISERS

0400

0001/25

N

ATTACKS BY VICTORIOUS
AIRCRAFT

0600

0226

10½M 192°

0306

0226

LAST CONTACT

0400

0328

0306

1300

0340

NORFOLK & PRINCE
OF WALES

BISMARCK

SUFFOLK 0400

0800/25

SCALE

0   5   10   15   20   25   N. MILES

Left:
Bismarck loses her shadowers and breaks for France.

1810 Original plotting error discovered [15] . Tovey alters course to east-southeast, 118°, without reply yet from Admiralty his signal of 1630 and without receiving the Admiralty's 1805 to *Rodney*.

1812 Based on a Bletchley Park decrypt of a Luftwaffe 'Enigma' message it is confirmed *Bismarck* is heading for France. Fleet advised accordingly and 'Ultra' signal received within an hour. (The Luftwaffe Chief of Staff was in Athens in connection with the invasion of Crete. His son was one of the many midshipmen in *Bismarck* and the General wished to know her destination. He was informed in the rapidly-broken Luft-

waffe 'Enigma' code. The only comfort for the soon-to-be-bereaved parent was that this breach of security was too late to affect the issue decisively.)

At the end of all this *Bismarck* and *King George V* were steaming roughly southwest, with *Bismarck* 150 miles ahead, but still 1,000 miles from home. *Rodney* was converging, steering northeast. *Norfolk*, *Prince of Wales* and *Suffolk* had broken off for Iceland or Scapa to refuel, but when France seemed certain *Norfolk* turned back again and headed for Brest.

Ark Royal and Vian

The only hope now was that *Ark Royal* and Force H, hurrying northward, might block or slow down *Bismarck*. Fuel shortages meant that the British capital ships were running dangerously low on destroyers. The poor troop convoy WS8B was therefore denuded of five destroyers led by Capt (later Admiral of the Fleet) Philip Vian in *Cossack*. In foul weather *Cossack*, *Sikh*, *Zulu*, *Maori* and the Polish *Piorun* were sent to join *King George V* and *Rodney*.

The situation for most of 25 May was a harrowing one for the British. Shortage of fuel had already forced *Prince of Wales* and *Victorious* to break off, other capital ships were running low and the capital ships rapidly were being denuded of destroyers, too, because of fuel shortages. The British had a far less elaborate system for refuelling at sea, unlike the Germans, perhaps spoilt by the variety of shore bases available to those with an Empire. Bad weather was slowing Force H down to 17kt from its original 27, *Bismarck's* position was uncertain and reconnaissance difficult because of the weather. To add to his troubles Adm Somerville with Force H felt obliged to cover the possibility of a breakout from Brest by *Scharnhorst* and *Gneisenau*, not being told by the Admiralty until the morning of the 26th that these two ships were not operational.

26 May

Ark Royal launched her first patrols just before 0900, with a deck rise and fall measured at 55ft. Launching the aircraft at all was a remarkable feat of airmanship; getting them back would be even more so.

However, it was a Catalina of Coastal Command, with an American 'adviser' as co-pilot and acting on the 'Ultra' information that first sighted *Bismarck* at 1030 . *Bismarck* opened fire on the Catalina and it has been said that by so doing she gave the game away. In fact the Catalina had already reported the vessel as *Bismarck* before she opened fire. The Germans had spent the previous day building a dummy funnel to disguise their silhouette but it was not yet rigged.

Half an hour after the Anglo-American Catalina had been driven away, two Swordfish from *Ark Royal* refined the contact to 49°19'N, 20°52'W. It was clear that only Force H and Vian's destroyers were within striking range. All hinged on *Ark Royal* being able to slow down *Bismarck*. At noon she had crossed *Bismarck's* line of advance and was 50 miles to the northeast of her. She had to gather in her patrols and rearm and fuel them, and it was not until 1450 that her 15 Swordfish started

Below:
The search for *Bismarck*.

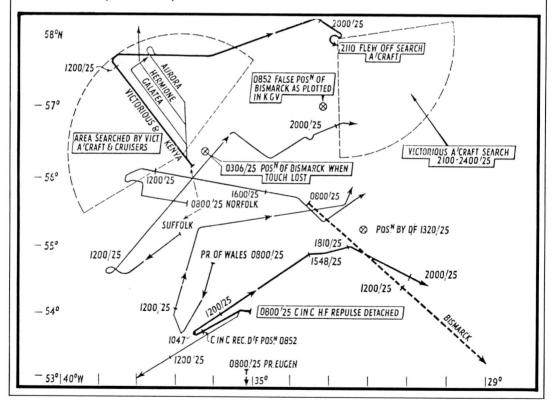

to fly off. That *Ark Royal* was not able to launch an immediate strike without waiting for her patrols, and that when she did she could only send a paltry 15 aircraft off, was the result of both the Admiralty's long-standing inability to get its hands on more than a trivial proportion of Britain's aircraft production resources, and its own equally long-standing inability to ask for the right kind of aircraft. Thus, one of the world's best aircraft carriers was operating some of its most obsolete aircraft, and precious few of them at that. After launching her strike, *Ark Royal* and Force H passed over *U556*, ironically a boat which had signed a pact of friendship and mutual support with *Bismarck*. *U556* had no torpedoes left, and could only watch as the sitting ducks passed her by.

Above:
HMS *Ark Royal* — her Swordfish were to cripple *Bismarck*. MPL

At 1315 Somerville had detached *Sheffield* to make contact with and shadow *Bismarck*. *Ark Royal* had missed the visual signalling of this order, and when the coded Admiralty signal, repeated to *Ark Royal*, was received it went to the bottom of the pile in a busy signals office. Capt Maund of *Ark Royal* was shown the signal an hour after his strike had flown off, and he ordered an immediate message to the flyers in clear language: 'Look out for *Sheffield*'; they had been told *Bismarck* was the only vessel in the area. The signal came too late for a force that had located a target through cloud as a blip on radar and which was committed to an attack before gaining visual contact.

When at 1540 Capt Larcom in *Sheffield* saw the Swordfish dip out of the clouds he immediately saw that they were taking up an attack formation. He ordered an increase to full speed, told his anti-aircraft crews to hold fire (which they did, with remarkable discipline) and frantically tried to dodge the torpedoes. Three crews recognised *Sheffield* and pulled out of the attack. 11 aircraft (one Swordfish had had to return to *Ark Royal*) did not, and launched their torpedoes. These had been armed with Duplex (magnetic) pistols for the warheads, designed to explode underneath a warship, its most vulnerable part. About half the torpedoes exploded on impact, the magnetic pistols being unreliable in very rough seas; the

HMS *Ark Royal*

Builder: Cammell Laird
(Laid down 1935; launched 1937; completed 1939)

Displacement: 22,000 tons (standard)

Dimensions: 800ft oa×94.75ft×22.75ft

Machinery: Geared turbines, 3 shafts, 102,000shp, 31kt

Armour: Main belt 4.5in; lower deck covering boilers and magazine 3.5in

Armament: 16×4.5in (8×2); 48×2pdr (6×8); 6×20mm (8×1)

Aircraft: 72 (she rarely carried more than two-thirds of this number)

Complement: 1,580

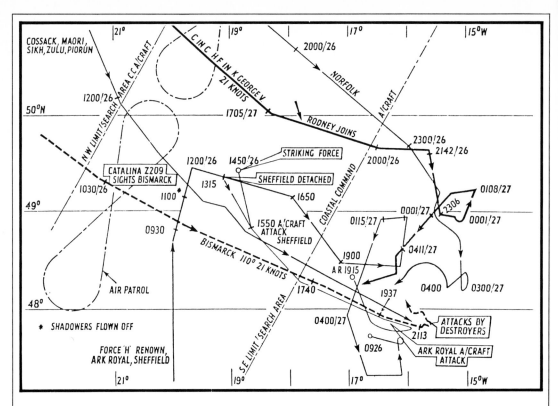

COSSACK, MAORI, SIKH, ZULU, PIORUN

21° 19° 17° 15°W

2000/26

C IN C H F IN K GEORGE V
21 KNOTS

N.W. LIMIT SEARCH AREA C.C A/CRAFT
1200/26

NORFOLK

A/CRAFT

50°N

1705/27

RODNEY JOINS

2300/26
2142/26

CATALINA Z209 SIGHTS BISMARCK

1200/26   1450/26   STRIKING FORCE

2000/26

0108/27

1030/26

1315   SHEFFIELD DETACHED

2306

49°

1100

1650

0001/27   0001/27

0930

1550 A/CRAFT ATTACK SHEFFIELD

0115/27

0411/27

BISMARCK 110° 21 KNOTS

1900
A R 1915

0400   0300/27

S.E. LIMIT SEARCH AREA

1740

1937

AIR PATROL

48°

COASTAL COMMAND

0400/27

2113   ATTACKS BY DESTROYERS

* SHADOWERS FLOWN OFF

0926   ARK ROYAL A/CRAFT ATTACK

FORCE 'H' RENOWN, ARK ROYAL, SHEFFIELD

21°   19°   17°   15°W

remainder ran true, and were successfully dodged by *Sheffield*, to the accompaniment of language that has not made its way into the official records. One aircraft signalled 'Sorry for the kipper' as it made its way morosely back to *Ark Royal*. In a

Above:
Disposition of vessels leading up to the final action.

Below:
HMS *Sheffield* as new. *Real Photographs S1114*

variation of the Nelsonian blind eye, Tovey was simply informed that the Swordfish had made no hits on *Bismarck*, which indeed they had not . . .

When Tovey received the 'No hits' signal it must have seemed as if the last card had dropped from his hands. *King George V* had only 32% fuel remaining, *Rodney* would have to break off at 0800 on the 27th (in theory; she somehow managed to stay longer than that on the day). *Ark Royal* could launch another strike but there was no reason to think it would be any more successful than the first, and this left Vian's destroyers — small ships on a wild night up against an opponent of awesome power and with proven fighting skill — as his last, very small chance.

Ark Royal Hits Home

At 1910 *Ark Royal* launched her second strike of 15 Swordfish. The three sub-flights lost contact

Below:
HMS *King George V*. *Real Photographs S1499*

Bottom:
HMS *Inglefield*, one of the destroyers escorting *King George V*. *Real Photographs 326*

with each other in the clouds but were starting their attack by 2047 [17], an attack which lasted for 40min. Conventional wisdom has it that *Bismarck* took two hits — one amidships, and a crippling one on the stern. Survivors' stories suggest there may have been another hit amidships. The remarkable fact that *Bismarck* failed to bring down one Swordfish in two separate attacks has been explained by the German anti-aircraft directors being calibrated for a minimum speed of 100mph from attackers, and hence firing consistently ahead of the British, and by the 'paint and paper' construction of the 'Stringbag' Swordfish, which allowed flak and splinters to pass through the fabric without destroying the aircraft. A more likely explanation is that in foul weather, with a wildly-manoeuvring ship, the inexperienced flak crews on *Bismarck* simply could not land home.

Although the one or two hits amidships increased *Bismarck's* list to port, it was the hit astern that shook *Bismarck* to her marrow. It jammed the rudders 12° to port and inflicted serious shock damage. The propellers were still operable but, whilst on trials, *Bismarck* had proved very difficult to steer on engines alone, with rudders amidships, because her propeller shafts were convergent or inward-facing, thus giving much less sideways thrust. With her rudder jammed to port and despite heroic efforts on the part of her Captain and engine room crew, she refused to steer on any course except head to wind, which happened to be from the north and hence straight into Tovey's fleet.

Argument has raged over whether or not *Bismarck* did enough to try and repair her damage, or cope with it. It was suggested that the rudders be blown off: divers did manage to enter the steering compartment in appalling conditions, but even this eventually ineffectual exercise was easier than placing a charge below the waterline in an appalling sea. Had it been possible, which seems unlikely, the chance of *Bismarck* simply blowing off her propellers was as high as that of removing the rudders. Sea anchors, even a U-boat to keep the ship steady might have been a possibility, but the non-availability of a U-boat and a ship of over 50,000 tons in a heavy sea make this possibility a dream for armchair strategists rather than a realistic proposal. Rather similar is a proposal suggested years later by German technical experts, of *Bismarck* reversing her engines and steering stern-first to Brest. It might — just — have worked; but one does not have to argue undue fatalism or sheer exhaustion on the German side to understand why it was never tried. As if in revenge for her hurt, *Bismarck*, now stumbling northwards into Tovey's arms, fired on the shadowing *Sheffield*.

It took a while for Tovey to realise his opponent had been delivered to him on a platter by the Swordfish. His first reaction to *Sheffield's* signals that *Bismarck* was heading north was to think that Larcom of the *Sheffield* had joined 'the reciprocal club', or made the extremely easy navigational error of reversing the bearings. *Bismarck's* stumbling course northwards was reported to Tovey at 2136 and at 2145. In between the signals Lutjens had signalled, at 2140, 'Ship no longer manoeuvrable — we fight to the last shell — long live the Fuhrer'.

Sheffield had lost three men killed and two wounded when *Bismarck* had fired six salvoes at her immediately after being hit. She directed Vian's destroyers on to *Bismarck*, the Polish *Piorun* sighting her first at 2238. Tovey altered course at 2306, deciding with his usual caution to defer engagement until dawn and approach *Bismarck* from the west, so as to have her silhouetted. This left Vian's destroyers to harry *Bismarck* and deliver her to Tovey in the morning. The destroyer action is summarised below.

Destroyer Action, 25/26 May

2238 Vian orders destroyers to take up shadowing positions.

2242 *Bismarck* opens fire on *Piorun* and *Maori*. *Maori* decides on alternative approach. *Piorun* closes and opens fire. After this single-handed attack she loses touch both with *Bismarck* and Vian.

2248 Vian decides to concentrate on shadowing and only attempt to damage *Bismarck* if it is possible without serious risks of damage. Destroyers signalled to shadow [18].

2324 Deteriorating weather tempts Vian to prepare for a synchronised attack, but this proves impossible because of weather.

2342 *Cossack* straddled at 8,000yd, suffers splinter damage.

2350 *Zulu* straddled, one officer and two men wounded.

2358 Adm Lutjens signals 'We fight to the last in our belief in you my Fuhrer, and in the firm faith of Germany's victory.' Hitler replies, 'What can still be done, will be done.' All that could be done was to order U-boats to gather near the scene.

0020 *Sikh* fired on; *Maori* tries to take over from *Sikh* as close shadower, but loses sight of

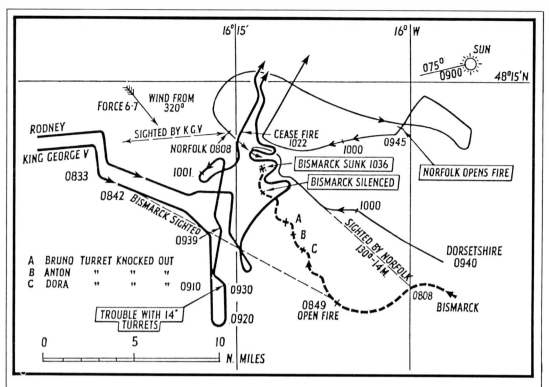

Labels within the map image (part of figure).

Above:
The final action.

Bismarck as the engines were used to alter the battleship's course.

0100 *Zulu* resights *Bismarck*.

0121 *Zulu* fires four torpedoes at 5,000yd and is, herself, fired upon; no hits.

0137 *Maori* creeps up unobserved whilst *Bismarck's* attention is on *Zulu*, and fires two torpedoes. Two possible hits reported, and *Maori* withdraws under heavy fire to 10,000yd.

0140 *Cossack* fires three torpedoes at 3,600yd, reports one hit.

0148 *Zulu* reports *Bismarck* stopped.

0218 *Sikh* fires four torpedoes from 7,000yd at stationary *Bismarck*; believes one to have hit. *Bismarck* underway again by 0240.

0325 *Cossack* fires one torpedo at 4,000yd; no hit, and vessel withdraws under heavy fire.

0400 Contact lost.

0600 Contact regained.

0650 *Piorun* ordered to Plymouth to refuel.

0650 *Maori* sights *Bismarck*, and at 0656 fires two torpedoes at 9,000yd, and is fired on.

A total of 16 torpedoes were fired during the night by the British destroyers. The British remained convinced that two, and possibly a third had hit; the Germans assert that none did. On balance it seems likely that, given the foul weather, the range at which most torpedoes were launched, and the erratic course steered by *Bismarck* there were no hits. In such conditions gun flashes were easily misinterpreted. Commentators in general have seen this night action as a model harrying exercise by destroyers, and an heroic one, both of which it was. It is also worth noting in the light of Tovey's decision to defer the final engagement that *Bismarck* was lost to sight twice for considerable periods, in either one of which she might have mended her steering and be steaming at 22 or 25kt towards the Luftwaffe. Tovey was a cautious commander — some might think too cautious.

It was a feature of German capital ship engagements throughout the war that their secondary armament appeared to perform less well than might have been expected. German survivors tell of arguments between the gunnery officers on board *Bismarck*, and certainly her secondary armament does not seem to have been handled with the crispness one might expect. This being said, the courage, tenacity and spirit of a young and exhausted crew on board a ship that was being delivered up to superior opponents is noteworthy. Perhaps, however, being kept up all night by Vian contributed to the relative weakness of German gunnery during *Bismarck's* final desperate fight.

27 May

At 0753 *Norfolk*, the old enemy, sighted *Bismarck*; indeed at first she thought it was *Rodney* and flashed a recognition signal, and ducked away without being fired on when the mistake was realised. At 0805 *Norfolk* sighted *King George V*, and at 0810 Adm Somerville steered southwest to open the range between *Renown* and *Bismarck*, at that time a mere 17 miles. *Maori* shadowed for *King George V* with *Bismarck's* speed at 10kt. Neither *Repulse*, long since detached to refuel, nor even the rebuilt *Renown* had any place in the C-in-C's plans for the *coup de grâce*. Risking such lightly-protected vessels could result in another *Hood* disaster. Neither was Tovey going to make Holland's other mistakes, and ordered *Rodney* to assume open order (6 cables distance) from the flagship and adjust her course as necessary. Steaming in line ahead, *King George V* sighted *Bismarck* at 0843, at a range of 25,000yd and a bearing of 118°.

Rodney opened fire first at 0847, followed by the flagship at 0848 [19]. *Bismarck* returned fire at 0850,

concentrating wisely on the older and more vulnerable *Rodney*, and straddled her with her third and fourth salvoes, forcing the aged *Rodney* into manoeuvres that would not have shamed the more spritely *Sheffield* at an earlier stage in the action. *Norfolk* joined in at 0854, at 22,000yd putting out of action *Bismarck's* fire control director 5min later, an important early blow for the British. At the same moment, 0859, *King George V* swung to starboard to open her 'A' arcs, with *Rodney* 2½ miles away soon following suit. Both British ships were now steering south, and *Bismarck* turned north, shifting her fire to *King George V* and putting the British and German ships on opposite courses. All the while Tovey was frantically closing the range.

The effect of this firepower on *Bismarck* was devastating: a 16in hit from *Rodney* at 0902 put *Bismarck's* forward turrets out of action (except for one last defiant salvo by the fore turret at 0927). At 0910 *Bismarck* shifted to her after fire control position. After four rapid salvoes, however, a 14in shell put this fire control station, too, out of action. The turrets went over to local control but by 0930 only one turret was in action and a minute later it, too, was silenced. Thus a powerful vessel was rendered impotent relatively

Below:
HMS *Rodney*. *MoD (Navy) OS/138*

early on without inflicting significant damage in return (one of *Bismarck's* last shots landed close to *Rodney* and jammed a torpedo sluice). German fire control positions seem to have been a particular weakness on *Bismarck:* perhaps her compact superstructure which bunched control facilities amidships around the enemy's centre of aim did not help. However, the real answer is that *Bismarck* was completely outgunned, surrounded and unable to manoeuvre effectively, and that lack of steering control raised huge problems for her own gunners. It was effectively a practice shoot for the British. However, they were not quite having it all their own way: the wind was blowing cordite smoke back on to them; too many ships were firing — making spotting difficult, and *King George V's*

main 14in turrets were showing their usual behavioural patterns. One turret was out of action for half an hour, others for shorter periods; for 7min her fire power was reduced by 80% and for 23min by 40%.

Above:
An erratic oilslick trail shows *Bismarck's* steering problems after her wounding by *Ark Royal's* Swordfish. *IWM C2450*

Below:
Debate still rages over whether it was HMS *Dorsetshire's* torpedoes or *Bismarck's* own scuttling charges that finally sank the German ship. *Real Photographs 1435*

Dorsetshire opened fire at 20,000yd at 0904, King George V's secondary 5.25in armament at 0905; fire from both was checked shortly afterwards as only adding to the confusion of shell-splashes. Around 0910 Rodney fired six of her heavyweight torpedoes at 11,000yd, and Norfolk four torpedoes at 16,000yd, but no hits were reported. At 0916 Rodney, falling astern of Bismarck, altered course 180° to starboard, bringing the range down to 8,600yd; the flagship followed suit at 0925. An eye witness reported:

'About this time, the coppery glow of our secondary armament shells striking the armoured upper works became more and more frequent, and one fierce flame shot up from the base of the bridge structure, enveloping it as high as and including the spotting top for a flickering second.'

By 1005 King George V had closed to 3,000yd. Rodney fired four more torpedoes, with one probable hit. A German survivor recorded the scene on Bismarck:

'Gradually the noise of combat became more irregular until it sank, to become nothing more than a series of sporadic crashes; even the control bells from the bridge stopped ringing. All three turbine rooms were filled with smoke from the boiler room; fortunately no shells had yet come through the plating protecting the engine room or the electric generators . . . Somewhere about 1015 hours I received an order over the telephone from the Chief Engineer: "Prepare the ship for sinking". That was the last order I received on Bismarck. After that all transmission of orders collapsed.'

Bismarck was a burning hulk, but was not sunk. At 1015 Tovey broke off the action, and at 1036 Dorsetshire was ordered to sink Bismarck with torpedoes. Of four torpedoes fired from 2,600yd two hit, and Bismarck sank at 1040. There has been fierce argument over whether British gunfire and torpedoes sank her, or the scuttling charges fired by her crew at approximately 1020; apart from understandable pride it matters little. As with all German-built ships, tight watertight subdivisions made Bismarck extremely difficult to sink, although they did give a slightly stronger tendency to capsize; as a fighting unit Bismarck was rendered useless long before she sank.

Conclusion

After the battle, 119 crew members were rescued by Dorsetshire, which unfortunately was forced to make off after a suspected U-boat sighting, and by *Maori*. Neither Adm Lutjens nor Capt Lindemann survived. Three men were rescued by *U75*, two more by the German weather and fishing vessel *Sachsenwald*. At 0925 on 28 May two destroyers, *Tartar* and *Mashona*, were caught by German bombers as shortage of fuel caused them to lag 100 miles behind the main fleet. *Mashona* was sunk, losing one officer and 45 men: small revenge for the Germans. *Prinz Eugen* refuelled at sea, but was forced to return home due to engine defects, a perennial feature of the 'Hipper' class heavy cruisers. She sailed into Brest on 1 June. *Bismarck's* supply vessels were picked off one by one until none survived.

It is easy enough now to argue that serious mistakes were made. On the German side *Bismarck* should have refuelled whilst off Bergen; had she done so her loss of fuel would have been less critical and she might have eluded her pursuers more easily. Nevertheless, her damage, even after her victorious fight with *Hood* and *Prince of Wales*, demonstrates the problems faced by a surface raider force challenging a dominant sea power. It was understandable that Capt Lindemann should have wanted to go after *Prince of Wales*. Had *Bismarck* sunk, or even more severely damaged *Prince of Wales*, the propaganda victory and the loss to the British fleet could have been serious. Nevertheless, it must be remembered that 'tonnage' — not ships flying the White Ensign — was still Lutjens's target at this stage. *Graf Spee*

showed what happened to German raiders which broke that golden rule. An error worthy of more serious criticism was the lengthy signal that gave away his position at a crucial time. Perhaps, finally more could have been done to get *Bismarck* into Brest, but it is hard to blame a crew who fought so well for so long.

On the British side again one can find apparent mistakes. Holland's dispositions when *Bismarck* was met were unwise, as were Wake-Walker's shadowing dispositions. Signalling and plotting confusion did not help the British and though, in the end it worked and a vast fleet was mustered, it should not be overlooked that at times the Admiralty had both considerable difficulty in marshalling forces and a confused attitude as to how to use the link between the Admiralty and those at sea. It took four capital ships, two aircraft carriers and a host of cruisers and destroyers, as well as many other capital and other vessels on the fringes of the action, to sink *Bismarck*. It is, however, wrong to describe the hit on *Bismarck's* stern — the Achilles heel of all battleships — as 'lucky'. Luck is the wrong word to use of a hit that was itself the culmination of over 20 years of development of British naval doctrine. Slowing the enemy down, 'fixing' him for the battleships was something the Fleet Air Arm had been preparing for. Even though the margins of British superiority were wearing disturbingly thin (notably in the Home Fleet's capital ship situation at the outset of the chase), Tovey perhaps summed it up best in his despatch, not published during the war: 'The *Bismarck* had put up a most gallant fight against impossible odds, worthy of the old days of the Imperial German Navy, and she went down with her colours flying.'

Below:
HMS *Mashona*, sunk by air attack on the way home from the *Bismarck* action. *Real Photographs S1658*

CHAPTER FIVE

The Sinking of *Prince of Wales* and *Repulse*

The loss of *Prince of Wales* and *Repulse* was pure tragedy: it was a bloody and violent ending to a series of horrific misunderstandings and misjudgements. The four preparatory factors in the tragedy are the strategic situation in the Far East, Japanese military capabilities, the decision to send out the pair of capital ships and the choice of British commanders on the spot. Over and above these factors there is the one overriding operational development that stands out from the early naval history of World War 2: the rapid changes that were taking place in the relative strength of the aircraft against the traditional capital ship. Both the Italian cruisers sunk at Matapan and the mighty *Bismarck* had been delivered up to surface ships by aircraft. The Italian battlefleet had been surprised and crippled in harbour by aircraft. Nevertheless, it was still possible to argue that aircraft had yet to sink a powerful, fully worked-up capital ship at sea. After 10 December 1941 even the most heavily protected battleships had to consider themselves vulnerable to aircraft wherever they were.

Below:
HMS *Prince of Wales*. *Real Photographs S1779*

Singapore and the Far East

Japan had been Britain's ally in World War 1 but the renunciation of that alliance as part of the Washington Treaty of 1922 made it much more likely that she would be an enemy in any future conflict. In any case, Japan was becoming a serious threat to British interests in the Far East. Her military leadership was aggressively expansionist, as the Russo-Japanese War and her consistent and violent pressure against China showed. Her desired expansion to the east, south and west was blocked by British and American interests. Indonesian oil and Malayan tin and rubber made British territory an inevitable and prime target for Japanese war aims, starved as she was of her own natural resources. Yet it was clear in the interwar period that Britain could not afford to station a large fleet in the Far East. Naval cuts dictated by Britain's parlous postwar economic state meant that she simply did not have the ships to do this, and those she had were designed for northern waters and tended to fare badly in warmer climes. One of the great mysteries of naval history remains the failure of the interwar Admiralty to install air-conditioning in warships designed largely to

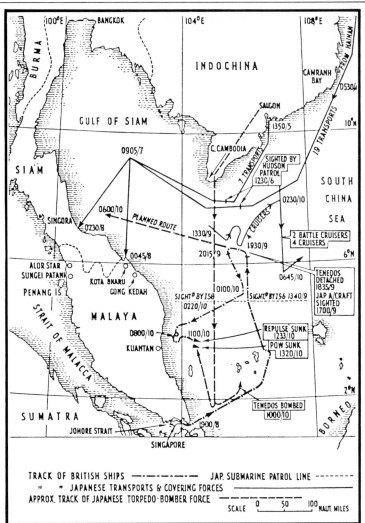

The map shows:

100°E — BANGKOK — 104°E — 108°E

BURMA

INDOCHINA

GULF OF SIAM

CAMRANH BAY
0530/4

SIAM

SAIGON
1350/5

C. CAMBODIA

0905/7

SINGORA
0600/10
0230/8
0045/8

PLANNED ROUTE

SIGHTED BY HUDSON PATROL 1230/6

7 TRANSPORTS

19 TRANSPORTS

SOUTH CHINA SEA

0230/10

10°N

4 CRUISERS

2 BATTLE CRUISERS
4 CRUISERS

1330/9
1930/9

2015/9

6°N

ALOR STAR
SUNGEI PATANI
KOTA BHARU
GONG KEDAH

PENANG IS

MALAYA

SIGHT? BY I58
0220/10

0100/10

SIGHT? BY I56 1340/9

0645/10

TENEDOS DETACHED 1835/9
JAP A/CRAFT SIGHTED 1700/9

STRAIT OF MALACCA

0800/10

KUANTAN

1100/10

REPULSE SUNK 1233/10
POW SUNK 1320/10

SUMATRA

JOHORE STRAIT

1900/8

TENEDOS BOMBED 1000/10

BORNEO

2°N

SINGAPORE

TRACK OF BRITISH SHIPS —·—·—·—   JAP. SUBMARINE PATROL LINE --------
    "   " JAPANESE TRANSPORTS & COVERING FORCES ————
APPROX. TRACK OF JAPANESE TORPEDO-BOMBER FORCE ————

SCALE 0   50   100 NAUT. MILES

Right:
The sinking of the *Prince of Wales* and *Repulse*.

Below:
HMS *Repulse* in a fine view taken before her reconstruction.
Real Photographs 1111

protect the Empire in tropical climates. This, however, was not a factor affecting deployment. Britain could not afford to build new home ports on the scale of the British dockyards and the bases in the Mediterranean. Therefore a fleet would have to be sent out to the Far East in a crisis and an operating base established that could hold off an enemy attack until that fleet could arrive. Hong Kong was the traditional British fleet base in the area, but as early as 1920 the War Office considered it indefensible with an affordable garrison. Sydney was too far away. Singapore — described by Lord Beatty, the First Sea Lord in 1924, as 'the finest strategical position in the whole world' — was the obvious choice for the new installation.

The amount of time for which Singapore was intended to hold out before the fleet arrived varied. The Admiralty estimated 42 days in 1922. By 1937-38 it had become 70 days, by July 1939, 90. Five days after war broke out in 1939 the Chiefs of Staff doubled even that to six months, and in the desperate summer of 1940 it was finally accepted that for the time being the fleet could not be sent at all, at least until Italy was defeated. This put an enormous strain on the defenders and necessitated the defence of all Malaya, not just Singapore Island. There were, however, insufficient troops available and reliance was placed on doubling air strength, with what extra troops were available defending the airfields and the naval base. Hardly surprisingly, even these plans proved too ambitious. Although reinforcements were brought in they fell far short of the 1940 plans, both on land and in the air. Most seriously, less than half the required aircraft were available and these included machines like the RAF Vildebeest torpedo-bomber that made even the Swordfish seem high technology in comparison. Liaison between the armed services was appalling. Realising that an attack on Singapore would mean an attack on Siam and the whole of Indo-China, the RAF had established air bases in the north of the country at Kota Bharu, Gong Kedah, Machang, Alor Star and Sungei Patani as well as further south. Despite their defence being the land forces' prime task there had been no consultation with the army on the location of airfields. They therefore tended to be both too dispersed in widely separated areas and placed too close to the sea so as to render them highly capturable. By December 1941, when *Prince of Wales* and *Repulse* arrived at Singapore, there were only 166 'first line' aircraft of all types in Malaya with 86 in reserve of which about a quarter were unserviceable. Apart from her famous guns installed when it seemed the Japanese would have to come by sea, Singapore's defences were woefully inadequate in 1941 when war with Japan began to loom, and this in itself determined that at some stage heavy units of the Fleet might well be sent there; these were the only mobile forces of any real power that were available. The Singapore strategy had been turned on its head.

Japanese Military Power

If British capital ships are seen as a plug to fill the gaping hole in Far Eastern defences, it is clear that the thinly-stretched British Fleet would be far too small to fill the gap. Other factors ensured that the gap was larger even than expected. Japanese naval development had proceeded at great speed in the interwar years, and in great secrecy spurred on by

Below:
HMS *Repulse* photographed in 1936.
Paul Silverstone Collection

a perception of numerical inferiority for which only technological and personal prowess could compensate.

By 1941 the Japanese had the most effective carrier striking forces and land-based naval air arm of any country in the world. Their pilots were trained with a dedication and ferocity that must have made actual warfare seem a comparative relaxation. Japanese naval aircraft were the best in the world, and they had the crews to go with them at the start of the war (although, later on, the inability to train a new generation would play a vital part in their defeat). For surface use the Japanese had — ironically — developed the oxygen-driven 24in 'long lance' torpedo as a result of a mistaken assessment that the British had developed the oxygen-driven torpedo for their new battleships *Nelson* and *Rodney*. They had not, but Japan did, producing a weapon with five times the range and 30% more destructive power than the best of her enemies' torpedoes. Submarines and aircraft did not have the 24in 'long lance'. The former carried a 21in variant and the complexities of oxygen did not seem worthwhile for the latter, essentially short range, use. Nevertheless, Japanese torpedoes were the best belonging to any navy at the outbreak of the war. The 17.7in Type 92 airborne torpedo carried a 150-205kg warhead 2,000m at over 40kt; the equivalent British torpedo carried a similar sized warhead less than 1½ times the distance less reliably. Most important of all, Japanese air-launched torpedoes could be released from up to 500ft at high speed and still run true.

Japanese air reconnaissance, though not without problems, was good, their command structure able to act promptly in case of emergency. Despite these technical strengths the British Admiralty tended to patronise and underestimate the Japanese, and place far too much faith in the destructive power of anti-aircraft guns, especially the multiple pom-pom. In another theatre of the war they also placed a similarly exaggerated faith in the power of Asdic to defeat the submarine menace.

Personalities and Politics

It is impossible to separate the fate of *Prince of Wales* and *Repulse* from the personalities of the British Prime Minister, Winston Churchill, the First Sea Lord, Dudley Pound, and Acting Adm Sir Tom Phillips. It is fashionable to denigrate great men, and Churchill has come in for the lion's share of the blame for the loss of the two vessels; to an extent this is fair. Churchill had an exaggerated belief in the power of the battleship and a tendency to interfere in naval matters, and in so doing displayed considerable ignorance. His

suggestion at the time of the hunt for *Bismarck* that British battleships should proceed even at the risk of running out of fuel and be towed back was an idea that would have shamed a *Boy's Own Paper* war story, and aroused fierce anger and an outraged amusement amongst serving officers. But Churchill was a totally dominant personality. There is no doubt that he forced the sending out of the two ships against the better judgement and wishes of Pound. Pound was immensely loyal and hard working, but also plagued by illness at the end of 1941, and was unable to resist Churchill. Churchill must take the greater part of the blame for the disaster which followed, but a warning note needs to be sounded, again arising from a tendency to write about the sinking of the ships as a purely military matter. In pure military terms the dispatch of *Prince of Wales* and *Repulse* was foolhardy, but recent research is suggesting that Australia's commitment to a European war was severely tested in 1939/40. The arrival of two major heavy units of the British Fleet at Singapore was the clearest possible declaration of intent on the part of Britain to defend Australia and pay back the men and money she was contributing to a war that, until late 1941, was being fought a long way from Australia. Cruelly, the sinking of the ships could only confirm that Australia would have to look elsewhere for her long-term security. But at least Britain had made the effort. Churchill's decision was militarily incompetent, and too small and too late to deter Japanese aggression. As an attempt to cement Australian commitment to the war it may still have had some justification.

Given this, disaster might have been averted if the third influential member of the command triumvirate, Phillips, had been other than he was. Tom Phillips, known as 'Tom Thumb', was a diminutive and aggressive naval officer who had got on well with Churchill in the prewar years, and also with Dudley Pound, and he became Vice-Chief of the Naval Staff in 1940. He was a brilliant Staff Officer, but his seagoing experience was limited and less successful. He was also a gunnery expert and, ominously, convinced of the superiority of capital ships over aircraft. He fell out with Churchill firstly over the issue of high-level bombing in Europe, and then more seriously over British involvement in Greece.

His promotion and appointment to command *Prince of Wales* and *Repulse* was a convenient way of ridding Churchill of a thorn in his side, whilst at the same time giving his opponent a prestigious seagoing command. Adm Sir James Somerville would have been an obvious and better choice but, in appointing Phillips, Churchill was doing what he had done with success in 1914: he had defused a similarly tense situation between himself, Fisher and Adm Sturdee by detaching the latter from the

Right:
Adm Sir Tom Phillips and his Chief-of-Staff Rear-Adm A. F. E. Palliser. Phillips' diminutive stature (he is on the right) is clear from this, hence his nickname of 'Tom Thumb'. *IWM FE486*

Staff and sending him off to hunt the German raiders *Scharnhorst* and *Gneisenau*. Phillips was never physically robust, and high intelligence did not make it any easier for him to listen and change his mind. In choosing Phillips, Churchill put the seal on disaster, sending out to face the Japanese naval air arm the officer who most of all doubted their ability to sink capital ships at sea.

The Ships

Though it hardly mattered in the final count, there were weaknesses in both *Prince of Wales* and *Repulse*. The former was something of a jinx ship: there had been a series of incidents when she was building and on trials, including an accidental firing of a pom-pom whilst in harbour. She had been forced to turn away against *Bismarck*, and had never properly worked-up. On paper she was an excellent design, with a dual-purpose secondary armament of 5.25in guns, and a heavy battery of lighter AA weapons. This was increased in July 1941 when the useless and dangerous UP rocket launchers on 'B' and 'Y' turrets were replaced by multiple pom-poms, bringing the total number of 2pdr barrels to 48. An undercurrent of worry about the 5.25in guns persists. It has been said that they were too light for effective surface work but too heavy for effective AA firing, that their director system was inadequate, and that they failed to score significant successes against enemy aircraft. More important was that power was lost to the turrets soon after a crippling hit landed on *Prince of Wales*'s stern. This was a possible design fault as the absence of electrical power rendered the turrets virtually useless.

Repulse was a battlecruiser, and she and her sister vessel *Renown* were known as 'Refit and Repair' among the Fleet because of the time they spent in dock. *Renown* had been almost completely rebuilt in the interwar period, but *Repulse* had received a far less extensive modernisation. She received more horizontal armour over her magazines and machinery spaces but was still inadequately protected by 1941 standards. She sailed to her death still with secondary armament of triple 4in guns that were obsolete and only suitable for low angle fire. Her

AA armament was limited to six old-fashioned 4in single open mountings, three octuple pom-poms, four quadruple 0.5in machine guns and eight recently fitted 20mm Oerlikons. She was an extremely happy ship, which *Prince of Wales* was not, but her only really viable use by 1941 was against commerce raiders such as *Graf Spee*.

The Sending of *Prince of Wales* and *Repulse*

By July 1941 the need for a fleet in the Far East was becoming clear, with the Japanese occupation of Saigon and Camranh Bay, a base from which they could control the South China Sea. The United States imposed a crushing trade and oil embargo, and the following month Roosevelt warned Churchill of the possibility of war. The need for a British fleet was, however, easier to see than to satisfy. Of 15 capital ships available to the British none could obviously be spared for the Far East.

Disposition of British Battleships, July 1941

Home Fleet, Scapa Flow	*King George V*, *Prince of Wales*
North Atlantic Convoys	*Ramillies*, *Revenge*
Mediterranean	*Queen Elizabeth*, *Valiant*, *Barham* based at Alexandria *Nelson*, *Renown* with Force H, based at Gibraltar
In refit or being repaired	*Warspite*, *Rodney*, *Repulse*, *Malaya*, *Resolution*, *Royal Sovereign*

One more 'King George V' class ship, HMS *Duke of York*, was to be ready by the end of 1941; two more by summer 1942.

The Admiralty preferred option was to assemble an Eastern Fleet, made up of *Nelson*, *Rodney*, *Renown* and the four obsolete 'R' class battleships. This would be supported by a carrier, 10 cruisers and two dozen destroyers, and would be assembled at Singapore by March 1942 once necessary refits had been completed. In August,

prompted by the American warnings, the Admiralty prepared plans for a more rapid deterrent deployment by the beginning of 1942, but still using the same ships. *Nelson*, *Rodney* and *Renown* would be concentrated at Singapore with the old light carrier *Hermes* with orders to withdraw to Trincomalee if deterrence failed; the old 'Rs' would remain in the Indian Ocean on convoy protection duties. The dispatch eastwards in September of one of the Mediterranean Fleet's capital ships was also suggested by the Chiefs of Staff, but the Admiralty refused to part with any of the Home Fleet's 'KGVs' because of the threat of the *Tirpitz*.

Churchill had his own plans: he insisted on a 'deterrent squadron . . . of the smallest number of the best ships . . . This powerful force might show itself in the triangle Aden-Singapore-Simonstown. It could exert a paralysing effect upon naval action.' The Prime Minister felt that what *Tirpitz* was doing to the British, his proposed squadron of a 'KGV', a battlecruiser and a modern carrier could do to the Japanese. Having set out these views by the end of August, Churchill lost interest and the Admiralty continued with its own plans. Phillips was appointed C-in-C designate of the new Eastern Fleet to fly his flag in *Nelson* or *Rodney*. In mid-October, however, these leisurely preparations were interrupted. The coming to power in Tokyo of the notorious hard-liner General Tojo seemed to signal an early crisis. In the War Cabinet's Defence Committee (Operations), Churchill again insisted on his fast, modern deterrent squadron. By then *Repulse* had been substituted for *Renown* and she was already on her way to the Indian Ocean. She should be joined, Churchill strongly suggested, by a 'KGV' and a carrier. Phillips set out the Admiralty's opposition; Pound was not present but he was called to discuss the matter at a subsequent meeting on 20 October. The First Sea Lord noted that the War Cabinet was prepared to take the responsibility for risks run in the Atlantic if a 'King George V' class ship was sent east. Pressed to send a 'really modern ship' by the Prime Minister and the Foreign Secretary, Anthony Eden — who both clearly underestimated the direct threat to Malaya — Pound compromised, agreeing that *Prince of Wales* should leave as soon as possible, but only proceed as far as Capetown, pending discussion of her further movements. This was the official Cabinet decision but no one appears to have had any intention of keeping to it. The Admiralty signalled those concerned that the ship was headed for the Far East four days before she left the Clyde, and on 11 November, four days before she reached Capetown, she was ordered to rendezvous with *Repulse* in Ceylon and proceed with her to Singapore.

Above:
A murky but dramatic picture of HMS *Prince of Wales*, revealing her low freeboard. *MPL*

Below:
HMS *Express*, an 'E' class destroyer.
Real Photographs 312

Departure

Prince of Wales left the Clyde on 25 October, with a meagre escort of two fleet destroyers (*Electra* and *Express*), which were all that could be spared.

She called briefly at Freetown on 5 November, and then at Capetown on 15 November. At Capetown, Phillips flew to see the Prime Minister, Field Marshal Smuts. He seemed to tell Phillips that he thought a fast battleship would deter Japanese aggression, but he signalled to Churchill his fear that the American fleet at Pearl Harbor and the British one at Singapore would be 'two fleets each inferior to the Japanese Navy . . . If the Japanese are really nippy there is here [an] opening for a first-class disaster'.

Prince of Wales, *Repulse*, *Electra*, *Express*, *Encounter* and *Jupiter* arrived in Singapore on

2 December to be welcomed by Phillips (who had flown on ahead) and every other available dignitary in a glare of publicity. Before this, on 1 December, Pound had signalled Phillips to consider taking his fleet away from Singapore; Pound sensed war was coming faster than expected, but there is a plaintive feel to his signal, just as there had been when he had 'considered' signalling Holland to place *Prince of Wales* in the van when attacking *Bismarck*. Phillips' response was to dock *Prince of Wales* for minor repairs, consider Darwin as a base and send *Repulse* for a short visit to North Australia.

War

By the morning of 8 December, Phillips' embryonic consultations with his allies had been overtaken by events. The night before, his time, the Japanese had launched their surprise attack on Pearl Harbor and crippled a significant part of the American Fleet. Singapore had been attacked by Japanese aircraft, and the South China Sea seemed full of Japanese invasion forces. In particular, two attacks had been launched at Malaya, with landings at Singora and Kota Bharu on either side of the Siam-Malaya boundary, and the Malayan airfields were under attack. The political reason for the sending of the force had now gone; deterrence had failed. The War Cabinet seemed to think the capital ships should withdraw amongst the numerous islands in the area, but actually sent a signal which simply asked Phillips what he proposed to do with his forces against invasion forces.

Phillips could stay in Singapore, in which case he would inevitably find himself under heavy air attack. He could retreat to Darwin or North Australia. He could try and hide in the islands, or he could sail and attempt to disrupt Japanese invasion forces. The latter were heavily escorted by cruisers and destroyers and a battleship covering force; the air threat would also be great. Phillips likened the whole operation 'to taking the Home Fleet into the Skagerrak without air cover'. Nevertheless, 'however extremely hazardous the prospects, we have got to do something'. It is hard not to agree with him.

Force Z Sails

Prince of Wales and *Repulse* — called 'Force Z' for signalling purposes — sailed for their last journey at 1735 on 8 December 1941. With them were the destroyers *Electra*, *Express* and two World War 1 veterans *Tenedos* and *Vampire*, the latter of the Australian Navy. Other ships were left behind, mostly because they needed repairs or were under refit, one old 'D' class cruiser because its limited World War 1 capabilities made it more of a hindrance than a help. Rear-Adm A. F. E. Palliser remained behind in Singapore as liaison officer with the Army and RAF. Phillips proposed to attack Vice-Adm Kondo's invasion transports off Singora on the morning of 10 December, and had asked the RAF, under Air Vice-Marshal C. W. H. Pulford, to provide air cover for them.

Below:
HMS *Tenedos* demonstrating her gaunt Great War-like lines. *Real Photographs N1031*

Above:
HMS *Electra*, launched on 15 February 1934, was lost a little over eight years later in the Java Sea. *MPL*

Under cover of darkness the British force steamed northeast at 17kt on the night of 8 December. On the morning of 9 December, Phillips received an ominous signal from Palliser in Singapore, stating that 'Fighter protection on Wednesday 10th will not, repeat not be possible.' Kota Bharu airfield, the only one close enough to give cover to Force Z on 10 December, had been evacuated, and other airfields were being neutralised by Japanese air attacks. Palliser also reported that the Japanese had large bomber forces stationed in southern Indo-China and possibly Thailand. Phillips has been criticised for not breaking off his action there and then. His instructions clearly demanded action; Singapore was a vital asset and he had not yet been sighted. However, there is another — and rarely offered — reason why his decision to press on was at least partly justified. He has been derided for underestimating the power of air attack against capital ships. The irony is that he was probably half-right in his assessment. High-level bombing against vessels at sea had signally failed to sink any capital ships to date in the war, despite the frequency with which it had been utilised by German and Italian forces.

This topic leads back to the absence of a fleet carrier with 'Force Z'. One had been planned, but the chosen ship, HMS *Indomitable*, had run aground while working-up in the West Indies and her departure east delayed. *Indomitable* had been built to a modified design with increased hangar capacity compared to the earlier armoured hangar carriers and carried two fighter squadrons — one of Fulmars and one of Sea Hurricanes in addition to 24 Albacores. Twenty-one fighters, however, was not much to pit against the high-performance bombers of the reinforced Japanese 22nd Air Flotilla, which also contained 36 superb Zero fighters, available — if required — for long-range escort duties. Perhaps reinforced from elsewhere these fighters would certainly have been com-mitted had a British carrier been reported. The relatively low-performance Fulmars and Hurricanes might well have shot down shadowers, the crucial factor in the Mediterranean, but 'Force Z' was first sighted by a submarine, not an aircraft. Given the strength of the Japanese air force in skill, material and sheer numbers, although *Indomitable* would have added significantly to the Japanese problems she would, in all probability, have been added to the butcher's bill had she been with 'Force Z'. Given what he had to go on, namely two years of ineffectual high-level bombing, absolutely no knowledge of Japanese technical superiority, and no experience of receiving skilfully carried out low-level torpedo attacks, Phillips had more right on his side than he is usually given credit for.

'Force Z' was sighted at 1400 on 9 December by the submarine *I65*. Reconnaissance aircraft from Saigon failed to make contact; aircraft from two cruisers did so, but lost it when darkness came. A torpedo strike from Saigon very nearly launched their torpedoes at Kondo's two fast battleships (rebuilt battlecruisers) covering the invasion force, and so at midnight the strike was recalled and ordered to wait for day. Had Phillips kept on his original course he would have run straight into these battleships, but the Admiral's skill when he knew he had been sighted is also often underestimated. 'Force Z' sighted the three aircraft from the Japanese cruisers *Kinu* and *Kumano* shortly before 1800. It continued on its northward course until 1900, after having detached *Tenedos* (short of fuel) to return to Singapore and signalled Palliser at 0800 the next morning that Phillips intended to break off the attack against Singora. By this Phillips was wisely guarding against his signals being intercepted. At 1900 Phillips swung west and increased speed to 26kt, giving the impression that he was heading for Singora. He then headed south to Singapore at 2015 when darkness had caused the shadowing aircraft to break off. In so doing he was using darkness to the full and an estimate of 5hr between sighting and attack, to both lose his enemy and send them chasing after him in the wrong direction.

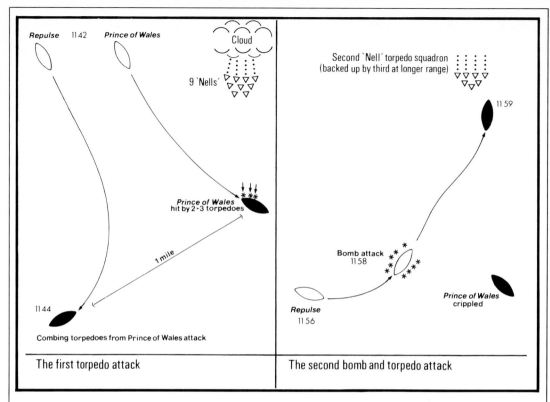

Repulse 11.42   **Prince of Wales**

Cloud

9 'Nells'

Prince of Wales
hit by 2·3 torpedoes

1 mile

11.44

Combing torpedoes from Prince of Wales attack

Second 'Nell' torpedo squadron
(backed up by third at longer range)

11.59

Bomb attack
11.58

Prince of Wales
crippled

Repulse
11.56

| The first torpedo attack | The second bomb and torpedo attack |

The real turning point in the action came with a signal from Palliser in Singapore at 0050 on 10 December. The signal, 'Enemy reported landing Kuantan', suggested that the Japanese were about to take a pair of scissors to one of the main arteries that linked Singapore with the north. At 24kt 'Force Z' could reach the area soon after dawn. Phillips altered course to the southwest at 0100. The speed with which he responded to the signal shows how clearly he felt that he had no option but to move in and attack. It is difficult to see how anyone could have supposed he would react any differently. Phillips clearly assumed Palliser would know he was heading to Kuantan and arrange air cover accordingly, particularly as Kuantan was much further south and could be covered by aircraft from Singapore airfields; an Australian squadron to cover 'Force Z' of Brewster Buffaloes was being kept at readiness at Sembawang airfield. For fear of giving his position away, Phillips made no signal declaring his intention to move on Kuantan. It is rather too easy to criticise this decision: Phillips' two overriding priorities throughout the action were to take the offensive and to avoid detection, and if he overestimated Japanese Radio Direction-Finding skills he erred on the right side of caution. Palliser can be excused, perhaps, for not knowing that Phillips would sail on to Kuantan; he ought,

however, to have taken steps to ensure air cover in case Phillips made that move. 'Force Z's' assigned Buffaloes could have been sent north to patrol over the area.

At 0220 'Force Z' was sighted by the Japanese submarine *I58* which launched five torpedoes at the vessels, scoring no hits. In the light of this knowledge the absence of an effective number of screening destroyers seems as significant an omission as the absence of a carrier with 'Force Z'. In response to the submarine's sighting report the Japanese launched an armada of 34 bomb-armed aircraft, 51 torpedo-carrying aircraft and nine reconnaissance planes, all before dawn. Phillips' change of course had done its job. Only one squadron found a target, the *Tenedos*, which had been detached earlier. By skilful manoeuvring *Tenedos* proved what Phillips had been arguing for years, and avoided major damage. *Tenedos* was sighted at 0950. The narrow margin between success and failure for 'Force Z' can be gauged by the fact that it was not itself sighted by Japanese aircraft until 1105, by a reconnaissance aircraft on its last leg of patrol and which was running short of fuel. The massive Japanese strike was still in the air, albeit for the most part starting to head home. As it was, the first attack was able to be launched at 1115. It is interesting to note in passing that though 'Force Z' had been sighted twice by

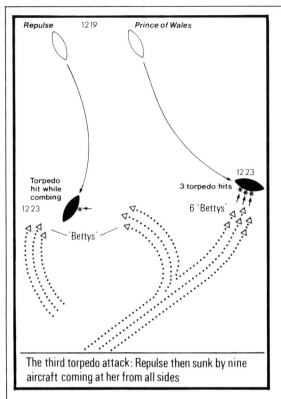

Repulse 1219   Prince of Wales

1223

3 torpedo hits

Torpedo
hit while
combing

1223

6 'Bettys'

'Bettys'

The third torpedo attack: Repulse then sunk by nine aircraft coming at her from all sides

Japanese aircraft on the previous day neither appears to have logged a sighting report; the Italian Navy and the Regia Aeronautica were not the only people to have problems with air reconnaissance. All Japanese air dispositions had been made on the basis of the submarine sighting.

Phillips arrived at Kuantan to find peace and calm prevailing. The report of a landing was false. Phillips was 500 miles from the Saigon airfields, the danger from which he was well aware of, within range of his own air cover and clearly not threatened by enemy warships. Thus he felt able to dawdle slightly at Kuantan, and then proceed to try and find a group of junks the fleet had passed shortly before dawn; this exploration was at the suggestion of Capt Tennant of Repulse. Whilst engaged on this hunt, at 1030, a signal was received from Tenedos — 'Am being bombed by enemy aircraft'. Phillips must have started to see the writing on the wall at this moment. He altered course immediately to the southeast, increased speed to 25kt, and called his crews to action stations.

Radar caught the reconnaissance aircraft before it was visually sighted, and here — if only here — a combat air patrol from Indomitable might have had at least a chance to postpone the day of judgement. However, the major and perhaps the only real mistake had already been made by

Phillips. For reasons that can hardly even be guessed at he failed to call for his assigned air cover when he received Tenedos's report that she was being bombed. There is simply no excuse for this. Flying time from Singapore was just over one hour; a call for air cover in time might have contributed to saving at least one of the British capital ships.

The Attack

The first attack came at 1115, a high level bombing attack from nine Mitsubishi G3M2 'Nell' aircraft. It was directed at Repulse. The AA fire (5.25in from Prince of Wales, 4in from Repulse) failed to make any impression — physical or spiritual — on the closely-spaced attackers. This was almost entirely Phillips' fault. The British Admiral first tried to manoeuvre the fleet together by flag signal which totally confused both ships' high angle fire control and masked their fire; the Japanese were allowed virtually undisturbed target practice. Repulse was 'straddled' by seven 550lb near-misses to port and one to starboard, but the ninth hit plumb on Repulse's hangar and went through it to explode on her armoured deck. A gout of flame shot up amidships, but within a few minutes the fire was well under control. Repulse was still doing 25kt and in fighting trim. Wisps of smoke rising through the bomb hole worried those on Prince of Wales and reassured Japanese observers, but serious damage was yet to be done. The Japanese were only equipped with ordinary 550lb and 1,100lb bombs: all heavy armour-piercing bombs had been allocated to the Pearl Harbor attack. Phillips was lucky that this first wave had the smallest bombs; he quickly learnt his tactical lesson and ordered the two ships to manoeuvre freely in future.

The next attack effectively killed Prince of Wales. Two squadrons of 'Nell' torpedo-bombers — 16 aircraft in all — flew through the short and long range flak barrage. Nine attacked Prince of Wales, the rest Repulse. They launched their torpedoes at 1,700yd or less, dropping their missiles at heights of about 100ft and at speeds of 150kt with a careless abandon that would have had a Swordfish pilot green with envy. The attack on Repulse was delayed and Tennant handled his ship brilliantly, turning first hard to starboard and then to port to comb the tracks. Prince of Wales shot down one of her attackers but was caught by two or three torpedoes: the first hit on the stern near the outboard propeller strut. The distorted shaft,

HMS *Repulse* (top right) hit by a Japanese bomb amidships. HMS *Prince of Wales* can be seen at bottom left. *IWM HU2763*

now unsupported, sent a vibration through the whole ship and opened a leak all the way into 'B' engine room, which was completely flooded in less than 20min. The bent shaft also tore a 12ft hole in the ship's plating, partly flooding the inboard shaft spaces.

A heavy explosion then occurred further forward, probably caused by the simultaneous detonation of two torpedo warheads. These defeated the underwater protective system and caused further widespread flooding. The port side electrical generators — both steam and diesel — in the immediate vicinity of these hits were quickly put out of action. The combined effects of the torpedoes compounded by some lax watertight door discipline was to put out of action half *Prince of Wales'* engine power and three out of seven electrical generator rooms. She took onboard some 2,400 tons of water and began to list to port 11.5°, her speed dropping to 16kt. The loss of electrical power was especially serious: not only did the generators in the flooded compartments fail but, perhaps through a combination of shock,

overloading and cooling water problems two more dynamos were soon out of action. The rear part of the ship lost all its power and never regained it. All pumps in the aft of the ship were put out of action as were the after 5.25in turrets. The lack of telephone communications in this part of the ship also helped prevent proper direction of the damage control parties. There was no lack of effort in *Prince of Wales'* damage control, but there is doubt as to whether the effort was applied correctly and with the right order of priority, particularly as regards restoring electrical power from the three surviving generators. A similar loss of electrical power had caused the aircraft carrier *Ark Royal* to sink after only one torpedo hit, when a list to port covered boiler uptakes and so caused a loss of power to the pumps which could and should have kept her afloat.

It was clear to Tennant in *Repulse* that the flagship was in serious trouble and, as if to confirm it, she hoisted the two black balls signifying she was no longer under her own control: her electrical steering motors — like much else — were without power. In fact *Prince of Wales* was in far more serious condition than *Bismarck* had been after her stern was hit, with half her engines gone, very serious flooding and her secondary armament either impaired or out of action. Even those turrets that were still operational could not train because of the list. Tennant was even more horrified when his signals office told him that no message had been sent to Singapore asking for air cover, but the signal that he sent off on his own initiative

111

reporting 'enemy aircraft bombing' which was received at 1204, was far too late to make any difference.

If there was a star in this tragedy it was Tennant and *Repulse*. Not only had his zig-zagging avoided the seven torpedoes of the second attack and the torpedoes which had missed *Prince of Wales* in the first (see diagram) but eight more torpedoes launched by a longer-ranged and uncharacter-istically half-hearted attack by a third 'Nell' squadron. The bombers also returned to make a brilliantly co-ordinated attack on the old battle-cruiser, dropping six 550lb bombs from 12,000ft which all fell within 100yd, soaking *Repulse's* crew. Finally, at 1202, the commander of the first 'Nell' squadron to attack *Repulse* — and whose torpedoes had hung up — mounted a solo attack. Once more Tennant's luck and skill held and the torpedo missed *Repulse* which now steered to the south to see if she could give assistance to *Prince of Wales*. In answer to a visual signal from the flagship, Tennant replied that 'thanks to Provi-dence' he had avoided any torpedo hits. His move towards the flagship may, however, have been his first and only mistake.

At 1220 no less than 26 torpedo-carrying 'Betty' aircraft swept in with the two ships only four cables apart. Initially, eight took on *Repulse*, dropping at long range from the starboard side. Tennant swung in that direction and successfully combed the tracks heading towards his ship, but then three of the nine aircraft attacking *Prince of Wales* suddenly swung away just when they seemed to be on the point of launching. *Repulse* was caught out. To comb the tracks on the starboard side, launched by the rogue aircraft that diverted from *Prince of Wales*, Tennant would have had to steer into the torpedoes launched at his port side. He could do little else but hang on and wait for a hit. As it was, *Repulse's* luck still had a little while to run. Only one torpedo hit on her port bulge, where she could best take it, and her speed did not drop from 25kt. *Prince of Wales*, unable to make any counter-manoeuvres, was not so lucky. Four of the six torpedoes launched at her hit, spaced out on the starboard side: one near the stem, one abreast 'B' turret, one near the stern. The water pouring in righted her list, but put her low in the water.

At 1225 came the attack that sank the brave *Repulse*. The third Japanese wave of nine aircraft was waiting its turn. As it wheeled in on *Repulse* it split its aircraft, coming in at the battlecruiser from all sides. *Repulse* downed two of her attackers, but four of the torpedoes launched at her hit, three on her port side and one to starboard, after she had swerved first to port and then hard to starboard in frantic evasive manoeuvres. This was too much for a ship that was essentially a World War 1 design. In Tennant's own words:

'When the ship had a list of 30 degrees to port I looked over the side of the bridge and saw the Commander and two or three hundred men collecting on the starboard side. I never saw the slightest sign of panic or ill-discipline. I told them how well they had fought and wished them good luck as they jumped into the oil-fouled sea. The ship hung for several minutes with a list of 60 or 70 degrees to port and then rolled over.'

At 1223 *Repulse* sank stern first into the depths. Tennant left her as she rolled over and, though stunned, survived to be rescued.

Phillips ordered *Encounter* and *Vampire* to pick up survivors. Then came eight more 'Nell' high level bombers, faced this time by only six of *Prince of Wales'* 5.25in guns. One 1,100lb bomb hit aft causing terrible casualties among the men using the Cinema Flat as a casualty station and rest area from the unventilated spaces in the stricken ship. *Prince of Wales* was already sinking, though Capt

Below:
Crew being taken off the listing *Prince of Wales* by the destroyer HMS *Express*. Note the 5.25in AA turret pointing skywards. *IWM HU2675*

Leach was still vainly trying to call up tugs from Singapore. At 1305 Capt Cartwright in the destroyer *Express* was ordered alongside to take off survivors. At 1318 *Prince of Wales* rolled over, scraping *Express* and nearly flipping her over to join the flagship. She took with her both Phillips and Leach, 18 other officers and 307 men from *Prince of Wales'* complement of 110 officers and 1,502 men. 42 officers and 754 men were rescued from *Repulse's* complement of 69 officers and 1,240 men. A total of 47 officers and 793 men were lost from both vessels. Some survivors heard screams from the quarter deck ventilators as *Prince of Wales* made her final roll. The survivors landed in Singapore at midnight; both ships had been less than half a day away from survival.

Arriving at 1318, four fighter pilots in their Brewster Buffaloes were in time to see *Prince of Wales* roll over and sink, and chase off the remaining Japanese aircraft. Flt Lt T. A. Vigors, the Officer Commanding No 453 Squadron, gave a widely-publicised report of the survivors cheerfully waving at the aircraft:

'During that hour I had seen so many men in dire danger waving, cheering and joking as if they were holidaymakers at Brighton . . . It shook me, for here was something above human nature. I take my hat off to them, for in them I saw the spirit which wins wars.'

Sadly, the survivors report that whatever cheering and waving there was, was certainly not in the spirit Vigors suggested.

Express left at 1415, with hardly any standing room on board. *Vampire* and *Electra* departed at 1600. Both hulls, now war graves, can still be seen by divers.

Conclusion

Little more remains to be said about the role and responsibility for what happened of the various participants. As with all disasters, it was the result of more than one man's errors. Those who write from a military viewpoint tend to deride all too easily political aims and ambitions, and none of us are free of the search for convenient scapegoats; but Indonesian and Malayan natural resources, Australian commitment to a European war and trade with India were the highest possible stakes to play for, and it is no more cruel than war itself to say that the stakes may have been worth the gamble of two capital ships. As did Iachino at Matapan, Tom Phillips made only one culpable error, and that was not to call for air support at 1030 on the day of the sinking. It may well be, however, that that decision reflected a more general problem. It is clear that Phillips did not

believe that he was facing a torpedo-bomber threat until the first 'Nells' carried out their attacks. Poor intelligence and a serious underestimation of Japanese technical prowess were to blame, spiced by Phillips' general prejudice against the dangers aircraft posed to capital ships.

What is more interesting is that *Tenedos* and *Repulse*, the oldest vessels present, emerged with more credit than the extremely modern *Prince of Wales*. *Repulse* avoided damage for longer than her flagship and downed more aircraft. Of course ship design matters — and matters greatly — in the business of who wins a sea battle, but the engagements so far examined suggest that luck, quality of command and training are, if anything, slightly higher in the list of priorities. The same is not true of air combat, but at sea it is often the use made of the ships that matters more than the ships themselves.

As a footnote, Tom Phillips had shared a flat in London before the war with John Slessor, later to become Marshal of the RAF. At a farewell party, Sir Arthur 'Bomber' Harris, also to become Marshal of the RAF, proposed a toast. Knowing of the arguments between Slessor and Phillips, good friends but with very different views of air power and its effectiveness, he said, 'Tom, when the first bomb hits, you'll say "My God, what a hell of a mine!" '.

HMS *Repulse*

Builder: John Brown
(Laid down 25 January 1915; launched 8 January 1916; completed August 1916). Major refits 1918-21 and 1933-36

Displacement: 38,300 tons (full load)

Dimensions: 794.2ft × 90ft (101ft to bulges) × 27ft

Machinery: Geared turbines, 4 shafts, 120,000shp, 28.3kt

Armour: Main belt 9in (lower), 6in (upper); turrets 7-11in; main deck 3.5-5.75in; lower deck over forward magazines 4.25in

Armament: 6 × 15in (3 × 2); 9 × 4in (3 × 3); 6 × 4in AA (6 × 1); 24 × 2pdr (3 × 8); 16 × 0.5in (4 × 4); 8 × 20mm (8 × 1); 8 × 21in torpedo tubes (4 × 2 fixed)

Sensors: 1 × Type 284 radar

Aircraft: up to 4

Complement: 1,181

Notes: In their original state *Repulse* and her sister ship *Renown* were rather inadequate battlecruiser designs, very lightly armoured and with only six 15in guns, fewer than the minimum deemed necessary for accurate shell-spotting in the days before radar. Both vessels were considerably changed in the 1920s and 1930s, but *Repulse* did not receive the major reconstruction given to her sister ship.
(For technical details of HMS *Prince of Wales*, see Chapter 4.)

CHAPTER SIX

The Escape of *Scharnhorst* and *Gneisenau*

When Dudley Pound telephoned Winston Churchill to tell him that the German battlecruisers *Scharnhorst* and *Gneisenau* and the heavy cruiser *Prinz Eugen* had escaped from Brest and sailed virtually unharmed up the English Channel to Germany there was a long pause on the end of the line. 'Why?' said Churchill, and rang off. It is a question that has been asked ever since.

Gathering Forces

Scharnhorst and *Gneisenau* entered Brest on 22 March 1941 after a three-month raiding cruise in the Atlantic during which they had sunk 21 merchant vessels totalling 105,784 tons. Earlier in the war 'Salmon and Gluckstein', as they were known to British sailors, had been among the more active of German capital ships, usually operating as a pair. They had sunk the armoured merchant cruiser *Rawalpindi* in 1939, and then run away from the British light cruiser *Newcastle*. In the

Norwegian campaign of 1940 both ships had a desultory gun battle with *Renown*, which landed two hits on *Gneisenau* and was hit twice in return before the German ships withdrew. In May 1940 the two vessels met and sank the British aircraft carrier *Glorious* and the destroyers *Ardent* and *Acasta*, at the tail end of the same Norwegian campaign, but not before *Acasta* had severely damaged *Scharnhorst* with a torpedo. *Scharnhorst* and *Gneisenau* had, therefore, earned themselves the title of the most effective and dangerous German capital ships of the war by 1941, even though on their raiding cruise they had turned away from the ancient battleships *Ramillies* and *Malaya*.

The two ships were surpassingly beautiful, and poised somewhere between battleship and battle-cruiser. In common with all German capital ships they were bad sea boats, despite having a flared 'Atlantic' bow fitted after completion. Enlargements of the earlier 'Panzerschiffe', both vessels suffered from having a light main battery of nine 11in guns and some secondary battery 5.9in guns mounted singly in weakly protected positions. 15in main armament was considered for these ships but this would have delayed completion too long. The triple 11in mounting was already available, although the guns themselves were of a new, more powerful model than those in the 'Panzerschiffe'. Another weakness, and one which has a bearing

Below:
The German battleship or 'battlecruiser' *Gneisenau*. She could be distinguished from her sister ship *Scharnhorst* by the fact that *Gneisenau* had her mast stepped abaft of the funnel. *Real Photographs S1802*

on both their escape up the Channel and the sinking of *Scharnhorst*, was their relatively weak deck armour.

As has already been noted, original plans for both ships to rendezvous with *Bismarck* came to nothing. *Scharnhorst* was shown to need a long refit (another consistent feature of almost all German surface vessels was the unreliability of their high-pressure boilers, which had been rushed into service without adequate testing), and *Gneisenau* was damaged by torpedo and bomb hits. Then it was *Scharnhorst's* turn to be badly damaged by bombs whilst on trials further south at La Pallice. Her deck armour was pierced, as *Gneisenau's* had been, and she was placed out of action until the end of 1941.

Above:
Prinz Eugen in dry dock. *IWM C2576*

Prinz Eugen had arrived in Brest on 1 June 1941 after her cruise with *Bismarck*. She was damaged by a bomb hit on 1 July 1941, which put her out of action until the beginning of 1942. To Adm Raeder the situation was by no means unhopeful; it was true that his plans for sorties into the Atlantic had come to nothing as a result of bomb damage, but the presence of three heavy units in France and *Tirpitz* at Trondheim both stretched and tied down a high proportion of the British fleet. Brest had excellent repair facilities, damage had so far not been fatal, and German defensive measures were improving all the time. The smoke screen that could now be generated meant that the British were forced into virtually indiscriminate bombing, which was both inaccurate and a source of hostility amongst the local inhabitants.

This favourable balance was tipped against Raeder by Hitler, and to a lesser extent Goering. Hitler disliked capital ships at the best of times; commando raids and his own intuition convinced him that a combined Anglo/Russian attack on Norway was imminent and Goering announced that he was unable to supply adequate fighter cover for the ships in Brest. Early in 1942 Hitler delivered an ultimatum: either the ships were to be brought back north, or their guns dismantled and sent to help defend Norway. This left Raeder little option, though some German officers thought temporary dismantling preferable to what seemed like a suicidal breakout. Here Hitler, land animal though he was, seems to have an intuitive and brilliant insight: the German ships could either head out into the Atlantic and then back through the Iceland-Faroes Gap, or simply dash straight up the English Channel. Hitler picked on the latter option almost immediately, and made it his own. At first glance it appeared suicidal — it demanded a course almost over England's doorstep, through minefields and narrow channels and within easy range of British aircraft, not to mention heavy gun emplacements commanding the Channel. The threat from submarines was considerable and there was a real possibility that the British Home Fleet might move to intercept. In addition *Scharnhorst*, *Gneisenau* and *Prinz Eugen* had been landlocked for months, many of their technical experts had been drafted away, and they had found little opportunity to exercise or work up to full operational efficiency.

Hitler based his support for the Channel dash on two points: the first was that the Brest group of ships were like 'a patient having cancer, who was doomed unless he submitted to an operation. An operation, on the other hand, even though it might have to be a drastic one, would offer at least some hope that the patient's life might be saved. The passage of the German ships through the Channel would be such an operation and had therefore to be attempted.' This was announced at a conference at Hitler's headquarters on 12 January 1942. Additionally, Hitler said that he believed the British had shown an inability in the past to take 'instant decisions' in the light of an unexpected situation. As time was to show, his appreciation was absolutely correct. There were, of course, factors in the German favour. The sheer impudence of the breakout — if secrecy could be maintained — might well, as Hitler guessed, confuse the British. Minefields could be swept, British radar jammed. A large escort of destroyers

and motor torpedo boats could be made available, and continuous fighter cover if the Luftwaffe co-operated.

Command of Operation 'Cerberus' was given to Vice-Adm Ciliax who commanded the Atlantic Squadron. He was an unpopular officer, a stickler for petty rules and cursed with a stomach complaint that helped make him even more short-tempered. Whatever his personal failings, his organisation was excellent. Almost from the start the Germans decided to depart from Brest under cover of night. This would place them in the narrowest part of the Channel in daylight, but this apparent risk was actually a distinct advantage, as it allowed maximum use of fighter cover and escorting vessels, as well as AA fire. If they forced the straits in darkness much of this weaponry would be unusable at the point where the attacks on them might be expected to be heaviest; better, therefore, to use darkness to cloak their escape and delay its discovery as long as possible.

It was not possible to hide the gathering of escorts in Brest, but this could be seen as part of normal exercises. Minesweeping operations could be hidden by taking place largely at night, and huge credit must go to Cdre Friedrich Ruge, in charge of minesweeping forces, who cleared the channels with the loss of only two vessels. By using German night-fighters, a force of 250 aircraft could be used; they were to fly 35min sorties over the German ships, with 16 aircraft in each sortie. As each relief wave would arrive 10min before the preceding one was to leave, there would be 32 fighters overhead for 20min in each hour. Older British radar could be jammed, but to avoid arousing suspicion selective jamming was undertaken by the Germans for short but increasing periods, this being interpreted as 'atmospherics' by the British operators. Marker boats would be left by the swept channels and radio beacons operated from the shore for navigational guidance all along the route. Tugs would also be on stand-by in ports along the route, and there would be a series of 'safe' harbours to which vessels could head if damaged.

The largest problem of all was secrecy. The navigating officer of *Scharnhorst* had to call for almost every chart available, slipping in those for the English Channel at the last minute as an apparent afterthought so as not to arouse suspicion. Tropical kit was loaded on to the vessels, rumours planted and, in an echo of Cunningham's ruse in Alexandria, invitations sent out for a dinner on board the German ships on the night they were to sail. Land-based flak crews were shipped on board the vessels, to augment their AA fire but also to lull suspicion, as such soldiers never went to sea. Fighter pilots were told their rehearsals were for escort duties for a vital convoy, and only told what they were escorting on the morning of the operation. Minesweeper crews were similarly briefed about convoys, but the marker boats — sent out to the side of nowhere and told to wait — were told nothing at all. A small number of ratings were allowed home on leave as the date of the operation loomed. Thus a remarkably complex operation was prepared and rehearsed in what seems to have been total secrecy — except, ironically, back home in Germany, where the wives of destroyer crews seem to have known what was happening. However, unlike the inhabitants of Brest, the local populace of Wilhelmshaven and Kiel were not interested in talking to the British.

Below:
HMS *Walpole*, a 1,100-ton Thornycroft 'W' class escort destroyer. *Real Photographs N1034*

Bottom:
HMS *Campbell* of the 'Scott' class of escort destroyer. *Real Photographs S417*

Ciliax needed maximum darkness and an east-running tide in the early morning hours to give him speed and his ships' screws deep water to bite on, as well as have the maximum chance of avoiding ground-moored mines. Fitting the bill was 11/12 February, and the forecast of reasonable visibility deteriorating in the afternoon was also excellent. *Gneisenau* had been damaged in an air raid on 6 January, but was repaired by 27 January, so 11/12 February was fixed on for the breakout.

British Preparations

The British had been aware of the danger of a breakout almost from the first moment the German warships arrived in Brest, and they held at least two aces up their sleeves which the Germans were unaware of. A French naval officer — codename 'Hilarion' and later to become Adm Philipon — was working in Brest, and able to brief the British on German ship movements and preparations at fairly frequent intervals. In addition, the British had 'Ultra', the secret of some German naval ciphers. The first source told the

Above:
**HMS *Sealion*, a 'S' class submarine, was armed with
6×21in torpedo tubes.** *Real Photographs S1504*

British that the German ships would be ready to proceed to sea by the end of January or start of February, the second showed increased German minesweeping activity, particularly off the Dutch coast and Frisian Islands. Indeed, in a series of messages, 'Hilarion' predicted almost exactly the time when the German ships would leave Brest. Then there was the concentration of destroyers and escorts at Brest. As a result the British gave a possible breakout the codename 'Fuller'. On 2 February the Admiralty issued an appreciation which considered the situation of the German ships, and concluded with a remarkably accurate prediction of what did actually take place:

'We might well, therefore, find the two battle-cruisers and the heavy 8in gun cruiser with five large and five small destroyers; also, say, twenty fighters constantly overhead (with reinforcements within call) proceeding up the Channel. To meet this sortie we have about six MTBs at Dover, but no destroyers with torpedo armament.'

The appreciation goes on to suggest that little reliance can be placed on bombers for destroying the ships, and that a mere nine Coastal Command torpedo-bombers would be available. It concludes:

'Taking all factors into consideration, it appears that the German ships can pass east up the Channel with much less risk than they will incur if they attempt an ocean passage.'

Six days later the C-in-C of Coastal Command, Sir Philip Joubert, issued an appreciation which predicted a Channel breakout 'any time after Tuesday, February 10th'. The British could read tide tables and the phases of the moon as well as the Germans; remarkably, they had almost the exact date pinned down in advance.

Steps were taken to increase offensive capacity. Six destroyers (*Mackay*, *Whitshed*, *Walpole* and *Worcester* of the 16th Flotilla at Harwich, and *Campbell* and *Vivacious* of the 21st Flotilla at Sheerness) were to wait in readiness at Harwich, operating under Dover Command. Six MTBs were ordered to Ramsgate; the minelayers *Welshman* and *Manxman* were to add to the mines already laid by *Plover* in the likely path of the German ships. Vice-Adm Ramsay ordered six Swordfish torpedo-bombers of 825 Squadron to Manston airfield from Lee-on-Solent. Coastal Command was ordered to fly nightly reconnaissance patrols in darkness: a western patrol known as 'Stopper' off the entrance to Brest, a central patrol 'Line SE' between Ushant and the Ile de Brehat, and an eastern patrol known as 'Habo' between Le Havre and Boulogne. These would be flown from dawn to dusk by radar-equipped Hudson aircraft, and complement the day time patrols by Fighter Command.

300 bombers were allocated to Operation 'Fuller' on 4 February 1942, at 2hr notice, and 450 aircraft from Fighter Command. In addition, Vice-Adm Sir Max Horton sent a modern submarine, *Sealion*, to lurk off Brest; the two older submarines in the area were unable to come close inshore.

Although superficially impressive, at least in terms of the air power available, this plan was riddled with weaknesses, some built-in and some accidental. It hinged on a co-ordinated attack by torpedo-carrying air and surface forces at the narrowest point in the Channel which it was assumed the enemy would traverse in darkness, an attack which would be lit by flare-carrying Hurricanes. This attack would force the German vessels into minefields and shallow waters, and hopefully disable them to allow bombing attacks and radar-ranged gunfire from land. The conviction that the German ships would sail from Brest in daylight and force the Channel in darkness underpinned all planning and thinking. It may have been a genuine appreciation, or it may have

been one of those 'truths' familiar to all those who have served on committees, where an early idea somehow escapes gritty analysis and establishes itself as correct with no one quite knowing how it has happened. It may also have been wishful thinking. Launching destroyers, MTBs and Swordfish at a large surface fleet with heavy air cover was sheer suicide; it was also all the British had available.

Vice-Adm Sir John Tovey had decreed that no British heavy units would sail south to engage the German forces. The distance from Brest to Ijmuiden is approximately the same (just over 500 miles) as that from Scapa to Ijmuiden. The Home Fleet could have intercepted, given sufficient warning, though on the day only *Duke of York* and three light cruisers were in Scapa. Tovey was desperately stretched in trying to guard against a breakout by *Tirpitz* and in escorting the massive WS troop convoys to the Far East. In addition, with *Prince of Wales* and *Repulse* recently sunk he was down two capital ships from an already meagre supply, and forcibly reminded of the

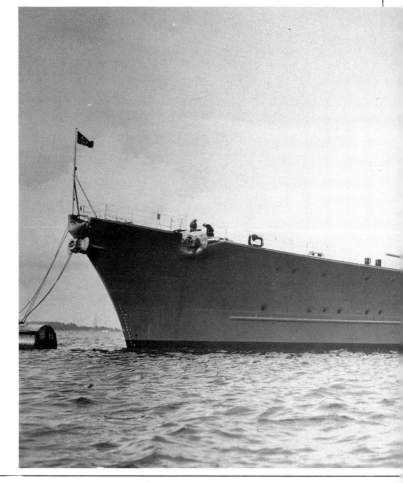

Right:
Prinz Eugen, newly completed in the late summer of 1940. The fire control equipment is trained to starboard; note the prominent radar on the main director. The main armour belt (3.25in maximum thickness) is clearly visible below the two rows of scuttles. Prinz Eugen was a huge ship, the size of a World War 1 battleship.
Paul Silverstone Collection

power of aircraft against capital ships. He simply could not risk his vessels within range of massive German air cover.

The naval plans, therefore, depended upon co-ordination and darkness in which to attack; the non-availability of either effectively castrated the whole naval response to the breakout. The same applied to the submarine *Sealion*, which at nightfall would have to retreat, surface and charge its batteries. All this would have mattered less if the Coastal Command and RAF position was stronger. Indeed, the relative weakness of the naval response was in part the result of the large air forces available to the British, with all along the primary thrust designed to be from the air. For unknown reasons 811 Squadron — at full strength and fully worked-up, at Arbroath — was not brought south: instead the six serviceable Swordfish from 825 Squadron were placed at Manston. The Beaufort torpedo-bombers of Coastal Command lacked practice in attacking fast-moving surface vessels; they also lacked knowledge of their likely target, with both Coastal Command

and the RAF maintaining an obsessive secrecy, to the extent that a large number of pilots simply had no idea of what they were flying out to attack. One pilot exclaimed 'I didn't think we had such beautiful warships!' when he caught sight of a vessel in the Channel. He was right — it was *Prinz Eugen*.

Three further factors cast a malign spell over the British side of the operation. 'Hilarion' in Brest had not been briefed that a Channel breakout was even a possibility; had he been so briefed it is possible that, given the importance of early notification of such an escape, he might have got information earlier to Britain that the ships had departed. Secondly, the guns on the Channel were manned by inexperienced crews, inadequate in numbers and for the most part could not target on fast-moving naval vessels. Thirdly — and most alarmingly — for a fortnight before the breakout a signals exercise had been planned, known as 'Tiger 11', which commenced with the news that *Scharnhorst* and *Gneisenau* had broken out of Brest and were proceeding up the Channel. In an

example of the left hand not knowing of the right hand's existence this exercise was not cancelled even when it became apparent that it was due to take place in the prime time for the real event. As it was, on the early morning of the breakout a signal was received in Corps Signal office, without the prefix that would have made it exercise only. An officer then added in the exercise prefix on the assumption that it had been left out of the signal at its point of origin by mistake. As a result the 'exercise' signal went to the bottom of the pile, and neither the RAF nor the Admiralty were informed. It has been suggested that the Germans planned the breakout for that day knowing of the exercise, but wind, weather and tides must have loomed far more significantly in their thinking. There was inadequate planning in Coastal Command to ensure that sufficient torpedoes were available at the right time and in the right place to arm the Beauforts. Of the three modes of aerial attack — torpedo, dive-bombing and conventional bombing — experience throughout the war had shown the last of these to be the least effective, yet this was the main strength of the RAF forces. The RAF had failed to develop before the war an effective armour-piercing bomb, and any such bomb has to be launched from considerable height to penetrate an armoured deck. This latter requirement meant that bad weather and a low cloud ceiling could render the bombers ineffectual.

The bombers, 300 in all, that were earmarked for Fuller on 4 February were as a result taken off night bombing attacks on Germany. Bomber Command resented this, and asked for their release on 7 February. The Admiralty requested the continuation of the bombers' availability, stating that a breakout was imminent. In a unilateral decision — and without informing the Air Ministry, Fighter or Coastal Command — the C-in-C of Bomber Command removed 200 of the bombers from 'Fuller', leaving the remaining 100 on stand-by at 4hr notice. AVM Baldwin was Acting C-in-C of Bomber Command (Harris was in the United States, about to return and take over); his decision to remove the aircraft from 'Fuller' reduced the sense of urgency over the operation, and severely weakened the British response. Underlying and affecting all the plans was the lack of co-operation and liaison between Fighter, Bomber and Coastal Commands, the Navy and the Army. No one person or agency had authority over Operation 'Fuller', and that fact alone was to have tragic consequences.

Operation 'Cerberus/Fuller'

The German plan, codenamed 'Cerberus', was rigid and allowed individual commanders no room for manoeuvre. The three vessels and their escorts were to clear Brest at 1930 on 11 February, *Scharnhorst* leading, followed by *Gneisenau* and *Prinz Eugen*. Speed would be 25kt, the aim to be in the Straits of Dover by 1130 on 12 February. A 2hr delay at the start of the operation was allowed for; any more and it was to be postponed. That 2hr was almost exceeded when a British bombing raid caught the ships just as they were getting underway in Brest harbour, but the smoke and flak did its job, and the ships were able to clear the harbour an hour-and-a-half late. *Sealion* missed them by a matter of hours having withdrawn out to sea to recharge her batteries. At 0012 on 12 February the

Below:
The German torpedo boat T8 of the type used to escort
Scharnhorst **and** *Gneisenau* **up the Channel.**
Real Photographs S1936

ships rounded Ushant and set course for the English Channel, 72min behind schedule. The crews cheered when they were told where they were heading; apart from a handful of officers it was the first they knew of the operation. It was a very dark but clear night, and tides and deep water let them make a steady 27kt.

There were six levels of reconnaissance that might have picked up the German ships; though the Germans were unaware of it as they steamed through the night, they had already avoided discovery from five of them. The bombing raid had failed to notice the departure of the ships; *Sealion* was out of the area. Then came the three Coastal Command patrols: 'Stopper', covering the immediate area of Brest, was flown off from Cornwall at 1827 on 11 February, but at 1907 it met a German Ju88 night-fighter, and switched off its radar while evading it. The inexperienced radar operator then switched on the set at full power from cold, instead of the regulation half power, and blew the set. The crew spent some minutes trying to mend the set but failed, and left the patrol line at 1940. On landing, 40min were spent trying to locate the fault, again without success. The pilot was ordered to take up a new aircraft, but this one

refused to start. 50min later the cause — a damp plug — was found out, but by the time another Hudson resumed the patrol at 2238 the 'Stopper' line had been unwatched for 3hr, during which time the German vessels had passed through its area.

The second line of patrol, 'Line SE', took off at 1848 and reached its designated area, between Ushant and the Ile de Brehat, at 1940. Its radar refused to switch on. The crew worked at it for an hour-and-a-half, with no success, so at 2113 the aircraft was ordered home. No relief aircraft was sent up, and the patrol line was left unwatched for the remainder of the night. The German ships passed through its patrol area between 0100 and 0400.

The third patrol line, 'Habo', was between Le Havre and Boulogne, flying from Thorney Island. The first aircraft flew a normal patrol. The third left its patrol line at 0615 instead of 0715; the Station Controller at Thorney Island thought fog was coming to blanket the base, and ordered the Hudson home so it could land safely. The German vessels passed through its area between 0630 and 0715.

Mechanical failure is excusable, although bad training that defies operating instructions and inability to trace a damp plug are less so. What is not excusable is firstly that relief aircraft were not sent up quickly enough (or at all) to cover the gaps, that an aircraft was brought home early simply because fog might hamper landings, and that no one was informed that the patrol lines had not been kept during the night. Secrecy is largely to blame; those at the sharp end of the business simply did not know that something big was brewing. The Germans had launched a feint with motor torpedo-boats against British shipping off Dungeness on the night of 11 February, to draw off and exhaust British light forces. The bait was not taken, but the fact that the German ships had broken with normal practice and stayed out all night might have triggered an alarm bell if the reconnaissance failures had been noted. Meanwhile the German ships were proceeding up the Channel, hardly believing their luck. Indeed, Ciliax began to wonder if a trap was not lying in wait for them, possibly with heavy units of the British Fleet. Fighter cover duly arrived at 0730, and at 0915, 10 torpedo boats joined the escorting forces. At 1025 the ships had to slow temporarily to 10kt; a minefield laid by HMS *Welshman* had

been discovered after the big ships had left Brest on 11 February, and a narrow channel swept through it. At 1156 the German force rounded Cap Gris Nez, following the channel marked by moored minesweepers acting as marker boats. More torpedo boats, motor torpedo boats and aircraft arrived; Ciliax knew he had been spotted at 1042, but still no action was being taken against his ships.

No less than four British officers spotted that something was up on the morning of 12 February. German jamming was by and large treated as atmospherics, but some air movement was picked up and some of the more modern sets could not be jammed. Naval Headquarters were not concerned with aircraft movement; No 11 Fighter Group at Hornchurch assumed the reports were of air-sea rescue operations, or escorts for a coastal convoy.

At 1016 the Station Commander of Swingate radar station near Dover picked up three large blips at a distance of 56 miles. His report was held up because both his lines to Dover were plugged into the same line at the local exchange; after much delay he eventually got through via Portsmouth. The Fighter Command Controller for the area studied the earlier plots and, disagreeing with No 11 Group, said he thought they might be *Scharnhorst* and *Gneisenau*. No one believed him. The Controller at Biggin Hill reached the same conclusion as the Controller at Fighter Command, independently. He telephoned No 11 Group to say he thought this might be 'Fuller'. No one at No 11 Group appeared to know what 'Fuller' was, so on his own initiative the Biggin Hill Controller rang the fighter station at Hawkinge and asked for a special reconnaissance. A further officer to

become worried was the air-liaison officer with Vice-Adm Ramsay at Dover. He was sufficiently alarmed to ask for a Spitfire reconnaissance at 1045. When told that one was already being flown (the 'Jim Crow' daylight reconnaissances were the fourth line of patrols after the Coastal Command patrols) he rang Lt-Cdr Eugene Esmonde at Manston, and told him to bring his six Swordfish to immediate readiness, and set his torpedoes to run deep.

In fact it was Spitfires that made the first confirmed sightings. The first 'Jim Crow' patrol sighted only normal coastal traffic. The patrol flown from Hawking at the request of the Biggin Hill Controller set off at 1020, and sighted what they took to be a large coastal convoy, but when they returned at 1050 one pilot correctly identified *Scharnhorst*. No 11 Group disregarded this, reporting merely a convoy to Naval Headquarters. Ironically, the sighting which brought the British response into action came from none of the planned reconnaissance patrols, but from Gp Capt Beamish and Sqn Ldr Boyd, who had 'privately' taken out two Spitfires in the hope of finding something to shoot up. They came upon the German force at 1042; standing orders demanded radio silence be kept whilst flying, and so Beamish waited until he landed at 1109 to make his sighting report. One word over the radio would have been all it needed. It says something for chain of command that the sighting report went from No 11 Group to Fighter Command Headquarters, then to the Air Ministry, then the Admiralty and finally to Dover Command, reaching Dover at 1125.

Let Battle Commence

The first shots fired at the German squadron came at 1210. The 9.2in battery on the South Foreland — the only guns able to target the German ships — fired 33 rounds at 27,000yd. The German ships were already passing out of range, visibility was bad and radar-guidance for the guns in its infancy. All the shots fell well astern.

Once the sighting was confirmed Ramsay acted quickly. Five motor torpedo-boats (MTBs) and two motor gunboats (MGBs) from Dover and three MTBs from Ramsgate were ordered to sea (three other modern boats had been damaged a short while earlier and were unavailable). The destroyer force, which should have reverted to 4hr notice at 0700, fortunately was at sea exercising;

Left:
MTB34, a Vosper '73' boat, similar to MTB32 that sortied against the 'Channel Dash'. *IWM A4245*

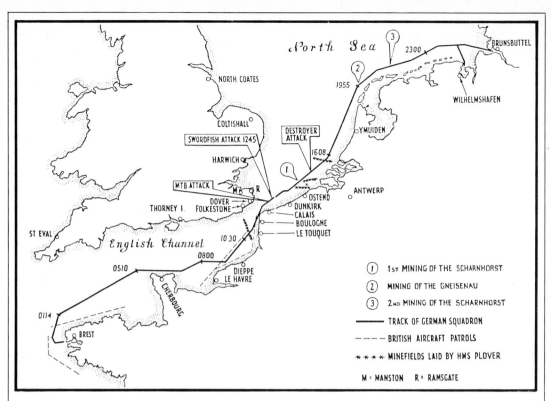

On the map:

North Sea

BRUNSBUTTEL
③ 2300
② 1955
WILHELMSHAFEN

NORTH COATES

COLTISHALL

SWORDFISH ATTACK 1245

DESTROYER ATTACK

YMUIDEN

1608

HARWICH

ANTWERP

MTB ATTACK M R

OSTEND

DOVER
THORNEY I. FOLKESTONE

DUNKIRK
CALAIS
BOULOGNE
LE TOUQUET

ST EVAL

English Channel

1030

0800

0510

DIEPPE
LE HAVRE

CHERBOURG

0114

BREST

① 1st MINING OF THE SCHARNHORST
② MINING OF THE GNEISENAU
③ 2nd MINING OF THE SCHARNHORST
———— TRACK OF GERMAN SQUADRON
– – – – BRITISH AIRCRAFT PATROLS
∗ ∗ ∗ ∗ MINEFIELDS LAID BY HMS PLOVER

M = MANSTON   R = RAMSGATE

Above:

The escape of the *Scharnhorst*, *Gneisenau* and *Prinz Eugen* from Brest — 12/13 February 1942.

they sped off immediately. The six Swordfish had already been brought to full alert, but there was no certainty that Eugene Esmonde would fly them off; in daylight his mission would be suicide, a fact of which he was well aware. He agreed to fly when No 11 Group offered three fighter squadrons as close escort, and two more to go in ahead to attract and disperse flak. The fighters were to rendezvous over Manston at 1220. When the 9.2in battery opened up the German ships were 10 miles west of Calais; a Swordfish strike launched at 1220 would still catch the German vessels in the narrows. Two further squadrons from Hornchurch were to assemble over the German ships, providing 84 fighters during the Swordfish and MTB attacks, which should have taken place at the same time, 1245. A suggestion to delay the Swordfish for an hour-and-a-half so their attack could coincide with that of Coastal Command Beauforts was turned down because it was hoped the Swordfish could cripple the German ships before they reached the shallow waters off the Belgian coast, and because the delay would mean a 2½hr flight for the vulnerable Swordfish. The different speeds of the Swordfish (80kt) and the Beauforts (150kt) would also mean separate fighter escorts. A later start time for the Swordfish would also deprive them of radar guidance on to the enemy, whereas a 1245 attack would bring them over the German fleet when maximum fighter cover was available.

MTBs Attack

Five MTBs and two MGBs left Dover at 1155 and proceeded to intercept at 36kt. British MTBs and MGBs were distinctly inferior to the German 'E-boat', having a slower speed, lighter armament and petrol engines that were both fragile and highly flammable in comparison with the German vessels' diesels. Lt-Cdr E. N. Pumphrey in MTB221 sighted smoke at 1210 (a smokescreen ordered by Ciliax after the vessels had rounded Cap Gris Nez) and then two flotillas of E-boats in two divisions, line ahead with about half-a-mile between the two flotillas. Pumphrey engaged the E-boats at 1,000yd, saw the three heavy German ships through the smoke about 4,000yd beyond the E-boats and signalled a sighting report at 1223, estimating their speed at 23kt. He hoped to cross ahead of the E-boats and attack from inside the screen, but twice in succession his engine failed, dropping his speed to 15kt and his bows almost beneath the waves. Thus crippled he ordered the rest of the flotilla ahead, and got within 800yd of the gap between the E-boat flotilla, launching his torpedoes at the lead ship, *Scharnhorst*, from about 3,000yd. Under heavy E-boat fire and

Above:
A German S-Boat ('E-Boat' to the British). These vessels were never equalled by the Allies. *IWM A29320*

Below:
A prewar picture of the German destroyer *Friedrich Ihn*. *IWM HU3211*

intermittent German fighter attack his boat was clearly headed for destruction in fairly short order, and would hence lose all chance of firing unless he took quick action. Pumphrey and, later, Ramsay were to complain bitterly about the relative weakness of the British boats, and the lack of fighter or MGB support to distract German E-boats and aircraft.

MTB219 (Temporary Sub-Lt M. Arnold-Forster and MTB48 (Lt C. A. Law) had been heavily attacked by German fighters and fallen slightly astern, but fired at a range of between 4,000 and 4,500yd between the gap dividing the two E-boat flotillas, at about 1233. MTB45 (Lt L. J. H. Gamble) had tried to work round the stern of the E-boats, realised he was not fast enough, and fired again between the gap at *Prinz Eugen*. A torpedo misfired so he made a second pass, but this time ran into the German destroyer *Friedrich Ihn*, so fired at her. Again the torpedo misfired, and she was being chased to the northeast by the German destroyer when the two Dover MGBs arrived, attacked *Friedrich Ihn* and laid a smoke screen to cover the withdrawal of the MTBs. MTB44 (Sub-Lt R. F. Saunders) had suffered an engine breakdown (one of the perennial weaknesses of British MTBs, as MTB211 had already shown), fell astern but managed to claw back on the beam of the German ships, 4,000yd away at the time they made a 90° turn to port to comb the tracks of torpedoes from the other MTBs. She fired one torpedo at *Prinz Eugen* and another at *Scharnhorst*, and thought, mistakenly, she had hit *Prinz Eugen*. All four MTBs and two MGBs escaped without serious damage or casualties.

Swordfish Attack

Meanwhile Eugene Esmonde's pathetically frail force of six Swordfish had launched their attack. All planning and exercises had assumed a night-attack. Esmonde had circled for 8min over Manston waiting for the arrival of his fighter escort — only 10 arrived. Feeling he could wait no longer Esmonde set off at 1228.

Esmonde's attack is one of the outstanding acts of heroism in World War 2. He was far too experienced not to know that he was flying to his death, but that did not and could not deter him. His two flights of three Swordfish apiece were jumped by German fighters 10 miles out of Ramsgate, with 12 miles to go. The Spitfires, which had to gyrate wildly about the sky in order to fly slowly enough to keep with the Swordfish, did what they could, but it was not enough to keep the Germans away from the biplanes, which flew on for seven or eight appalling minutes under continual attack, conducting wild evasive manoeuvres and with torn fabric and struts flapping. When the aircraft saw the German capital ships, ringed with E-boats and destroyers all hurling up a curtain of flak, several jinked away as if in shock. Esmonde's aircraft did not, and the two flights crawled on through the barrage. Esmonde's lower port wing was blown off, but still he flew on, until at 3,000yd he was hit again, and

his aircraft plunged into the sea. Swordfish W5983 had its pilot (Sub-Lt Rose) hit in the back and its air gunner killed. Rose still managed to fire at *Gneisenau* from about 2,000yd, then had his petrol tank holed, and managed to ditch 500yd from the German escort screen, where they were later picked up by a British MTB. Both Sub-Lt C. M. Kingsmill and Sub-Lt Samples of W5907 were wounded and their aircraft set on fire, but they too dropped their torpedo at under 3,000yd, and ditched when a burst of fire from *Gneisenau* ripped the top off their engine. The second sub-flight vanished over the escort screen and were never seen again. No one knows if Esmonde launched his torpedo before dying, or if the second sub-flight fired before their deaths; the two torpedoes which were definitely fired both missed. There were five survivors, all wounded, from the 18 men who had flown out on the hopeless mission, and were all picked up by MTBs. The attack was over by 1245. It was almost exactly 20min since the six Swordfish had set off; that is how close the German ships were. The three MTBs from Ramsgate took longer to arrive, made fleeting contact with the screen but could not penetrate it and withdrew.

Chaos was piling on chaos. No 217 Squadron of Coastal Command at Thorney Island had seven Beauforts on hand, but only four were at operational readiness. These set off to pick up a fighter escort at Manston; they had not been briefed what their target was, or where it was. They separated on the way to Manston, and were unable to receive orders because they had recently been converted to voice radio communications, whereas the ground persisted in signalling to them in morse. Their leader eventually landed at Manston, picked up orders and instructions, and set off with one of his aircraft. The other two did not see him set off, continued to circle Manston, and then decided in the absence of anything better to do to tag along with the line of other aircraft that all seemed to be heading off somewhere with at least a degree of certainty. All four made unco-ordinated attacks in increasingly bad weather and visibility, but failed to hit. The remaining three aircraft at Thorney Island set off later in the afternoon; one was shot down by a fighter before firing its torpedo, the other two made unsuccessful attacks.

Unbelievable things were happening with and to the Beauforts of No 42 Squadron, based originally at Leuchars in Fife. Ordered south on 8 February their departure had been delayed by bad weather in eastern England, and only nine of the 14 aircraft had torpedoes. They were ordered to land at the Coastal Command Station at North Coates in Norfolk, but North Coates had failed to clear its runway of snow, so the Beauforts were diverted to Coltishall fighter station, which of course had no

Left:
HMS *Vivacious*, **launched on 13 November 1917.** *MPL*

torpedoes. The Beauforts landed at Coltishall at 1145. The Mobile Torpedo Servicing Unit based at North Coates had been set up to deal with just such an emergency but, unused for two years, its huge convoy finally arrived with spare torpedoes at Coltishall just as the German ships were entering German waters. Thereafter the Unit became known as the 'Immobile' Unit. As had happened with the Thorney Island aircraft, the nine serviceable Beauforts were held back for the five unserviceable ones, for 2½hr. Eventually the nine Beauforts set off, arriving over Manston only 3min late for rendezvous with fighters, and Hudson bombers; the latter were to make a bombing attack whilst the Beauforts went in low. They arrived over Manston at 1453, and tucked in behind the 11 Canadian Hudson bombers as ordered; the delay had at least allowed the Beauforts to receive orders. Not so the Hudsons. They too had just been converted to radio telephone, but no one had told Manston Control, who repeatedly tried to give them their orders in Morse. The Hudsons turned and tucked in behind the Beauforts, and ring-a-roses took place for several minutes. Just as the previous Beaufort squadron had done, No 42 Squadron finally had enough of going in circles, and set off. The Beauforts set off, and six Hudsons followed them, an exact reversal of what had been ordered. They left Manston at 1530; the orders

they had received had been to attack a convoy. No further details had been given. They arrived over the target area at 1600, by now separated from the Hudsons, two of which were shot down and the remaining four of which scored no hits with their bombs. Four Beauforts managed to fire at the German ships, three fired at British destroyers which had just made their attack, and two never found the enemy. None of the torpedoes hit. The final fling of the Beaufort squadrons was made by No 86 Squadron from St Eval. They were ordered to Thorney Island, which they reached at 1430, then on to Coltishall for a fighter escort, which they reached at 1640. None was available, so they set off in the dusk to find the enemy. Two were shot down by enemy fighters; the remainder never made contact.

The Beauforts — relatively fast and modern aircraft with trained crews and the best weapon for deployment against capital ships — were the strongest weapon against the German ships that the British had. Fifteen made contact with the enemy, 10 dropped torpedoes at the German ships and three at British ships. Three were lost, and none of the torpedoes hit. None of the blame for this failure can attach to the crews. The aircraft were held back when they need not have been, and the sent off in dribs and drabs with an obsessive and fatuous secrecy ensuring that they often did not know where they were going and what they would be firing at. Co-ordination was a joke, communications a farce and fighter cover unavailable. The fact that the aircraft made contact at all was due almost entirely to personal initiative on the part of the crews. The day of reckoning for all

Above:
HMS *Whitshed*, a modified 'W' class short-range escort destroyer. *MPL*

Left:
Torpedo attacks by British destroyers.

the bureaucratic jealousies which split Bomber, Fighter and Coastal Command came on 11 February. It was an appalling tragedy that so many brave men had to pay that reckoning.

The Last Assault

If the Beauforts had attacked earlier they might have had a better chance, but worsening visibility and weather severely hampered operations. The weather was a stroke of luck for the Germans and so was the fact that at 1330 the German ships passed, without incident, over a minefield laid by HMS *Plover*. The luck came to a partial end at 1432; *Scharnhorst* was brought to a grinding and wallowing halt when a mine exploded on or near her. Ciliax transferred his command to the destroyer *Z39* with what seemed to *Scharnhorst's* crew to be indecent haste; obeying orders, *Gneisenau* and *Prinz Eugen* overtook and vanished into the gloom at 27kt. Here was the moment

the British had been waiting for: if only there had been an aerial radar picket and a snapping horde of MTGs and destroyers to go in after a massive air onslaught with bombs and torpedoes, they would have found *Scharnhorst* immobile and virtually devoid of escort. Nothing happened. *Scharnhorst's* magnificent engineering branch had her underway again in 17min, working up to 25kt and catching up on the rest of the fleet. By 1500 she was off the mouth of the River Maas, almost two-thirds of the way home.

At 1411 the British passed naval control to the Nore Command, whose destroyers were the only naval force still able to attack. Capt C. T. M. Pizey was in overall command of *Campbell*, *Vivacious*, *Worcester* (21st Destroyer Flotilla), and *Mackay*, *Whitshed* and *Walpole* (16th Destroyer Flotilla). Pizey had taken his ships to sea that morning; told that the German ships were steaming at 20kt, he soon realised from the radar plots he was receiving that the Germans' speed was actually 27kt. He could only hope to intercept them, off the River Maas, if he increased to 28kt and went directly across a minefield. His destroyers were of World War 1 vintage, and lacked high-level AA guns. The 'Hunt' class escort destroyers which might have given some cover could not be got to sea in time and were in any case too slow to keep up.

At 1318 Pizey gave the order to cross the British minefield at 28kt; at least one report suggests the minefield had never actually been laid. Then *Walpole* stripped a bearing and had to turn back. On her way she was attacked by two British bombers which were then chased off by German fighters which 'escorted' *Walpole* for a while, realised their mistake and made off after strafing her. At 1445 *Worcester* was attacked by a British bomber which missed. Then at 1517 *Campbell* picked up *Gneisenau* and *Prinz Eugen* on radar at 9½ miles, and *Scharnhorst* (now slightly astern) a few minutes later. Visibility favoured the British, being reduced to four miles or less. Many German aircraft thought the destroyers were friendly; a number of British attacked their own ships, some were even fired at. *Campbell* sighted gun flashes at 1542, then *Gneisenau* and *Prinz Eugen* shortly afterwards. The British destroyers, in line ahead, turned to attack in two divisions — *Campbell*, *Vivacious*, *Worcester*, and *Mackay* and *Whitshed* — zig-zagging as they did so. They were under continuous air attack, and being fired on by every gun the Germans possessed, from 11in downwards. At 1542 *Mackay* and *Whitshed* saw *Prinz Eugen* steering towards them; she had thought they were German destroyers, and at that moment was avoiding a torpedo from a Beaufort of No 217

Squadron. *Mackay* launched her torpedoes at 1546 and *Whitshed* at 1549, but *Prinz Eugen* swung round to the south and the torpedoes passed ahead. Mercifully a sudden squall then hid the British ships. *Campbell* and *Vivacious* were being continually straddled, and both launched their torpedoes at *Gneisenau* at 1547, whilst the torpedo tubes still had a ship under them. The range was 3,500yd, but *Worcester* pressed on, under severe fire. She was hit at 1550, launched her torpedoes in local control at an incredible 2,400yd, brought to a halt by two hits in her boiler rooms, and was then repeatedly hit for 10min more. The German gunnery officer in *Prinz Eugen* checked fire because he did not want to waste shells on a ship that was clearly sinking; a jammed shell case temporarily stopped *Gneisenau's* fire. No one would believe the story of *Worcester* if it had not actually happened. Torn apart by a succession of 11in, 8in and lighter calibre hits the order 'Prepare to abandon ship' was given, in the chaos understood by some to mean 'Abandon ship'.

Various crew abandoned ship. *Campbell* and *Vivacious* appeared and rescued these men, during which time *Campbell* had to go hard astern in order to avoid three torpedoes launched at her by Beauforts of No 42 Squadron. Then *Worcester* announced she had got up steam for 6kt, by using salt water in her boilers. *Campbell* and *Vivacious* sped off to reload with torpedoes, and *Worcester* began an epic and harrowing journey back to port, losing power twice from her engines, but finally making it home to a hero's welcome at dawn on 13 February. 27 of her crew were dead; only 57 were unwounded.

Bomber Command were the final hope on the British side. They launched a total of 242 aircraft in three waves between 1445 and 1700. Every type of bomber aircraft available to the RAF (with the exception of the Whitley) flew: 92 Wellingtons, 64 Hampdens, 37 Blenheims, 15 Manchesters, 13 Halifaxes, 11 Stirlings and 10 Bostons were despatched in the largest Bomber Command daylight operation of the war so far. Official reports state that only 39 found the enemy and dropped their bombs, but 15 bombers were lost

and many of these may actually have sighted the German ships. The pilots had little or no experience of bombing moving naval targets, inadequate briefing, and because of low cloud many of the aircraft were armed with high explosive rather than armour-piercing bombs. In all 675 RAF aircraft took off to attack the German ships: 398 fighters, 242 bombers, and 35 Coastal Command Hudsons and Beauforts. There were no bomb or torpedo hits on the German vessels apart from one bomb hit on the torpedo-boat *Jaguar* and splinter damage to *T13*. *Z39* was also damaged when an AA shell exploded in an overheated barrel, and splinters holed her boilers. All three vessels limped into Rotterdam. As a final gesture 20 aircraft of Bomber Command took off to lay mines in the approach to Kiel at 2300; none of the German ships passed near them. Mines laid by Bomber Command earlier were, however, to inflict some last Parthian shots on the German ships.

The German Return

Prinz Eugen and *Gneisenau* had become separated as a result of their manoeuvring to avoid the destroyer attack, and *Scharnhorst* had been forced to drop back to 21kt. At 1955, north of Vlieland, *Gneisenau* detonated a mine but suffered only slight damage, and was working up to 25kt after

Below:
The German destroyer *Z28* taken late in the war with her designed armament. *Real Photographs S1863*

only a few minutes. She and *Prinz Eugen* reached the western entrance to the Kiel Canal at 0700 on 13 February. *Scharnhorst* was not so lucky: she hit another mine at 2134, lost her port engine completely and shipped over 1,000 tons of water. It took 50min to restart her centre and starboard engines, and even then she could only limp at 12kt. Ironically, it was in this final stage — and only then — that the German organisation failed. No tugs or pilots were available for any of the German ships, and *Scharnhorst* in particular was in desperate straits. The Germans showed the least interest in their ships when they were virtually in home waters. *Scharnhorst* made her own way in and docked at Wilhelmshaven at 1030 on 13 February.

Mopping Up

There was huge outrage in England at the escape of the German ships, summed up by a leading article in *The Times:* 'Vice-Admiral Ciliax has succeeded where the Duke of Medina Sidonia failed. Nothing more mortifying to the pride of our sea power has happened since the seventeenth century.' Uniquely the Government set up an independent Board of Enquiry, the findings of which were kept secret until the end of the war, and then shown to be a damp squib anyway. The Bucknill Report was presented as a White Paper in March 1946, slapped a few wrists, and left it at that.

For once Grand-Adm Raeder was more right than the British public. Whilst Germany chuckled and trumpeted over their triumph he wrote 'We have won a tactical victory and suffered a strategic defeat'. The German ships were still within bomber range in northern waters, far less well-placed for a breakout. The British could now redeploy much-needed ships and aircraft. The 'Channel Dash' was also the 'Retreat from Brest' but, like Dunkirk, it was a defeat that could be made to look like a victory.

It is easy now to see where things went wrong. The British plan had a rotten apple at the bottom of its barrel right from the start when it was decided that the Germans would force the Channel in darkness. Inadequate forces — naval and air — were deployed, and the operation cloaked with an obsessive secrecy that was wholly counter-productive. The Royal Navy and the three operational commands of the RAF failed almost totally to co-operate with each other. The Army threw in its joker with the exercise 'Tiger 11'. The crucial factor was the failure of the three-tier reconnaissance patrols, because the result of their failure was the British forces being at least 2hr behind for most of the day. Up to the level of Lt-Cdr, heroism, commonsense and initiative were

there in plenty; beyond it confusion and ineptitude held sway. No heads rolled in the British camp, partly because in Cabinet circles, if not in the public eye, the fall of Singapore two days later took precedence. Furthermore, no ships were lost and the British were delighted that the German heavy units were out of Brest.

In the welter of chaos and confusion that surrounded Operation 'Fuller', commentators have possibly failed to give sufficient prominence to the fact that Swordfish, Beauforts, destroyers and MTBs all managed to launch torpedoes at the German heavy units without a single hit being scored. Admittedly many were launched at excessive range but German observers saw at least one torpedo explode as it hit the water. Well over 30 torpedoes were launched at the German vessels. Few if any, however, were of the best type, being either 18in air-launched weapons or old World War 1 models. These inadequate British torpedoes might well be unsuspected villains that deprived the British of at least a consolation prize. That this number of torpedoes were launched points to the real operational tragedy of the day. The forces and the opportunity were present on the day for a co-ordinated attack: fighters to draw off air cover and strafe ships, and either Swordfish or Beauforts to make a torpedo attack, whilst bombers and either MTBs or destroyers made a surface attack. The lack of preparation for a daylight attack meant that no section of the air or surface forces had been briefed to punch a hole through the ring of escorts and open up a path to the big ships. Surely it should also have been possible to mount airborne radar surveillance of the German ships, using the cloud cover that increased during the afternoon, and so concentrate on and pick off *Scharnhorst* when she was left without power and with a puny escort of only four torpedo boats for over quarter-of-an-hour. What actually happened was that no sense of urgency before the action was replaced by a frantic rush on the day, with each branch hurling in its forces as they came to hand. The British threw handfuls of gravel at the Germans when, if they had stopped, compacted the gravel and chosen an aiming point, they could have thrown at least one big rock.

Neither *Gneisenau* nor *Prinz Eugen* ever reached Norway to fulfil Hitler's wishes. *Gneisenau* was crippled by a force of 49 bombers in Kiel on 26/27 February — only a fortnight after her arrival — and was eventually sunk as a blockship off Gdynia. *Prinz Eugen* was torpedoed by the British submarine *Trident* on 23 February, returned to Kiel, and spent the rest of the war in the Baltic, ending her life at the Bikini atomic bomb tests. Only *Scharnhorst* made it to Norway in February 1943, and her story is continued in Chapter 10.

Forces Engaged

Scharnhorst and Gneisenau

Builders:

Scharnhorst — Wilhelmshaven Dockyard
(Laid down 16 May 1935; launched 30 June 1936; completed 7 January 1939)

Gneisenau — Deutsche Werke, Kiel
(Laid down 3 May 1935; launched 8 December 1936; completed 21 May 1938)

Displacement: 31,847 tons (standard), 38,092 tons (full load)

Dimensions: 772.3ft × 98.4ft × 32.5ft

Machinery: Geared turbines, 3 shafts, 157,811shp, 31.65kt (*Scharnhorst*), 30.7kt (*Gneisenau*)

Armour: Main belt 13.78in (tapering to 6.69in); upper deck 1.97in, main 3.5in-4.14in. Turrets 14.17in (face), 7.09in (side), 13.77in (rear)

Armament: 9×11in (3×3); 12×5.9in (4×2 and 4×1); 14×4.1in (7×2); 16×37mm (8×2); 34 (*Scharnhorst*) 22 (*Gneisenau*) ×20mm (10×1, 3 or 6×4); 6×21in torpedo tubes (2×3)

Aircraft: 3

Complement: 1,800

Notes: Extra AA guns were placed on board for the Channel Dash, and torpedo warheads removed to minimise damage if hits were scored on deck.

(For details of *Prinz Eugen* see Chapter 4.)

Richard Beitzen

Builder: Deutschwerke
(Laid down 1935; launched 1935; completed 1937)

Displacement: 1,625 tons (standard), 3,156 tons (full load)

Dimensions: 391.5ft × 37ft × 13.1ft

Machinery: Geared turbines, 2 shafts, 70,000shp, 38.2kt

Armament: 5×127mm (5×1); 4×37mm; 4×20mm; 8×21in torpedo tubes (2×4)

Complement: 315

Notes: The Type 34 destroyers were less ambitious than *Z25* and *29*, but their main armament is sometimes considered to have been too heavy. *Richard Beitzen* (*Z4*) was given a tripod mast in 1940, and a clipper bow in 1944. After being surrendered to the British when the war ended she was used for target practice, and broken up in 1949.

Z25 and Z29

Builders:

Z25 — Deschimag, Bremen
(Laid down 1939; launched 1940; completed 1940)

Z29 — Germaniawerft, Kiel
(Laid down 1939; launched 1940; completed 1941)

Displacement: 2,600 tons (standard), 3,600 tons (full load)

Dimensions: 416.7ft × 39.3ft × 15ft

Machinery: Geared turbines, 2 shafts, 70,000shp, 38.5kt

Armament: 4×5.9in (4×1); 4×37mm, 5×20mm, 8×21in torpedo tubes (2×4)

Complement: 321

Notes: These were from the fourth batch of German destroyers to be built after World War 1, the Type 36A group. They were large, fast, and well armed, but the twin turret intended to be mounted forward arrived late. When eventually fitted to *Z23*, *Z24*, *Z25* and *Z29* it proved unsatisfactory, weighing over 100 tons and helping to make the vessels bad sea boats. German destroyers and larger surface vessels were plagued throughout the war by unreliable high-pressure steam machinery.

Paul Jacobi, Friedrich Ihn, Hermann Schoemann

Builders:

Paul Jacobi (Z5) — Deschimag, Bremen
(Laid down 1935; launched 1936; completed 1937)

Friedrich Ihn (Z14) — Blohm und Voss, Hamburg
(Laid down 1935; launched 1936; completed 1938)

Hermann Schoemann (Z7) — Deschimag, Bremen
(Laid down 1935; launched 1936; completed 1937)

Displacement: 1,625 tons (standard), 3,110-3,165 tons (deep load)

Dimensions: 397ft × 37ft × 13.1ft

Machinery: Geared turbines, 2 shafts, 70,000shp, 38.2kt

Armament: 5×127mm (5×1); 4×37mm; 4×20mm; 8×21in torpedo tubes (2×4)

Complement: 315

Notes: All these vessels were Type 34A. *Hermann Schoemann* was scuttled after being damaged by HMS *Edinburgh* and destroyers in the Barents Sea on 2 May 1942. *Friedrich Ihn* was allocated to the USSR and not disposed of until the 1960s.

T2, T4, T5, T11, T12, T13, T14, T15, T16, T17

General purpose coastal warfare vessels these 'torpedo boats' were launched between 1938 and 1939, and completed in 1940.

Displacement: 839-844 tons (standard), 1,088 tons (deep load)

Dimensions: 269.66ft × 28.25ft × 6.25ft

Machinery: Geared turbines, 2 shafts, 27,000shp, 36kt

Armament: 1 × 4.1in, 1 × 37mm, 5-8 × 20mm, 6 × 21in torpedo tubes (2 × 3)

Complement: 119

Kondor, Falke, Seeadler

All built by Wilhelmshaven, completed 1926-28.

Displacement: 924 tons (standard), 1,290 tons (deep load)

Dimensions: 287.75ft × 27.6ft × 9.2ft

Machinery: Geared turbines, 2 shafts, 24,829shhp, 33.6kt

Armament: 3 × 4.1in (3 × 1), 7 × 20mm (1 × 4, 3 × 1); 6 × 21in torpedo tubes (2 × 3)

Complement: 127

Notes: Based on World War 1 designs these 1923-Type ships were originally classified as destroyers; they became 'torpedo boats' in 1934. A slightly enlarged 1924 Type was built which included *Iltis* and *Jaguar* also used in the operation.

HMS *Campbell* and HMS *Mackay*

Builders:

Campbell — Cammell Laird
(Laid down 1917; launched 1918; completed 1918)

Mackay — Cammell Laird
(Laid down 1917; launched 1918; completed 1919)

Displacement: 1,530 tons (standard), 2,010 tons (full load)

Dimensions: 332.5ft × 31.75ft × 12.25ft

Machinery: Parsons turbines, 2 shafts, 40,000shp, 31kt

Armament: 5 × 4.7in, 1 × 3in AA, 6 × 21in torpedo tubes (2 × 3)

Complement: 138

Notes: Old World War 1 flotilla leaders allocated to coastal convoy protection duties; they carried the World War 1 Mk IV torpedo in their tubes. At this time, they also still carried their original gun armament, like the 'V' and 'W' class destroyers of similar vintage with which they operated.

World War 1 Ships

All but one of these (*Worcester*) were properly modified for escort duties later in the war. *Vivacious* lost a boiler and a funnel as a long range escort; *Walpole* acquired specialised anti-E-Boat capabilities. Their weak AA protection was a problem in the Channel although the temporary retention of a full torpedo armament helped against big enemy ships. The old Mk IV torpedoes, however, had only about half the range of the later Mk IX.

Coastal Forces

German motor torpedo boats — 'E-Boats' to the British and 'S-Boats' to the Germans — were 92.5 tons standard displacement and carried 2 × 21in torpedo tubes and 1-2 × 20mm guns (later increased to 3 × 20mm plus one 20mm/37mm/40mm). The British MTBs used in this operation were as follows:

Number	Type	Displacement	Armament
18	British Power Boat 60ft	18 tons	2 × 18in torpedoes; 4 × 0.303in MG
32	Vosper 73ft	35 tons	2 × 21in torpedoes; 2 × 0.5in MG; 2 × 0.303in MG
44, 45, 48	White 72ft	37 tons	2 × 21in torpedoes; 2 × 0.5in MG; 2 × 0.303in MG
71	Vosper 61ft	25 tons	2 × 18in torpedoes; 6 × 0.303in MG
219, 221	Vosper 72ft	32 tons	2 × 21in torpedoes, 2 × 0.5in MG; 2 × 0.303in MG

MTBs 44, 45, 48, 219 and 221 were at Dover, the remaining three at Ramsgate. This mixed bag of boats included one — MTB71 — built originally for Norway and one — MTB18 — of the original prewar type. These boats relied for support on specialised motor gunboats (MGBs). Only two were available, which had a serious effect on the potential effectiveness of the MTB attack. MTBs also usually carried older and/or less effective torpedoes.

41, 43 MGB 24 tons 1 × 20mm, 2 × 0.5in MG, 2 × 0.303in MG

British Power Boat 60ft vessels being built for Norway and Sweden as MTBs, taken over as anti-submarine vessels (MA/SBs) but eventually used as gunboats. Britain was not intending to fight in the Channel before World War 2 and was having to improvise coastal forces from whatever resources were at hand. As usual, Britain could simply not afford to be strong everywhere at once.

CHAPTER SEVEN

The Battle of the Coral Sea

By the early spring of 1942 Japanese forces had conquered Burma, Malaya, the Dutch East Indies and the Philippines. In addition, they had dealt a savage blow to the American Navy at Pearl Harbor, sunk *Prince of Wales* and *Repulse*, defeated an Allied naval task force at the Battle of the Java Sea, and driven a superficially imposing British Eastern Fleet across the Indian Ocean, sinking in the process the heavy cruisers *Cornwall* and *Dorsetshire*, as well as the small aircraft carrier *Hermes*. It seemed that nothing could stop their forces. Fortunately for the Allies this was a belief held as strongly by the Japanese as by the Allies themselves, and the 'victory disease' of over-confidence was to play its part in the Battle of the Coral Sea where, for the first time in the war, the Japanese Navy took losses without achieving its objective.

Below:
At the heart of the early battles in the Pacific: a Japanese troop convoy at sea. *Bur Mar Hist vd Marinestaf*

Fierce rivalry existed between the Japanese Army and Naval commands, almost as fierce as anything displayed on the battlefield. The Navy itself was, however, divided on the next step: Adm Yamamoto, its dominating figure, realised all too well that the American carrier fleet had not been hit at Pearl Harbor and that the American economy was far better geared to a long war than that of Japan — two factors which made it imperative that the American carriers be brought to battle and destroyed at the earliest possible opportunity. Yamamoto saw that an attack on Midway Island and the Aleutians would inevitably draw out the American carriers, and believed that once this had been done they could be overwhelmed by superior Japanese forces. However, parts of the Japanese Naval Staff also favoured ambitious assaults on either Australia or India and Ceylon. There was also a variant of the Australia option, a sweep southeast against the Allied base of Port Moresby in Papua which was one of the few initial Japanese objectives not yet in their hands. This would then continue and engulf the Solomon Islands, New Hebrides, New

Caledonia, Fiji and Samoa, thus cutting off Australia from the United States and perhaps forcing her out of the war.

An uneasy compromise resulted from the battle of prejudices between and within the various arms of the Japanese military and naval establishment. The Army, anxious not to withdraw troops from the Asian mainland, rejected Australia outright and was hardly happier about the India and Ceylon options. It was eventually decided on 5 April that Port Moresby would be occupied by the beginning of May, with operations against Midway and the Aleutian Islands following in early June 1942. This would both allow Yamamoto his decisive battle, and keep open options in the southwest Pacific, if these were still necessary.

The Japanese Plan: Operation 'MO'

Throughout the war Japanese plans tended to be highly complex; Operation 'MO' was no exception, and it suffered from the weakness of all such plans in that it divided forces and objectives. It was influenced by the false intelligence that the Americans had only one carrier available for the Coral Sea, and by the need to make use of existing forces so as not to draw strength from the proposed confrontation at Midway. No less than eight separate forces were to be involved in the attack on Port Moresby, as follows:

Operation 'MO' (Adm Inoue at Rabaul)

1 **Tulagi Invasion Force** *(Rear-Adm K. Shima)*
   One minelayer, one converted minelayer transport, two old destroyers converted to double as transports, five minesweepers and two submarine chasers to seize and hold the island of Tulagi.

2 **Support Force** *(Rear-Adm K. Marumo)*
   Two light cruisers, one seaplane transport, three gunboats and one minelayer to establish advanced airbases, firstly on Santa Isabel and then the Louisiade Archipelago.

3 **Transport Group** *(Rear-Adm K. Abe)*
   Eleven transports, five Navy, six Army; one minelayer, three minesweepers, one oiler, one supply ship to carry the troops to Port Moresby.

4 **Attack Force** *(Rear-Adm S. Kajioka)*
   One light cruiser and six destroyers to support the Transport Group and command the landing phase of the operation.

5 **Main Body Support Force** *(Rear-Adm A. Goto)*
   One light aircraft carrier, four heavy cruisers, one destroyer, one tanker, to cover Port Moresby invasion forces.

6 **Carrier Striking Force** *(Vice-Adm T. Takagi)*
   Two large aircraft carriers, two heavy cruisers, six destroyers and one tanker to provide distant cover and attack any encroaching American warships.

7 **Look-out Group** *(Capt Ishizaki)*
   Five submarines to form a patrol line across the southern Coral Sea.

8 **Land-based Air Group** *(Rear-Adm S. Yamada)*
   To provide shore-based air cover.

The aim was to trap any American vessels approaching Port Moresby in a sandwich of Goto's forces to the west and Takagi's to the east.

Below:
USS *Lexington* prewar; her closed hangar design was not perpetuated in later US carriers. *MPL*

Top:
USS *Lexington*. Note the huge deck park. The US Navy pioneered the techniques of operating very large numbers of carrier aircraft prewar. *Real Photographs S1253*

Above:
USS *Yorktown*: again the huge deck park is noteworthy. *MPL*

American Response

The Americans had broken the Japanese 'purple' naval code. They knew that a light carrier and two heavy carriers had set sail, saw clearly that an invasion was planned but did not know where, except that it was the Coral Sea area. Port Moresby was the obvious choice. Adm Chester W. Nimitz, Commander-in-Chief of the US Pacific Fleet, could muster two fleet carriers, *Lexington* and *Yorktown*, 141 aircraft, seven heavy cruisers, one light cruiser, 15 destroyers and various submarines; this included a force of Australian and American vessels (Task Force 44) under the overall command of Rear-Adm J. C. Crace RN. Nimitz decided to concentrate all his forces in the Coral Sea under the command of Rear-Adm F. J. Fletcher, their object being to keep open the vital lines of communication between the United States and Australia.

1 May-4 May
At 0615 on 1 May 1942 *Yorktown* and *Lexington* met about 250 miles west of Espiritu Santo. *Lexington* was the flagship of Adm Fitch, and had

Above:
Vice-Adm Frank J. Fletcher. *US Navy*

been the centre of Task Force 11 until the meeting with Fletcher put him in overall command and produced what was now known as Task Force 17. At this time all the Japanese forces were at sea except for the main invasion convoy, which was still at Rabaul, sweeping down in a line from the north on to the position of the American fleet, with the strike force of fleet carriers at the eastern edge. Adm Crace's covering force of cruisers had not yet formed, its vessels still making their way to the rendezvous point.

The American division into separate task forces allowed each Admiral freedom of manoeuvre, but also produced an atmosphere in which each Admiral tended to do his own thing; this was very visible in what should have been a unified task force. Fletcher ordered both the *Yorktown* and the *Lexington* group of ships to refuel, but Fitch's

tanker, the *Tippecanoe*, was delayed and his replenishment took longer than it should have done. He signalled to Fletcher that he would not be able to start refuelling until the evening of 4 May; in the meantime, Fletcher had Port Moresby confirmed as the Japanese target, and received news of enemy vessels to the northwest. Fletcher felt an urgent need to block the Jomard Passage from the south, which he correctly assumed to be the route the Japanese forces would take, and so hurried ahead. Soon the two carriers were 100 miles apart, observing total radio silence and so completely unaware of each other's position.

Fitch actually finished refuelling at 1310 on 3 May — 24hr early — but failed to inform Fletcher. This had the seeds of disaster within it, even more so when at 1900 Fletcher was informed of landings at Tulagi and heavy enemy forces to the northwest. There was a 300-mile wide area of bad weather which stretched almost from the bows of Fletcher's force to the edge of Tulagi, good cover but extremely risky for aircraft to fly through

140

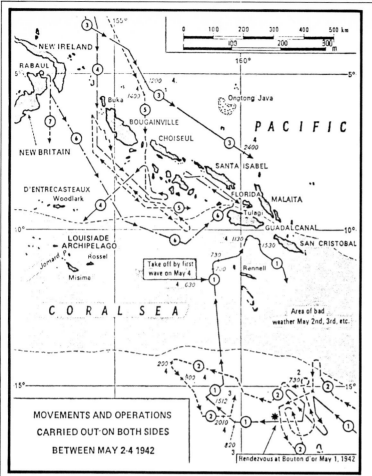

Left:

Movements and operations carried out on both sides between 2-4 May 1942.

Time notes: eg 730=0730hrs (am)

1 Course followed by Task Force 17 under Adm Fletcher
2 Course followed by ex-Task Force 11 under Adm Fitch
3 Course followed by Japanese striking force under Adm Takagi
4 Course followed by Japanese support group under Adm Marumo
5 Course followed by Adm Goto's support group
6 Course followed by Adm Shima's naval group
7 Course followed by Japanese landing force making for Port Moresby

and find their way home. Despite this, Fletcher decided to attack Tulagi, partly for fear of being spotted by seaplanes based there. Fletcher had planned to rendezvous with *Lexington*. Instead he sent the tanker *Neosho* and the destroyer *Russell* to the original rendezvous, with instructions for all his forces to make a new rendezvous 300 miles south of Guadalcanal at dawn on 5 May. He himself set off with *Yorktown* to a point about 100 miles south of Guadalcanal from which he could launch his attack on Tulagi, reaching it and launching his first strike of 11 Douglas Devastator torpedo-bombers and 28 Douglas Dauntless dive-bombers at 0630 on 4 May. At the same time Fitch, 250 miles away, was hearing for the first time of the new arrangements from *Neosho*. *Lexington* made her way slowly to the new rendezvous.

Fletcher was playing with fire: he had split his forces at a crucial time, thus doubling the chances of them being discovered and laying them open to Japanese attack. He had also failed to maintain effective communications and risked *Yorktown* in

an uncertain venture that could just as easily have been an attempt to lure him into a trap. It would have mattered less if in his playing with fire he had burnt some Japanese fingers, but the 'Battle of Tulagi' was close to farce. Most of the Japanese landing and naval forces had left Tulagi earlier, their mission complete. Nevertheless *Yorktown* launched three waves of strikes at the base, and a smaller fighter strike against a nearby seaplane base. For three American aircraft lost *Yorktown's* strikes managed to sink one destroyer-transport, three minesweepers and a handful of smaller craft, and expended vast quantities of bombs and torpedoes in the process. Inexperienced American aircrews told of huge successes, but the truth was that the Americans had hit several times with a huge sledge-hammer an already dead and rather small animal, and in so doing had told the Japanese that an American carrier was in the area. It was lucky for Fletcher that a delay in passing on signals from Rabaul meant that Goto's covering force was too far north to reach *Yorktown*, and that the strike force with its two large carriers was

141

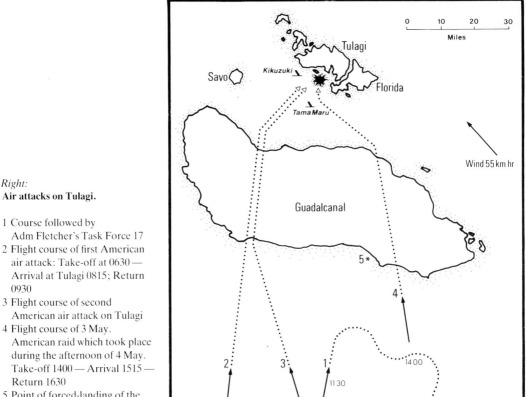

Right:
Air attacks on Tulagi.

1 Course followed by
  Adm Fletcher's Task Force 17
2 Flight course of first American
  air attack: Take-off at 0630 —
  Arrival at Tulagi 0815; Return
  0930
3 Flight course of second
  American air attack on Tulagi
4 Flight course of 3 May.
  American raid which took place
  during the afternoon of 4 May.
  Take-off 1400 — Arrival 1515 —
  Return 1630
5 Point of forced-landing of the
  two Wildcat fighters early in the
  afternoon of 4 May

refuelling when news of Tulagi came through. *Yorktown* retired south to make the new rendezvous.

5 May

Yorktown and *Lexington* met again at 0815 on 5 May. For most of the day the ships were hidden in the same belt of bad weather that had protected Tulagi. A notable first was scored when a Wildcat fighter was vectored in by radar guidance alone to shoot down a Japanese reconnaissance aircraft. The ships cruised southeast, still formed around the original task group designations of Task Force 11 (*Lexington*), Task Force 17 (*Yorktown*) and Task Force 44 (Adm Crace's cruisers), and *Yorktown* refuelled. The vessels then emerged into clear weather and the Coral Sea at the same time, and at 1930 headed northwest, adhering now to the original plan for blocking the Jomard Passage. If Japanese battle plans were complex they had some similarity with the American command structure in the Pacific. One result of a fragmented organisation was that long-range reconnaissance was the responsibility of Gen MacArthur, who had insufficient aircraft to cover his vast designated area. Nimitz had 12 PBYs (Catalinas) that could have helped, but because command areas did not overlap they could not be placed where they could be of any use for the Coral Sea. Furthermore, in an echo of German practice that was to prove disastrous in the sinking of *Scharnhorst*, MacArthur's reconnaissance reports were passed to Brisbane, and only those 'considered to be useful' then passed on to Fletcher. Thus Fletcher knew that numerous Japanese units were heading to Port Moresby, but did not have sufficient detail to plan a major action. Had he but known it, the Port Moresby invasion force was well on its way by 5 May, with the support force and the striking force to its east and west threatening to squeeze the American Task Force in a pincer grip.

6 May

At 0730 on 6 May the three separate Task Forces officially amalgamated to become Task Force 17. At 0830 Adm Goto's support force finished refuelling and headed southwest. Adm Takagi's strike force headed south at 0930. Fletcher spent most of the day refuelling, an operation which

Left:
Vice-Adm Aubrey W. Fitch.
US Navy

Bottom:
**Battle of the Coral Sea —
movements of both sides between
5-8 May 1942.**

1 Course followed by
  Adm Fletcher's Task Force 17
2 Course of Task Force 11
  formerly under Adm Fitch
  before they merged with Task
  Force 17
3 Course followed by the
  American tanker *Neosho*
4 Course followed by
  Adm Crace's Task Force 44
5 Course followed by Japanese
  striking force under
  Adm Takagi
6 Course followed by Adm Goto's
  support force
7 Course followed by Japanese
  naval force under Adm Shima
8 Course followed by Port
  Moresby Landing Force
9 Course followed by support
  group under Adm Marumo

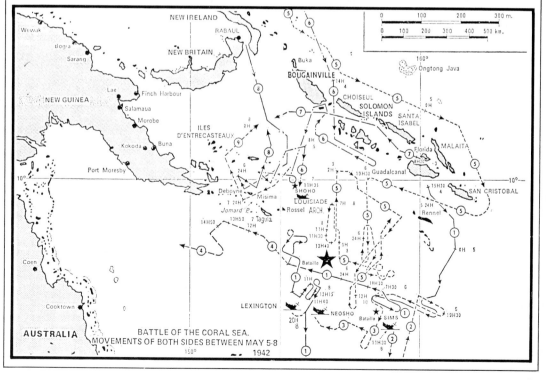

BATTLE OF THE CORAL SEA.
MOVEMENTS OF BOTH SIDES BETWEEN MAY 5-8 1942.

Task Force 17 seemed to dawdle over. Fletcher's reconnaissance patrols stopped only a few miles short of Takagi's group; inexplicably Takagi sent out no reconnaissance patrols, but he might have caught Fletcher refuelling if an accurate sighting made by a land-based seaplane at 1100 had been passed on to him. As it was, the report did not reach the strike force until the following day.

Fletcher was told that MacArthur's B-17s had made an unsuccessful attack on the light carrier *Shoho* of Goto's support force at 1200, and that an invasion force was heading south from Rabaul. Fletcher's aircraft, launched in the afternoon, flew over Takagi's carriers without seeing them. Takagi found nothing, and so turned north at slow speed to refuel when he was within 70 miles of Fletcher's

force. Unwittingly, the two forces had headed slowly away from each other whilst refuelling. Fletcher detached the almost empty tanker *Neosho* and the destroyer *Sims* to head south.

The situation at the end of 6 May was that the *Shoho* Main Body Support Force was on the left flank of the Port Moresby invasion group and the heavy carrier group on its right flank, whilst the Americans were moving up from the south. By dawn on 7 May all three groups would be within striking range of each other.

7 May
Adm Hara with the *Zuikaku* and *Shokaku* fleet carrier strike force has claimed that he felt a premonition of American forces in the area,

sufficient for him to persuade Takagi to break off refuelling, proceed south again and launch intensive air reconnaissance at 0600 on 7 May. At 0730 one of his aircraft reported an aircraft carrier and a heavy cruiser at the eastern extremity of the search area. Even Japanese pilots made mistakes; the vessels sighted were actually the luckless *Neosho* and *Sims*. Assuming he had found the American carrier force, Hara launched an immediate strike of 78 aircraft, starting at 0810. He realised his mistake by 0900 when a garbled report from a cruiser's seaplane put one American carrier and 10 other vessels 280 miles to his northwest.

It was too late to call back his aircraft; Hara could only wait for them to return, and then launch another attack. A single reconnaissance aircraft had found *Neosho* and *Sims* at 0900, dropped a single bomb, and then chased off after bigger prey. The *Zuikaku* and *Shokaku* aircraft eventually found the American vessels at 0954. *Neosho* and *Sims* avoided two attacking waves, but the third wave of 36 'Val' dive-bombers, arriving at noon, landed three bombs on *Sims* which broke in half and sank, taking all but 15 of her crew with her. *Neosho* was hit by seven bombs and an aircraft on her stern. In an echo of HMS *Worcester* in the Channel Dash, the order 'Prepare to abandon ship' was taken as 'Abandon ship', and several crew were lost as a result. *Neosho* drifted until 11 May on which date 123 men were taken off her and she was scuttled. The sacrifice of the two vessels was hardly in vain, as they had drawn off Hara's forces at a crucial time, and allowed Fletcher's carriers a free hand.

Adm Crace's Division

Before *Neosho* and *Sims* were attacked, Fletcher took an extraordinary decision: at 0645 he ordered Adm Crace's Task Group 17, the Australian heavy cruiser *Australia* and light cruiser *Hobart* and the American cruiser *Chicago* with three US destroyers to head northwest to attack the Port Moresby invasion force. The carriers would turn north and prepare to attack Takagi's carriers. His aim was obviously to achieve two objectives — stopping the invasion and attacking the carriers — but he was also splitting his forces, seriously weakening his AA fire for the carriers and sending the cruisers into an area where they would be within range of the massive Japanese land-based air power and have no immediately available air cover themselves. It was a decision that had elements of *Prince of Wales* and *Repulse* in it. It was also a decision that succeeded, and so history has tended to describe it as 'bold', whereas a better term might be foolhardy.

It is worth following Crace's fortunes for the rest of the day. He was sighted at 0810, at which time he formed his ships up into the 'lozenge' formation that had proved to be the most effective against air attack. He increased speed to 25kt, suffered a false alarm when he sighted American bombers at 0940 and 1130, and was south-southwest of the Jomard Passage (where Fletcher had ordered him to) at 1400, when the first wave of 11 shore-based bombers attacked him. In rapid succession these were followed by 12 torpedo planes and 19 high-level bombers. Rear-Adm Yamada at Rabaul believed there was a battleship with Crace's force, was fearful of their impact on the Port Moresby landing group and unwisely chose to fling his aircraft at the vessels he could see rather than wait for the appearance of an American carrier. Remarkably — and uniquely as far as the war to date had gone — the Japanese scored no hits and lost five aircraft into the bargain. The Allies had learnt a lot about ship handling the hard way and the cruisers packed a fearsome AA barrage. Fletcher took gambler's luck, aided by Crace's tactical skill. He had drawn off Japanese forces, was still blocking the invasion and had lost no American ships. He was handed a bonus of huge proportions when the Japanese aircraft that had attacked Crace reported sinking a battleship of the 'California' class, damaging a cruiser of the 'Augusta' class and putting a battleship of the 'Warspite' class out of action; the famed but tired Japanese aviators were making the same mistake as the inexperienced American pilots had done at Tulagi, but the result was that no more planes were sent out from Rabaul, the Japanese considering the job had been done.

The Sinking of *Shoho*

The Japanese light carrier *Shoho* was 30 miles southwest of the invasion force by dawn on 7 May, and launched reconnaissance aircraft just before dawn. Fletcher did the same from his two carriers. A sighting by the Japanese at 0820 gave them, by 0830, the exact position of Fletcher's group. *Shoho* made aircraft ready to repel an attack, but Headquarters at Rabaul was worried by the sighting of Crace's force. At 0900, well before the Japanese pilots had reported their 'success' against this force, Adm Inoue at Rabaul ordered the Port Moresby invasion force to temporarily reverse course. At this moment the cards were stacked in Fletcher's favour. *Shoho* had too few aircraft to mount an offensive and had in any case to cover the invasion force; *Shokaku* and *Zuikaku* had sent their aircraft chasing off after *Neosho* and *Sims*. The Port Moresby invasion force had reversed course, and though Fletcher's position had been discovered the Japanese were in no position to make capital out of it for the present. Then one of Fletcher's aircraft reported sighting two carriers

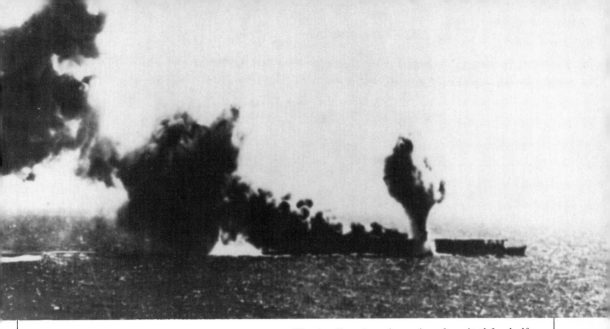

and four cruisers 235 miles to the northwest, at 0815. Unfortunately the pilot was wrong; what he had actually sighted was Rear-Adm Marumo's minor landing group with its two cruisers and light escorts.

Fletcher knew he had been sighted, though he did not know that the main Japanese air strike was headed towards *Neosho*. Thinking he had found the main Japanese carrier squadron he turned north and started to launch a strike of 93 American aircraft from both *Lexington* and *Yorktown* at 0925; this left 47 aircraft (mostly fighters) to protect his own ships which, by 1030, were firmly in the bank of bad weather that had already influenced operations. However, soon after 1030 when the last of the aircraft were on their way, the reconnaissance pilots returned to reveal that the pilot had seen only two cruisers; his sighting report had become garbled because of a wrongly-arranged coding pad. Fletcher's force was committed. He had little option but to let his aircraft carry on in the hope that somewhere, in what was obviously an invasion area, they might strike heavier Japanese forces. One mistake was to cancel another; the leading Dauntless from *Lexington* flew north over Tulagi and was off course when it spotted Goto's covering force, with *Shoho*, bathed in clear sunlight, at 1022. The Japanese were unable to launch many fighters immediately as their aircraft were being refuelled after flying covering and reconnaissance missions.

The leading American aircraft waited for half-an-hour while the remainder of the strike force gathered. The Japanese trusted primarily to gunfire and evasion to deal with the first attacks. Three waves of American aircraft attacked: three Dauntless bombers of the command group, followed at 1110 by 10 Dauntless scout bombers and finally a combined attack by the *Lexington's* torpedo squadron and *Yorktown's* whole attack group beginning at 1117. By the time the main attack went in *Shoho* was steaming straight and into wind to launch her aircraft — a sitting duck.

The first attack was close enough to blow five aircraft off the stern of *Shoho*, and the subsequent assaults hit her with 13 bombs and seven torpedoes. A small carrier stood no chance against hits such as these, and she sank at 1135, her fighters continuing a heroic defence right until the end, and plunging after the American aircraft regardless of their own ship's AA fire. Only 100 survivors were picked up, and three of her 18 aircraft escaped to ditch near Deboyne Island. The Americans lost three aircraft from their 93. The American vessels broadcast the aircraft's wireless traffic over their Tannoys, and so most of the crews heard Cdr R. E. Dixon's famous message at 1130 — 'Scratch one flattop! Dixon to aircraft carrier: I repeat: Scratch one flattop!' It was a momentous event. For the first time American and Japanese forces had met each other in a straight carrier against carrier fight, and the Americans had won. Perhaps equally momentous, though less remarked upon, was Crace's dodging of Japanese aircraft, further proof that Tom Phillips was not entirely wrong, at least with small to medium sized vessels against limited numbers of torpedo-bombers. The Japanese were also not at their best,

Right:
USS *Lexington* in action at Coral Sea; note the aircraft off the ship's bow. *US Navy*

Below:
A Japanese Zero fighter beached on a reef at the Battle of the Coral Sea. *US Navy*

launching at too long a range. Japanese replacement pilots were, apparently, closer to the unskilled prewar stereotype than the highly trained crews with which Japan had started the war. Even at this early stage attrition was beginning to tell on the shallow veneer of Japanese naval expertise.

The American carriers were 100 miles to the southeast of where *Shoho* had been sunk, their 90 aircraft back on board by 1335. The American pilots had reported four heavy cruisers and two destroyers with *Shoho* and though a second strike was prepared and ready to take off at 1450, Fletcher held it back. Prudence was beginning to enter into his calculations. He might miss a chance at the remaining Japanese carriers if he launched at the less significant force, and if he did launch in the late afternoon his inexperienced crews would face some of their journey back in darkness. By this time *Neosho's* radio operator had signalled that his ship was 'as full of holes as a colander', but also given a wrong position which placed *Neosho* (and hence the Japanese carriers) too far to the east.

Takagi was powerless to act when first he heard news of *Shoho's* sinking, his own aircraft being still on their way back from the red-herring mission against *Neosho*. When they did return he faced the same problem as Fletcher with regard to a night action, but his pilots were more experienced and Takagi thought he knew the position of the Americans. He therefore picked the very best of his pilots and launched 12 'Val' dive-bombers and 15 'Kate' torpedo-bombers at 1630, hoping to catch the Americans under cover of dusk. It was always a risky decision, but it had disastrous consequences. Fletcher was actually much nearer than Takagi suspected, and the Japanese aircraft failed to find the Americans in the prevalent foul weather on their outward leg. Disconsolate they jettisoned their bombs and torpedoes and headed back to find their own carriers, without the benefit of radar or homing beacons. They had failed to find the Americans on the outward leg; going back they flew almost over the Task Force, still unable to see it (and powerless to act if they had), but were suddenly faced with Wildcat fighters vectored on to them by *Yorktown's* radar at 1800. The Wildcat fighters shot down seven 'Kates' and one 'Val', losing three of their own aircraft, one which could not find its carrier in the darkness.

The other two Japanese groups headed out to where they thought *Shokaku* and *Zuikaku* should be, and fanned out to find them. What they found instead was *Yorktown*. Expecting to find their own vessels they saw what they wanted, and at 1900 three aircraft flashed recognition signals at *Yorktown* and attempted to land on her. Gunfire blasted them on their way back to their own carriers. None was shot down, but a further three aircraft tried again at 1920, and this time *Yorktown's* gunners brought one of them down. The Japanese took the risk of turning on their searchlights to ensure a relatively safe arrival for the survivors and about 18 undamaged aircraft landed on the two carriers. Recovery was complete by 2100.

A communications tangle was to mar the last hours of American victory. *Lexington's* radar picked up a number of circling aircraft at 1930, and it was assumed quite correctly that this marked the position of the Japanese carriers. However, Adm Fitch was not able to get this message to Fletcher until 2200 because of trouble with the low-power transmissions necessary if detection was to be avoided. Fletcher decided against sending surface vessels in against the Japanese, partly because the force was by now 95 miles away, and partly because he felt he would need his cruisers' and destroyers' AA fire on the morning.

Japanese plans for night attacks were also dropped. Takagi and Hara, unused to defeat, considered sending their two heavy cruisers and destroyers in for a night attack. The idea was dropped when Rear-Adm Abe, in command of the invasion transports, asked for air cover and support at dawn on 8 May. As covering the invasion force was the designated task of the Japanese it was felt that to divert at night against the Americans, who might in any event have superior numbers of surface vessels, conflicted with their prime objective. It was also true that both the Japanese and the American Admirals felt that 8 May would see the decisive outcome to the battle, and neither wished to split their forces in advance of this. The Japanese headed north at 2200, the Americans southeast at 1200.

8 May

At 0822 on 8 May a Japanese reconnaissance patrol spotted and correctly identified the American carriers. At 0915 the Japanese carriers launched their remaining aircraft, 69 in all. The pilot who made the sighting, Flight Warrant Officer K. Kanno, lost his own life when he turned to lead the Japanese strike force on to the position of the American carriers, knowing that if he did so he would have insufficient fuel to return to his carrier. The Americans also made a sighting a few minutes later, at 0835, but the position given was

45 miles out. When the true position was established, at 0930, the strike force from *Yorktown* and *Lexington* was already on its way, a total of 85 aircraft: 48 Dauntlesses, 21 Devastators and 16 Wildcat escorts.

Yorktown's Dauntless bombers found the enemy first, at 1030, and circled in cloud for half-an-hour to await the arrival of the *Yorktown's* nine Devastator torpedo planes. Rear-Adm Hara had been reinforced by two more heavy cruisers during the night, and was now in a belt of bad weather. As a result he split up *Zuikaku* and *Shokaku* into two separate squadrons, each with two heavy cruisers, in the hope that the freedom of action thus allowed would let one or both of the carrier groups slip under cloud cover as and when it became available. This was precisely what happened. Whilst *Shokaku* launched more Zero fighters *Zuikaku* made off into a rain squall and played no further part in this stage of the action. At 1057 the *Yorktown's* torpedo planes attacked *Shokaku*.

American Mk 13 airborne torpedoes were slow, and at this stage of the war both bad at depth keeping and prone not to explode even when they hit. Their only advantage was relatively long range which encouraged the American pilots to launch them too far out. *Shokaku* avoided all the torpedoes, but the Dauntless dive-bombers had better fortune. One bomb hit on the starboard side of the Japanese carrier close to the bow and started a serious fuel fire. Even worse, the flightdeck was seriously damaged, preventing aircraft flying off. This was some return for the sacrifice of Lt Powers who had dived far too low before releasing his bombs, a feat for which he was awarded a posthumous Congressional Medal of Honour. The second bomb hit starboard and aft, and destroyed an aircraft engine repair shop on the lower deck. *Shokaku* was burning, but still able to receive aircraft even though she could not launch. *Lexington's* air group might have provided the *coup de grâce*, but because of the initial sighting mistake and inadequate fuel loads 12 of her Dauntless dive-bombers failed to locate the target, leaving only 11 Devastators with torpedoes and three Dauntless scout-bombers (the Dauntless was used by the USN for two roles — dive-bombing and scouting; in a normal carrier group one squadron specialised in each role. The scouts usually carried less bomb-load than the specialised dive-bombers — up to 700lb as opposed to 1,000lb; the scouts could range 775 miles, the bombers less than 500). Again the torpedoes missed, but a Dauntless scored a third hit on *Shokaku* (though not seriously). *Shokaku's* crew soon brought her fires under control as *Zuikaku* emerged from her squall. She had been hit by three bombs, and suffered 108 dead and 40 of her crew injured, but

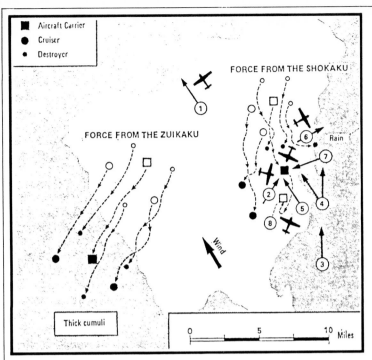

Legend:
- ■ Aircraft Carrier
- ● Cruiser
- • Destroyer

FORCE FROM THE SHOKAKU

FORCE FROM THE ZUIKAKU

Rain

Wind

Thick cumuli

0   5   10 Miles

Above:

Movements of the Japanese Fleet before and after the attack on 8 May 1942.

The blank symbols indicate the position of the Japanese ships at the moment when they were spotted. The filled-in symbols represent the same ships at the time when the Americans attacked.

1 Group of dive-bombers from the *Lexington* lost in the clouds before reversing course and returning to their carrier without attacking
2 Group of dive-bombers from the *Yorktown*
3 Attacking aircraft from the *Lexington*
4 Group of torpedo aircraft passing close to the Japanese Fleet without seeing it
5 Four Dauntless bombers from the *Lexington* attacking the *Shokaku*
6 The *Lexington's* torpedo aircraft gathering in the clouds
7 The same aircraft attacking the enemy in their turn once they had spotted the Japanese planes
8 Position of the *Shokaku* after attack when it had just received permission to return to Japan for repairs

she was still seaworthy. Most of her aircraft were transferred to *Zuikaku* before she was ordered to proceed to Truk at 1300. Ironically she was nearly lost en route when an insistence on too high a speed opened up hull plates weakened by

near-misses, as she was caught in a gale. The Americans lost five aircraft in this action.

The Japanese Attack

The Japanese and American air strikes had passed each other on reciprocal courses, though thick cloud precluded any sighting. The Japanese force consisted of 18 torpedo-bombers, 33 bombers and 18 fighters, a well-balanced force that had been accurately directed to its target and which was acting as a single unit. *Lexington* detected the Japanese aircraft at 1055, at a range of 70 miles. Inexperience brought disaster to the Americans. Despite the fact that Capt Sherman of *Lexington* had worked out almost to the minute when the Japanese aircraft would arrive, Task Force 17 had only eight Wildcat fighters in the air when the attack was detected, all short of fuel and waiting to land; nine Wildcats had only just landed and were refuelling. Aviation fuel taps were left on in order to finish the refuelling, and the nine Wildcats were launched too late to gain height over the enemy. Shortage of fuel meant that *Lexington's* Fighter Direction Officer stationed the Wildcats too close to the American vessels, and to add to what was a rather bad day for him he put these eight aircraft at 10,000ft. The Japanese dive-bombers were at 18,000ft and the fighters and torpedo-bombers at 6,000ft, so the combat air patrol was not able to break up either attack in its early stages. In what was almost a panic measure, Adm Fitch launched his remaining Dauntlesses to join those already on anti-submarine patrol with orders to contribute to the air-defence of the carrier, if required. Unfortunately the Japanese torpedo-bombers simply flew in at 6,000ft and straight over the Dauntlesses, which took on the Japanese Zero fighters in rather unequal combat.

The Japanese attack began at 1118, as usual sending in their torpedo aircraft first. These divided into three groups, dropping to between 60ft and 150ft. Two of these attacked *Lexington*, six aircraft in all, with three converging on each

bow — the classic 'anvil' attack. Launched at 1,000yd, one torpedo hit on the port side forward at 1120, followed almost immediately by another hit on the port side below the bridge. Then the dive-bombing began. A number of the available Wildcats had chased off after the torpedo planes, giving the bombers almost a clear field. At 1125 a 120lb bomb hit *Lexington* on the port bow, landing on a ready-use ammunition box, the other, a 500pdr, hit by the funnel causing more serious damage. Several near-misses shook hull plates and ruptured her fuel tanks and her siren jammed full on.

Yorktown had fared rather better. *Lexington* was just over 43,000 tons fully laden, and had a turning circle of 1,650yd. *Yorktown's* 25,500 tons let her turn in 1,000yd, and with the advantage of being attacked from only one side she managed to avoid the torpedoes fired at her, though one torpedo reportedly came within 10yd of her hull. However, at 1120 a 500lb bomb landed close to the

Below:
Movements of the American aircraft carriers on 8 May 1942.

1 Course followed by the aircraft carrier *Yorktown* under Japanese attack
2 Course followed by the aircraft carrier *Lexington* under Japanese attack
3 Attack made by 'Kate' torpedo aircraft
4 Attack on the *Yorktown* by Japanese torpedo aircraft
5 Attack by 'Val' dive-bombers on the *Yorktown*
6 First attack on the *Lexington* by Japanese dive-bombers
7 Second attack by 'Val' dive-bombers on the *Lexington*

Right:
USS *Lexington*: the fatal explosion. *US Navy*

Below right:
USS *Lexington* ablaze and abandoned at the Battle of the Coral Sea. *US Navy*

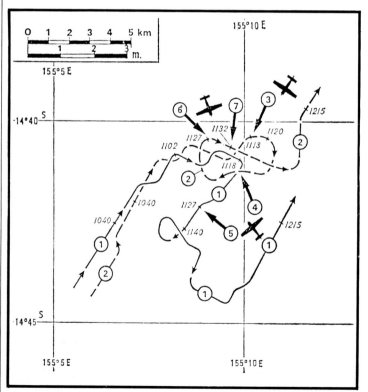

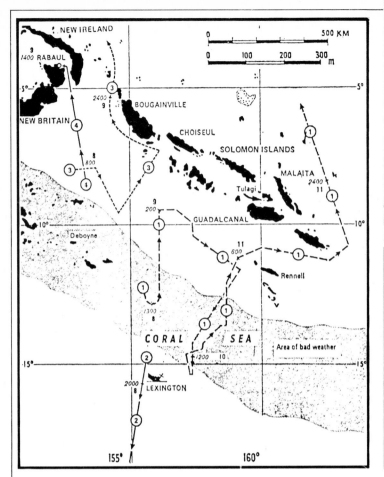

Above:
Movements of both sides between 8-11 May 1942.

1 Course followed by Japanese striking force reinforced by units from Goto's group
2 Course followed by the retreating Task Force 17
3 Course followed by the retreating Japanese support group on its way to Truk
4 Course followed by the retreating close-support group and the Japanese landing forces retreating to Rabaul

island, penetrated three decks and exploded on the fourth, starting a large fire, killing 37 men and wounding 33 others.

The engagement had lasted some 19 or 20min. At the end of it *Lexington* had a 7° list to port, three of her boiler rooms flooded and three fires still burning. *Yorktown*, on the other hand, had managed to put out her fire, and had found to her delight that the bomb damage was near enough to her island not to restrict flying operations. The crew of the 'Lady Lex' responded magnificently.

By 1230 pumping had reduced her list, her fires were out and the flightdeck ready for air operations as she began to recover the strike she had launched earlier. As 1240 Cdr H. R. Healy, head of Damage Control, felt able to make what has since become a famous report:

'. . . We have stopped up the holes made by the torpedoes, the fires are now out and the vessel will be almost back on an even keel in a few moments; but may I suggest, Captain, that if you intend to be hit by any other torpedoes it would be as well to take them on the starboard side!'

Cdr Healy's delight was short-lived. He himself was seriously injured when at 1247 a massive explosion erupted from within *Lexington*. The 'whipping' of the hull from the hits and near-misses had fractured aviation fuel supply lines and allowed volatile gas to seep through the ship. A sparking motor generator had been left running which ignited the fumes, and the first explosion was followed by several smaller ones. Despite this apparently crippling blow *Lexington* continued to

Above:
Despite damage, the USS *Lexington* managed to land her air group at Coral Sea. Here they are seen on deck at about 1500hrs, 5 August. *US Navy*

recover aircraft for a few more minutes, and was able still to steam at 25kt. However, the huge black cloud which now engulfed the ship and the threat of further explosions caused air operations to be halted, and by 1430 the fires were getting out of control. At 1445 another large explosion deprived the engine rooms of ventilation, forcing their evacuation. Air operations had been resumed but were stopped again at 1515, with 19 further aircraft being directed on to *Yorktown*. By 1630 *Lexington* lay dead in the water and the fires were rampaging through her hull, despite the assistance of the destroyer *Morris* alongside. The order to abandon ship was given at 1707. This was carried out with remarkable discipline and control, and is arguably one of the most efficient exercises of its kind ever carried out. 2,735 officers and men were saved, or all except those killed directly by enemy action or the explosions which followed. *Lexington's* torpedo store blew up at 1830. The destroyer *Phelps* fired five torpedoes into her and she slowly sank at 1952 to the accompaniment of a huge final explosion, taking the bodies of 216 of her crew with her.

American pilots had reported sinking one large Japanese carrier and damaging another, but their Japanese counterparts were equally, if not more, optimistic, and claimed the destruction of two large American carriers. This report was accepted by the Japanese at least early on, and contributed to the decision to send *Shokaku* back to Truk. It was also to play a decisive part in the Battle of Midway. What it does not explain is why Adm Inoue in Rabaul ordered the carrier strike force to withdraw, and turned back the Port Moresby invasion force, rescheduling it for 3 July, after Midway. According to his reports there were now no American carriers to block the invasion, and Adm Crace's heavy cruisers were far to the south, heading for Australia. The way was therefore clear for the original Plan 'MO', the invasion of Port

Moresby. That was not the way it seemed to Adm Inoue. His decision seems to have been based primarily on fear of land-based air attack on the invasion force that would now face a much depleted air cover, with the loss of *Shoho*, the withdrawal of *Shokaku* and the serious damage inflicted on *Zuikaku's* air group. Adm Yamamoto did not share Inoue's caution or his belief in the total obliteration of the American forces. He ordered the forces of Takagi and Goto to reverse their course and sail south in pursuit of the American forces at midnight on 8 May, a fruitless search which was broken off on the afternoon of 11 May.

On the American side the two carriers *Enterprise* and *Hornet*, which had been sent by Nimitz in the hope that they might assist Fletcher, were called back to Pearl Harbor. *Yorktown* and her cruisers were together until 11 May, when the carrier separated from the cruisers and also headed back to Pearl Harbor for the repairs that were to allow her to fight at Midway, and die there. At Pearl Harbor, Nimitz had toyed briefly with the idea of a further engagement, but had rejected it as he had only one carrier in the area and needed to gather and preserve all his forces for the major Japanese offensive his intelligence told him to expect. The only incident to enliven *Yorktown's* withdrawal was the sighting of a carrier 175 miles northwest of her position. Gen MacArthur's staff sent 14 bombers out to what proved to be white breakers on a very small island. The incident did little to improve relations between the Army and Navy, which were at a low ebb anyway after a force of American bombers had attacked Crace's cruisers just after they had beaten off their last Japanese air attack.

Significance

The Battle of the Coral Sea has always tended to be overshadowed by the Battle of Midway, and some commentators have therefore felt prompted to make strident claims for its importance. There should be no need for this. It was both less dramatic and less decisive than Midway, but if the seeds of Japanese defeat at sea were to be seen anywhere they were first made visible at Coral Sea and confirmed at Midway.

As with the Battle of Jutland many years previously, the figures for losses do not tell the whole story. On paper the Japanese won a resounding victory; they sank a large aircraft carrier, a destroyer and a tanker for the loss of 92 aircraft. The Americans sank a light carrier, a destroyer, a supply vessel, three minesweepers and four smaller vessels totalling less than half the tonnage, losing 66 carrier aircraft in the process.

The loss of the *Lexington* was far more serious to the Americans than the loss of *Shoho* to the Japanese. However much these figures suggest a naval and tactical victory on the part of the Japanese they conceal the fact that by winning at Coral Sea the Japanese made a significant contribution towards losing at Midway. *Shokaku* and *Zuikaku* were Japan's two most modern and effective carriers; neither were available for Midway, the former through battle damage, the latter through the loss of trained aircrews. A profligate wastage of pilots and inadequate training capability were to bedevil the Japanese Navy throughout the war, and in downing 92 aircraft and their crews the Americans dealt a savage blow to the Japanese. Furthermore, Coral Sea — again like Jutland — was a strategic victory even while it was a tactical defeat. For the first time in the war the Japanese failed to achieve their objectives; they were never to capture Port Moresby, or to venture so far south again. For the first time Japanese forces had retreated; the significance of this in symbolic terms and for the future of Australia was immense.

There were surprising similarities between the two forces. Both suffered from faulty reconnaissance, though Japanese activity in this area was both more active and more successful. Both mistakenly attacked minor targets, and both failed to realise at times how close they were to each other. Equally, the greater experience and skills of the Japanese showed through strongly. American aircraft were inferior to those flown by the Japanese, their torpedoes almost ineffective and their pilots less efficient and relatively poorly trained for combat. Their air strikes were less well-organised than the Japanese, and their use of fighters for combat air patrol inexpert. Their radar proved of limited use, and the weaknesses of US carrier design were shown up. Any US fleet carrier had striking power at least twice that of its British counterpart. Nevertheless a price had been paid for this in inherently more hazardous fuel arrangements. The seawater fuel isolation system used in British carriers might well have prevented *Lexington's* accident. Also, it might well have prevented her deploying and operating a modern air group of 71 aircraft.

The American command structure which allowed Fletcher freedom of action and gave Nimitz in Pearl Harbor an essentially advisory role was preferable to the complex Japanese system with its three elements of Yamamoto, Inoue at Rabaul and Takagi at sea, together with a plethora of subordinate commanders. The Japanese were shown to be weakest when their enemy did not do what was expected of them, and Inoue at least vacillated when his carefully-laid plan began to go adrift. Japanese land-based aircraft flown by inexperienced crews performed badly after their success against *Prince of Wales* and *Repulse*, and the Japanese disregard of casualties which helped create these problems could only make the situation steadily worse.

Fletcher remains an enigma, and his decision to detach Crace's cruisers has been subject to mixed judgements. By blocking the invasion force and distracting land-based bombers it may have swung the battle America's way, at least in strategic terms. It is equally possible that with the gunfire support of heavy cruisers, *Lexington* might not have been sunk. Only two torpedoes and three bombs hit the two American carriers; with figures such as these the effective bombardment which Crace's cruisers had proved they could launch might have drastically reduced the number of aircraft able to reach an effective launching position. Furthermore, Fletcher would have been in deep trouble if the Japanese had launched a night attack; the absence of heavy cover would have left Fletcher's ships open to vastly more experienced Japanese vessels. Apart from the one instance when he cancelled his own planned night attack, Fletcher's policy was simply to charge at the enemy wherever and whenever he found them. Unfortunately they were not always there when he arrived, as happened at Tulagi and with Crace's cruisers.

As a final note, it was at Coral Sea that the Americans found out how the Japanese launched their torpedoes from such high altitudes and at such high speeds. Observers saw Japanese torpedoes being dropped with wooden casing round the warhead and fin sections, which cushioned these sensitive areas against shock even as they disintegrated on impact, thus allowing the torpedoes to run straight and true. Measures were taken to copy the technique and apply it to American airborne torpedoes.

Below:
Shokaku ablaze after bombing runs by American aircraft in the Battle of the Coral Sea. *US Navy*

Zuikaku and Shokaku

Builders:
Zuikaku — Kawasaki, Kobe
(Laid down 25 May 1938; launched 27 November 1939; completed 25 September 1941)

Shokaku — Yokosuka Naval Dockyard
(Laid down 12 December 1937; launched 1 June 1939; completed 8 August 1941)

Displacement: 25,675 tons (standard), 32,105 tons (full load)

Dimensions: 844.8ft × 85.3ft × 29ft

Machinery: Geared turbines, 4 shafts, 160,000shp 34.2kt

Armament: 16 × 5in (Type 89) AA guns (8 × 2); 42 × 25mm (14 × 3)

Aircraft: 72 (+12 reserves)

Complement: 1,660

Notes: The vessels were amongst the best built by the Japanese for World War 2. They were bigger and more heavily protected than their predecessors *Hiryu* and *Soryu*. The armoured belt was 3.5in over the machinery spaces and 5.9in over the magazines; 1-2.2in armour covered these spaces below the hangar. The flightdeck was wooden; it had originally been intended to put both superstructure and boiler uptakes on different sides to facilitate group air operations but above average numbers of accidents with previous carriers with port side superstructures led to both ships having small starboard islands. As was usual with Japanese carriers there were no conventional funnels, but instead uptakes curved downwards on the starboard side to vent fumes. They combined high speed, large aircraft complement and good defensive armament.

Shoho

Builder: Yokosuka Naval Dockyard
(Laid down 3 December 1934; launched 1 June 1935; completed 15 June 1938; converted 26 January 1942)

Displacement: 11,262 tons (standard)

Dimensions: 671.9ft × 59.75ft × 21.75ft (flightdeck 590.5ft × 75.5ft)

Machinery: Geared turbines, 2 shafts, 52,000shp, 28kt

Armament: 8 × 5in (4 × 2); 8 × 25mm

Aircraft: 30

Complement: 785

Notes: Launched as a high speed oiler and named *Tsurugizaki*, *Shoho* was completed as a submarine tender and only became an aircraft carrier in 1942, following her sister ship *Zuiho*, completed as a carrier at the end of 1940. She had no island and downward sloping funnel on the starboard side.

USS Lexington

Builder: Fore River
(Laid down 8 January 1921; launched 3 October 1925; completed 14 December 1927)

Displacement: 37,681 tons (standard), 43,055 tons (full load)

Dimensions: 888ft × 105.5ft (130ft flightdeck) × 27.5ft

Machinery: Geared turbines, 180,000shp, 33.25kt

Armour: Main belt 5-7in, 2in protective deck above belt, 3-4.5in deck over steering gear

Armament: 12 × 5in (12 × 1); 48 × 1.1in (12 × 4); 18 × 20mm

Sensors: CXAM-1 search radar

Aircraft: 71

Complement: 2,122 (up to 2,951 carried in wartime)

Notes: *Lexington* and her sister ship *Saratoga* were probably the most successful conversions by any navy of battlecruiser designs to aircraft carrier. It was thought at the time that her size made her vulnerable, which may have partly proved her downfall at Coral Sea, but it allowed for a very high number of aircraft to be carried, and for the retention of much of the original protection. Unlike later US carriers the hangar was closed and an integral part of the hull, thus reducing its potential size. The flightdeck was made of 40lb steel covered in wood. Original aircraft complement was 90. The 'Lady Lex' bred fanatical loyalty in her crew; as well as being amongst the best-disciplined of the US Navy, many wept openly when she finally went down.

USS Yorktown

Builder: Newport News
(Laid down 1933; launched 1934; completed 1936)

Displacement: 19,872 tons (standard), 25,500 tons (full load)

Dimensions: 809.5ft × 83ft (flightdeck 802ft × 86ft) × 21.5ft

Machinery: Geared turbines, 4 shafts, 120,000shp, 32.5kt

Armour: Main belt 3.25-4in, protected deck above belt 1.5in

Armament: 8 × 5in (8 × 1); 16 × 1.1in (4 × 4); 24 × 20mm (24 × 1)

Aircraft: 72

Complement: 1,889 (up to 2,919 in wartime)

Notes: The three ships of this class were probably the best prewar American carrier designs. Original aircraft complement was 96. They had wooden flightdecks and open hangars; shutters in the side of the hull rolled back for ventilation. (This allowed running up aircraft engines before moving them to the flightdeck thus facilitating putting large numbers of aircraft into the air.) Despite this they also showed themselves able to take a large amount of punishment.

CHAPTER EIGHT

The Battle of Midway

The Battle of Midway was the turning point of the Pacific war, and arguably the most decisive naval engagement of the 20th century.

The Japanese Plan

For the Japanese the Battle of the Coral Sea was little more than a diversion, and one at which they thought they had scored a major victory. It was at Midway that they would finish off the job started at Pearl Harbor. The operation against Midway, known as Operation 'MI', was the brainchild of Adm Yamamoto who had to fight it through against considerable opposition. Yamamoto used his political skills to the utmost, but the vast prestige he carried as the victor of Pearl Harbor and the man whose Navy had won a string of victories for the six months that the war had been

in operation was the factor his opponents could not defeat. Yamamoto was as shrewd as he was aggressive; he knew the United States from first-hand experience, and he knew that Japan's only hope for victory lay in a quick, knock-out blow that would not allow the United States to bring the vast resources of its economy and industry to bear. Midway was simply an excuse to draw out the post-Pearl Harbor remnants of the American fleet and destroy it. At the top level of decision Yamamoto was absolutely correct: a knock-out blow was Japan's only hope, and an assault on Midway — the corner of the whole Hawaiian chain — would and did draw out the American fleet. It was at the second level, the actual detail of the operation, that Yamamoto slipped, and slipped disastrously.

The Americans had so few ships that they had, of necessity, to concentrate them when an action

Right:
Fleet-Adm Isoroku Yamamoto, Commander-in-Chief, Imperial Japanese Navy, and the dominant figure in Japanese naval planning in early 1942. *US Navy*

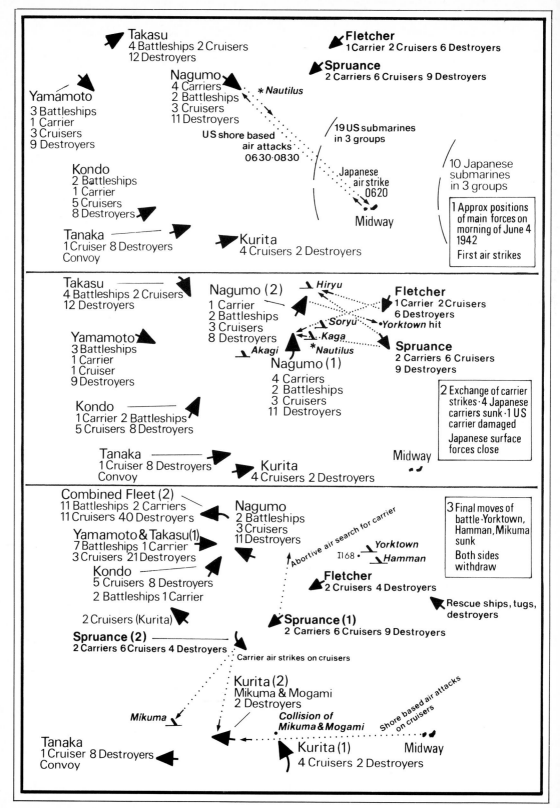

Takasu
4 Battleships 2 Cruisers
12 Destroyers

Fletcher
1 Carrier 2 Cruisers 6 Destroyers

Spruance
2 Carriers 6 Cruisers 9 Destroyers

Nagumo
4 Carriers
2 Battleships
3 Cruisers
11 Destroyers

Nautilus

Yamamoto
3 Battleships
1 Carrier
3 Cruisers
9 Destroyers

US shore based
air attacks
0630·0830

19 US submarines
in 3 groups

10 Japanese
submarines
in 3 groups

Kondo
2 Battleships
1 Carrier
5 Cruisers
8 Destroyers

Japanese
air strike
0620

Midway

Tanaka
1 Cruiser 8 Destroyers
Convoy

Kurita
4 Cruisers 2 Destroyers

1 Approx positions
of main forces on
morning of June 4
1942

First air strikes

Takasu
4 Battleships 2 Cruisers
12 Destroyers

Nagumo (2)
1 Carrier
2 Battleships
3 Cruisers
8 Destroyers

Hiryu

Fletcher
1 Carrier 2 Cruisers
6 Destroyers

Yorktown hit

Soryu

Kaga

Akagi

Nautilus

Spruance
2 Carriers 6 Cruisers
9 Destroyers

Yamamoto
3 Battleships
1 Carrier
1 Cruiser
9 Destroyers

Nagumo (1)
4 Carriers
2 Battleships
3 Cruisers
11 Destroyers

Kondo
1 Carrier 2 Battleships
5 Cruisers 8 Destroyers

Tanaka
1 Cruiser 8 Destroyers
Convoy

Kurita
4 Cruisers 2 Destroyers

Midway

2 Exchange of carrier
strikes · 4 Japanese
carriers sunk · 1 US
carrier damaged

Japanese surface
forces close

Combined Fleet (2)
11 Battleships 2 Carriers
11 Cruisers 40 Destroyers

Nagumo
2 Battleships
3 Cruisers
11 Destroyers

Abortive air search for carrier

Yorktown

I168

Hamman

3 Final moves of
battle · Yorktown,
Hamman, Mikuma
sunk

Both sides
withdraw

Yamamoto & Takasu (1)
7 Battleships 1 Carrier
3 Cruisers 21 Destroyers

Kondo
5 Cruisers 8 Destroyers
2 Battleships 1 Carrier

2 Cruisers (Kurita)

Fletcher
2 Cruisers 4 Destroyers

Rescue ships, tugs,
destroyers

Spruance (2)
2 Carriers 6 Cruisers 4 Destroyers

Spruance (1)
2 Carriers 6 Cruisers 9 Destroyers

Carrier air strikes on cruisers

Kurita (2)
Mikuma & Mogami
2 Destroyers

Mikuma

*Collision of
Mikuma & Mogami*

Shore based air attacks
on cruisers

Tanaka
1 Cruiser 8 Destroyers
Convoy

Kurita (1)
4 Cruisers 2 Destroyers

Midway

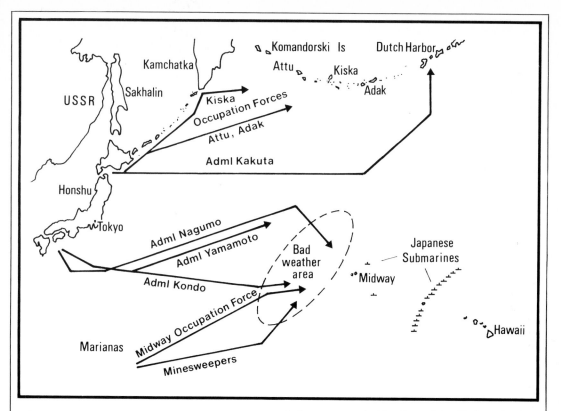

Above:
1 — Sortie of Japanese Forces.

loomed. The Japanese were under no such restrictions, and this was reflected in Yamamoto's plan. Perhaps above all it was the plan of a brilliant military mind that had never had its edge blunted by defeat, or by the enemy failing to behave as predicted. It might have won an immediate distinction as an exercise undertaken at a Staff College, but a less intelligent and more experienced combat officer might have looked at its complexity and its division of forces over a vast area of ocean and wondered if, after all, the human element in it was lacking. In the final count it was human error as much as anything else which brought disaster to the Japanese at Midway.

The plan had the actual Midway landing force sailing from the southwest. It consisted of three elements: the first was a Landing Force of 5,000 men under Capt M. Ota in 12 transports and three ex-destroyer patrol craft. With them were one light cruiser, 10 destroyers and an oiler, the whole force being commanded by Rear-Adm R. Tanaka. The second was a Minesweeping Group under Capt Miyamoto, consisting of an ammunition ship, four converted minesweepers and three small anti-submarine escorts. The third element was a Seaplane Tender Group under Rear-Adm Fujita, consisting of three seaplane tenders and a destroyer. They were to set up a seaplane base on Kure Island, 60 miles northwest of Midway. Close support for the Landing Force would be provided by four heavy cruisers, two destroyers and an oiler under Vice-Adm T. Kurita. Further support would be provided by the Invasion Force Main Body under Vice-Adm Kondo. He would guard the southern flank of the invasion force with two fast battleships (*Hiei* and *Kongo*), the light carrier *Zuiho*, four heavy cruisers, one light cruiser and eight destroyers. The actual occupation force was, therefore, split into three groups; it had two covering groups of warships, with by far the heaviest stationed to the south.

The main group of warships — those with which the Americans would be destroyed — were stationed to the north. One side of the cutting blade was Vice-Adm Nagumo's carrier strike force, consisting of the four carriers *Akagi, Kaga, Hiryu* and *Soryu* (72 fighters, 72 dive-bombers, 81 torpedo-bombers, plus reserves), the fast battleships *Haruna* and *Kirishima*, two heavy cruisers,

one light cruiser and 11 destroyers. These would be stationed some 250 miles northwest of Midway, and pulverise its defences from the air before turning to destroy the American carriers which would inevitably be sent out to Midway. Behind them, roughly 300 miles further to the northwest, would be Yamamoto himself, with the huge 18in-gun battleship *Yamato*, two further battleships (*Nagato* and *Mutsu*), the small training carrier *Hosho*, one light cruiser, nine destroyers and two seaplane tenders. When the Japanese aircraft carriers had crippled their American counterparts the battleship force, assisted by Kondo if necessary, would move in and finish the destruction. Yamamoto also planned to split American forces and divert them by mounting a diversionary attack, Operation 'AL', on the Aleutian Islands. Three of the islands, Kiska, Adak and Attu would be occupied, whilst Dutch Harbour further east would be bombed by aircraft

from the carriers *Ryujo* and *Junyo*; the whole Aleutians force would consist of the two carriers, three heavy cruisers, three light cruisers and 12 destroyers, under Adm Kakuta. Vice-Adm Takasu would be deployed as a guard force for the Aleutians venture, with four battleships (*Hyuga, Ise, Fuso, Yamashiro*), two light cruisers and 12 destroyers. If the Americans took the bait at the Aleutians it was obvious that Takasu would need a strong force to deal with them, but he could also be called down from the north to trap American forces at Midway between himself and the Yamamoto/Nagumo forces.

In addition, three separate patrol lines were placed to spot American vessels sailing out from Pearl Harbor towards Midway, and it was planned to occupy French Frigate Shoals and from them mount a last-minute reconnaissance of Pearl Harbor itself. The total forces deployed by the Japanese were 11 battleships, four large and two small carriers, 10 8in cruisers, six smaller cruisers, 53 destroyers and 15 submarines. The carriers mustered 319 aircraft, and a further 162 aircraft were available from shore bases. The Japanese actually overestimated the force the Americans

could gather in response. As it sailed from Pearl Harbor it consisted of three large carriers (225 aircraft), seven 8in cruisers, one light cruiser and 17 destroyers. Battleships there were, but as they were slower than the carriers — and in some cases weaker than the Japanese vessels — they were left behind.

Despite this overwhelming paper superiority there were numerous weaknesses in Operation 'ALMI', the most obvious being the huge dispersal of forces over such a wide area. The Aleutians expedition was a feint, but it had to be constituted so as to be able to land a knock-out blow if it succeeded in its aim. In this it took away from the main strike forces two carriers and very valuable AA firepower. This main strike force could have been increased by at least one large carrier. *Shokaku* was damaged after Coral Sea and *Zuikaku* had a much-depleted air group, but a transfer of *Shokaku's* pilots to *Zuikaku* would have produced one very valuable and battle-hardened extra carrier; complacency saw that it was not done. The greatest weakness in the plan was its assumption of total surprise: the American fleet would not sail until the attack on Midway was launched, and the carriers would have ample time to pulverise Midway before shifting their attention to a carrier-versus-carrier battle.

There were other less tangible worries. Vice-Adm Nagumo had been criticised for failing to launch a second strike against Pearl Harbor. Officers who knew him well sometimes suggested that he was tired and had lost his fighting edge. His whole carrier force had been in continuous operation for six months without rest for men or ships, and he himself was worried by the poor quality of some of the aircrew replacements drafted to his carriers. The elite force of the Japanese naval aviators was never able to produce the mass-recruitment and training that was so necessary for all-out war.

Other factors of which the Japanese had no knowledge were preparing nails for their own coffin. Masterly code-breaking and Intelligence work gave Adm Nimitz at Pearl Harbor advance warning of the attack on Midway, and in broad outline at least what forces would be used and when it would take place. He was, therefore, able to order out his own forces to a position 200 miles north of Midway where they were unlikely to be sighted on 28 May 1942, when the Japanese forces themselves had only sailed between 26 and 28 May. The Americans had already set up their own seaplane base on French Frigate Shoal, so the Japanese were unable to use it for long range reconnaissance of Pearl Harbor and its approaches; the American ships had long passed over the Japanese submarine patrol lines when the actual submarines took up station. Nimitz also

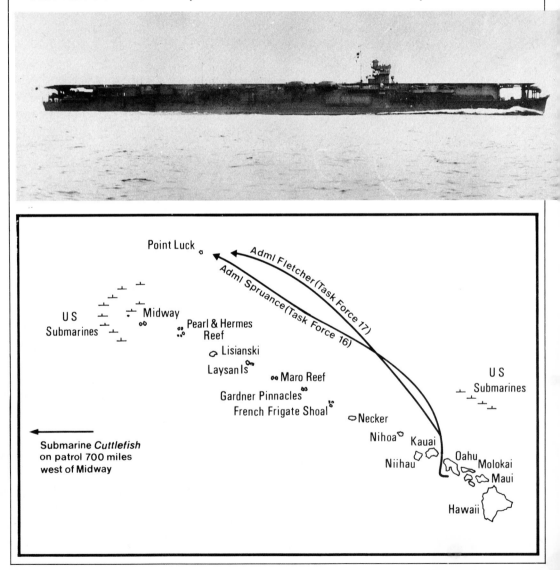

knew enough to ignore the Aleutians operations, and concentrate on Midway, although he did send five cruisers and 10 destroyers to harass the Aleutians operation. Thus even before most of the Japanese fleet had set sail their early warning patrol lines had been by-passed and the one advantage they relied upon — surprise — had been passed over wholly to the Americans.

The American Response

The carrier *Yorktown* had limped into Pearl Harbor after Coral Sea needing repairs that were estimated at taking three months. Instead 1,400 men, working round the clock, managed to patch her up sufficiently so that she was able to fight in a

mere three days. Unfortunately the torpedo-damaged *Saratoga* and two battleships from San Diego were unable to sail early enough to make the battle. The two large carriers *Enterprise* and *Hornet* sailed from Pearl Harbor on 28 May. Designated Task Force 16 they were under the command of Rear-Adm R. A. Spruance. Spruance was a surprise choice, and on paper he was surprisingly similar to Nagumo and, ominously, Tom Phillips of the British *Prince of Wales*. He was an aloof, reserved man with little carrier experience and a reputation of being a brilliant staff officer. He was, however, to prove an inspired choice.

Rear-Adm Fletcher remained flying his flag in *Yorktown*, which sailed on 30 May and was designated Task Force 17. Fletcher had overall

Left:
Soryu. *IWM MH6490*

Right:
Rear-Adm R. A. Spruance — the unlikely victor. *US Navy*

Below left:
2 — Sortie of American Forces.

command, but as was usual this in practice left Spruance with considerable room for independent manoeuvre. Ahead of him lay 'Point Luck' where the two Task Forces were to meet, and 15 submarines positioned east of Kure.

The cause of all this attention, Midway, was two scraps of land only six miles in diameter, 1,135 miles away from Pearl Harbor and commanding the approaches to it. It had been hastily reinforced to a strength of just over 3,000 fighting men, and its triangular airstrip had 28 fighters, 34 scout-bombers, six torpedo-bombers, 32 PBY (Catalina) flying boats, four twin-engined B-26 Marauder torpedo-bombers and 19 huge B-17 Flying Fortresses. However, there were only 30 pilots for the scout bombers, the majority of the fighters were the obsolete Brewster Buffaloes, and even the newer Wildcats were inferior in performance to the Japanese Zeros.

Thus the Americans, despite the disparity in size between their forces and those of the Japanese, had a roughly equal number of carrier aircraft, and the advantages of radar and surprise. The Japanese had better aircraft and torpedoes, and better pilots. Most of all, the Japanese had the knowledge that in the war to date their forces had sunk two Allied carriers (*Lexington* and the British *Hermes*), nine battleships, a seaplane tender, four heavy cruisers, three light cruisers and 17 destroyers, all for the loss of a light carrier, six destroyers, a seaplane tender and a minelayer. Nimitz's orders to Fletcher were as follows:

'. . . you will be governed by the principles of calculated risk, which you shall interpret to mean avoidance of exposure of your forces to attack by superior enemy forces without good prospect of inflicting, as a result of such exposure, greater damage on the enemy.'

History has let Nimitz off a little lightly for these orders, which in plain English said sink the enemy but do not get sunk yourself. Perhaps there was little else he could say.

30 May-3 June
Spruance and Fletcher met at 'Point Luck' on 2 June, 325 miles northwest of Midway, and there waited in tense expectancy, air reconnaissance showing nothing but empty ocean. The Japanese had been under way since 26 May, but their approach to Midway was covered by cloudy weather. The first sighting of the Japanese was made by an American PBY from Midway at 0848 on 3 June, and shortly afterwards another PBY tagged the main invasion force; the first sighting had been of the minesweeping group. Tanaka's invasion force was still 600 miles from Midway, and unable to drive off his shadower. Yamamoto

knew from signals interception that a strong body of American submarines lay in his path, and at this point should have known that he had lost surprise. He pressed on. Nine B-17s flew off from Midway and bombed the invasion force from between 8,000ft and 12,000ft, with majestic splendour and absolutely no success, yet another instance of the failure of high level bombing against surface vessels. This did not stop the Army pilots claiming hits on two battleships or heavy cruisers and other vessels, but Fletcher correctly spotted the group as the invasion force. At 1950 on 3 June he turned his three carriers to the south and headed for a position 200 miles north of Midway, from where he could launch an air strike against Nagumo's carrier force, unseen as yet but almost certainly on its way. The B-17s had attacked at 1624.

4 June
At 0014 the invasion force was attacked by four PBYs with torpedoes. One tanker was hit in the bow but was able to steam on at the convoy speed of 19kt, unaffected.

At 0430 Nagumo's carriers began to launch their strike force against Midway from *Akagi*, *Kaga*, *Hiryu* and *Soryu*, consisting of 72 bombers and 36 fighters. It was at this point that the essential contradiction in his orders became apparent. Nagumo was to smash the American carriers, but firstly he had to pulverise Midway, and as well as requiring large numbers of aircraft a strike against land required the aircraft to be armed with different weapons; the 'Kates' would operate as level bombers with 1,770lb bombs and the 'Vals' would also carry general purpose bombs. He thought he had a day to deal with Midway before facing American carriers, and he was a cautious man. This latter fact meant that he had a second strike of aircraft armed up for anti-ship attack waiting on his flightdecks almost as soon as the Midway strike departed, in case reconnaissance revealed American carriers within range. Despite this the double role his aircraft had to perform was to prove his undoing.

Nagumo also launched reconnaissance patrols: a plane apiece from *Akagi* and *Kaga* to search to the south, and seaplanes from the heavy cruisers *Chikuma* and *Tone* to search for 300 miles to the east. The American fleet lay firmly within the search arc of *Tone's* second aircraft. The first departed at 0442, but the second was delayed for half-an-hour by a catapult fault. This apparently insignificant error was to have far-reaching results.

It was a PBY that first sighted the Japanese carriers, at 0520. It then played a hair-raising cat and mouse game with Japanese Zeros amongst the cloud, signalling to Fletcher at 0534 'enemy carriers in sight', following this by a report of 'many' aircraft heading for Midway. The first signal was certainly not the most misleading of the war, but it must have been one of the most infuriating; it did not tell Fletcher where the carriers were, or how many of them there were, and the PBY was obviously in a position to be shot down at any minute without giving this essential information. Finally, at 0603, details of course and composition were received. *Yorktown* still had 10 reconnaissance aircraft in the air. In his urgency to get to grips with the Japanese carriers before they could reach him, Fletcher ordered *Enterprise* and *Hornet* to detach, head southwest and 'attack enemy carriers when definitely located'. The Japanese carriers were 200 miles west-southwest of *Yorktown*, Midway itself 240 miles to her south. *Yorktown* would race to catch up once she had recovered her aircraft, but Fletcher's massive urgency demanded that *Enterprise* and *Hornet* steam near enough to launch an attack against the Japanese carriers before they in their turn spotted his ships; Spruance and his carriers turned away to the southwest at 0607.

The Attack on Midway

In the midst of all this excitement at sea, Midway picked up the incoming Japanese strike on radar at 0553, and immediately scrambled every available aircraft. The bombers rose and set off to attack the Japanese carrier force. Eighteen Marine Corps Dauntless scout-bombers were followed by 12 Vindicator scout-bombers; two Dauntless and one Vindicator had to abort their missions. The Dauntless was a relatively modern plane, but the accidental destruction of much of Midway's aviation fuel meant that the Dauntless pilots had clocked up a few bare hours on the aircraft. The Vindicators were obsolete and slow. Four Army Martin Marauder twin-engined bombers then took off, each armed with a 21in torpedo. Sixteen Flying Fortresses had already taken off before dawn; six new Grumman Avenger torpedo-bomber aircraft were also available. Midway's operational fighters, 18 obsolete Brewster Buffaloes and eight Wildcats, rose to break up the incoming Japanese strike. One had to return with engine trouble, the rest engaged the enemy.

It was a confused and murderous air battle — the Midway fighters suffered severely. For all their courage and hopeless heroism the Japanese Zero fighters were faster, more manoeuvrable and better armed than the American fighters, which were ruthlessly cut up before they could reach most of the bombers. Of the 25 American fighters, 13 were shot down and seven more so badly damaged as to be written off. The Japanese lost 11 aircraft, probably mostly to ground fire; three

more were write-offs. The bombers had missed their main target, Midway's bombers. They turned to bomb hangars, oil tanks and power installations, doing severe damage but leaving the runway still usable.

The Japanese strike leader, Lt Tomonaga, surveyed the damage done to Midway, and at 0700 advised Nagumo that a second strike was necessary. The next 15min were to decide the course of the whole battle. While Adm Nagumo hesitated over sending a second strike against Midway, Spruance was starting to launch his air strike against the Japanese carriers. He had taken one of the most momentous decisions of the battle. He would not reach his ideal flying-off position for another 2hr, at 0900, but his calculations revealed that if he launched 2hr early at the extreme range of his aircraft he might catch Nagumo's carriers at their most vulnerable time, when they were landing on and refuelling the aircraft which had flown against Midway. This was one of the most brilliant pieces of operational judgement of the Pacific War. Spruance started to launch at 0702, knowing as he did so that many of his aircraft would not make it back to his carriers and would have to try and land on Midway. *Hornet* launched all but one of her Dauntlesses, 35 each with a 500lb bomb, 15 Devastator torpedo-bombers and an escort of 10 Wildcat fighters. *Enterprise* launched 15 Dauntless dive-bombers with 1,000lb bombs, 17 Dauntless scouts with 1×500lb and 2×100lb bombs, 14 Devastators and 10 more Wildcats, a total of 116 aircraft. Here at last was the vindication of those who had fought in the prewar years for large carriers and the aircraft to put on them.

However, not all problems of launching such a massive strike had been solved. It took over half-an-hour for this armada to launch and assemble in the air, and before all the aircraft had been launched the Americans were forced to commit their forces piecemeal. First went *Enterprise's* dive-bombers under Lt-Cdr C. W. McClusky, which had been launched first as they required the full length of the flightdeck. Their restricted endurance meant that they could not hang around the carriers for long. *Hornet* managed a more co-ordinated launch, although the strike soon strung out into two groups — one of Dauntlesses under Cdr S. C. Ring with the Wildcat escort, and a second of torpedo planes (Lt-Cdr J. C. Waldron).

Distance and cloud had disastrous consequences for the cohesion of the group. The fighters from *Enterprise*, led by Lt J. S. Gray were above but out of contact with Waldron's *Hornet* torpedo squadron. *Hornet's* fighters never made contact with Waldron either, and so ended up escorting their own dive-bombers. Lindsey's *Enterprise* torpedo

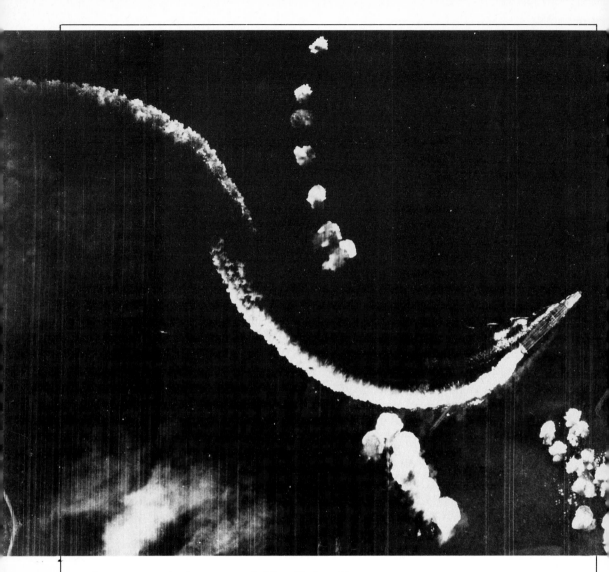

squadron was completely unescorted. Thus Task Force 16's aircraft advanced in four separate groups, all independent of each other: McClusky's dive-bombers, *Hornet's* dive-bombers and fighters, *Hornet's* torpedo squadron and *Enterprise's* torpedo squadron. Despite the need to escort the vulnerable torpedo squadrons, these were the ones that ended up with no escort at all.

However, if there was confusion on the American side it was matched by the Japanese. It will be remembered that Nagumo had a torpedo-armed strike ready to launch on his flightdecks, but at 0700 had received the news that Midway needed a second strike. As he was agonising over whether to strike his aircraft below for rearming, the first wave of American aircraft from Midway came into view at 0705. The first wave consisted of six Avenger and four Marauder torpedo-bombers.

Only one Avenger and two Marauders escaped; the remainder were cut to ribbons by the Zero fighters or AA fire, and the few which launched their torpedoes all missed. The strike did have one effect: it persuaded Nagumo that a second strike against Midway was justified, and at 0715 he ordered the torpedo-armed 'Kates' on *Kaga* and *Akagi* to be struck down and rearmed with bombs. This was a lengthy and laborious process. It had hardly been started when the 'Jake' seaplane launched half-an-hour late from *Tone* radioed a bombshell at 0728: 'Sighted estimated 10 enemy surface ships bearing 10° distant 240 miles from Midway. Course 150°, speed over 20kt.' That was all. It was the first news of any sort that Nagumo had received of American surface vessels in the area. But did the American force contain carriers? At 0747 he signalled tersely to the 'Jake': 'Ascertain ship types and maintain contact'. But he was already in trouble. He had an American squadron on his flank and closing, his decks cluttered still with second wave aircraft and his hangars full of aircraft being rearmed, a returning air strike due to land on and a need to fly off fighters to replace those lost or short of fuel as a result of the recent combat. If the American force contained no carriers he could recover his first strike, launch a second against Midway and have the first strike rearmed and ready to hit the American ships before they came within gun or torpedo range; but if the Americans did have carriers then 200 miles was already far too close, and a torpedo-armed strike was a matter of maximum urgency. Furious signals were sent out to *Tone's* plane to identify the American ships; nothing was heard. Agonised, Nagumo finally ordered a halt to the rearming, which was now half complete. Nagumo ordered an attack on the American squadron by the half of his aircraft which still had torpedoes slung beneath them. Before that strike could be launched further trouble hit Nagumo in the form of the remainder of the Midway aircraft: 16 Dauntless dive-bombers flew in, using glide rather than dive-bombing techniques because of the crews' lack of training. Only eight dive-bombers returned to Midway, two of those so damaged as to be useless, and one with no less than 259 bullet holes in it. Again all the aircraft missed their target, but the attack was much closer than the torpedo onslaught had been, with nine or 10 bombers launching their bombs, and for a heart-stopping moment it looked as if the carrier *Hiryu*, the centre of the attack, had been hit. Then the huge B-17s sailed over at 20,000ft, 16 of them. This time their bombs came closer, but again — despite no less than 108 being dropped — there were no hits; the pilots nonetheless reported that two carriers had been hit.

Having survived these attacks with no losses, Nagumo must have been a very relieved man when the *Tone's* floatplane finally signalled at 0809 'enemy is composed of five cruisers and five destroyers'. This argued clearly for available aircraft to launch a second strike against Midway, and the returning first strike to rearm and go out against the American ships. He was to have 11min of jubilation remaining to him; even those minutes were reduced in intensity — if not in length — when the final stones in Midway's sling were flung

at him, in the shape of 11 aged Vindicator dive-bombers. Zeros and AA fire pushed most of these over on to the battleship *Haruna*, but no hits were scored. Nine Vindicators survived the attack.

The Bells Toll

At 0820 the *Tone* floatplane signalled the news that spelt doom for the Japanese carriers, and which Nagumo had been dreading: 'The enemy is accompanied by what appears to be a carrier'. To add to his problems the American submarine *Nautilus* chose that moment to pop up her periscope bang in the middle of a sizeable portion of the Japanese battlefleet just as it was manoeuvring wildly to avoid the Vindicator attacks. *Nautilus* fired at the battleship *Kirishima*, dived and was heavily depth-charged. The destroyer left behind to sink the submarine, the *Arashi*, was to play an unwitting and decisive part in the later action.

Thus Nagumo had to take his decisions amidst the crash of exploding depth charges. He was in the most agonising situation of any modern naval commander; he had first of all armed his second wave with torpedoes, then changed this to bombs at 0715. At 0745 he had changed these and ordered the remaining aircraft with torpedoes to set off against the reported American ships. Before any action could be taken, his ships had been repeatedly attacked and then a signal stating there were no American carriers had caused him to relax. At 0820 he learnt of an American carrier, and knew that a strike from it must even then be heading towards him. Yet by this time his situation was even more complicated, because at 0830 he sighted his own first Midway strike force returning. Some of these aircraft were damaged, all were short of fuel. If he delayed their landing-on by launching the torpedo planes he had, many of the Midway first strike would be lost and have to ditch. If he sent off the dive-bombers and torpedo-carrying aircraft that he did have available from *Hiryu* and *Soryu*, which had been less heavily involved in the Midway strike, they would be virtually without fighter cover. The fighters with the Midway force and those which had been defending his ships against the American land-based attacks were reaching the end of their endurance; with an incoming American strike probably headed his way he could not denude himself of an effective combat air patrol to escort an attack on the American ships.

The second-in-command of the carrier force, Rear-Adm Yamaguchi, argued desperately for a makeshift strike to be launched against the American carrier from *Soryu* and *Hiryu*: but soon after 0830 Nagumo made his fateful decision. The Midway strike force would be recovered in its

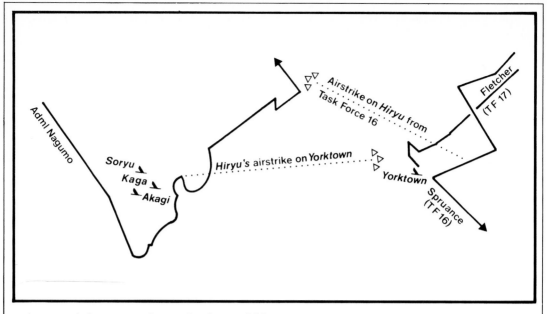

Adml Nagumo

Soryu
Kaga
Akagi

Hiryu's airstrike on Yorktown

Airstrike on Hiryu from
Task Force 16

Fletcher
(TF 17)

Yorktown

Spruance
(TF 16)

Above:
3 — Turning of the tide.

entirety, and then a complete strike force of 36 dive-bombers, 54 torpedo-bombers and 12 Zeros would be launched against the American ships at 1030. It is easy to see his reasoning: he was already suffering from a shortage of trained pilots and, with a carrier battle looming, simply could not afford to throw away pilots and aircraft by failing to recover the Midway strike. He had seen what had happened to unprotected bombers and torpedo-bombers when his own fighters had made mincemeat of the unescorted aircraft from Midway; if there was only one American carrier, his success earlier in the day must have helped him believe that his massive flak and superb fighters could brush its attack aside, and allow his carriers to mount a massive and decisive counter-strike. Nagumo took exactly the opposite view to Spruance, who put speed of attack before all thoughts of co-ordination and precision, and flung his aircraft at the Japanese regardless of likely losses. It was a strange reversal of roles for the Japanese Navy to be so cautious of its pilots and aircrew.

It is also easy to see what Nagumo should have done. Immediately on hearing of the American carrier he should have launched whatever he had against it from *Hiryu* and *Soryu*. Better still, he should have always kept one — or even two — of his carriers for a strictly anti-shipping role, having them ready to launch a strike at a moment's notice regardless of Midway. He took his obligations towards the landing too seriously, and believed far too implicitly that American carriers would not be waiting for him off Midway. As a result of his decisions Nemesis had bought its ticket, and was due to arrive over his head at 0928.

Yorktown

Yorktown had sent *Enterprise* and *Hornet* on ahead so that she could recover her reconnaissance aircraft. At 0838 Fletcher launched from *Yorktown* 17 dive-bombers (Lt-Cdr M. F. Leslie), 12 torpedo-bombers (Lt-Cdr L. E. Massey) and six Wildcats (Lt-Cdr J. S. Thatch). Fletcher was beset by a fear of an unknown Japanese force that might have remained undiscovered, and so kept his scout-bombers back to mount a small second strike. It is interesting to note that the two most experienced commanders on each side, old enemies from Coral Sea, were the ones who showed the most caution.

The American Attack

Between 0837 and 0918 Nagumo's carriers recovered the Midway strike force and readied their second anti-shipping wave, the last aircraft from the Midway strike landing on *Akagi* at 0918. Frantic preparations were underway to get the second wave airborne, and as more and more aircraft began to appear on the flightdecks, fully fuelled and armed, it must have seemed as if the Japanese were going to make it after all. Then, from 0905 onwards, reports began to come in from combat air patrols of large numbers of carrier aircraft heading towards the Japanese fleet. Nagumo had signalled earlier to *Yamato*, a confusing and confused report which nevertheless told Yamamoto of the existence of an American carrier and Nagumo's intention to attack it. Yamamoto was, however, too far away to be of any assistance. The luckless pilot of *Tone's* floatplane had signalled hopefully 'I am homeward bound', but had been sternly ordered by his captain to overstay his endurance and maintain contact. These mattered little. At 0918 Nagumo turned his carriers from southeast to north-northwest and cracked on speed to close with the American carrier and attack it. It was too late.

Nagumo's change of course threw at least some of the American aircraft into confusion. The four separated air groups from Task Force 16 (*Enterprise* and *Hornet*) arrived at Nagumo's estimated position and found nothing. *Hornet's* dive-bombers gambled on Nagumo having turned towards Midway, followed a southeasterly course and missed contact completely. Some aircraft landed on Midway, some back on *Hornet*; the fighters were all forced to ditch. Lindsey and Waldron's torpedo squadrons, VT-6 and VT-8 respectively, saw smoke to the north, turned towards it and sighted the Japanese carriers at shortly before 0930. Lt Gray, *Enterprise's* fighter escort leader, was flying high so as both to protect the Dauntlesses and to gain some advantage over the Zeros. He was, however, looking for the vulnerable torpedo-bombers to support if required and found *Hornet's* aircraft, not his own. VT-6 had arranged to call down Gray's fighters when it launched its attack, but VT-8 could not so so due to a different radio frequency. Gray, circling above in the clouds, out of range of VT-6, thus never knew either torpedo attack was about to take place. First to go in was Waldron's VT-8 from *Hornet*. It was a suicide run — and Waldron knew — as was clear from messages he left before the battle. Eight miles out, and before he was in effective flak range, he had lost four of his 15 aircraft to the 50 or more Zeros that were in the air. Five more of the lumbering aircraft went within minutes, then three more. Only the last aircraft, piloted by Ensign G. Gay, made it to launch position, dropped its torpedo at a carrier (it missed) and then belly-flopped, leaving Gay to swim clear. He was the only survivor from 30 men.

Then it was the turn of VT-6's 14 aircraft from *Enterprise*. Lindsey was attacking a fully-alerted enemy, and he had to waste valuable minutes working round to a new attack position to compensate for the gaps opening up in the Japanese carrier's tight box formation. The Devastators were intercepted five miles out, in two wedges trying to attack *Akagi* from either side of the bow. One by one they toppled until only about seven managed to launch their torpedoes, surprisingly at *Hiryu* rather than *Akagi*. Both carriers avoided being hit; miraculously four aircraft made it back to *Enterprise*. Lindsey was not amongst the

survivors. The cordite smoke had hardly had time to clear from the decks when at 1000 Massey's 12 torpedo planes from *Yorktown* started their attack. It should have been a co-ordinated attack in company with the same carrier's 17 dive-bombers and six Wildcats. They had set out an hour-and-a-quarter after the Task Force 16 aircraft but had steered a more northerly and accurate course, so making up lost time. However, when the combined strike force first sighted the Japanese they veered hard right, the bombers climbing high above the torpedo-planes, hitting cloud and losing both visual and radio contact. Massey's torpedo squadron, VT-3, at least had six Wildcats with them, but the Zeros overwhelmed these: only five of VT-3 made it to launch point. None of their torpedoes hit, and only two aircraft made it back to *Yorktown*.

However, as *Yorktown's* dive-bombers clawed their way upwards they met McClusky's dive-bombers from *Enterprise*. They too had arrived to find empty sea, but had then seen the destroyer *Arashi* heading at full speed back to the main fleet after trying to put down *Nautilus*. By following her, McClusky had arrived over the Japanese carriers arriving from the southwest, whilst Leslie's force came in from the southeast. McClusky had 32 bombers, Leslie 17, though Leslie's aircraft and three others had inadvertently jettisoned their 1,000lb bombs when an electrical arming device malfunctioned.

It was 1027 when Leslie's *Yorktown* dive-bombers launched their attack on *Kaga*. The Japanese had completed rearming; their strike was on the flightdecks ready to start flying off at 1030. The carriers were at their most vulnerable, their fully-armed and fuelled aircraft a damage control nightmare if they were to be hit. The hopeless torpedo attacks had not been in vain. They had drawn the Zero fighter cover down virtually to ground level, leaving the dive-bombers a clear and unimpeded run down on to the carriers. With no radar to provide early warning, proper fighter control was an impossible task for the Japanese. Both visual lookouts and fighter pilots were understandably distracted by the torpedo-bombers: it would have taken almost superhuman self-control not to have been. In these circumstances, concerns about the presence of hypothetical threats — however likely — were all too easily forgotten. However, where there were torpedo-bombers, there might well also be dive-bombers . . .

There is still no complete certainty about which aircraft attacked which carriers; the latter had lost their formation avoiding torpedoes and were probably in rough line ahead. The most likely answer is that Leslie's *Yorktown* bombers for the most part hit *Soryu*, *Enterprise's* dive-bombers

Kaga, and scout-bombers *Akagi*; *Hiryu* had become separated to the north, and so was not attacked. It was 1024: in 6min the Japanese carriers would start launching their strike, massed on deck now and fully fuelled and armed. It seems probable that refuelling and rearming of the first strike was still taking place in the hangars below. Then the scream of the bombers was heard and, taken totally by surprise, the Japanese looked up in horror.

McClusky led his dive-bombers down on *Kaga* but he and his first two companions, missed the target. The following Dauntlesses had better luck. The first 1,000lb bomb hit on the starboard quarter among 'Kates' waiting to be launched. The next two were near *Kaga's* island, exploding a petrol bowser in a sheet of flame and killing all those on the bridge. The fourth hit in the middle of the flightdeck. It, and the other bombs, ploughed through the deck and its crowded aircraft and into the hangars; the carrier was a blazing wreck within seconds. She still took until 1925 to sink, but was a dead vessel for many hours before this.

With *Kaga* clearly done for, the last of *Enterprise's* dive-bombers joined the scouts in diving on the flagship, *Akagi*. The first bomb plunged into the midships lift, igniting bombs and torpedoes which had not been stowed away due to the hurried rearming; the effect was devastating. A second hit was scored on the port side of the

flightdeck aft; many of the pilots — already in their aircraft — burnt alive whilst inside them, unable to escape. *Akagi* was dead. Adm Nagumo had to be almost forcibly led from the smoking bridge as explosion after explosion rumbled through the ship, and only with great difficulty did he transfer to the light cruiser *Nagura*. As with *Kaga*, *Akagi* lingered on, a gutted hulk. Her entire engine room crew, unhit but trapped, went down with her when Yamamoto finally allowed her to be torpedoed at dawn on 5 June (0455). He had earlier refused permission, hoping against hope that the ship could be saved.

Soryu fared no better. Leslie, without his bomb, led his squadron down on a strafing run. *Yorktown's* Dauntlesses hit her at 1026 with a bomb that smashed through the centre of the flightdeck just before the forward lift, exploding in the hangar and threw the massive lift floor against the island. Two more bombs hit aft, and the same appalling carnage was wreaked as in the other carriers. A smaller vessel than the other two, she was not to sink until 1913, Capt Yaganimoto remaining on the bridge, holding his ceremonial sword and singing the Japanese national anthem as

Below:
Damage to the flightdeck of USS *Yorktown* in the early stages of the Battle of Midway. *US Navy*

she went down. She took with her 718 of her crew, *Kaga* over 800 and *Akagi* over 270.

It was the most successful air strike in history, but not achieved without cost: although it is unlikely that any Dauntlesses were shot down by the carriers, 16 of *Enterprise*'s Dauntlesses were forced to ditch because of confusion over the carrier's position and insufficient fuel margins. Two were forced to land on *Yorktown* whose own Dauntlesses — two of which ditched — brought less welcome followers. Between 1024 and 1030 three of Japan's most mighty weapons had effectively been sunk — but not all. *Hiryu*, to the north, had escaped. Rear-Adm Abe of the battleship squadron assumed temporary command, with Rear-Adm Yamaguchi in charge of air operations, on board *Hiryu*. Her first strike was getting airborne at 1040 — 18 'Val' dive-bombers and six Zeros. She was a small carrier, and it was all that could be made ready at that moment. The strike headed towards *Yorktown*, 20 miles away from *Enterprise* and *Hornet*, and the only carrier the Japanese had sighted. Meanwhile the battle-ships of Kondo, Takasu and Yamamoto, and the light carriers *Ryuzo* and *Junyo*, were all being ordered or steaming of their own volition flat out to join Nagumo's force. It was all far too late; the concentration should have been made earlier.

Nagumo abandoned *Akagi* at 1047; only a few minutes later, at 1159, *Hornet*'s radar picked up the *Hiryu* strike coming in from the west, the strike that might still turn the tables and wreak Nagumo's revenge on Fletcher. But radar allowed *Yorktown* to discover the Japanese at 40 miles range, and vector in fighters at 20 miles (though it did not let her shoot down the cruiser reconnaissance aircraft that were now giving a stream of accurate sighting reports on the Americans). *Yorktown* went to 30kt, emptied her fuel lines, and waited. Lt M. Kobayshi's aircraft had followed several American aircraft back to their carriers but his escort of six Zeros broke off to attack the American Daunt-lesses, using up both fuel and ammunition and coming off the worst in their encounter with two damaged aircraft forced to turn back. The Zeros did even worse against the combat air patrol (CAP) — all but one being lost. The CAP was able to shoot down or disable 10 of the 18 bombers; cruiser fire knocked out another, but seven survived to release their bombs, one of them disintegrating to cruiser AA fire just as its bomb fell clear. Another Japanese pilot shook his fists at the Americans as his aircraft passed close over *Yorktown*. The bomb dropped by the stricken 'Val' burst on the flightdeck on the starboard side of No 2 lift, and started a hangar fire. A second hit penetrated the flightdeck from the port side crossing the ship to burst at the base of the uptakes to the ship's funnel. A third hit forward, penetrated to the fourth deck, where it started a fire in a compartment adjacent to a magazine. Prompt flooding prevented an explosion, but *Yorktown* was dead in the water and afire by 1220.

As Nagumo had done before him, Fletcher transferred his flag to a cruiser, in this case *Astoria*, and Spruance was given a free hand with flying operations. The cruiser *Portland* was ordered to tow *Yorktown* back to Pearl Harbor; two cruisers and two destroyers were sent over by Spruance, 20 miles away, to reinforce the AA screen. It looked as if the tow would not be needed. *Yorktown*'s damage control (after Coral Sea and the recent attacks the most experienced in the US Navy) soon had four boilers operating, and was able to steam at 18-20kt by 1340. Three things of significance had happened in between Fletcher leaving her and her getting underway again. At 1331 *Hiryu* had launched a second strike of 10 'Kate' torpedo-bombers and six Zero fighters. Lt J. Tomonaga led the strike knowing that a hole in his fuel tank from the attack on Midway earlier on gave him only enough petrol for a one-way trip. The second event had been the report from a fast 'Judy' reconnaissance aircraft from *Soryu*, launched before her destruction, of three enemy carriers in the area, correctly identified as *Yorktown*, *Enterprise* and *Hornet*. The third event was the ubiquitous submarine *Nautilus* which had launched three torpedoes at the burning hulk of *Kaga* at 1359. In the manner of American torpedoes at this stage of the war, two ran wide, one hit the hull, bounced off, lost its warhead and was used as a float by Japanese survivors.

Tomonaga's force found *Yorktown* at about 1425. They knew of the report of three American carriers in the area, and coincidentally all three vessels named were of the same class, and so similar in appearance. *Yorktown* was steaming when sighted, had fighters on deck and showed no signs of fire. They automatically assumed this was a second carrier they had sighted, not the one attacked by *Hiryu's* dive-bombers earlier. In any event, two torpedoes hit *Yorktown* to port at 1442. The torpedo planes had split into two separate groups to attempt a scissors attack. One group was knocked out of the sky by US fighters and AA fire from *Yorktown's* reinforced screen. The other five made it to launch position, and four successfully launched their torpedoes at pointblank range — 500yd. Two scored devastating hits; *Yorktown* lost all power and took on a 17° list. Within half-an-hour it was 26°, and at 1456 Capt Buckmaster gave the order to abandon ship. Only five torpedo-bombers and three Zeros returned to *Hiryu*, but their news that they had damaged what they thought to be a second American carrier was cheering indeed. It left only one American carrier; if *Hiryu* could only be kept afloat until next day she would be joined by the battleships and by the carriers *Ryujo* and *Junyo*, a force which could wipe out the remnants of the American fleet. *Hiryu* had a mere five 'Vals', four 'Kates' and six Zeros. Despite the pitifully small nature of this strike, Yamaguchi ordered it to be prepared for a dusk strike against the third American carrier. It was never to be. Just as *Soryu* had sent out reconnaissance aircraft before her demise, so Fletcher had launched patrols hunting for *Hiryu*, which was spotted at 1445, 110 miles northwest of *Yorktown*.

At 1530 Spruance launched 25 dive-bombers from *Enterprise*, the heroes of the morning's attacks, and 16 from *Hornet*. One of the aircraft turned back, leaving 10 from *Enterprise*, all with 1,000lb bombs and 14 from *Yorktown's* group, all armed as scouts with 500 pounders. There was no fighter escort — there were simply not enough Wildcats if a CAP was to be left over the ships. The attackers did not quite achieve the same surprise that they had earlier in the day but the result was the same. The fighter defences were soon exhausted and at 1703 a direct 500lb hit rolled the forward deck back and blasted the lift platform against the bridge. Three 500lb hits went straight to the ship's vitals. Seeing she was doomed, two of *Hornet's* aircraft went for the battleship *Haruna* which was missed yet again. As had been the case with the other Japanese carriers, *Hiryu* refused to sink despite clearly being a total loss. Twelve Flying Fortresses near-missed her burning hulk at 1810, also near-missed *Haruna*, *Chikuma* and *Tone* and, as usual, claimed hits. A sortie of Vindicators — brave as ever — from Midway failed to find *Hiryu*. It was not until 0315 on 5 June that she was abandoned, with roughly 750 of her crew lost, 8hr after her bombing. Adm Yamaguchi and *Hiryu's* captain refused to leave the ship. The transfer of the Emperor's portrait (the ritual that was always observed immediately prior to a vessel sinking, and which acknowledged its loss as a fighting vessel) was carried out, and two destroyers fired torpedoes at her at 0510, with the senior destroyer officer, Capt Abe, reporting her sunk, and withdrawing. In fact she remained afloat until 2100 on 5 June.

To plot the Japanese response it is necessary to go back to 1130 on the morning of 4 June, when Nagumo (who still had *Hiryu* battleworthy) was told by a *Chikuma* scout plane that the American carrier or carriers had an escort of only seven cruisers and five destroyers, and was a mere 90 miles away. Nagumo's two fast battleships and two heavy cruisers could handle this with ease, and at 1156 the order was given to advance on the Americans. Then his confidence began to ebb even further. *Tone's* aircraft signalled that the Americans were withdrawing, presumably hoping to wear down the Japanese by air strikes, so Nagumo substituted a night attack that would nullify American air power. Then he heard of *Hiryu's* destruction and at 1733 a further message that the Americans were withdrawing. Finally, at 1830 *Chikuma's* aircraft reported four American carriers, six cruisers and 15 destroyers. Nagumo was ready to believe anything by this stage. He threw in the towel and set course for home.

Yamamoto, far to the rear, had only a fragmentary idea of what was happening. Nagumo's signals were neither profuse nor lengthy; when his three carriers had been blasted to hell and beyond he had described them as 'inoperational'. However, at 1915 Yamamoto sent one of the most remarkable signals of the war. He knew he had lost all four carriers, that it would be two or three days before any carrier reinforcements could arrive and that at least one American carrier was unscathed. His signal read:

'1. The enemy fleet has practically been destroyed and is retiring eastward.
2. Units of Combined Fleet in vicinity are preparing to pursue the remnants and at same time to occupy AF (Midway).'

He then gave his own position and ordered almost all the remainder of his forces to 'immediately make contact with and destroy the enemy'.

In response, at 2130, Nagumo signalled Yamamoto: 'Total strength of enemy is five carriers . . . They are steaming westward . . . I am supporting *Hiryu* and retiring northwest, speed 18kt'. There were not five carriers, they were not steaming west but east, and Nagumo had left *Hiryu* a burning wreck behind him. At 2250 Nagumo signalled: 'There still exist four enemy carriers . . . These are steaming westward. None of our carriers are operational.' By that time his carriers were indeed not operational. It was clear to Yamamoto, whose will to fight was still there, that Nagumo had lost his nerve. He radioed back relieving Nagumo of his command, giving it to Adm Kondo and making Nagumo responsible for the burning hulks of *Akagi* and *Hiryu*. Kondo injected a little steel and purpose into the Japanese forces, but it was far too late. Spruance refused to play ball, and skilfully withdrew during the night in a manner that put him beyond the reach of the Japanese surface forces, but near enough by morning to cover Midway (whose invasion might still be planned for all he knew) and launch a strike against the Japanese surface fleet.

5 June

It did not take long for realism to enter into Yamamoto's plans. Shortly after midnight he began to call back his forces. At 0255 he issued the instructions that admitted defeat, beginning 'Occupation of Midway is cancelled'. He could not risk the surface ships with an intact and powerful American carrier force at sea; he could not reach them to attack by night, and he could not pit his men and his ships against Midway's bombers and largely-intact shore batteries.

Two further footnotes to the great battle remained to be written. When Yamamoto ordered his general retirement, four heavy cruisers of Adm Kurita's support force were steaming through the night westwards to deliver a dawn bombardment against Midway. They reversed course on Yamamoto's order, but at 0342 caught sight of the American submarine *Tambor*. The signal for an emergency turn to port was flashed down the line, but the last cruiser, *Mogami*, failed to see it and crashed into the one ahead, *Mikuma*. Both damaged cruisers were dive-bombed from Midway and by Spruance's aircraft, the latter having given up hope of finding the main Japanese fleet. *Mikuma* was overwhelmed, but the *Mogami* survived an almost unbelievable amount of damage, and reached the Japanese base at Truk looking more like a wreck than a warship.

Yorktown had been abandoned with a heavy list, but stubbornly refused to sink. Destroyers and a salvage party were sent back to her, and it looked

Right:
A remarkable picture of the USS *Hammann*, sinking after a torpedo hit from a Japanese submarine; taken from the USS *Yorktown*, itself soon to follow. *US Navy*

as if she would make it home, too, until the Japanese submarine *I-168* found and torpedoed her; in the process sinking the destroyer *Hammann*, tied up alongside. It was a sad end for a fine ship; she sank at 0600 on 7 June, and even then the old lady showed how tough she was, having been torpedoed at 1330 on 6 June.

Conclusions

The huge scale of Japan's defeat at Midway — four carriers and a heavy cruiser lost, against one carrier and one destroyer — has tended to obscure how very close-run a thing it was. If *Tone's*

seaplane had been launched on time, instead of half-an-hour late, Nagumo would have received a sighting report of an enemy squadron when he had a fully armed anti-shipping strike ranged on his flightdecks, and time in between the first and second air attacks from Midway to launch them. With that strike in the air his carriers would have been far less vulnerable and might even have survived bomb hits as did *Yorktown*. It is impossible to predict what damage the second wave would have done to the American carriers; on the evidence of what a scratch force from *Hiryu* did, it would not have been small. The crucial decision was that taken by Nagumo at 0715 on 4 June, to rearm his second wave for an attack on Midway, but even having got that wrong he was only minutes away from launching a strike when *Hornet's* and *Enterprise's* torpedo-bombers arrived. A few minutes separated Nagumo and a very different outcome to Midway. Diversion of forces, over confidence, reliance on achieving surprise and forcing the carriers to undertake both landing support and anti-carrier operations were weaknesses in Yamamoto's plan, but were it not for a faulty catapult and one wrong decision it might have worked well enough to produce at least a draw, if not a Japanese victory.

If the Battle of Midway proves one thing it is that rules are made to be broken. The Japanese are criticised even now for wasting their most precious asset — their pilots — throughout the war, yet in this battle it was Nagumo who decided to land on a returning strike rather than send off his second wave, and Spruance who flung his aircraft at the enemy in an unco-ordinated attack at extreme range. By all the rules the American attack should have failed; its torpedo planes did so, disastrously, and were it not for a great deal of luck the dive-bombers might never have arrived, and could have been knocked out of the sky by Zeros if they had.

Midway did more than turn the tide of the war in the Pacific: it marked the final end of the battleship as the measure of a fleet's strength. For all Yamamoto's strength in battleships, the American carriers denied him the chance of getting near enough his enemy to engage. Fletcher's carriers did more than sink four of their Japanese opposite numbers — they beat 11 Japanese battleships as well, for the most part without ever making contact with them. A new era in naval warfare had arrived.

Above left:
USS *Yorktown* sinking at the Battle of Midway. *US Navy*

Left:
The savagely damaged Japanese cruiser *Mogami*.
IWM NYF7584

USS *Enterprise* and USS *Hornet*

Builders:

Enterprise — Newport News Shipyard
(Laid down 16 July 1934; launched 3 October 1936; completed May 1938)

Hornet — Newport News Shipyard
(Laid down 25 September 1939; launched 14 December 1940; completed October 1941)

Notes: *Hornet*, the last of the class, was built to the existing *Yorktown* pattern as in 1938 the US navy's designers were concentrating on the 'Iowa' class battleships. She seems to have been more or less identical with her two sisters except for new 5in gun directors and a revised foretop layout. By Midway, *Enterprise* was carrying 32×20mm AA guns. For other details see *Yorktown* (Chapter 7).

Akagi

Builder: Kure Naval Dockyard
(Laid down 6 December 1920; launched 22 April 1925; completed 25 March 1927)
Rebuilt 1935-38 at Sasebo Navy Yard

Displacement: 36,500 tons (standard), 42,750 (full load)

Dimensions: 855.2ft×102.7ft (flightdeck)×28.6ft

Machinery: Geared turbines, 4 shafts, 133,000shp, 31.2kt

Armour: Main belt 10in

Armament: 6×8in (6×1); 12×4.7in (6×2); 28×25mm (14×2)

Aircraft: 66 operational plus 25 reserve

Complement: 2,000

Notes: *Akagi* was laid down as a battlecruiser but then converted to a carrier and further rebuilt and modernised between 1935 and 1938. In her final form, like *Hiryu*, she was supplied with a portside island, partly in the hope that it could facilitate operations with *Kaga* and *Soryu* (built with starboard islands), but the concept did not work. *Akagi* had one large funnel venting down from the side of the hull, just forward of the island on the starboard side. As with most Japanese carriers her bow was not plated in. Her flightdeck had a slight 'peak' amidships, an attempt to give extra speed on take-off and slow down planes on landing.

Kaga

Builder: Kawasaki, Kobe
(Laid down 19 July 1920; launched 17 November 1921; completed 31 March 1928)
Rebuilt 1935-38

Displacement: 38,200 tons (standard), 43,650 tons (full load)

Dimensions: 812.5ft×106.6ft×31ft

Machinery: Geared turbines, 4 shafts, 127,400shp, 28.34kt

Armour: Main belt 11in

Armament: 10×8in (10×1); 16×5in (8×2): 30×25mm) 15×2)

Aircraft: 72 operational plus 18 reserve

Complement: 2,016

Notes: Laid down as a battleship, and hence relatively slow. Converted to a carrier when *Akagi*'s sister ship *Amagi* was destroyed by earthquake. Her superstructure was on the starboard side forward, ahead of her amidships placed, downward-facing funnel.

Soryu and *Hiryu*

Builders:

Soryu — Kure Navy Yard
(Laid down 20 November 1934; launched 23 December 1935; completed 29 December 1937)

Hiryu — Yokosuka Navy Yard
(Laid down 8 July 1936; launched 16 November 1937; completed 5 July 1938)

Displacement: 15,900 tons (standard — *Soryu*); 17,300 tons (standard — *Hiryu*)

Dimensions: *Soryu*: 746.5ft×69.9ft×25ft; *Hiryu*: 745.9ft×73.25ft×25.75ft

Machinery: Geared turbines, 4 shafts; *Soryu* 152,000shp, 34.5kt; *Hiryu* 153,000shp, 34.3kt

Armament: 12×5in (6×2); *Soryu* 28×25mm; *Hiryu* 31×25mm

Aircraft: *Soryu* 53 plus 18 reserve, *Hiryu* 57 plus 16 reserve

Complement: 1,101

Notes: *Hiryu* differed from *Soryu* by being laid down after the expiry of the London Naval Treaty, and after storm damage to several vessels in 1935 had forced changes on Japanese designers. *Hiryu* had her bridge on the port side, *Soryu* to starboard. Both ships had twin sideways-facing stacks on the starboard side.

CHAPTER NINE

The Battle of the Barents Sea

'The entire action shows that the ships are utterly useless and nothing but a breeding ground for revolution, idly lying about and lacking any desire to get into action. This means the passing of the High Seas Fleet; it is now my irrevocable decision to do away with these useless ships.'

Thus spoke Adolf Hitler in January 1943 after the heavy cruisers *Hipper* and *Lützow* (the latter a redesignated pocket battleship) had been driven off from an Arctic convoy by a handful of destroyers and two light cruisers, suffering the loss of a German destroyer in exchange for the sinking of one British destroyer. This was the Battle of the Barents Sea. Its significance lies not so much in what happened — though from the British viewpoint the action was one of the most inspiring

Below:
The German heavy cruiser (ex-'Panzerschiffe') *Lützow* seen in her 1942 state with large funnel cap. Originally named *Deutschland* and renamed in 1939, she was the first, smallest and most weakly-armoured of the pocket battleships. *Real Photographs S1950*

of the whole war — but rather in the fact that it snapped the fragile bond of faith between Hitler and his surface forces. That bond had never been strong, and Hitler had never forgiven his Navy for the loss of *Graf Spee* and *Bismarck*; nor had he ever understood sea power. Barents Sea caused Hitler to order the scrapping of the German surface fleet, and though that decision was not fully carried out the whole affair and its aftermath marked, arguably, the greatest defeat suffered by the German Navy's surface ships in the war.

Background

Hitler had already used the threat to dismantle Germany's heavy ships to bring pressure on his Navy to make the Channel Dash (see Chapter 6). In June 1942 the Germans had smashed Convoy PQ17 on the Arctic run; in one of the greatest tragedies of the war PQ17 had been ordered to scatter by Dudley Pound when it seemed to the First Sea Lord, contrary to intelligence advice, that heavy German surface forces were sailing against it. In fact the big ships had never sailed. It was planned to sail them from Altenfjord to attack

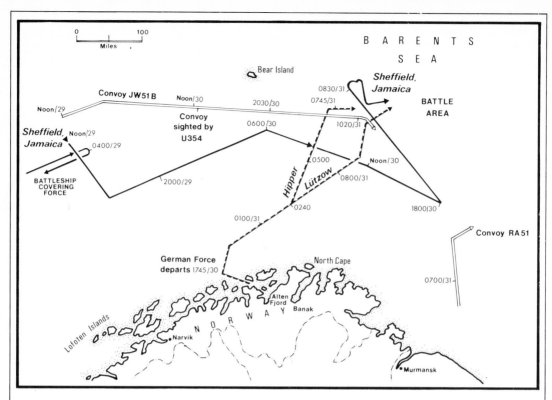

Miles 0 — 100

BARENTS SEA

Bear Island

Convoy JW51B Noon/30 2030/30 0830/31 0745/31 Sheffield, Jamaica BATTLE AREA

Noon/29

Convoy sighted by U354 0600/30 1020/31

Sheffield, Noon/29
Jamaica 0400/29

BATTLESHIP COVERING FORCE

2000/29

0500 Noon/30
Hipper Lützow 0800/31
0240 1800/30

0100/31

Convoy RA51

0700/31

German Force departs 1745/30

North Cape

Alten Fjord Banak

N O R W A Y

Lofoten Islands

Narvik

Murmansk

Above:

Overview of the Battle of the Barents Sea.

PQ18, but this too was cancelled by Hitler's chronic fear of his ships being sunk. Hitler tied his Navy to a doctrine of minimum risk; it was not a healthy atmosphere for commanders, ships or their crews.

Russian convoys were suspended after PQ18 in September, but planned to resume again in December 1942. Rather than sail one massive convoy of 30 or 40 ships, it was decided to split each outward-bound convoy into two and give them the designation 'JW', perhaps a symbolic break from the memories that attached themselves to the 'PQ' designation. Homeward-bound convoys would carry the designation 'RA'. Each outward-bound convoy would carry a local escort. Ships in this with limited endurance would detach when destroyer escort proper joined the convoy, this usually having sailed from Iceland to extend its range. It joined the convoy well before it reached the danger zone for attack. A separate force of cruisers was assigned as cover with the heavy units of the Home Fleet as more distant support. In December the first of these paired convoys, JW51, set sail. Cruiser cover was provided by two light, 6in-gun ships — *Sheffield* and *Jamaica* — which would cover the convoys, the so-called 'Force R'. This was not to come nearer than 50 miles from the convoy, for fear of submarine attack. Adm Tovey, Commander-in-Chief of the Home Fleet, had lost the light cruiser *Edinburgh* when only 15 miles

ahead of QP11, and wished no repetition of the loss. In addition, limited air cover could be provided for a few days on the outward leg from Scotland and Iceland. The cruisers were commanded by Rear-Adm R. L. Burnett, a veteran of the summer convoy battles. Burnett was no intellectual; he used to slap the seat of his trousers and inform listeners that that was where his brains were, but he was immensely popular with his crews and a genuine fighting sailor whose instincts for battle were to prove remarkably sharp when later he met *Scharnhorst*. He was also considered lucky, unlike his predecessor. Adm Bonham-Carter had had two cruisers shot from under him within a few weeks, after which the ratings used to refer their lifejackets as 'Bonhams'.

The Germans had also made their plans. Operation 'Regenborgen' (Rainbow) was a detailed plan for an attack by the heavy cruisers *Hipper* and *Lützow* and six destroyers to sail from Altenfjord, only 200 miles or so off the likely convoy route, and attack an as yet unspecified convoy.

Above:
HMS *Obdurate*, postwar. She survived after the war with two periods of service in 1946-47 and 1953-56 before being broken up in 1964. She always retained her old 4in guns.
Real Photographs 2163

18-28 December

Convoy JW51A sailed from Loch Ewe in Scotland on 15 December 1942, 14 merchant ships in all, covered by a distant battleship force to the far south and 'Force R' (*Jamaica* and *Sheffield*). It arrived at Kola without loss on Christmas Day 1942.

Convoy JW51B sailed from Loch Ewe on 22 December. It consisted of 14 merchantmen, which between them carried 202 tanks, 2,046 vehicles, 87 fighters, 33 bombers, 11,500 tons of fuel oil, 12,650 tons of aviation spirit and 54,321 tons of other supplies, giving some idea of the massive aid being supplied to Russia at this time. The local escort for JW51B was provided by the minesweeper *Bramble* (Cdr M. T. Rust DSO), three 'Hunt' class escorts (*Blankney, Chiddington* and *Ledbury*), three corvettes (*Hyderabad, Rhododendron* and *Circe*) and two trawlers (*Northern Gem* and *Vizalma*). The convoy and its local escort were only the first instalment of a complex series of ship movements, all with the protection of JW51B as their prime aim. Of the nine vessels in the initial close escort, only two corvettes (*Hyderabad* and *Rhododendron*) and the two trawlers would remain with JW51B all the way to Russia, together with *Bramble*. The three 'Hunt' class and the corvette *Circe* would return home just east of Iceland, where the fleet destroyer escort would join the convoy to take it through to Russia. When JW51B sailed on 22 December the seven fleet destroyers were either in or heading for Seidisfjord in Iceland. They were commanded by Capt R. Sherbrooke in *Onslow*, who had been in command of the 17th Destroyer Flotilla for only four weeks. He was a reserved, refined and impassive man who had failed to make a particularly good impression on his flotilla in that time. He had attended the pre-convoy conference of JW51B in Loch Ewe, and then raced away to Iceland ahead of the convoy to meet up with the remainder of his flotilla. Two other destroyers were also steaming for Seidisfjord, but being just behind *Onslow* the bad weather she had just missed. The destroyer *Bulldog* was so badly damaged by the storm that she had to turn for home; *Achates* sprung her new topmast, but made it to Seidisfjord at 1130 on 24 December. She hardly had time to refuel and restay her mast before the flotilla, consisting now of only six destroyers (*Onslow* [Captain (D)], *Achates, Oribi, Obedient, Obdurate* and *Orwell*) sailed from

Seidisfjord to rendezvous with JW51B. By 2320 on 24 December they were all steaming past the boom at the entrance to the anchorage.

The next force to move was the battleship covering squadron, led by *Anson* from Scapa, which sailed on 26 December. With limited endurance they could only cover a surface attack on the convoy from the south. 'Force R' (*Sheffield* and *Jamaica*) sailed from Kola, where it had arrived on 24 December after covering JW51A, on 27 December. No less than nine submarines were stationed around the entrances to Altenfjord, from which any German surface vessels would sail.

Sherbrooke's destroyers made a successful rendezvous with the ships of JW51B at 1430 on 25 December. He signalled his position to Burnett and 'Force R' at 1700 and, having rounded up stragglers, set a speed of 8kt. Sherbrooke, with the convoy, had been signalled by the Admiralty that there was a westbound U-boat in his vicinity, and that there had probably been a sighting of the convoy by a German Focke-Wulf reconnaissance aircraft also on 24 December. There was little Sherbrooke could do; the escorts for JW51B had already been well-briefed on what to do in the event of an attack by enemy surface units. The minesweeper *Bramble*, the corvettes *Hyderabad* and *Rhododendron* (the latter being blessed with the codename 'Pansy' by *Onslow's* signals office) and the two trawlers *Northern Gem* and *Vizalma* would form up on the convoy; the remaining destroyers would form up on *Onslow*, except for *Achates*, which would stay with the convoy and lay a smoke screen.

Trouble started for JW51B on 27 December when it was south of Bear Island. A full gale began to blow, with the ships rolling wildly and ice forming on their decks, and visibility seriously reduced. It blew its worst throughout 28 December during which the destroyer *Oribi* suffered a compass failure and lost the convoy. She was eventually to steam on alone and make her own way to Russia, in so doing steaming out of the story of the battle. Radio was not much help in a situation such as this, the most that could be used for fear of being pinpointed by the enemy being very low power — and hence short range — transmissions on the Fleet waveband; even these were frowned upon. Also on 28 December the merchant ship *Jefferson Myers* had to heave-to and then steer a course more into the wind for fear of capsizing as a result of her bulky deck cargo. A destroyer and a merchant ship thus went astray on 28 December; worse was to follow on 29 December. At 0200 four merchant ships and the trawler *Vizalma*, most of the port wing of the convoy, also lost touch. When the weather began to ease at about noon the sight that met Sherbrooke was not a cheering one: only nine of

his 14 merchant ships were left with him, and in addition there was no sight of a destroyer and a trawler. Because all the missing vessels were from the port wing of the convoy, Sherbrooke hoped they might be together. *Bramble* had an effective radar fit and so she was detached at 1230 to search for the missing ships. It was the last time she would be seen by any British eyes. To cap a perfect day *Onslow* and *Orwell* narrowly avoided colliding that night. Sherbrooke sent a savage signal requiring a written explanation from *Orwell*; he later cancelled the order from his hospital bed after the action.

Burnett and 'Force R' reached their patrol position by 29 December. He believed he was 60 miles southwest of JW51B, and between it and Altenfjord. However, the reality was that JW51B had been blown off course and southwards by the gale, and Burnett was due south of it. At 1600 on 29 December the Commander-in-Chief of the Home Fleet signalled a position for JW51B that put it almost 150 miles east-northeast of its true position, its speed having been overestimated. This false position was to affect Burnett's own movements quite seriously later on.

30 December

This was a crucial day for JW51B and the German forces that were sent out against it. By 1130 three of the lost merchant sheep had rejoined Sherbrooke's flock. This still left *Oribi*, *Vizalma* and two merchant ships still untraced. Sherbrooke did not know it, but the trawler *Vizalma* had met the merchant ship *Chester Valley* in their mutual wanderings. In hoping to catch up the convoy they in fact managed to overtake it to the north of its course, where later they were to confuse 'Force R's' radar operators and draw 'Force R' away from the enemy. Sherbrooke pressed on at 9kt, short now of a destroyer (*Oribi*), a minesweeper (*Bramble*) and a trawler (*Vizalma*) from his escort. He had been warned of increased signal traffic from Norwegian coastal stations, but if he was worried about the implications of this for JW51B he showed no signs of it.

Then came the moment that launched Operation 'Regenborgen'. At 1240 *U354* sighted JW51B, her torpedo attack failing only because of a last-minute zig-zag by the convoy. *U354* was then pinned down and depth-charged by *Obdurate* and *Obedient* later in the day, at 2015, as she was trying to work ahead for a new attack. The two destroyers had to pull back to the convoy after the 2hr search time that was all they were allowed expired, and *U354* was able to surface and make what was her third signal to base, the first having gone off just after noon. She put the convoy on a course of 120° whereas it was actually steering nearer 090°, and gave a speed for JW51B of 13kt as distinct from her actual speed of 9kt, but these mistakes were not to stop an extremely accurate interception by the German surface vessels the next day.

The German response to *U354's* sighting report was almost immediate. Raeder was optimistic. The convoy appeared to be escorted only by destroyers, and the distance of under 200 miles from Altenfjord to interception meant little chance of the German ships' retreat being cut off. In fact the situation was even more promising than Raeder knew. The convoy escort was minus four ships (*Bulldog, Bramble, Oribi* and *Vizalma*), and the covering force of cruisers way out of position. The battleship covering force had turned for home at 0400 on 29 December: JW51B was as vulnerable as any convoy was ever likely to be. Operation 'Regenborgen' had already been planned; all that remained was to activate it, and this was done with sufficient speed to allow for a planned sailing time of 1700 that evening, 31 December. A message was sent to Hitler, who was in conference at the time sorting out an inter-service wrangle about the command of troop transports in the Mediterranean. The message said effectively that the operation would take place unless Hitler vetoed it. After a tirade against the German Navy and its surface fleet he then began to show some interest in the operation, demanding to be kept fully informed of its progress. The operation would be led by Adm Kummetz, Flag Officer (Cruisers) in Altenfjord, under the authority of firstly Adm Klüber (Flag Officer, Northern Waters) and secondly Group North (Adm Karls, operating

from Kiel). Instructions were simple: the task was to destroy JW51B, and the German force was to 'avoid a superior force'. It was also warned that whilst it might be advisable to capture a ship so its captain and officers could be interrogated, 'the rescue of enemy survivors by enemy forces is not desirable'.

The German force consisted of the heavy, 8in-gun cruiser *Admiral Hipper*, escorted by the destroyers *Friedrich Eckholdt, Richard Beitzen* and *Z29*, and the ex-pocket battleship *Lützow*, escorted by the destroyers *Theodor Riedel, Z30* and *Z31*. It was a powerful force. *Hipper* carried eight 8in guns, *Lutzow* six 11in and eight 5.9in. The German destroyers were armed with either five 5in or four 5.9in guns. Kummetz's plan was simple: *Hipper* and *Lützow* would separate during the night and by 0800 on 31 December would be 75 miles apart, with *Hipper* to the north. Each ship would station its three destroyers 15 miles apart and 15 miles ahead so as to cover the maximum search area, and both groups would turn east to search along the track of the convoy. When it was found, *Hipper* was to attack first from the north, draw off the escorts and delivery the convoy to the guns of *Lützow*.

The two German ships were held up when a tug failed to arrive, and then *Hipper's* engines started to give trouble — as we have seen previously a perennial feature of the German high-pressure boilers. At 1745 the eight ships finally got under way. Then at 1840 Adm Klüber sent the following signal to Kummetz: 'Contrary to operational order regarding contact with the enemy . . . use caution against enemy of equal strength because it is undesirable for the cruisers to take any great risks.' Commentators have seen in this a symbol of the whole doctrine of caution that afflicted the German surface fleet, and which may have reduced its morale and its performance. The

German destroyer *Z31* with twin turret fitted forward.
Real Photographs 1861

significance of this may have been overestimated; it is true that any force with the capacity to sink a cruiser could be seen as 'equal', and that included even a single destroyer armed with torpedoes. It is also true that German ships tended to turn away when faced with a battleship escort, even if it was far inferior in numbers and quality to the German ships. It is also true that the doctrine of caution was not confined to German Admirals. Tovey displayed it when he refused to bring capital ships down south to meet the threatened escape of *Scharnhorst* and *Gneisenau*, when the battleship escort for JW51B was turned back so far west, and when he refused to let cruisers come closer than 50 miles to a convoy. A capital ship is so vast an expenditure of resources and so great a symbol that all navies tend to spend as much time worrying about how to stop them being sunk than about how to use them. The Germans were not alone and, given the huge inferiority of their surface fleet, the greatest weapon they had was its mere existence, which tied down large numbers of enemy ships. It made tactical and strategic sense for them to preserve their heavy ships, and any other policy would have been madness.

There was one weakness in the German plan, which was the scheme known as Plan '*Aurora*' whereby *Lützow* would proceed on from Operation '*Regenborgen*' to undertake independent commerce raiding. It has been argued that Capt Stange of *Lützow* was too concerned to avoid damage to his ship for him to take the correct offensive action when he met JW51B. Rear-Adm Fricke, the German Chief of the Operational Staff, had personally telephoned to emphasise that there must be absolutely no risk to the ex-pocket battleship.

31 December

The two German ships began their planned divergence of course at 0230 on 31 December. By the early morning of that day considerable confusion still attended JW51B. *Vizalma* (the trawler) and one merchant ship were still adrift from the convoy, actually 40 miles to the north of it and steaming 2kt faster, although neither party was aware of it. *Bramble* was still hunting lost sheep, 15 miles northeast of the convoy. Burnett and 'Force R' thought he was crossing the wake of the convoy 50 miles astern, and turning to follow it. He was *actually* 30 miles north of it, only 10 miles or so away from *Vizalma*. To add to Sherbrooke's worries, he had been informed in the early hours of the morning that signals from a German destroyer had been picked up somewhere in the region of North Cape, revealing that there was one U-boat ahead of the convoy and one to his south. Sherbrooke appears to have read the signals at 0800: he ordered that his crews should have finished their breakfast by 0900, and changed into clean underwear — the traditional precaution when heading into action, taken to minimise the risk of infection amongst those wounded. Unbeknown to Sherbrooke, JW51B had already been sighted.

Kummetz's interception plan had worked brilliantly. He sighted silhouettes from *Hipper* at 0718, and at 0725 ordered the destroyer *Friedrich Eckholdt* to investigate. It was nearly 2hr before the first shots of the Battle of the Barents Sea were to be fired. The delay came about because Kummetz was waiting for more light, necessary to avoid hitting his own ships, for spotting his fall of shot and to exploit fully his matchless optical range finders. At first Kummetz thought it was some of his own destroyers he had spotted, and it was not until 0753 that he knew for certain it was the convoy. Kummetz wrote that he wanted a speedy action, his main fear being that a torpedo attack from destroyers would cripple his ship. It is clear also that he was very concerned about bad visibility, and the risk that his own destroyers were in among the convoy. It still seems that he spent an immense amount of time shadowing the convoy, and was hampered by fairly chronic indecision. At 0800 the confirmation that it was a convoy dispelled some of this indecision; Kummetz put *Hipper* at 20kt to catch it up.

At 0820 the corvette *Hyderabad* sighted two destroyers. Unfortunately she had received a signal earlier that Russian aircraft might be coming out to cover the convoy, decoded this wrongly as referring to Russian destroyers, and assumed the destroyers she sighted were Russian. Unfortunately she failed to inform Sherbrooke. At 0830 *Obdurate* also sighted the destroyers. Not wishing to break radio silence she informed *Obedient* by signal lamp of the sighting, for *Obedient* to pass it on by similar means to the flotilla leader, *Onslow*, where it was received at 0845. Sherbrooke sent *Obdurate* to investigate. She sighted three destroyers and made the challenge to them at 0915. Russian forces were something of a standing joke with convoy forces, and so the failure of the 'Russian' destroyers to reply need not have been unusual. However, even Russian destroyers usually refrained from opening fire on their British allies, and when one of the German destroyers fired at *Obdurate* the matter of identification was settled beyond reasonable doubt. Almost at once Sherbrooke's plan rolled into motion. *Onslow* steered to support *Obdurate*,

Left:
The action — 0942-1000.

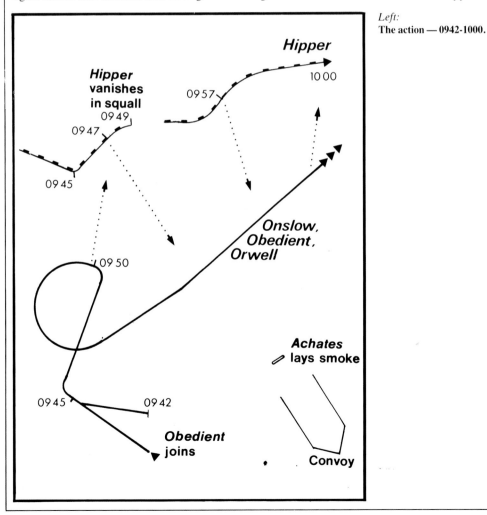

185

and at 0933 signalled 'Join me' to *Obedient*, *Obdurate* and *Orwell*, *Achates* remaining behind with the convoy to lay a smoke screen. At 0939 Sherbrooke in *Onslow* sighted the vast bulk of *Hipper* emerging from a snow squall and heading straight for the convoy. Immediately he headed for her without waiting for the remaining destroyers.

Despite problems with their armament, the German destroyers had opened a desultory fire on *Obdurate* at 0930. They were almost directly astern of the convoy, and turned northeast almost as soon as they opened fire to shadow it. *Obdurate* also turned away sharply to the east, to join with *Onslow* which was stationed ahead of the convoy to port. At this time *Hipper* was to the northwest of the convoy, and by 0930 was steaming astern of it to the northwest, running almost parallel with its course.

Almost immediately after *Onslow* sighted *Hipper*, *Achates* started to make smoke, but this drew *Hipper's* attention to her, and she opened fire with her main battery at *Achates* at around 0941. At the same time *Onslow* opened fire on *Hipper*. Her four 4.7in guns were insufficient to penetrate *Hipper's* armour and two of her guns were iced up, only 'B' and 'Y' mountings being able to fire. Despite the expected loss of her forward fire control radar with the first salvo, and icing of her excellent optics, *Hipper's* fire was relatively accurate, and a near miss on *Achates* on the port side, just forward of the bridge, riddled her with splinters, broke steam and power lines and reduced her speed to 15kt. However, *Hipper* suddenly caught sight of *Onslow* charging straight at her. Sherbrooke knew that a torpedo attack was the one real threat to *Hipper's* safety and that, at

Right:
The action — 1000-1020.

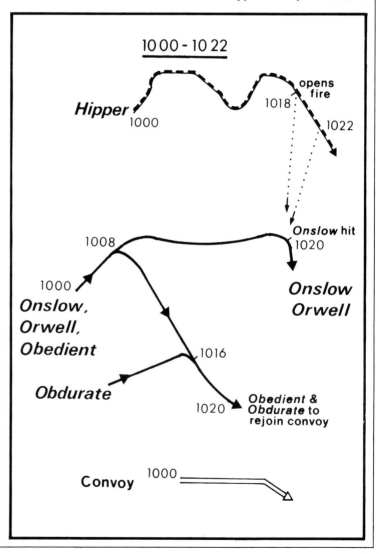

186

the ranges he would be firing, the threat of torpedoes was almost as potent a weapon as the missiles themselves. At 0944 *Onslow* swung hard over to port, describing a huge circle and then proceeding northeast. Kummetz was deceived into thinking torpedoes had been launched (a look-out on *Hipper* actually thought he saw one approaching), and so Kummetz swung *Hipper* sharply round to port, presenting her stern to the supposed torpedoes and combing their 'tracks'. This course took him north and away from the convoy, exactly as Sherbrooke had planned, and shortly after 0949 *Hipper* vanished into a snow squall. By this time Sherbrooke, with *Onslow*, *Obedient* and *Orwell*, was some eight miles away from the convoy, which had turned sharply to starboard when firing started, and which was now heading off to the southeast, putting as much ocean between itself and *Hipper* as it could. This was exactly what Kummetz had planned. JW51B's 'dash' to the south should lead it straight on to the guns of *Lützow*.

Realising how far away he had been drawn from JW51B, Sherbrooke ordered the less well-armed *Obedient* and *Obdurate* to rejoin the convoy, fearful that undiscovered German warships might be lying in wait to the south, as indeed they were. His fears were added to by a signal from 'Force R' which revealed that the cruisers were to the north, rather than in their planned position to the south. Sherbrooke's position was not enviable. 'Force R' had not signalled where it was, or when it would arrive, and *Onslow's* navigation officer put the arrival of the cruisers at between 1-4hr, the best he could do with the sightings and positions he had. Sherbrooke knew he had to fight off a heavy cruiser and three heavily-armed destroyers, and knew that *Lützow* and a light cruiser were at least — in theory — available to the Germans.

Twice more, at 0957 and 1004, *Hipper* dipped out of snow squalls and opened fire on the British destroyers with accurate salvoes. Then at 1013 Kummetz decided to try and smash his way through the British destroyers. Had he but known it at the time, *Onslow's* gun crews were trying to close the breech of one gun by hammering at it with shells, a procedure which they had certainly not been instructed in at Whale Island.

It was only a matter of time before *Onslow* was hit. At about 1020 *Hipper's* after fire control radar managed to obtain hits with two consecutive 8in salvoes. The first hit *Onslow* between her funnel and the bridge, wrecking her radar office, putting boilers out of action and sending a hail of splinters through the ship. Sherbrooke had the left-hand side of his face smashed by splinters, and his left eye was hanging down his cheek. He continued to give orders in a normal voice. The next salvo landed two rounds on the British destroyer: the

first hit at deck level between 'A' and 'B' guns, tore a 6ft by 5ft hole, and killed all 'A' gun's crew. The second hit the edge of 'B' gun deck in front of the bridge, killed most of the crew and started a huge fire in the Chief Petty Officers' Mess, which was directly under the bridge. Sherbrooke turned away to starboard, reduced speed to 15kt so as not to fan the flames out of control and started to lay a smoke screen. *Orwell*, coming up behind *Onslow*, had already been engaged by *Hipper's* 4.1in secondary armament. Now she found herself in the limelight as *Hipper* transferred her main armament to her. *Orwell* had two choices: she could either carry on her solo dash towards *Hipper* and try to launch torpedoes — or at least dupe *Hipper* into thinking she had — in which case she would most likely be blown out of the sea; or she could retire and try to give cover to the wounded *Onslow*. The decision was taken for her when a snow squall separated the two sides. If *Hipper* had smashed through *Orwell* it could have turned the battle, but Kummetz did not appear to realise how badly hit *Onslow* had been (40 men killed or wounded within 2min), and was obviously still worried about torpedo attacks. As it was, *Hipper* turned east-northeast with her three destroyers, the convoy at this time being some 12 miles distant.

At 1036 *Hipper's* turn brought her within sight of the minesweeper *Bramble*. *Bramble* had time to send off a sighting report, but the corvette *Hyderabad* which received this failed to pass it on, as she had earlier failed to report the first sighting of the German destroyers. *Hipper* pulverised *Bramble* with 8in and 4.1in fire. At 1046 Kummetz ordered the destroyer *Friedrich Eckholdt* to finish off *Bramble*, which he thought was a destroyer, and then turned back towards the convoy, hoping by these intermittent attacks to keep the escort off balance and draw it away northwards. He has been criticised for not pressing forward his attacks with greater determination, but it is possible to argue that his tactics were exactly right. The erratic appearances of *Hipper* meant that some at least of the escorting force had to be kept to the north to guard against her forays, and ensured that the convoy would stay steaming south and into *Lützow*. *Hipper* was also never around long enough for a torpedo attack to take place, and was using her greater range of gunnery and her speed to best advantage. In fact, Kummetz's conduct of the operation to this point deserves the highest praise. He had arrived precisely at the convoy's position with his forces deployed exactly as he wished them. He had effectively sunk *Bramble* and severely damaged *Achates* and *Onslow*, avoided damage himself and delivered JW51B straight into *Lützow's* armoured lap.

Sherbrooke had passed command of the destroyers on to *Obedient*, and taken *Onslow* back

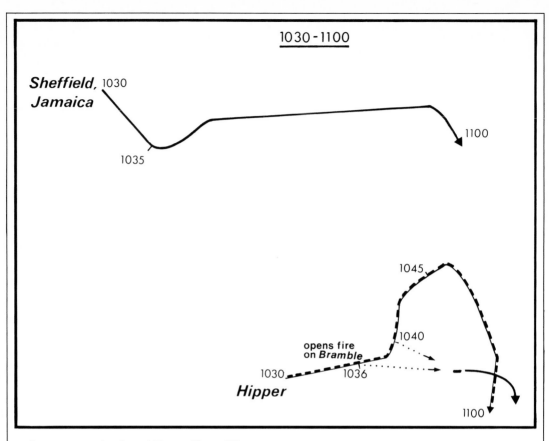

Above:
The action — 1030-1100.

to the convoy so that it could home 'Force R' on to its position.

Lützow had come up from the south as planned, and sighted silhouettes at 0922. For 50min after receiving *Hipper*'s report that she was in action (0951), Capt Stange steered slowly northeast, across the bows of the convoy. He had been sighted by *Hyderabad* who, for the third time, had failed to report the sighting; by 1050 he was some 2-3 miles ahead of the convoy, escorted by three destroyers and with no effective British escort to stop him doing whatever he wanted with the merchant ships. The plan for Operation 'Regenborgen' had succeeded to an extent rarely achieved by such plans. The convoy was at his mercy.

Lützow did nothing. Her log entries are of little help in explaining this apparent huge failure to do precisely what the mission had been set up to do. It reads 'Several targets sighted through snow squalls . . . No identification possible', and that at 1050, 'Impossible at first to ascertain whether dealing with friend or foe because of the poor light, and the smoke and mist on the horizon. To avoid observation from *Lützow*, being obscured by the snow squalls and smoke drifting south, I decided to proceed at slow speed in the vicinity of the convoy,

clear of snow squalls, in order to take advantage of opportunities for attack as visibility improved.'

At 1115 *Lützow* signalled to *Hipper* 'Enemy lost to sight' and turned east. At 1126 she saw *Hipper* in action, and Stange turned *Lützow* west to help *Hipper*. On her way there she sighted destroyers, but 'the intended engagement of these vessels is abandoned due to darkness and extremely poor light'.

Stange's failure to engage is explained, from his viewpoint, solely in terms of bad light and poor visibility. He knew at least some of the ships he sighted were the convoy, as he shows by referring to them as 'targets' and 'enemy'. He knew roughly where *Hipper* was, and should have known where his own destroyers were. The light certainly was appalling, but that was why recognition signals were invented.

Obdurate sighted *Lützow* at 1055, and a second sighting occurred, including this time two destroyers, at 1100. The German force was five miles to the east of the British destroyers, steering south. Immediately Cdr D. C. Kinloch in *Obdurate*, who was now leading the flotilla, led *Obedient*, *Obdurate* and *Onslow* out to meet this new threat. At 1115 he asked *Achates* to join him, for by this time *Hipper* had made her fifth appearance. *Achates* replied that she was down by the bow and able to steam only at 15kt, and so instead she was ordered to join up with *Onslow*. Doing this meant that she had to leave her own smoke screen, and immediately she did so she was picked out by *Hipper* and badly hit on the bridge. Only a young lieutenant was left to take over, the bridge personnel having been wiped out, and the ship was heeling 20° to port in a tight circle. Then *Hipper* hit again on the port side, followed by another near-miss to port, both of which raked the deck and hull with splinters: *Hipper* was firing high explosive rather than armour-piercing shells, partly to obtain greater damage with splinters, and

of course, because she was firing at opponents with no armour. With 40 dead, a 15° list to port and the ship down by the head, *Achates* was in deep trouble; but *Hipper* suddenly turned to starboard as if to cross the stern of the convoy and switched target to *Obedient* at 1126, steering 305° at a range of four miles. The British destroyers dutifully open fire, but at 1128 *Obedient* was straddled and lost her wireless aerials. Command was transferred to *Obdurate*, but then *Hipper* turned away once more. The destroyers also turned and started to lay a smoke screen. At approximately 1130 *Hipper* signalled to *Lützow* that there were no cruisers with the convoy. It was tempting fate, and there can rarely have been such an immediate and contradictory reply to such a signal. A minute or two after signalling *Lützow*, 6in shells began to burst around *Hipper*: 'Force R' had arrived.

'Force R'

It had been a morning of mixed fortunes for 'Force R' which, as has already been noted, thought it was 50 miles astern of the convoy but which was actually to its north. At 0858 *Sheffield's*

Below:
The action — 1100-1126.

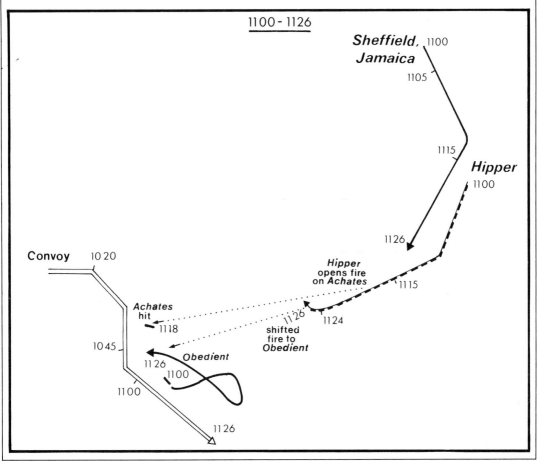

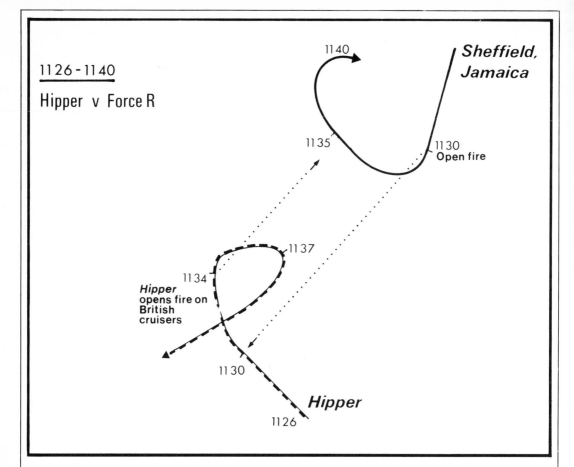

Above:
The action — 1126-1140.

Above right:
The action — 1140-1200.

Right:
The cruiser HMS *Jamaica*, a cramped but effective design. MPL

1126-1140

Hipper v Force R

1140

Sheffield, Jamaica

1135

1130
Open fire

1137

1134

Hipper opens fire on British cruisers

1130

Hipper

1126

radar picked up two vessels travelling at 10kt, which were in fact the trawler *Vizalma* and the merchant ship *Chester Valley*. Burnett was rightly suspicious, and decided to trail these vessels, a correct decision if he had been where he thought he was; it could well have been a German force following the convoy. At 0932 *Sheffield* spotted gunfire, which was actually the German destroyers opening the engagement by firing at *Obdurate*, but this was dismissed as AA fire. At 0946 heavy gunfire was seen (*Hipper* firing on *Achates*) and Sherbrooke's sighting report of three enemy destroyers received. There was a strange delay at this point; it was not until 0955 that Burnett ordered 'Force R' to 25kt and headed on a course of 170° towards the gunfire. The delay is explained by the fact that Burnett did not know where the convoy was, and the action he was witnessing might have been some distance from the convoy which it was his duty to protect. What if the vessels his radar was tracking were heavy enemy units, and Sherbrooke's destroyers a diversion? Kimmetz was not the only confused man at sea that day.

At 1020, and steaming now at 31kt, Burnett saw two gun actions to the south, one dead ahead, one

on the port bow. At 1030 *Sheffield's* radar picked up a large echo 10 miles distant steering east, then a second large echo at 1032, 15 miles on the port bow, steering northeast and closing. At 1035 *Sheffield* and *Jamaica* turned to port, parallel with the first target, so as to put what light there was behind the enemy. Between 1054 and 1112 'Force R' altered course to conform with the first target (*Hipper*); at 1128, just after she had turned to starboard to open fire on *Obedient*, she came broadside on to the cruisers and was at that moment correctly identified. At about 1130 *Sheffield* and *Jamaica* opened fire.

Hipper was taken completely by surprise, and

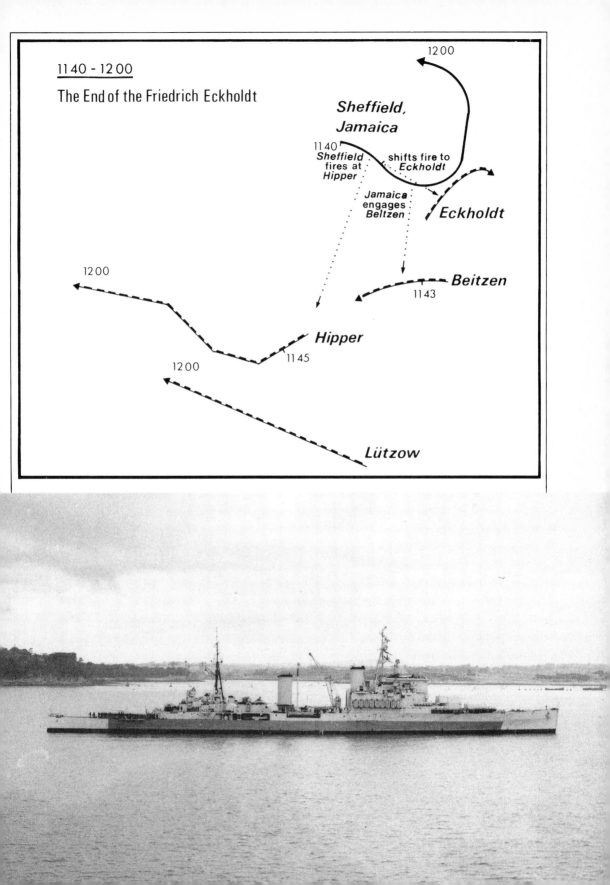

1140 - 1200

The End of the Friedrich Eckholdt

1200

Sheffield, Jamaica

1140
Sheffield fires at Hipper

shifts fire to Eckholdt

Eckholdt

Jamaica engages Beitzen

1200

Beitzen
1143

Hipper
1145

1200

Lützow

Above:
The cruiser HMS *Sheffield*; note the armour belt.
Real Photographs S9969

Below:
***Lützow's* indecisive manoeuvres.**

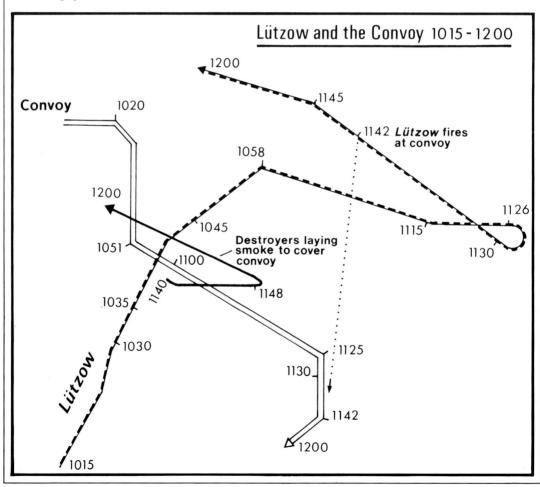

Lützow and the Convoy 1015-1200

1200

Convoy 1020

1145

1142 *Lützow* fires at convoy

1058

1200

1126

1045

1115

Destroyers laying smoke to cover convoy

1051

1130

1100

1148

1140

1035

1125

1030

Lützow

1130

1142

1200

1015

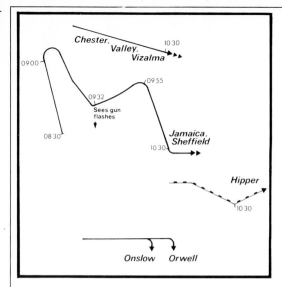

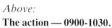

Above:
The action — 0900-1030.

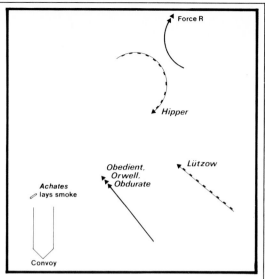

Above:
Relative positions at 1130.

the British cruisers were firing fast and accurately. As *Hipper* making smoke, heeled over on a starboard turn towards her assailants, a 6in shell penetrated under the starboard armoured belt and damaged a boiler to the extent of reducing the cruiser's speed to 23kt. *Hipper* still burning, took two hits on the port side, starting a fire between decks in the aircraft hangar, all this in the space of 5min. Taken by surprise, she fired her first 8in salvo at the cruisers at 1134, her shooting suffering from iced-up optics. The shells fell short and a second salvo went unobserved as a result of her turn. The hangar fire obscured the aft director and icing had once more furred-up the forward optics. *Hipper* thus fired only 20 rounds at her assailants. She made off into the smoke screen being laid by her own destroyers. Sighting destroyers, *Sheffield* turned towards them to comb any torpedo tracks, fired nine more salvoes at *Hipper*, and then spotted the German destroyer *Friedrich Eckholdt* at two miles range. She opened fire. The two destroyers — *Friedrich Eckholdt* with *Richard Beitzen* behind her — thought *Sheffield* was *Hipper*, and flashed a recognition signal at her. When *Sheffield* opened fire the captain of *Friedrich Eckholdt* actually signalled to *Hipper* 'You are firing on me!' *Sheffield* savaged the German destroyer, but was thrown into confusion when *Jamaica's* salvoes were seen to be going well over the target: actually *Jamaica* had sighted *Richard Beitzen* behind *Friedrich Eckholdt*, and realising that the first destroyer was being well looked after transferred her fire to the second, which managed to slip away before being hit.

At 1137 Kummetz, sandwiched between two cruisers and the convoy's escorts, signalled 'Break off action and retire to west'; *Friedrich Eckholdt* was probably sunk trying to obey this order. *Hipper* and *Lützow* turned away, and by 1200 *Hipper* was steaming away to the west with 'Force R' 13 miles away on *Hipper's* starboard quarter. There was no question of charging in after the German ships with the British cruisers, who were somewhat outgunned, had no destroyer escort and whose prime duty was to protect the convoy. At 1202 Burnett signalled: 'Enemy cruiser hit. Have lost touch. Enemy destroyer left sinking.' However, *Hipper's* course west took her back towards the convoy, now southwest of her whilst *Lützow*, steering northwest to join with *Hipper*, passed within nine miles of the convoy. At 1142 she finally opened fire on it, despite furred optics and inadequate radar. She succeeded only in damaging one merchant ship (*Calobre*) slightly with splinters. The convoy turned away to the southwest, and *Obedient*, *Obdurate* and *Orwell* also turned northwest, putting themselves between *Lützow* and the convoy and making smoke to cover its rear. *Lützow* continued sailing northwest, but then *Hipper* appeared at a range of four miles, straddled *Obdurate*, and vanished as quickly as she had come. The destroyers turned back to the convoy.

Then it was *Sheffield's* turn. Both British cruisers had come round in a circle and followed *Hipper* when she had broken off the action, but were north of *Hipper*, *Lützow* and the convoy. At 1223 *Sheffield* sighted silhouettes on her port

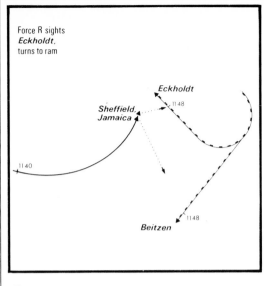

Force R sights
Eckholdt,
turns to ram

Eckholdt

1148

*Sheffield,
Jamaica*

1140

Beitzen

1148

1148

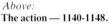

Above:
The action — 1140-1148.

beam, which were actually *Lützow's* destroyers. *Lützow* herself was directly behind her destroyers, so at first was not seen. *Lützow* sighted *Sheffield* at about the same time, but her twin funnels and the direction from which she was coming persuaded her that it was *Hipper's* destroyers. *Lützow* challenged *Sheffield* twice; *Sheffield* merely flashed the same signal back at her. *Sheffield* opened fire at 1229. Her Gunnery Officer, high in the ship, saw the bigger bulk of *Lützow* behind the destroyers and switched target to her, straddling with her first salvo. One minute later, at 1230, *Lützow* opened fire, the range being eight miles. *Lützow* was firing short, but not so *Hipper* which had joined the action by 1234 and straddled *Sheffield* with what might have been her first salvo. Burnett, with the cruisers, was in an extremely dangerous position. Two large German ships were off his port side, and a number of German destroyers were also lurking in the darkness and squalls. He had no destroyers, and *Graf Spee* had shown that the German pocket battleships, if not 8in cruisers, could withstand any amount of 6in gunfire. Burnett turned away at about 1237 and *Lützow* also turned to break off the action at the same time 'as the enemy's fire was accurate'. *Lützow* especially feared destroyers and their torpedoes, and thought the two cruisers were actually destroyers.

'Force R' continued to shadow on radar, despite *Jamaica's* set being put out of action by gunfire; a problem that did not only affect the Germans. *Sheffield's* exhausted and freezing operators finally lost contact at 1400. Burnett took his cruisers on a sweep south until 1609, then turned north, but

there was no further contact with the German ships. At 1233 Kummetz signalled 'No contact with *Eckholdt*. Enemy is shadowing the formation. Detachment of *Lützow* impossible.' Operation 'Aurora' was therefore cancelled. The final fling of the action came when the ex-German *U570*, captured by the British and named *Graph*, fired at the German destroyers escorting the German squadron off the coast of Norway. She missed.

Hipper had fired 375 rounds of 8in and 203 rounds of 4.1in; *Lützow* 86 rounds of 11in and 76 of 5.9in. Their reward was to sink one minesweeper, *Bramble*, and one destroyer, *Achates*, which went down later in the afternoon. She suffered over 100 casualties, whilst the battered *Onslow* had 14 dead, three dying and 23 wounded. She survived with her wounded Captain on board, and was cheered in by other ships when she made it back to Scapa. For their part the Germans lost *Friedrich Eckholdt* and her crew. An explosion seen at 1328 might have been the German destroyer blowing up; both she and *Bramble* sank alone and unseen in some of the cruellest waters in the world. Convoy JW51B arrived intact, some at Murmansk, some where they had been routed further east at Archangel. No one could argue with the C-in-C of the Home Fleet's verdict on what came to be known as the Battle of the Barents Sea. Adm Tovey wrote that it had been 'one of the finest examples in either of the two world wars of how to handle cruisers and destroyers in action with heavier forces'. The award of the Victoria Cross to Capt Sherbrooke recognised this verdict, and his own heroism.

Aftermath

The real victory won that day was hidden from the Allies until after the war. At the height of the action the captain of *U354* signalled: 'According to our observation the battle has reached its climax. I see nothing but red.' This signal aroused high expectations. Radio silence meant nothing transmitted on the journey home, and an almost comic series of errors made it many hours before anything like a full report of the action reached Hitler.

First news of the action came from Allied radio. When it did come it seemed to Hitler that his forces had suffered an ignominious and shameful failure, driven off from a rich convoy by a handful of inferior escorts. Summoning Vice-Adm Theodor Krancke, Raeder's representative at Hitler's *'Wolfsschanze'* Headquarters, he announced his 'unalterable resolve' to scrap the surface ships and mount their guns on land. The Navy were an embarrassment, a source of ridicule, and completely useless. Five days later Hitler harangued Grand-Adm Raeder for 90min hardly

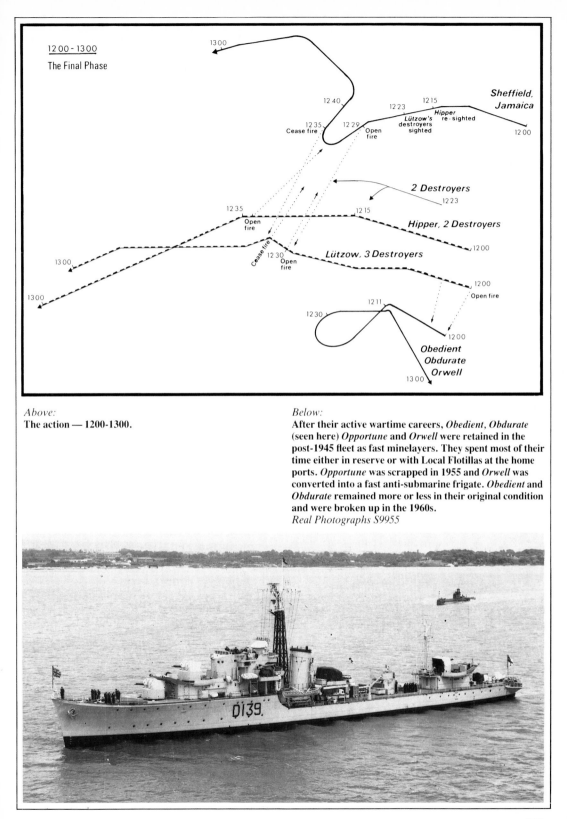

12 00 - 13 00

The Final Phase

1300

12 40

12 23

12 15

Sheffield,
Jamaica

Lützow's
destroyers
sighted

Hipper
re-sighted

12 00

12 35
Cease fire

12 29
Open
fire

2 Destroyers

12 23

12 35
Open
fire

12 15

Hipper, 2 Destroyers

1200

1300

12 30
Open
fire

Cease fire

Lützow, 3 Destroyers

1200
Open fire

1300

1211

12 30

1200

Obedient
Obdurate
Orwell

1300

Above:
The action — 1200-1300.

Below:
After their active wartime careers, *Obedient*, *Obdurate* (seen here) *Opportune* and *Orwell* were retained in the post-1945 fleet as fast minelayers. They spent most of their time either in reserve or with Local Flotillas at the home ports. *Opportune* was scrapped in 1955 and *Orwell* was converted into a fast anti-submarine frigate. *Obedient* and *Obdurate* remained more or less in their original condition and were broken up in the 1960s.
Real Photographs S9955

pausing for breath, repeating his earlier allegations, and worse. The outcome was inevitable; Raeder resigned on 15 January 1943, after having produced a lengthy document which showed totally the stupidity of Hitler's viewpoint, and pointed out that for a total of 13 coastal batteries and a handful of men Hitler would hand the Allies their largest ever naval victory without making them even fight for it.

It was no use; but when Adm Karl Doenitz — previously head of the U-boat arm — took over from Raeder, Hitler had a shock. Despite early compliance with Hitler's wishes, Doenitz was too much of a sailor not to dig his heels in. He produced his own plans: the cruisers *Hipper*, *Leipzig* and *Köln* would be removed from active service together with Germany's two old, pre-Dreadnought battleships, but *Tirpitz*, *Scharnhorst*, *Admiral Scheer*, *Lützow*, *Prinz Eugen* and *Nurnberg* would be retained with attendant destroyers in northern waters to defend Norway and attack Russian convoys. Hitler was furious at this change of heart and the accusation — delivered bluntly enough by Doenitz — that the surface fleet had suffered from too many political restrictions, but he could not afford to lose another Admiral so soon, and with exceeding bad grace he grudgingly acceded to Doenitz's request. Yet even if some of the ships were saved, the effects of the aftermath were considerable.

Goodwill is an intangible feature, but if the goodwill concerned was Hitler's, its removal brought with it a place very low down in the pecking order in a dictatorship that was increasingly running short of oil, raw materials and men. Without effective air support every sortie from Norwegian waters was a running jump taken blindfold, and Hitler's outrage ensured that Goering felt even less pressure to divert Luftwaffe resources for naval use. Doenitz stopped the head being lopped off the surface fleet; he could not prevent its slow strangulation. It also meant that Doenitz had a point to prove to Hitler. At the end of 1943 it was Doenitz's urging that sent *Scharnhorst* out to her death.

HMS *Jamaica*

Builder: Vickers-Armstrong, Barrow
(Laid down 28 April 1939; launched 16 November 1940; completed 29 June 1942)

Displacement: 8,530 tons (standard)

Dimensions: 555.5ft × 62ft × 16.5ft

Machinery: Geared turbines, 4 shafts, 72,500shp, 31kt

Armour: Main belt 3.25-3.75in; deck 2-3.25in; turrets 2in

Armament: 12×6in (4×3); 8×4in (4×2); 9×2pdr (4×2 and 1×1); 8×0.5in (2×4); 6×21in torpedo tubes (2×3)

Sensors: As *Sheffield*

Aircraft: 3

Complement: 733-900

Notes: These were designed under the 1936 London Naval Treaty and managed to cram most of the 'Town' features on to a smaller hull. The price was paid in very cramped accommodation, but protection was good and all vessels of the class performed with distinction throughout the war.

HMS *Sheffield*

Builder: Vickers-Armstrong, Tyne
(Laid down 31 March 1935; launched 23 July 1936; completed 25 August 1937)

Displacement: 9,100 tons (standard), 11,350 tons (full load)

Dimensions: 591.5ft × 61.7ft × 17ft

Machinery: Geared turbines, 4 shafts, 75,000shp, 32kt

Armour: Main belt 4.5in; decks 1.25-2in; turrets 1-2in

Armament: 12×6in (4×3); 8×4in (4×2); 8×2pdr (2×4); 9×20mm (9×1); 6×21in (2×3) torpedo tubes

Sensors: Radars Types: 273 (surface search); 281 (air warning); 282 (2pdr direction); 283 (main armament AA 'blind-fire'); 284 (main gunnery direction); 285 (secondary armament HA fire control)

Complement: 796

Notes: The 'Town' class cruisers were produced in three batches, *Sheffield* being of the first 'Southampton' group. These handsome, well-balanced and extremely successful ships were designed at Chatfield's insistence, when First Sea Lord, in response to the trend towards large 6in cruisers encouraged by the London Naval Treaty. *Sheffield's* comprehensive radar fit, especially the centimetric 273 radar, was an enormous help in the murk of the Barents Sea.

HMS *Achates*

Builder: John Brown, Clydebank
(Laid down 1928; launched 1929; completed 1930)

Displacement: 1,350 tons

Dimensions: 323ft × 32.25ft × 8.5ft

Machinery: Geared turbines, 2 shafts, 34,000shp, 35kt

Armament: 2×4.7in (2×1); 2×20mm (2×1); 4×21in (2×4) torpedo tubes; Hedgehog ASW weapons; depth charges

Complement: 138

Notes: One of the first full flotillas of post-World War 1 destroyers, modified for escort work and hence weakly armed for surface warfare.

A heavily retouched view of *Hipper* in her original condition with straight stem and no funnel cap. By the outbreak of war she had acquired both fittings. The Germans put great store in a uniform appearance for their ships which, among other things, upset enemy gunnery calculations. *Paul Silverstone Collection*

HMS *Bramble*

Builder: Devonport Dockyard
(Launched 1938)

Displacement: 815 tons (standard)

Dimensions: 245ft × 33.5ft × 6.75ft

Machinery: Geared turbines, 2 shafts, 1,750shp, 17kt

Armament: 2 × 4in (2 × 1); 4 × 20mm (4 × 1)

Complement: 80

Notes: One of the 21-strong 'Halcyon' class of minesweepers.

HMS *Onslow*

Builder: John Brown
(Laid down 1940; launched 1941; completed 1942)

Displacement: 1,500 tons (standard)

Dimensions: 345ft × 35ft × 9ft

Machinery: Geared turbines, 2 shafts, 40,000shp, 34kt

Armament: 4 × 4.7in (4 × 1); 4 × 2pdr (1 × 4); 4 × 20mm (4 × 1); 8 × 21in (2 × 4) torpedo tubes

Complement: 217

Notes: The 'O' class were the first 'utility' destroyers ordered under the war construction programme, built on reduced 'Javelin' class hulls with more sheer to the bow to reduce wetness. *Onslow* differed slightly from *Obdurate*, *Orwell* and *Obedient*, as a flotilla leader. The later three were also intended primarily for minelaying duties and thus carried 4 × 4in old World War 1-pattern Mk 2s, one of which could be landed along with the torpedo tubes to take on 60 mines. The guns also reflected wartime shortages of better weapons and were also fitted to the following 'P' flotilla.

Lützow and *Admiral Hipper*

Lützow was originally named *Deutschland*, but had her name changed when it was thought that her loss might achieve symbolic importance. She was built by Deutschwerke at Kiel, laid down on 5 February 1929, launched on 19 May 1931, and completed at the beginning of April 1933. She had her original 3.9in AA guns replaced by 6 × 4.1in in 1940. She also originally had slightly smaller torpedo tubes. Her armour was thinner than *Graf Spee's*: 2.4in side plus 1.8in internal bulkhead (lower) and 0.8in (upper), 1.6in deck. Other details are generally as for *Graf Spee* (see Chapter 1), but standard displacement was 11,700 tons.

Admiral Hipper was built by Blohm und Voss, laid down on 6 July 1934, launched 6 February 1937, and completed in April 1938. She was smaller than *Prinz Eugen* (14,050 tons, 665.7ft long) and differed from her slightly, although armament and protection was similar.

Friedrich Eckholdt (*Z16*)

Builder: Blohm und Voss, Hamburg
(Laid down 1935; launched 1937; completed 1938)

Displacement: 1,625 tons (standard); 3,165 tons (deep load)

Dimensions: 397ft × 37ft × 13.1ft

Machinery: Geared turbines, 2 shafts, 70,000shp, 38.2kt

Armament: 5 × 127mm (5 × 1); 4 × 37mm; 4 × 20mm; 8 × 21in torpedo tubes (2 × 4)

Complement: 315

Notes: A destroyer Type 34A, *Theodor Riedel* (*Z6*) was similar. (For *Richard Beitzen* (*Z4*) and *Z29-Z31* see Chapter 6.) These ships had still not received their twin 5.9in forward mountings. *Z31* was the first of a new slightly modified 1936A (mobilisation) type.

CHAPTER TEN

The Sinking of the *Scharnhorst*

The year that separated the Battle of the Barents Sea from the last sortie of the *Scharnhorst* saw major changes both in the ships and the people that dominated northern waters. Grand-Adm Doenitz proved that he was far better at manipulating Hitler than Raeder had been when he persuaded Hitler to backtrack on his decision to dismantle all the German heavy surface units. Doenitz was unable or unwilling to save *Hipper* and the light cruisers *Leipzig* and *Köln*, which were decommissioned, but by March 1943 he had assembled a powerful force in Norway, consisting of the battlecruiser *Scharnhorst*, the pocket battleship *Lützow* and the battleship *Tirpitz*, sister ship of the *Bismarck*. The presence of these ships in Norway pleased Doenitz, who saw the Russian convoys as presenting the German Navy's surface units with one of its few remaining possibilities for offensive action, and though they did not please Hitler they at least offered some answer to his fear of an Allied invasion of Norway.

Sadly for the Germans, their strength was to be short-lived. The Russian convoys were suspended during the summer months of 1943, partly because of the German force lying at Altenfjord. All that was left for *Tirpitz* and *Scharnhorst* to do was a bombardment of the island of Spitzbergen, and in September 1943 *Tirpitz* was crippled by an attack from British midget submarines whilst at anchor; *Scharnhorst* was away on gunnery practice at the time. Immediately afterwards, also in September, *Lützow* left for an extended refit. With Luftwaffe strength stepped down and only five destroyers left to shepherd *Scharnhorst*, the Germans were in a far weaker position to mount any effective action. This weakness and pressure from the Russians caused the convoys to be restarted in November 1943, under essentially the same arrangements as had applied for JW51B at the Battle of Barents Sea.

Yet a major change had taken place on the British side, where Adm Sir Bruce Fraser had replaced Tovey as Commander-in-Chief, Home Fleet. Fraser was one of the most loved and respected officers the Royal Navy ever produced. A gunnery officer (the traditional foundation for promotion in the Royal Navy), his career had been one of undiminished brilliance from its commencement, and he was a symbol of how much the balance had swung the way of the British since the days when *Graf Spee* and *Bismarck* had been harried to their deaths. Fraser was an outstanding tactician, with one of the most efficient groups of staff officers gathered round him that the Royal Navy had ever seen. Four years of bitter warfare had hardened and honed the Royal Navy into an immensely strong and experienced force. It was not only that new battleships of the 'King George V' class swung round the anchors at Scapa; one of the most underestimated and undervalued achievements of the Royal Navy were the training schemes and camaraderie that produced efficient fighting units out of ships that might have up to 80% of their crews at sea in uniform for the first time. The British also had 'Ultra', the ability to decode Germany's top secret naval code. There were still weaknesses in the system, as the escape of *Lützow* from Norway to Gdynia in September 1943 proved, but the run-down of German forces in Norway and the fact that the surface ships had become the poor relation of the German armed forces put many of the top cards in British hands. However, the fact that the British were to face *Scharnhorst* at the Battle of North Cape did something to redress the balance. She had been both a lucky and a successful ship, and many of her crew had been together since the start of the war, producing a happy and efficient ship. She still retained her 11in guns as main armament, but against this was her ability to sustain higher speeds in heavy weather than the British 'King George V' class battleships.

November-December 1943

Starting in November the British sailed three outward- and two homeward-bound convoys on the Russian route without incident, excepting only a few submarine attacks. Ironically, Doenitz believed that the failure to attack no less than five convoys would lull the British into a false sense of security, and on 20 December he decided that *Scharnhorst* would attack the next convoy. Fraser, on the other hand, by December had an almost intuitive belief that *Scharnhorst* would no longer be able to resist the bait, and would attack a convoy in the near future. He sailed from Scapa

Flow in the battleship *Duke of York* on 12 December, covering JW55A all the way to Murmansk. He sailed from the Kola inlet for Iceland on the 18th. Before Fraser had arrived at Akureyri on the 23rd he had received 'Ultra' information that *Scharnhorst* was likely to attack JW55B, which had already left Loch Ewe.

The convoy consisted of 18 merchant ships, sailing in three columns. Local escort was to be provided by the destroyer *Scimitar*, but she was later replaced by the two corvettes *Borage* and *Wallflower*. In addition the local escort had two minesweepers, *Hound* and *Hydra*. Through escort

was provided by the minesweeper *Gleaner*, the two escort destroyers *Whitehall* and *Wrestler*, and two corvettes, *Honeysuckle* and *Oxlip*. The fleet destroyer escort consisted of *Onslow* and *Orwell*

Above:
HMS *Orwell*, escort for Convoy JW55B.
Real Photographs S1670

Below:
HMS *Ashanti*, a 1,870-ton 'Tribal' class destroyer.
Real Photographs 1017

(veterans of Barents Sea), and *Scourge, Onslaught, Impulsive, Iroquois, Haida* and *Huron*. The designation 'Force 1' was given to the three cruisers — *Belfast, Norfolk* and *Sheffield* — that would cover both the outward-bound JW55B and the homeward-bound RA55A. 'Force 1' was commanded by Vice-Adm Burnett in *Belfast*. Finally heavy battleship distant cover was to be provided by 'Force 2', with Fraser in *Duke of York*, escorted by the light cruiser *Jamaica*, and the destroyers *Savage, Saumarez, Scorpion* and *Stord*. 'Force 2' would patrol in the area of Bear Island for about 30hr, thus covering the danger point where both convoys passed each other and were nearest to the German bases in Norway. 'Force 2' was already at Akureyri in Iceland, whilst 'Force 1' (the cruisers) would sail with RA55A (the homeward-bound convoy) from Kola. The

fleet destroyer escort would sail from Skaalefjord in Iceland.

The complexity of these convoy operations can be judged from the fact that 18 merchant ships and their local and through escorts had first of all to be assembled at Loch Ewe in Scotland, and then sailed to synchronise with the sailing of the fleet destroyer escort and the battleship covering force from two separate points in Iceland, and convoy RA55A and the cruiser escort from the other side of the ocean at Kola. Additional forces deployed were a submarine stationed off *Scharnhorst's* likely exit route and air cover to the limit of fuel endurance from Iceland. The sequence was led off by JW55B's sailing on 21 December (postponed from 19 December because of bad weather). At 2345 that day the fleet destroyer escort sailed from Iceland. Convoy RA55A would then leave Kola

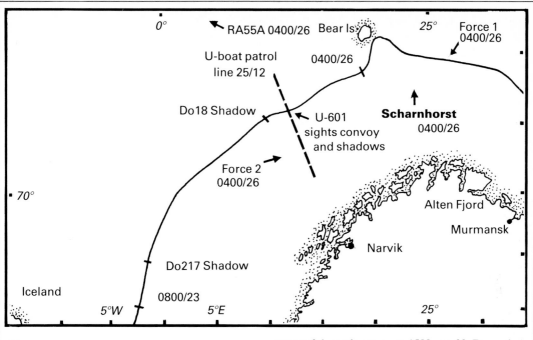

RA55A 0400/26   Bear Is.   25°   Force 1
                                           0400/26
U-boat patrol   0400/26
line 25/12

Do18 Shadow   ← U-601   **Scharnhorst**
                       sights convoy   0400/26
                       and shadows

Force 2
0400/26

70°   Alten Fjord

                                           Murmansk

                         Narvik

Do217 Shadow
Iceland
          5°W   5°E   25°
0800/23

Above:
The passage of Convoy JW55B.

on 22 December with 'Force 1' sailing from Kola on 23 December and 'Force 2' from Iceland on the same day.

21-24 December

JW55B left Loch Ewe at 0800. It was not to be a convoy that endeared itself to its escorts, with two vessels failing to make a course alteration later that night, steaming off on their own and having to be shepherded back to the convoy by *Whitehall*, the convoy having to reduce speed to 8½kt while they were found. The first real crisis came at 1059 on 22 December when *Gleaner* spotted an aircraft that was definitely not the Sunderland flying boat that was providing anti-submarine cover for the convoy passing astern. This aircraft, a German Dornier Do217, was on a meteorological flight, and signalled that she had sighted 40 troop transports, cruisers and 'presumably an aircraft carrier'. The Germans initially thought this might presage an invasion of Norway, and ordered seven submarines of Group '*Eisenbart*' away from their patrol area round Bear Island to the area off Vest Fjord; *Scharnhorst's* battle group was also put on 3hr notice for steam before the Germans realised that this was a conventional convoy. To be sighted so early was bad luck, but there was nothing to be done. The fleet destroyer escort was guided on to JW55B by the Sunderland flying boat, and made a

successful rendezvous at 1500 on 22 December, when the local escort was detached to return to Iceland.

Further bad news came on 23 December, when two Dornier Do217 aircraft picked up the convoy and shadowed it from astern at 1140, and continued to do so despite an alteration of course from the convoy to throw them off until 2305. It was much the same story on 24 December, when another shadower followed the convoy for most of the morning. Foul weather lost the convoy its airborne anti-submarine escort (by now a Catalina rather than a Sunderland) and partially scattered the convoy, which had to reduce speed at one stage to 7kt to allow the columns to re-form. Yet another shadowing aircraft appeared at 1225, all this when the convoy was a mere 400 miles from the German base at Altenfjord. The Germans had never ventured as far west as this before, but Fraser in *Duke of York* realised a very real chance of a massacre was looming, with 'Force 1' and 'Force 2' too far away to provide help, and the convoy defended only by destroyers. At 1325, therefore, Fraser broke radio silence to order JW55B to reverse its course for 3hr, until 1700, and increased his own speed to 19kt, to postpone any action until such time as his battleships and cruisers could be there.

However, JW55B was proving a pig to handle, had dropped below its scheduled speed of 9kt and was 20 miles west of where it should have been when the signal was received. In the heavy weather it was a daunting prospect to try to turn round ships that had shown an unwillingness to stay together even in a relatively straight line, and the coloured light signalling necessary for the alteration might reveal the convoy's position. This latter point seems a convincing one, but the convoy had been spotted from the air anyway, and it was undoubtedly the seakeeping difficulties of the exercise that persuaded the senior officer, Capt McCoy, to drop speed instead to 8kt which, given JW55B's earlier lack of progress, would put it in the same position as actually turning about. What is significant is Fraser's decision to break radio silence, an act he was to repeat several times during the action, in order to muster and control his forces. From the convoy's point of view it was entirely justified, as JW55B had already been sighted; from the point of view of luring out *Scharnhorst* it was far more risky, in that common sense and past behaviour suggested that *Scharnhorst* would not be sent out if there was any suspicion of a battleship covering-force in the vicinity. In fact some of Fraser's signals were picked up by the Germans, but not interpreted correctly, a fact that perhaps more than anything else was to contribute to the destruction of the *Scharnhorst*.

25 December

By the early morning of Christmas Day 1943 Fraser had realised that JW55B and RA55A would not cross paths in the vicinity of Bear Island as planned, because JW55B was not making its scheduled speed. It had not yet been sighted, so Fraser ordered it far to the north and out of the way of any likely surface action, at the same time requesting the transfer of four fleet destroyers from RA55A's escort to JW55B. At 0200 the 36th Division — *Musketeer, Matchless, Opportune* and *Virago* left RA55A to rendezvous with JW55B. However, the forces and the elements were combining against JW55B. It was sighted by *U603* at 0901 and by a Do18 shadowing aircraft at 1115. At 1135 a further U-boat bearing was picked up by the escort, which was soon battling through a Force 7 wind and prolonged sleet showers. 'Ultra' gave the Admiralty in London, and hence Fraser at sea with 'Force 2', details of nearly all the German sightings almost before they reached the Germans to whom they were initially sent, and he also knew that *Scharnhorst* and her battlegroup were at 3hr notice for steam, though the 'Ultra' information was severely restricted in its circulation, to avoid the secret being captured or discovered by the Germans. It was some comfort to JW55B — but also felt to be an ominous portent of things to come — when the four extra destroyers from RA55A joined JW55B at 1255. As they did so two destroyers were 10 miles to port of the convoy, chasing a radio-direction bearing on a submarine (actually *U601*) and picking up another one on a different bearing as they did so.

It was not only German submarines that were showing an increasing interest in JW55B. Soon after noon on 25 December further air reconnaissance was rendered impossible because of the appallling weather, but with U-boats in contact and shadowing, Rear-Adm Klüber — the German Flag Officer for North Norway — ordered the *Scharnhorst* battlegroup to 1hr notice for steaming at 1215. *Scharnhorst's* crew were convinced this was an exercise by the Staff Officers designed simply to ruin their Christmas; they changed their tune when they heard they were going out to attack a convoy, and cheered wildly.

Operation 'Eastern Front' — the name given to the sortie — was finally launched by a signal from Doenitz at 1415, ordering the operation to start at 1700. There seems to have been considerable disquiet about the operation on the German side, enthusiasm for it being at a peak with Doenitz and diminishing rapidly the nearer one got to Norway and Altenfjord. A Force 7 wind and visibility at two miles meant no German air reconnaissance, and hence no chance of spotting — visually at least — any battleship covering force, something which had always been considered an essential prerequisite before sending out *Scharnhorst*. The weather also put a question mark over *Scharnhorst's* five destroyers, which were few enough in number anyway and bad sea boats in such conditions. Adm Schniewind at Kiel went so far as to ask Doenitz for a postponement of the action, and both he and Rear-Adm Bey, who would actually command the battlegroup, suggested an alternative plan whereby the destroyers should go in against the convoy, and *Scharnhorst* lie off in support. Doenitz rejected this, believing that a swift hit-and-run raid could inflict serious damage on the convoy. Three destroyers would shadow in front, two remain with *Scharnhorst*, and the whole force sweep in on the convoy when visibility improved on the morning of 26 December with the destroyers fighting a rearguard action if heavy forces were met, *Scharnhorst* using her better speed to escape.

Doenitz's reading of the situation should have been correct. His orders signalled caution, but much less so than had been normal with German surface forces, and they also contained remarks clearly designed to stiffen the offensive spirit of his ships and avoid a repetition of the Barents Sea debacle. However, even the newest of brooms takes time to get below the top layer of dust, and Doenitz's commanders on the day let him down, as Kummetz had been let down by Capt Stange at Barents Sea. There has been considerable discussion of Bey's part in the action, some of the most implicitly hostile coming from Doenitz himself. The fact that Bey was a destroyer man with no big ship experience need mean nothing; plenty of successful admirals in charge of big-ship operations achieved their experience in destroyers, not least A. B. Cunningham. What did matter was that Bey had a scratch naval staff, little apparent confidence in the sortie from the start and had partaken of the generally negative atmosphere that permeated the German surface fleet at that time. Bey was in charge because Kummetz, who had led the Barents Sea operation, was on leave.

It took a considerable while for Bey to transfer his staff from *Tirpitz* to *Scharnhorst*, and he sailed — misgivings and all — at 1900, preceded by three small minesweepers. With him in *Scharnhorst* went a total of 1,968 officers and men, the numbers swollen by Bey's staff and officer-cadets under

training. *Scharnhorst* was accompanied by the destroyers *Z29*, *Z30*, *Z33*, *Z34* and *Z38*. It was bad weather for the minesweepers, and had they but realised it they picked up a foreshadowing of the bad communications that were to dog *Scharnhorst*; one minesweeper Captain had his head bitten off for trying to signal *Scharnhorst* for instructions and eventually the sweepers took their own orders to detach, none having been received from *Scharnhorst*. Throughout the action British communications were to be superb, handling almost effortlessly the foul weather, vast distances and a hugely complex network. The German communications suggested a battle squadron that had become too accustomed to messages that could be sent by picket boat and telephone.

The wind was now Force 8, and the German battlegroup appears to have made 25kt in all this, heading northwards to the convoy's expected position. The over-armed '1936A' destroyers were in trouble. At least the latter three were carrying their full armament of 5×5.9in guns but these potentially powerful weapons were unusable and the ships' steering almost impossible. Bey was clearly having doubts, signalling at 2116 that 'Use of destroyer weapons' was 'gravely impaired'.

Below:
The German destroyer Z34. *Real Photographs 1738*

Bottom:
The German destroyer Z38. *Real Photographs S1935*

Doenitz was not impressed, though this particular signal did not reach him until over 6hr later, this delay being typical of German signals throughout the action. His own orders reached Bey just before midnight. They pointed out the need to assist German troops on the Eastern Front by destroying the convoy, ordered *Scharnhorst* and destroyers to attack, and then said: 'The tactical situation must be exploited with skill and daring and the attack must not end in stalemate.' Barents Sea had left its mark on Doenitz. Bey was given freedom to disengage at will, and automatically if he encountered a superior force — habitual German caution at war with new-found aggression.

26 December

At 0216 Fraser received an 'Ultra' signal informing him that *Scharnhorst* had probably sailed the evening before. An Admiralty signal timed 0319, received by Fraser at 0339, is often given as the time when he knew for certain his prey was at sea; this latter signal was actually the 'cover' signal to Capt McCoy, Senior Officer of the fleet destroyer escort, who was not privy to 'Ultra' and was therefore informed separately on the basis of a conventional Admiralty appreciation.

By 0400 the British forces were well grouped for the coming attack. JW55B was 50 miles south of Bear Island, steering east-northeast at between 6-8kt, just about still in formation. RA55A was well clear of the danger area, about 200 miles west of Bear Island. 'Force 1' (Burnett's cruisers) were 150 miles east of JW55B, aiming to be 30 miles ahead of its likely position by dawn. Fraser and 'Force 2' were 210 miles southeast of the convoy, steaming at 24kt. *Duke of York* was furthest away of all the forces from where she needed to be, and was making heavy weather of it. Always bow-heavy, she was driving through the seas as much as over them, and taking in a lot of water. Ventilation trunking and some light guns had been torn off the bow, leaving gaps in the deck through which the water could pour.

Fraser risked breaking radio silence again at 0401, ordering JW55B to turn on to a more northerly course, and Burnett to report 'Force 1's' position. He was ordered to close the convoy by Fraser at 0628.

The reaction to Bey's worries about his destroyers had been a signal at about 0300 telling him to go it alone like a commerce raider, if he deemed it suitable. He did not, and kept his destroyers with him. Effective Luftwaffe reports had ceased, but U-boat sightings had not: U71 had been forced down by the convoy's escorts at 0327, and signalled a position back to base which suggested *Scharnhorst* was on a course for interception. Bey's battlegroup had altered course to 030° at 0423, and back to 004° at 0500. At 0700 Bey ordered his squadron into a reconnaissance formation on a course of 250° at 12kt, the five destroyers 5-10 miles ahead of the battleship, spread out in line abreast. At 0755 Bey ordered a course change to 230°; by luck and judgement he had placed himself on an excellent course for interception, and by an hour later he was just over 30 miles from JW55B.

Bey had made one crucial mistake: his orders had placed his destroyers 10 miles ahead of *Scharnhorst*, way beyond visual signalling range and a glaring opportunity for contact to be lost or mistaken identity to take place. Perhaps in so doing Bey was clinging to a vestige of the plan to send the destroyers in alone, holding *Scharnhorst* back until the opposition revealed itself fully, yet at the same time appearing to be holding to his orders to attack with the destroyers. The plan might have worked, and the convoy escorts lured on to the destroyers, if Bey had not turned north at 0820. It may have been a fleeting radar contact which caused him to do so, or it may have been the signal at 0814 from U716. In any event the German destroyers received no news of *Scharnhorst's* turn; they proceeded on a southwest heading, with *Scharnhorst* now heading away from them at right angles. It can never be known for sure what Bey

Right:
The situation at 0840.

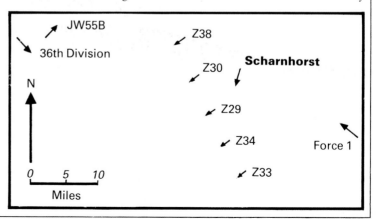

Above:
HMS Belfast, taken just after her repairs in 1942.
Real Photographs S1012

was doing; records went down with him and his ship. In any event, the destroyers were to play no further part in the action — a disastrous loss. Yet despite this failure Bey had managed to place himself squarely between JW55B and the cruisers of 'Force 1'. Burnett had gone too far to the east, and was almost 50 miles eastwards of JW55B, coming up from the southeast, allowing *Scharnhorst* to drive between 'Force 1' and the convoy. It was a brilliant approach, but also something of a misjudgement on Burnett's part to allow himself to get so far ahead of JW55B, particularly when Fraser's willingness to radio positions had so reduced the fog of confusion that normally surrounds such engagements. Burnett had been caught napping.

Contact

At 0834 *Norfolk's* surface search radar picked up an unidentified target, bearing 280°, range 33,000yd. Then came *Belfast* (0840, 295°, 35,000yd) and *Sheffield* (0850, 278°, 30,500yd). Hearing of the sightings, Capt McCoy ordered the fleet destroyer escort to take station six miles ahead of JW55B, with a mile between each destroyer. Between 0900 and 0930 Burnett's cruisers also held on to a second echo, bearing 299°, range 24,000yd. It could have been a straggler from the convoy, or the German destroyer Z38 which was roaming about off position to the north; at 0855 Capt Johannesson

(the Senior Officer) in Z29 had sent off a sighting report to *Scharnhorst*, only to realise that the vessel he was about to open fire on was Z38. In any event, Burnett ignored the second sighting, guessing quite correctly that the first and largest was *Scharnhorst*, which had altered course back to the south at approximately 0850. At 0904 Burnett ordered his cruisers to a line of bearing of 180° to the *Scharnhorst* echo, and then to 160° at 0915. *Scharnhorst* was drawing rapidly to port and aft of 'Force 1', because Burnett was running past *Scharnhorst* rather than at her, heading for the convoy. This meant that there was a risk of the cruisers fouling the range of any cruiser on their starboard or disengaged side, a result of Burnett's dispositions on the day.

Sheffield was first to sight *Scharnhorst*, at 0921 and at a range of 13,000yd. At 0924 *Belfast* opened fire with starshell: it took *Scharnhorst* totally by surprise. Because of the German phobia of radar emissions being picked up she was probably not using her radars. *Belfast* failed to illuminate *Scharnhorst*, so at 0927 Burnett orderd *Norfolk* to fire starshells; she too failed to illuminate the German ship. At the same moment *Scharnhorst* altered course 30° to port, heading on a course of 150°. By 0930 Burnett had had enough, and *Norfolk* was ordered to open fire at a range of 9,800yd. She was masking the fire of *Belfast* and *Sheffield*, and had no flashless cordite either. This did not stop her firing six broadsides with her 8in guns, dropping back as she did so to clear the turrets of *Belfast*. As *Norfolk* opened fire at 0930 Fraser altered course to port on a new course of 265°, and then a much larger alteration to port at 0938 on a course of 105°. The effect of this was to bring his cruisers right round *Scharnhorst* and put them between her and the convoy. Furthermore, *Norfolk's* firing had been both fast and accurate. She had scored two hits on *Scharnhorst* with her

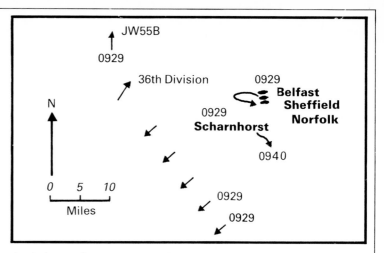

JW55B
0929

36th Division

0929
Scharnhorst

N

0929
0940

0929

0929

0   5   10

Miles

0929
Belfast
Sheffield
Norfolk

Right:
The situation at 0930-0940.

second or third salvoes. One landed on the portside high angle director, abreast the bridge, and not only destroyed the director but also the FuMo27 radar with its large mattress aerial on the foretop. The other shells hit between a portside 5.9in turret and the torpedo tubes, failed to explode, penetrated the deck and finished in a Petty Officers' Mess. *Scharnhorst* altered course immediately to 150° and increased speed to 30kt, firing back from her after 11in triple turret ('Caesar') as she did so. The weather meant that the cruisers could only make 24kt.

Burnett's actions at this point, and later, have been criticised. He had deployed his cruisers too far ahead, probably because of being given a wrong position for the convoy earlier in the morning, and when he had deployed them it had been in a manner that masked the fire of two out of the three of them. He had waited a long time under the circumstances to follow *Scharnhorst's* turn to port (11min, 18min after the first sighting), and with *Scharnhorst* making 30kt this meant the range opened very rapidly before Burnett turned to follow. Then at 1014 he turned away completely, deliberately losing contact.

It is this latter action that has received the most criticism, though Roskill's official history excuses him. To turn away from an enemy went deeply against everything the Royal Navy held holy, but it was the right decision. Burnett felt that *Scharnhorst* would work round to try to attack the convoy from the north. If she could lure the cruisers away from the convoy her 6kt speed advantage over them and the foul weather gave her an excellent opportunity of losing the cruisers, and then using her extra speed to cut back to the convoy. Burnett would have been stranded with *Scharnhorst* between him and the convoy yet again. Burnett felt that his prime duty was to protect the convoy, that *Scharnhorst* would come round again and waiting for her was both more

certain and less risky. His mistake was not in turning away, but in failing to turn more quickly when *Scharnhorst* turned away. There had been indecision in Burnett's handling of the cruisers at the Battle of Barents Sea, and it came at exactly the same time in the action, when initial contact had been established but before the enemy's intentions had been made clear. At such moments Burnett became extremely cautious — even indecisive — waiting for the enemy to move and make his mind up for him.

Fraser had ordered JW55B to turn north when *Scharnhorst* was sighted, and detached four destroyers from JW55B to give assistance to the cruisers — *Musketeer*, *Matchless*, *Opportune* and *Virago*. They joined 'Force 1' at 1024. Burnett signalled to Fraser at 1035: 'Have lost contact with the enemy who was steering north. Am closing convoy.' This put Fraser and his ships on a broad ziz-zag some 10 miles ahead of the convoy, his four destroyers thrown out ahead as a screen.

Burnett's signal that he had lost touch with *Scharnhorst* came as a severe blow to Fraser with 'Force 2' in *Duke of York*, and put him in a desperate predicament. His destroyers were starting to run low on fuel, and Fraser would soon have to make a decision to turn back or proceed to Kola. If *Scharnhorst* was heading home there was clearly no point in carrying on, as 'Force 2' was too far west to intercept her. If she was going to turn back and attack the convoy he needed to remain on his present course east. But there was the appalling possibility that *Scharnhorst* had broken out to the west, in which case *Duke of York* was heading in exactly the wrong direction, and Atlantic shipping open to her. If *Scharnhorst* was heading west into the trade routes Fraser would be remembered as the Admiral who fell for the biggest naval trick of the whole war. He had to know where *Scharnhorst* was — and the cruisers had just knowingly relinquished contact with her.

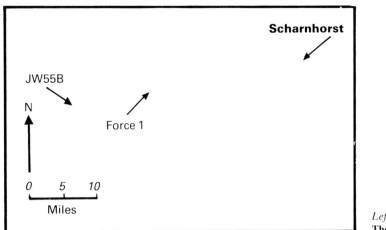

Scharnhorst

JW55B

N

Force 1

0   5   10

Miles

Left:
The situation at 1205.

At 1058 Fraser sent a signal to Burnett that threw the latter into a heart-searching passion: 'Unless touch can be regained by some unit, there is no chance of my finding enemy.'

Things were simpler from the German viewpoint, though Bey was starting to become troubled by the whereabouts of his destroyers. Perhaps the hits from *Norfolk* startled his memory. He signalled Johannesson, commanding the destroyers, 'Report your situation' at 0945, Johannesson, who had sighted the starshell of *Scharnhorst's* brief engagement with the cruisers, showed lack of initiative (at least) by stoically ignoring what he saw and steaming southwest. At 1027 Bey signalled the destroyers to come towards him again; at 1135 he gave his own position and finally, at 1158, he ordered the destroyers to steer for the convoy's position, as reported at 1000 by *U277*. Bey was also headed for that position, and was trying to draw his forces together, but he had left it too late and Johannesson was clearly not the man to take the initiative.

With hindsight, it is easy to see that Bey should have tried to blast his way through the cruisers and get to the convoy, but this was the one thing that German commanders in the war were never able to do. They were not only victims of political factors, but also of the law which dictates that capital ships are too valuable to be risked, particularly if that particular navy only has one of them operational. The most ominous events from the German viewpoint were not taking place in the sea around JW55B, but many miles away. 'Force 2', the *Duke of York* and all, was spotted by German air reconnaissance at 1012; the aircraft actually reported a large ship in the force it had detected at 1135. But these sightings were made by radar, and the Germans consistently underestimated the effectiveness of their own technology. At the Lofoten Islands, from where the aircraft originated, the reference to 'heavy

vessel' was deleted; *Scharnhorst* had no radio equipment that could communicate directly with or pick up the aircraft's signals. In addition, the Germans had been picking up signal traffic to an unidentified force or source throughout the morning. There was no definite proof it was a heavy force at sea which could cut off *Scharnhorst's* escape. There was every reason for guessing this was so, but remarkably no one seems to have warned Bey of the danger. His crew were told of a heavy covering force 150 miles away.

After shaking off the cruisers, Bey worked round to the north and, after several course changes, began to head down on it from the northeast, almost the exact bearing from which Burnett had gambled the German force would appear. History has tended to give Bey the lion's share of the blame for what happened to *Scharnhorst*; a fairer judgement would be to blame Doenitz. He had ordered the sortie to take place against the wishes of many of those under him. He had given it orders that demanded an outcome to the action, pressed for an offensive spirit but at the same time added the habitual note of caution. The result was that Bey, in following his orders, felt obliged to take neither the most aggressive and dangerous option of blasting his way through the cruisers nor the safest one, turning back for home when he met a screening force of enemy cruisers. Instead he compromised by trying to work round the cruisers and try for a 'safe' attack, whilst all the time 'Force 2' was ploughing eastwards to cut off his escape. Doenitz must also take some of the blame for the fact that it took so long for air reconnaissance reports to reach *Scharnhorst*. His U-boats had a highly complex and effective sighting and signalling procedure; of all people, Doenitz as C-in-C or Grand-Adm should have seen the need to tidy up communications for his surface fleet. In trying for a second attack Bey was merely trying to carry out the spirit of his orders.

The Second Engagement

Fraser had actually ordered 'Force 2' to reverse course, for fear of *Scharnhorst* breaking out to the west, when at 1210 *Sheffield's* Type 273 radar picked up an unidentified echo 12 miles off, some 3hr after *Scharnhorst* had broken off the first action. 'Force 1' was steering 045° with *Belfast* the northernmost ship, and *Sheffield* and *Norfolk* in that order due south of *Belfast* in line abreast. The four destroyers of the 36th Division (*Musketeer*, *Matchless*, *Opportune* and *Virago*) had by now joined the cruisers, and were two miles ahead of them off their starboard bow; *Scharnhorst* was steering a course of 240°, and thus heading almost exactly between the cruisers and the 36th Division destroyers and virtually straight at them. This time Burnett had positioned his force superbly to intercept *Scharnhorst*. He altered the course of 'Force 1' first to 090° and then to 100°, in order to intercept the German ship rather than pass her by, so as to block her passage to the convoy.

At 1221, with the range down to 11,000yd and the two forces closing at a combined speed of nearly 40kt, 'Force 1' opened fire, *Belfast* leading with starshell and then following with main armament. At the same time Burnett ordered the 36th Division to close and attack with torpedoes. It was unfortunate that the destroyers were deployed in line ahead rather than abeam, as this made for a very difficult torpedo shot with *Scharnhorst* heading directly at them; the issue became academic when *Musketeer's* signals staff received the message to attack but failed to deliver it to the bridge, possibly as a result of simple exhaustion.

The engagement was to last 20min. At first sight *Scharnhorst* seemed to want to make a fight of it, altering course slightly to the west, but at 1225, with the range down to just over 4,000yd, she turned away south on a course of roughly 135°. In the time she was in range she showed what she might have done. Taken by surprise and being fired on by three cruisers and two destroyers she still managed to give a very good account of herself. She straddled *Sheffield* and riddled her with splinters, and then concentrated on *Norfolk*, which was firing without the benefit of flashless cordite. At 1227 an 11in shell hit 'X' turret, put it out of action and produced a huge red column of fire that was seen both by the British cruisers and from *Scharnhorst*. A second shell penetrated the

Left:
HMS *Duke of York*, showing the angle of elevation of her 5.25in secondary armament. At the time of the *Scharnhorst* engagement *Duke of York* was probably the best-equipped ship in the fleet as regards radar.
MoD (Navy) BS/DOY/4

deck amidships. As a result of the two hits one officer and six ratings were killed, five others seriously injured, all radar put out of action and the magazine for 'X' turret flooded as a precaution. Miraculously, *Norfolk's* speed was not affected.

The British thought they had hit *Scharnhorst* but she seems to have emerged from this exchange of fire unscathed; her fighting capacity was unaffected anyway. *Scharnhorst* could almost shrug off cruiser fire, but this is not to blame Bey for turning away; he did so just at the time when his ship was coming into torpedo range from seven enemy vessels. Without his own destroyers to block and distract their British counterparts a closer approach would have been foolhardy. The fact that his destroyers were far away at the time he needed them is another matter altogether. Indeed, Bey seems to have lost all interest in them after he broke off action for the second time. They were still ploughing northwest to engage the convoy after his order of 1158 when he signalled them to break off at 1343, and to return to base at 1420. At their closest the destroyers passed within some 9-10 miles of the convoy, and were to play no effective part in the action whatsoever.

Sheffield was typical of the cruisers in firing 96 rounds of 6in during this part of the action. She had fired salvoes instead of broadsides for 7min, because bad visibility and an unserviceable Type 284 gunnery control made spotting fall of shot difficult. In the first few minutes of the engagement the British cruisers had been forced to fire by radar, and again at the end as *Scharnhorst* drew away. *Musketeer* managed as many as 52 salvoes, and *Virago* only six.

The cruisers had all checked fire by 1241, *Virago* being the last British vessel of all to fire at 1247. *Scharnhorst's* turn to the south had placed her on a perfect course for *Duke of York* and the rest of 'Force 2' to intercept. Burnett followed *Scharnhorst* round and with visibility at seven miles shadowed just beyond, from 7½ miles. He had no desire to disturb *Scharnhorst* from her run to the south, and so did not fire at her. Ironically 'Force 2' continued to be shadowed by a German reconnaissance aircraft until 1400, but as had already been noted the relaying of signals to *Scharnhorst* was immensely slow, and the reference in the sighting report to a heavy ship was deleted. It is at this stage that *Scharnhorst* sealed her fate. If she had known and been told of *Duke of York* steaming towards her she could have altered course to the southwest, pushing her shadowing cruisers into the seas which would inevitably have slowed them down, and might also have drawn her destroyers in between *Duke of York* and herself. As it was, Bey was content to alter course to 155° at 1300 which, at 28kt would

bring him comfortably back to base by midnight; he was 240 miles away. He and his crew were undoubtedly exhausted. He appeared to know he was still being shadowed by cruisers, and perhaps his major mistake of all was not to ponder on why three British cruisers were content to tail him quietly for so long without either they or their destroyers trying to cripple his vessel. In any event, he missed his golden opportunity later in the afternoon.

At 1603 a fire flared up in one of *Norfolk's* wing compartments, and at 1610 *Sheffield* stripped a port inner shaft bearing, reducing her speed to 8kt. This left one 6in-gun cruiser and four destroyers tailing *Scharnhorst*; it remains a mystery to this day why *Scharnhorst* did not turn round and dispose of *Belfast* (fortunately for the British the one cruiser whose radar had functioned faultlessly throughout the action). *Scharnhorst's* FuMo27 radar could detect a surface ship at about 12 miles, but the after set was not switched on so as to avoid detection by the British. A price is always paid for such electronic abstinence: in *Scharnhorst's* case a heavy one.

The Final Action

At 1647 on 26 December 1943 — without warning from look-outs or radar — *Scharnhorst* was suddenly flooded by the light of British starshell. It was the beginning of the end.

Duke of York had the best radar fit of any ship in the Royal Navy at the end of 1943. Her Type 273 radar detected *Scharnhorst* at 45,500yd — or nearly 23 miles — bearing 020°; *Scharnhorst* from the north and *Duke of York* from the west were on almost converging courses. The time was 1617. Fraser pressed on, refusing a long-range engagement; at 1636 the range was 13 miles. At 1637 Fraser signalled to *Savage* and *Saumarez* to his port and *Scorpion* and *Stord* to starboard: 'Take up most advantageous position for firing torpedoes but do not attack until ordered.' This order was to have unfortunate consequences later in the action. At the same time *Belfast* picked up *Duke of York* on her radar; 'Force 1' and 'Force 2' had finally joined up, and a veritable wolf pack was gathering round *Scharnhorst*.

At 1642 *Scharnhorst* appeared to alter course to port. 'Force 2' altered course to starboard to open her 'A' arcs, and *Belfast* was ordered to open fire with starshell, which she did at 1647. As had been the case before, the starshell failed to illuminate the German ship, so *Duke of York* opened fire with starshell from her 5.25in secondary armament, also at 1647. The four British starshells hung limply behind the vast, silvery-grey shape of *Scharnhorst*; her turrets were still trained fore and aft.

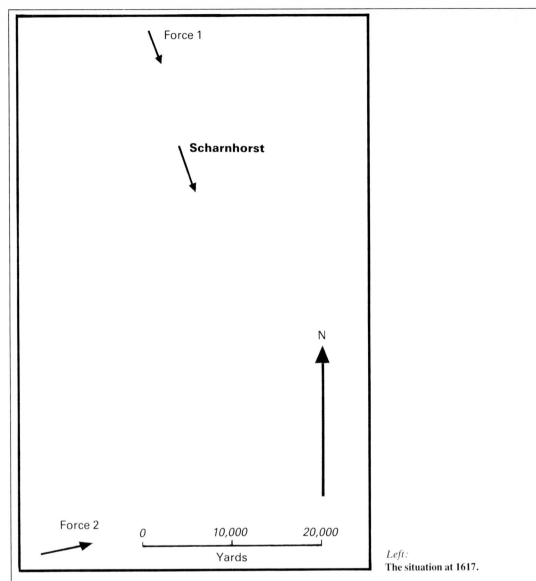

Force 1

Scharnhorst

N

Force 2

0   10,000   20,000

Yards

Left:
The situation at 1617.

Duke of York fired her first, full 10-gun 14in broadside at 1651. It was extremely accurate, straddling *Scharnhorst* with one shell landing abreast of the fore turret ('Anton') on the starboard side, putting the turret out of action and jamming it in its firing position with its barrels elevated. *Jamaica* opened fire at 1652, and straddled and hit with her third broadside. A shell which probably came from *Duke of York's* third salvo landed near to 'Caesar' turret, destroyed the aircraft hangar and caused considerable damage to the superstructure, killing many of the AA gun crews. The remaining crews were ordered into shelter, but this included those for the 4.1in guns which would have been very useful in fighting off destroyers; the order was never countermanded,

and *Scharnhorst* was left with inadequate anti-destroyer fire at a crucial stage in the battle, a fact which some survivors held to be the cause of her defeat.

Scharnhorst altered course to the north at 1655, and *Duke of York* swung to 060° to comb the tracks of any torpedoes that might have been fired. At 1657 *Belfast* and *Norfolk* opened fire, *Sheffield* still lagging behind. All this while there was no shortage of targets for *Scharnhorst*, who opened fire at 1646, a creditable 5min only after having sighted her enemy. Her early salvoes — with six guns only — were short, but she soon picked up the range and began to straddle *Duke of York*, those going over coming dangerously close to *Jamaica*. *Norfolk* had no flashless cordite, neither

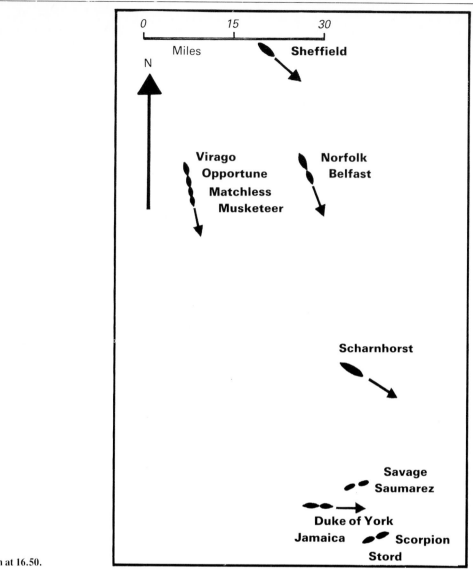

0   15   30

Miles

N

Sheffield

Virago
Opportune

Matchless
Musketeer

Norfolk
Belfast

Scharnhorst

Savage
Saumarez

Duke of York
Jamaica   **Scorpion**
Stord

Right:
The situation at 16.50.

did *Duke of York's* secondary 5.25in turrets, and both provided good aiming marks. In addition, *Savage* and *Saumarez* were so near to *Scharnhorst* that they were illuminated by *Duke of York's* starshell, and the accuracy of *Scharnhorst's* fire caused them actually to sheer away from the German vessel at one stage. The order for them to make a torpedo attack never came, and an opportunity was wasted that did not occur again for a very long hour-and-a-half.

At 1713 Fraser ordered his four 'S' class destroyers to close and fire torpedoes, but by that time *Scharnhorst* was using her superior speed and drawing away from her pursuers. At 1708 she had swung round on an easterly course of 111°, and by then had increased her range from 'Force 2' to

17,000yd. She was firing all the while at *Duke of York* with her aft turret, 'Caesar', and occasionally swinging round to open her 'A' arcs and firing six-gun salvoes with both 'Caesar' and 'Bruno' turrets. At 1656 Bey had signalled giving his position and adding 'Heavy battleship. Am in action', but he was handling his ship with skill. It was true she was being hit, and quite severely. A 14in hit on 'Bruno' turret pierced its ventilation trunking and soon made the turret inoperable, and another hit knocked out the foremost 5.9in turret on the starboard side, penetrated the deck and blew a hole half a yard wide in the ship's side, only 2ft above the waterline. Yet despite this, the range had increased to 18,000yd by 1742, when *Jamaica* had to cease fire after 19 broadsides. *Savage*

Saumarez, Scorpion and Stord were still 12,000yd away at 1800, and in turn almost 10 miles from Duke of York, and hardly making any headway. The cruisers of 'Force 1' were even further away to the north. Duke of York's stern turret was trained on its extreme forward bearing, and at that angle the 4° yaw of the ship was making accurate fire difficult. Furthermore, two 11in shells from Scharnhorst had passed through the mainmast, destroying the aerial of the Type 281 air warning set and temporarily putting out of action the Type 273 surface warning set. At 1824 a fault in the Type 284 gunnery control radar, caused by the shaking it had received from repeated salvoes forced Duke of York, who had been firing 'blind' by radar for a considerable while, to check fire. Lt H. Bates RNVR climbed the mast to resplice damaged wires. It looked as if Scharnhorst had escaped. Duke of York had fired 52 salvoes and made 13 hits. The range when she ceased fire was 21,400yd. Scharnhorst in her turn ceased fire at about 1820.

Now came one of the cruellest blows ever to strike the German Navy, or indeed any navy.

Shortly after ceasing fire, Fraser had admitted defeat and signalled to Burnett 'I see little hope of catching Scharnhorst and am proceeding to support convoy'. Bey for his part signalled at 1819 that he was under fire by radar at over 18,000yd, and that his speed was 26kt. Then, at about 1820, a 14in shell fired at long range as part of Duke of York's last gasp scored a hit which penetrated the starboard side and effectively destroyed No 1 boiler room, severing a steam pipe. Her speed dropped to between 8-10kt, then picked up to 22kt after some remarkable damage repair by Cdr Otto König, Scharnhorst's Chief Engineer; but it was not enough. Scharnhorst had been made to stumble at the last fence, and had lost her vital speed advantage.

There was elation when it was realised on board the British flagship that the destroyers were gaining on Scharnhorst. By 1840 Savage and Saumarez were astern of Scharnhorst, Scorpion and the Norwegian Stord about 10,000yd away, on her starboard side. Savage and Saumarez were approaching from the northwest, and drew

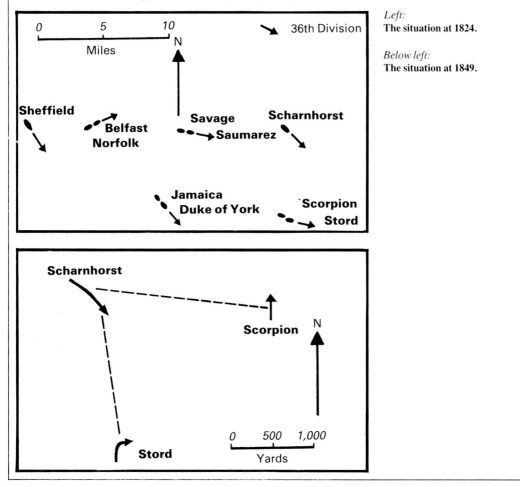

Left:
The situation at 1824.

Below left:
The situation at 1849.

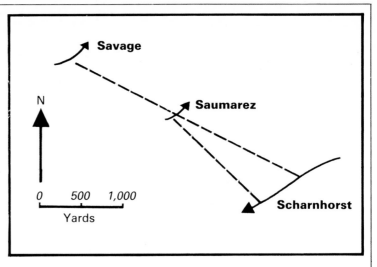

Right:
The situation at 1855.

Scharnhorst's fire whilst the remaining two destroyers approached unseen from the southeast. The German fire was rapid but erratic. There appear to have been differences of opinion amongst the German gunnery officers about how to handle the secondary armament, and many of the AA crews were still at their 'safe' stations. *Savage* and *Saumarez* opened fire at 7,000yd; *Scorpion* and *Stord* held their fire in order to remain undetected. It seemed to the crews on all four destroyers that they were going close enough to board *Scharnhorst. Scorpion* and *Stord* were suddenly spotted by *Scharnhorst*. She was heading southeast — almost directly at the two destroyers — presenting a very difficult onrushing target and already partially combing the likely torpedo tracks. Instead of smashing through the two destroyers *Scharnhorst* flung her helm over to starboard, continuing round until she was heading southwest. The result was to present *Scorpion* and *Stord* with almost a beam-on as distinct from an end-on target. *Stord* at 1,800yd and *Scorpion* at 2,100yd fired full salvoes before hauling round and away. As *Scorpion* turned away, an Ordinary Seaman yelled 'Out wires and fenders port side!'.

Scharnhorst's sudden change of course did wonders for *Savage* and *Saumarez* too, They had been chasing her from astern; she was now conveniently heading straight past them on their starboard side. *Saumarez* was in trouble: an 11in shell had passed through her Director Tower without exploding, but still wreaking havoc. Near-misses swept the decks with splinters, wiped out almost a whole torpedo crew and damaged the starboard engine, reducing speed to 10kt. She lost 11 killed and 11 wounded, but at about 1853 she still managed to fire four torpedoes at a range of 1,800yd. *Savage* simultaneously fired all eight torpedoes at 3,500yd. It is impossible to say exactly

how many of these hit: *Scorpion* and *Stord* got at least one hit on the starboard side, *Savage* and *Saumarez* at least three on the port, whilst repeatedly hitting *Scharnhorst* with their 4.7in main armament. The starboard side hit was just forward of the bridge; the port torpedoes hit the bows, a boiler room and aft. There was serious flooding aft, and speed fell again from 22kt to nearer 8-10kt. Again 22kt was restored, or nearly so, but *Scharnhorst* was entering her final agonies. As if giving a preliminary overture, *Norfolk* fired two salvoes before the confusion of radar echoes caused her to cease fire.

Duke of York and *Jamaica* opened fire at 1901, the range being 10,400yd. The destroyers' and her own vital hit had given her an unmissable second chance, and *Duke of York* even had her Type 284 gunnery radar back in action. Her first salvo seemed to hit the quarterdeck square, hitting the remains of the aircraft hangar and causing a large fire that took 20min to control. Again *Scharnhorst* seemed unaware of the British battleship's approach. She switched fire from the destroyers immediately, but only 'Caesar' turret was operational, and after a short while this had to be fired in local control, ammunition being manhandled to it from the forward turret magazines. At 1915 *Belfast* opened fire to add to *Scharnhorst's* troubles, but Bey and Capt Hintze seem to have realised the inevitable a few minutes before. At 1900 *Scharnhorst* had signalled: 'We shall fight to the last shell: *Scharnhorst* ever onwards.' But she was being battered into a blazing hulk. By 1912 *Scharnhorst* was making only 10kt and listing to starboard — yet she was not sinking. At almost 3,000yd *Duke of York's* shells had a virtually flat trajectory, not the plunging fire that would sink her. Her final moments were an echo of *Bismarck's*. Her

armoured deck had not been pierced, though as it was situated low down in the ship, communications and passageways above it had been demolished, and the ship ruined as a fighting instrument. *Duke of York* checked fire after 80 salvoes at 1929, having ordered *Jamaica* at 1919 to 'finish her off with torpedoes'.

Above:
HMS *Jamaica*. *Real Photographs S1659*

Below:
HMS *Savage*, seen postwar and showing the unusual twin 4.5in turret forward. She was used for shaft and propeller experiments in the early 1950s, finally being scrapped in 1962. *Real Photographs S9965*

It was easier said than done. At 1925 *Jamaica* fired three torpedoes at 3,500yd — one misfired because of an improperly closed breech; the other two missed, the bad visibility and huge clouds of smoke having led to a miscalculation of *Scharnhorst's* speed. *Scharnhorst* was still firing with all her serviceable secondary armament. 'Abandon ship' appears to have been ordered on *Scharnhorst* at 1930, but when *Jamaica* fired her starboard tubes at 1937 guns were still firing on board the German ship; there were two possible hits. Fraser had ordered *Belfast* in with torpedoes as well at 1920. She fired three at 1927, and claimed one disputed hit. She was unable to fire her remaining torpedoes because by this time the 36th Destroyer Division had arrived. *Scharnhorst* was moving at under 3kt, her bows submerged and her decks awash on the starboard side as she listed over. *Musketeer* fired four torpedoes at 1,000yd at

1933, and claimed three hits. As she turned away she nearly collided with *Matchless*, who was unable to fire because of storm damage. From the starboard side *Opportune* fired four torpedoes at 1931 and four more at 1933, from 2,500yd. She claimed two hits, and *Virago* also claimed two hits when she fired seven torpedoes at 1934 from a range of 2,800yd.

At about 1945 there was a huge explosion from *Scharnhorst*, and she had vanished when *Belfast* arrived to make a second torpedo attack at 1948. She had been hit by numerous shells of all calibres and by 11 modern Mk IX 21in torpedoes, capable of defeating her underwater protection. There were 36 survivors, none of them officers. Bey was never seen; Capt Hintze and his Executive Officer, Dominik, both gave their lifejackets away to sailors without them, but made it to the water. Hintze died before he could be picked up, and

Dominik actually had his hands on a line before he slipped back into the sea and died. Survivors were picked up mainly by *Scorpion*, with all the destroyers, *Belfast* and *Norfolk* detached for this purpose. The survivors went back to Scapa on board *Duke of York*, via Kola. Convoy JW55B survived various submarine scares and made it to Kola without loss.

Conclusion

From the German viewpoint *Scharnhorst* fought with exceptional courage, but was defeated almost before she sailed by much more than the physical odds against her. The 'Ultra' code organisation and German signalling, coupled with inadequate radar, was a combination she could not beat. Luftwaffe reconnaissance, in fact, did an excellent job on the day; it was German failure to believe

Right:
The *Scharnhorst* sinks.

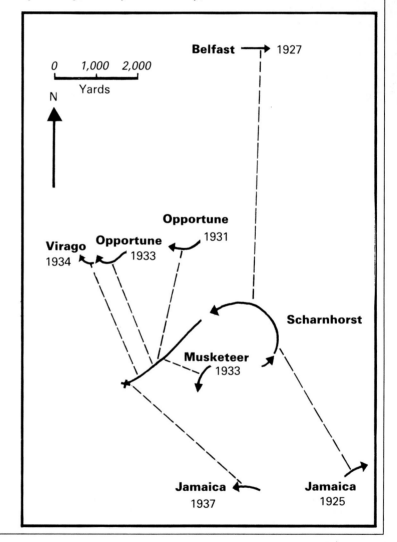

Above:
Survivors from *Scharnhorst* on board *Duke of York*.
IWM A21172

their own pilots and pass on all information that dogged *Scharnhorst*. Despite this it is possible to claim, in common with a number of German authorities, that *Scharnhorst* had appallingly bad luck. The hit that slowed her must have penetrated her relatively weak deck armour, but she had already survived a veritable battering. Without that hit there is every chance that she would have made it back to Altenfjord. For his part Bey made one mistake, which was to lose his destroyers; had he been able to fling them at *Duke of York* and force her to comb tracks, that decisive hit might have been averted. It is possible, however, that the significance of this might have been overestimated; with their overwhelming superiority of surface vessels a run against the battleship by five German destroyers would have been a suicide mission.

A worrying factor from the British point of view was the performance of *Duke of York's* main armament, dogged by malfunction just as *Prince of Wales'* had been against the *Bismarck*. From 80 broadsides fired, the third gun on 'A' turret missed no less than 71. The third gun on 'Y' turret missed 43, the second gun on 'A' turret 33, the second gun on 'B' turret 30. Ten 14in guns firing 80 broadsides should have sent 800 shells on their way to

Scharnhorst — in fact 446 shells were fired, meaning that for much of the battle *Duke of York* was firing with the effectiveness of a five- or six-gun ship. It is often stated that after the *Bismarck* hunt the problems with the quadruple 14in turrets were ironed out. *Duke of York's* gunnery log suggests that is a slight exaggeration. Some of the other British margins were also, in retrospect, disturbingly narrow. If the one shadowing cruiser that remained by the end had been shaken off or sunk, Fraser would not only have been too far away to protect JW55B but also too far away to catch *Scharnhorst*. Communications, radar and the ability to land telling hits swung the Battle of North Cape the way of the British. But it was a very close-run thing.

HMS *Duke of York*

Duke of York was built by John Brown at Clydebank, laid down on 5 May 1937, launched on 28 February 1940 and completed in November 1941. Details are as for *King George V* and *Prince of Wales* (see Chapter 4), except that by 1943 *Duke of York* carried more light AA guns, and a greatly enhanced electronics fit, with Types 273QR (surface warning×1); 281 (air and surface warning×1); 284 (14in gunnery×2); 285M3 (5.25in gunnery×4); 243 (aircraft IFF, working with 281×1); 253 (IFF×1); 91FV1 (detection of enemy transmissions×1). For technical details of *Norfolk* see Chapter 4, for *Sheffield* and *Jamaica* see Chapter 9.

Above:
The victors — from left to right: **Capt The Hon Guy
Russell** (*Duke of York*); **Cdr Lee Barber DSO** (*Opportune*);
Cdr E. L. Fisher DSO (*Musketeer*); **Cdr Meyrick**
(*Savage*); **Adm Sir Bruce Fraser**; **Capt J. Hughes Hallett
DSO** (*Jamaica*); **Lt-Cdr E. N. Walmsley DSC** (*Saumarez*);
Lt-Cdr Clouston (*Scorpion*) and **Lt Shaw** (*Matchless*).
IWM A21164

HMS *Belfast*

Builder: Harland & Wolff, Belfast
(Laid down 10 December 1936; launched 17 March 1938;
    completed 3 August 1939)

Displacement: 11,500 tons (standard)

Dimensions: 613.5ft × 66.3ft × 17ft

Machinery: Geared turbines, 4 shafts, 80,000shp, 32kt

Armour: Main belt 4.5in; deck 2-3in; turrets 2in

Armament: 12×6in (4×3); 12×4in (6×2); 16×2pdr (2×8);
    18×20mm (5×2, 8×1); 6×21in torpedo tubes (2×3)

Sensors: Type 273, 281, 282, 283, 284 and 285

Aircraft: 3

Complement: 850

Notes: Enlarged 'Town' class cruisers with enhanced protection,
    these two vessels had an unsightly gap between bridge and
    funnels to accommodate aircraft. *Belfast* was badly damaged by
    a magnetic mine in November 1939, not re-entering service for
    almost three years. The bulges fitted to restore her broken back
    enlarged the beam by 3ft. Her sister, *Edinburgh*, was sunk in
    May 1942.

'Savage' Class Destroyers

Builders:
Savage — Hawthorn Leslie
(Laid down 1941; launched 1942; completed 1943)

Saumarez — Hawthorn Leslie
(Laid down 1941; launched 1942; completed 1943)

Scorpion — Cammell Laird
(Laid down 1941; launched 1942; completed 1943)

Stord — J. S. White
(Laid down 1942; launched 1943; completed 1943)

Displacement: 1,780 tons (standard), 2,535 tons (full load)

Dimensions: 362.75ft × 35.75ft × 13ft

Machinery: Geared turbines, 2 shafts, 40,000shp, 36.75kt

Armament: 4×4.7in (4×1); *Savage* 4×4.5in (1×2, 2×1);
    Savage 12×20mm (6×2); *Scorpion* 4×2pdr (1×4);
    Saumarez and *Stord* 8×21in torpedo tubes (2×4); 2×40mm
    (1×2); *Scorpion, Saumarez* and *Stord* 8×20mm (4×2)

Sensors: Type 271 (surface warning — *Savage* only); 272 (surface
    warning — *Saumarez* and *Stord* only); 282 (40mm and 2pdr
    fire control — *Saumarez, Scorpion* and *Stord*); 285 (main
    armament fire control — all); 291 (primarily air warning —
    all)

Complement: 180

Notes: *Savage* mounted an experimental twin 4.5in turret, later
    mounted on 'Battle' class destroyers. The impressive radar fits
    of these modern ships were a great help in the Arctic night. The
    air warning 291 gave especially good results against surface
    targets: *Stord* detected *Scharnhorst* at 17,000yd on her Type
    291. *Savage's* 271 was masked by the bridge and could not
    detect targets ahead.

Select Bibliography

The following books are a selection of those available on the period and the engagements covered in this volume; sadly, a number are now out of print. A number of the works given below in their paperback form originally appeared as hardbacks; wherever possible either the cheapest good edition or the most readily available has been given.

Technical

Breyer, S. *Battleships and Battlecruisers 1905-1970* (Macdonald and James 1973).

Campbell, J. *Naval Weapons of World War Two* (Conway 1985).

Cocker, M. *Destroyers of the Royal Navy 1893-1981* (Ian Allan 1981).

Conway's All the World's Fighting Ships 1922-1946 (Conway Maritime Press 1980).

Fraccaroli, A. *Italian Warships of World War 2* (Ian Allan).

Friedman, Norman *Battleship Design and Development* (Conway Maritime Press 1978).

Garzke, William H. and Dulin, Robert O. *Battleships: Allied Battleships in World War II* (Naval Institute Press 1980) and *Battleships: Axis and Neutral Battleships of World War II* (Naval Institute Press 1986).

Jane's Fighting Ships (Sampson Low & Marston), all editions 1935-48.

Man o' War series (Arms and Armour Press), various.

Lenton, H. T. and Colledge, J. J. *Warships of World War 2* (Ian Allan).

German Warships of the Second World War (Macdonald and Janes 1975).

Lyon, H. *The Encyclopedia of the World's Warships* (Salamander 1978).

Raven, Alan and Roberts, John *British Battleships of World War Two* (Arms and Armour Press 1976) and *British Cruisers of World War Two* (Arms and Armour Press 1980).

Silverstone, P. H. *US Warships of World War 2* (Ian Allan).

Stephen, G. M. *British Warship Designs Since 1906* (Ian Allan 1984).

Taylor, J. C. *German Warships of World War 2* (Ian Allan).

Warship International, various.

Warship Profile series (Profile Publications), individual and collected volumes.

Warship Specials series (Conway Maritime Press), various.

Watton, Ross *The Battleship* Warspite, Anatomy of the Ship Series (Conway Maritime Press 1986).

Watts, A. J. *Japanese Warships of World War 2* (Ian Allan).

Battleships, World War 2 Fact Files (Jane's 1979).

Allied Cruisers, World War 2 Fact Files (Jane's 1979).

Axis Cruisers, World War 2 Fact Files (Jane's 1979).

General Historical

Beesly, Patrick *Very Special Intelligence* (Hamish Hamilton 1977).

Very Special Admiral (Hamish Hamilton 1980).

Bekker, Cajus *Hitler's Naval War* (MacDonald and Jane's 1974).

The German Navy 1939-1945 (Hamlyn 1974).

Brown, David *Carrier Operations in World War 2*, Volumes I and II (Ian Allan 1974).

Churchill, Sir Winston *The Second World War* (Cassell 1967).

Cooper, Bryan *The Battle of the Torpedo Boats* (MacDonald 1970).

Cunningham, Viscount of Hyndhope *A Sailor's Odyssey* (Hutchinson 1951).

Doenitz, Adm Karl *Memoirs: Ten Years and Twenty Days* (Weidenfeld and Nicholson 1959).

Dull, Paul S. *A Battle History of the Imperial Japanese Navy* (Naval Institute Press 1978).

Garrett, Richard *Scharnhorst and Gneisenau: The Elusive Sisters* (David and Charles 1978).

Hinsley, F. H. *British Intelligence in the Second World War* (HMSO 1979).

Humble, R. *Fraser of North Cape* (Routledge and Kegan Paul 1983).

Macintyre, Donald *The Battle for the Pacific* (Pan 1975).

The Naval War Against Hitler (Batsford 1971).

Marder *Old Friends, New Enemies* (Oxford University Press 1981).

Martinsenn, Anthony *Hitler and His Admirals* (Secker and Warburg 1948).

McClachlan, Donald *Room 39* (Weidenfeld and Nicholson 1968).

Morison, Samuel Eliot *A History of United States Naval Operations in World War 2* (Brown and Co/Oxford University Press 1947).

Padfield, P. *Dönitz: The Last Führer* (Gollancz 1984).

Potter, E. B. and Nimitz, Chester W. (eds) *The Great Sea War: The Story of Naval Action in World War 2* (Harrap 1961).

Preston, Antony *An Illustrated History of the Navies of World War 2* (Bison 1982).

Purnell's History of the Second World War, Volumes I-IV.

Raeder, Adm Erich *Struggle for the Sea* (Weidenfeld and Nicholson 1957).

Roskill, Capt S. W. *The War at Sea*, Volumes I-IV (HMSO 1954-61).

The Navy at War (Collins 1960).

HMS Warspite (Collins 1957).

Ruge, Vice-Adm Friedrich *Sea Warfare 1939-1945: A German Viewpoint* (Cassell 1957).

Salewski, Michael *Die Deutsche Seekriegsleitung 1935-1945*, Volumes I-III (Bernard and Graefe 1970).

Thomas, David A. *Japan's War at Sea: Pearl Harbor to the Coral Sea* (Andre Deutsch 1978).

Proceedings of the United States Naval Institute (various).

Vian, Sir Philip *Action This Day* (Frederick Muller 1960).

Whitley, M. J. *Destroyer! German Destroyers in World War 2* (Arms and Armour Press 1983).

German Cruisers of World War 2 (Arms and Armour Press 1985).

Woodward, David *Sunk! How the Great Battleships were Lost* (Allen and Unwin 1982).

Specific Engagements

Ash, Bernard *Someone Had Blundered: The Story of the* Repulse *and* Prince of Wales (Michael Joseph 1960).

Bennett, G *The Battle of the River Plate* (Ian Allan 1972).

The Loss of the Prince of Wales *and* Repulse (Ian Allan 1973).

Naval Battles of World War II (Batsford 1975).

Bradford, Ernle *The Mighty* Hood (Hodder and Stoughton 1961).

Busch, Fritze Otto *The Sinking of the* Scharnhorst (Futura 1974).

Fuchida, Mitsuo and Okumiya, Masatake *Midway: The Battle That Doomed Japan* (Hutchinson 1957).

Hough, Richard *The Hunting of Force Z* (Fontana 1964).

Kemp, P. *Escape of the* Scharnhorst *and* Gneisenau (Ian Allan 1975).

Kennedy, Ludovic *Pursuit: The Sinking of the* Bismarck (Collins 1974).

Layton, Edwin T. *And I Was There: Pearl Harbor and Midway — Breaking the Secret* (William Morrow 1985).

Lord, Walter *Incredible Victory* (Hamish Hamilton 1968).

McIntyre, W. D. *The Rise and Fall of the Singapore Naval Base* (Macmillan 1979).

Middlebrook, Martin and Mahoney, Patrick *Battleship: The Loss of* Prince of Wales *and the* Repulse (Allen Lane 1977).

Millington Drake, E. *The Drama of the* Graf Spee *and the Battle of the River Plate* (Peter Davies 1964).

Mullenheim-Rechberg, Baron von *Battleship* Bismarck (Bodley Head 1980).

Neidpath, J. *The Singapore Naval Base and the Defence of Britain's Eastern Empire 1919-1941* (Oxford University Press 1981).

Newton, Don and Hampshire, Cecil A. *Taranto* (Kimber 1959).

Ogden, Lt-Cdr Michael *The Battle of North Cape* (Kimber 1962).

Pack, S. W. C. *The Battle of Matapan* (Pan 1968).

Night Action off Matapan (Ian Allan 1972).

Pope, Dudley *73 North* (Weidenfeld and Nicholson 1958).

The Battle of the River Plate (Pan 1974).

Potter, John Deane *Fiasco* (Heinemann 1970).

Prange, Gordon W., with Goldstein, Donald M. and Dillon, Katherine V. *Miracle at Midway* (Penguin 1984).

Robertson, Terence *Channel Dash* (Evans 1958).

Schofield, Vice-Adm B. B. *Loss of the* Bismarck (Ian Allan 1972).

The Attack on Taranto (Ian Allan 1973).

The Arctic Convoys (Macdonald and Jane's 1977).

Smith, Peter C. *The Battle of Midway* (New English Library 1976).

Watts, I. *The Loss of the* Scharnhorst (Ian Allan 1970).

Willmott, H. P. *The Barrier and the Javelin* (Naval Institute Press 1983).

Winton, John *The Death of the* Scharnhorst (Granada 1980).

INDEX

221